Training Kit

Microsoft®

SECURITY+
CERTIFICATION

CompTIA
Exam SYO-101

Microsoft Corporation with
Andy Ruth and Kurt Hudson

PUBLISHED BY
Microsoft Press
A Division of Microsoft Corporation
One Microsoft Way
Redmond, Washington 98052-6399

Library of Congress Cataloging-in-Publication Data
Security+ Certification Training Kit / Microsoft Corporation.
      p. cm.
    Includes index.
    ISBN 0-7356-1822-4
    1. Electronic data processing personnel--Certification.   2. Computer security--Examinations--Study guides.   I. Microsoft Corporation.

   QA76.3 .S43   2003
   005.8--dc21   2002043072

Printed and bound in the United States of America.

1 2 3 4 5 6 7 8 9   QWT   8 7 6 5 4 3

Distributed in Canada by H.B. Fenn and Company Ltd.

A CIP catalogue record for this book is available from the British Library.

Microsoft Press books are available through booksellers and distributors worldwide. For further information about international editions, contact your local Microsoft Corporation office or contact Microsoft Press International directly at fax (425) 936-7329. Visit our Web site at www.microsoft.com/mspress. Send comments to *tkinput@microsoft.com*.

Acquisitions Editor: Kathy Harding
Project Editor: Jean Trenary
Technical Editor: Bob Dean

Body Part No. X08-94874

Contents

About This Book

Welcome to the *Security+ Certification Training Kit*. This training kit introduces the basic concepts of computer security. It is designed to prepare you to take the Security+ Certification exam administered by the Computing Technology Industry Association (CompTIA). The Security+ Certification program covers the computer security technologies most commonly used today. Passing the Security+ Certification exam means you are certified as possessing the basic knowledge and skills needed to work in computer security. However, this book is not just about getting you through the exam. The lessons in these chapters also provide you with knowledge you'll use to create a more secure computing environment.

Each chapter in this book is divided into lessons. Most lessons include hands-on procedures that allow you to practice or demonstrate a particular concept or skill. Each lesson ends with a short summary and a set of review questions to test your knowledge of the lesson material.

Intended Audience

This book is appropriate for anyone who has experience working on computer networks and wants to learn more about computer security. This book is specifically designed for candidates preparing to take the CompTIA Security+ examination SY0-101. CompTIA describes the Security+ certified professional as follows:

"Those holding the Security+ certification have demonstrated the aptitude and ability to master such knowledge areas as: general security concepts, communications security, infrastructure security, basics of cryptography, and operational/organizational security."

Prerequisites

No one is prevented from registering for or attempting the Security+ exam. However, you are more likely to achieve the Security+ certification if you meet certain prerequisites. At a minimum, you should be capable of installing, configuring, and connecting computers to the Internet before reading this book. Security+ Certification candidates should also have A+ and Network+ certifications or equivalent knowledge and skills, in addition to at least two years of experience in computer networking, and a thorough knowledge of Transmission Control Protocol/Internet Protocol (TCP/IP). This book will make the most sense to people who meet those criteria.

Reference Materials

Throughout this book, you will find references to RFC (Request for Comment), NIST (National Institute for Standards and Technology), and CC (Common Criteria) documents which supplement the topic being discussed. Unless otherwise noted, these documents can be found at the following Web sites:

CC: *http://www.commoncriteria.org*

NIST: *http://www.csrc.nist.gov/publications*

RFC: *http://www.icann.rfceditor.org*

For your convenience, some key RFC, NIST, and CC documents are included on the Supplemental Course Materials CD-ROM. These documents are provided as supplemental information. However, we recommend that you go to the respective Web sites to get the most up-to-date documents if you intend to use the information to manage your security issues.

About the CD-ROM

The Supplemental Course Materials CD-ROM contains a variety of informational aids that can be used throughout this book.

- **eBook**.   A complete electronic version of this training kit.

- **Preview content**.   Three preview chapters from the *Microsoft Windows Security Resource Kit* are included on the CD-ROM in the \WinSecureRK folder.

- **RFC articles**.   Included on the CD-ROM in the \RFC folder.

- **NIST publications**.   Included on the CD-ROM in the \NIST folder.

- **Common Criteria standards**.   Included on the CD-ROM in the \CC folder.

- **Practice test**.   To practice taking the certification exam, you can use the practice test provided on the CD-ROM. The sample questions help you assess your understanding of the concepts presented in this book.

For additional support information regarding this book and the CD-ROM, visit the Microsoft Press Technical Support Web site at *www.microsoft.com/mspress/support*. You can also e-mail TKINPUT@MICROSOFT.COM or send a letter to Microsoft Press, Attn: Microsoft Press Technical Support, One Microsoft Way, Redmond, WA 98052-6399.

Features of This Book

Each chapter has a "Before You Begin" section, which prepares you for completing the chapter.

The chapters are broken into lessons. Some lessons contain practice exercises that give you an opportunity to use the information presented or to explore the part of the application being described.

The "Lesson Summary" section at the end of each lesson identifies key points discussed in the text.

The "Lesson Review" section at the end of each lesson allows you to test yourself on what you have learned in that lesson.

Appendix A, "Questions and Answers," contains all the book's questions and provides the appropriate answers.

Notes

Several types of notes appear throughout the lessons.

- Notes marked **Note** contain supplemental information.
- Notes marked **Tip** contain explanations of possible results or alternative methods for performing tasks.
- Notes marked **Important** contain information that is essential to completing a task.
- Notes marked **Caution** contain warnings about possible loss of data.

Notational Conventions

The following notational conventions are used throughout this book.

- Characters or commands that you type appear in **bold** type.
- *Italic* in syntax statements indicates placeholders for variable information. *Italic* is also used for book titles and to indicate newly introduced terms.
- Names of files and folders appear in initial capital letters except when you are to type them directly. Unless otherwise indicated, you can use lowercase letters when you type a file name in a dialog box or at a command prompt.
- File name extensions, when they appear without a file name, are in lowercase letters.
- Acronyms appear in all uppercase letters.
- Monospace type represents code samples.

- Square brackets [ ] are used in syntax statements to enclose optional items. For example, [*filename*] in command syntax indicates that you can choose to type a file name with the command. Type only the information within the brackets, not the brackets themselves.

- Braces { } are used in syntax statements to enclose required items. Type only the information within the braces, not the braces themselves.

- Icons represent specific sections in the book as follows:

Icon	Represents
	Supplemental course materials. You will find these materials on the Supplemental Course Materials CD-ROM.
	An exercise containing questions about the lesson just presented. Answers to the exercises are contained in Appendix A, "Questions and Answers," at the end of the book.
	Lesson review questions. These questions at the end of each lesson allow you to test what you have learned in the lesson. You will find the answers to the review questions in Appendix A, "Questions and Answers," at the end of the book.

Keyboard Conventions

- A plus sign (+) between two key names means that you must press those keys at the same time. For example, "Press ALT+TAB" means that you hold down ALT while you press TAB.

- A comma (,) between two or more key names means that you must press each of the keys consecutively, not together. For example, "Press ALT, F, X" means that you press and release each key in sequence. "Press ALT+W, L" means that you first press ALT and W together, and then release them and press L.

- You can choose menu commands with the keyboard. Press the ALT key to activate the menu bar, and then sequentially press the keys that correspond to the highlighted or underlined letter of the menu name and the command name. For some commands, you can also press a key combination listed in the menu.

- You can select or clear check boxes or options in dialog boxes with the keyboard. Press the ALT key, and then press the key that corresponds to the underlined letter of the option name. Or you can press TAB until the option is highlighted, and then press SPACEBAR to select or clear the check box or option button.

- You can cancel the display of a dialog box by pressing the ESC key.

Chapter and Appendix Overview

This self-paced training kit combines notes, exercises, and review questions to help you prepare for the Security+ Certification exam. The book is designed to be worked through from beginning to end, but you can choose a customized track and complete only the sections that interest you. (See the next section, "Finding the Best Starting Point for You," for more information.) If you choose the customized track option, see the "BeforeYou Begin" section in each chapter. Any hands-on procedures that require preliminary work from preceding chapters refer to the appropriate chapters.

The book is divided into the following chapters:

- The section you are reading, "About This Book," contains a self-paced training overview and introduces the components of this training course. Read this section thoroughly to get the greatest educational value from this course and to plan which lessons you will complete.

- Chapter 1, "General Networking and Security Concepts," overviews many of the concepts discussed throughout the book. This chapter discusses the "big picture" of organizational and operational security, including security threats, intrusions, and defenses.

- Chapter 2, "TCP/IP Basics," presents an overview and review of the TCP/IP suite of protocols. This chapter also illustrates ways in which the TCP/IP protocol suite can be compromised.

- Chapter 3, "Certificate Basics," explains how encryption and certificates help you to increase security. The chapter describes cryptography and encryption keys, Public Key Infrastructure (PKI), and certification authorities.

- Chapter 4, "Network Infrastructure Security," describes a wide variety of security concerns related to the network infrastructure, including network device and cabling security, security zones, and monitoring network resources.

- Chapter 5, "Communications Security," describes ways to secure remote connections using a variety of encrypted connections and tunnels. You also learn about wireless security in this chapter.

- Chapter 6, "Application Security," explains the ways in which your e-mail, Web browser, and File Transfer Protocol (FTP) clients might be compromised by attackers. Further, you learn measures you can take to increase the security of those components.

- Chapter 7, "User Security," describes access control measures, such as mandatory and role-based authentication. This chapter also explains how you can increase security by using Kerberos, Challenge Handshake Authentication Protocol (CHAP), biometric authentication, and mutual authentication.

- Chapter 8, "Security Baselines," covers measures to increase the security of your network by ensuring that your hosts and devices are as safe as possible. This chapter focuses on how to keep servers secure, whereas Chapter 6 focused on how to secure client software.

- Chapter 9, "Operational Security," draws your attention to ways that your information security systems might be compromised by attacks from the world outside the computer. Issues such as social engineering, fire suppression, and disaster recovery are discussed. The chapter also discusses user and group management, removable media, and ways to protect your business continuity.

- Chapter 10, "Organizational Security," focuses on the policies, procedures, laws, and regulations that apply to your organization. Further, you learn to identify risks and methods for promoting your security policy and educating users.

- Chapter 11, " Incident Detection and Response," looks at the types of attacks your organization might encounter. This chapter also discusses intrusion detection systems and how to handle intrusions.

- Appendix A, "Questions and Answers," lists all of the exercise and review questions from the book, showing the page number where the question appears and the suggested answer.

- Appendix B, "Ports and Protocol IDs," reiterates the Transmission Control Protocol (TCP), User Datagram Protocol (UDP), and Internet Protocol (IP) identifiers that you should know. This appendix is assembled as a study reference for your convenience.

- The Glossary provides definitions of key networking terms used throughout the book.

Finding the Best Starting Point for You

Because this book is self-paced, you can skip some lessons and revisit them later.

If You	Follow This Learning Path
Are preparing to take the CompTIA Certification Exam SY0-101	Read the "Getting Started" section. Then work through the remaining chapters in any order.
Want to review information about specific topics from the exam	Use the "Where to Find Specific Skills in This Book" section that follows this table.

The following tables provide a list of the skills measured on certification exam *Security+ Examination SY0-101*. The table lists the skills, as defined in the objectives for the exam, and where in this book you will find the lesson relating to a particular skill.

Note   Exam objectives are subject to change without prior notice.

Domain 1.0: General Security Concepts

Skill Being Measured	Location in Book
1.1. Access Control	Chapter 9, Lesson 1
■ MAC/DAC/RBAC	Chapter 7, Lesson 2 Chapter 9, Lesson 2
1.2. Authentication	Chapter 7, Lesson 3
■ Kerberos	
■ CHAP	
■ Certificates	
■ Username/Password	
■ Tokens	
■ Multi-Factor	
■ Mutual Authentication	
■ Biometrics	
1.3. Non-essential Services and Protocols	Chapter 8, Lesson 1
1.4. Attacks	Chapter 11, Lesson 1
■ DoS/DDoS	
■ Back Door	
■ Spoofing	
■ Man in the Middle	
■ Replay	
■ TCP/IP Hijacking	
■ Weak Keys	
■ Mathematical	
■ Social Engineering	
■ Birthday	
■ Password Guessing	
Brute Force	
Dictionary	
■ Software Exploitation	
1.5. Malicious Code	Chapter 11, Lesson 1
■ Viruses	
■ Trojan Horses	
■ Logic Bombs	
■ Worms	

Domain 3.0:   Infrastructure Security

Domain 4.0:   Basics of Cryptography

Skill Being Measured	Location in Book
4.1. Algorithms	Chapter 3, Lesson 1
■ Hashing	
■ Symmetric	
■ Asymmetric	
4.2. Concepts of Using Cryptography	Chapter 3, Lesson 2
■ Confidentiality	
■ Integrity	
Digital Signatures	
■ Authentication	
■ Nonrepudiation	
Digital Signatures	
■ Access Control	
4.3. PKI	Chapter 3, Lesson 1
■ Certificates	
Certificate Policies	
Certificate Practice Statements	
■ Revocation	
■ Trust Models	

Domain 4.0:   Basics of Cryptography

Domain 5.0:   Operational/Organizational Security

Getting Started

This self-paced training kit comes with a companion CD-ROM, which contains additional material to enhance and supplement the text. The following sections discuss the hardware and software required to complete the exercises and view the items on the companion CD-ROM.

Hardware Requirements

You can perform most exercises without any computer at all. However, a few exercises ask you to install and use certain security programs. To perform these exercises, you will need a computer and an operating system. Almost any computer produced after 1994 can be used for the computer-related exercises in this book.

However, the exercises themselves were written on an Intel-compatible system running the Microsoft Windows 2000 Professional operating system. If you choose to utilize Windows 2000 Professional to complete all of the exercises in this book you'll require a minimum of:

- 133-MHz Intel-based Pentium level processor
- 64 MB of random access memory (RAM)
- 650 MB to 1.5 GB of free space on a 2-GB hard disk
- CD-ROM drive
- Mouse or pointing device
- SVGA monitor
- Network connection or modem (allowing Internet access)

The most important requirement is to be sure that your computer supports the software and operating system that you load on it. This information can be obtained from the manufacturer of your operating system. Many of the exercises that involve a computer require you to connect to the Internet.

Software Requirements

There is no particular operating system required to work with the software referenced in this book. The step-by-step instructions were written to work precisely on a Windows 2000 Professional computer, but they should work similarly on any Windows 95 or later operating system. If you have another operating system, you might need to look up specific steps on how to install the software referenced in this book on your particular operating system. All other software you require to perform any exercise can be downloaded for free from the Internet.

To view the eBook you must have Microsoft Internet Explorer 5.01 or later and the proper Hypertext Markup Language (HTML) components on your system. If your system does not meet these requirements, you can install Internet Explorer 6 Service Pack 1 from the CD-ROM prior to installing the eBook.

Note   You must have the Supplemental Course Materials CD-ROM inserted in your CD-ROM drive to run the eBook.

Setup Instructions

To perform these exercises, you must set up your computer according to the manufacturer's instructions. All other instructions should be accurate for a Windows 2000 Professional operating system and very similar for Windows 95 or later operating systems. As previously mentioned, you should already be capable of installing, configuring, and connecting computers to the Internet before reading this book or attempting any of these exercises. Those tasks must be accomplished according to your software and hardware vendor instructions before you attempt any computer-related exercise in this book.

The eBook

The companion CD also includes a fully searchable electronic version of the book (eBook).

▶ **To use the eBook**

1. Insert the Supplemental Course Materials CD-ROM into your CD-ROM drive.

Note If AutoRun is disabled on your machine, run StartCD.exe in the root folder of the CD-ROM or refer to the Readme.txt file on the CD-ROM.

2. Click eBook on the user interface menu and follow the prompts.

Note If AutoRun is disabled on your machine, run StartCD.exe in the root folder of the CD-ROM or refer to the Readme.txt file on the CD-ROM.

The Sample Exam Questions

The CD-ROM also includes an assessment tool that generates 50-question practice exams with automated scoring and answer feedback.

▶ **To install the sample exam questions on your hard disk drive**

1. Insert the Supplemental Course Materials CD-ROM into your CD-ROM drive.

Note If AutoRun is disabled on your machine, run StartCD.exe in the root directory of the CD-ROM or refer to the Readme.txt file on the CD-ROM.

2. Click Sample Exam Questions on the user interface menu and follow the prompts.

The Security+ Certification Program

The CompTIA Security+ Certification is a testing program sponsored by the Computing Technology Industry Association (CompTIA) that certifies the knowledge of networking technicians who have accumulated 24 months of experience in the information technology (IT) industry. You can find more information about CompTIA certifications at *http://www.comptia.org/certification*.

Leading experts from all sectors of the IT industry developed the *Security+ Certification Exam SY0-101*. CompTIA conducted a multilevel review process for all questions to ensure that they are accurate as well as psychometrically sound.

Benefits of Certification

For most individuals, Security+ Certification is the first step on the path to becoming a security professional. It can also be thought of as the next step after CompTIA's A+ and Network+ certifications for people who want to specialize in computer security. Passing the Security+ examination certifies you as possessing the basic knowledge and skills needed to become a computer security specialist. If you are interested in becoming a Microsoft Certified Systems Engineer (MCSE), the *Security+ Certification Training Kit* provides just the foundation you need to get on your way with confidence.

With Security+ Certification, you will receive many benefits, including the following:

- **Recognized proof of professional achievement**.   The Security+ credential asserts that the holder has reached a level of competence commonly accepted and valued by the industry.
- **Enhanced job opportunities**.   Many employers give hiring preference to applicants with Security+ Certification.
- **Opportunity for advancement**.   The Security+ credential can be a plus when an employer awards job promotions.
- **Training requirement**.   Security+ Certification is being adopted as a recommended prerequisite to enrollment in certain vendors' training courses.
- **Customer confidence**.   As the general public learns about Security+ Certification, customers will request that only certified technicians be assigned to their accounts.
- **Improved productivity**.   Certified employees perform work faster and more accurately. Statistics show that certified employees can work up to 75 percent faster than employees without certification.
- **Customer satisfaction**.   When employees have credentials that prove their competency, customer expectations are more likely to be met. More business can be generated for the employer through repeat sales to satisfied customers.

The Security+ Exam

The text in this book prepares you to master the skills needed to pass the Security+ exam. By mastering all course work, you will be able to complete the Security+ Certification exam with the confidence you need to ensure success. Individuals are permitted to take the exam as many times as they like.

The exam is broken down into five sections, called objective domains. The following table lists the objective domains and the extent to which they are represented in the examination.

Security+ Certification Domain Area	Percentage of Examination
1.0 General Security Concepts	30 percent
2.0 Communications Security	20 percent
3.0 Infrastructure Security	20 percent
4.0 Basics of Cryptography	15 percent
5.0 Operational/Organizational Security	15 percent

Registering for the Security+ Exam

Anyone can take the Security+ exam. There are no specific requirements or prerequisites, except payment of the fee. However, exam content is targeted to computer technicians with 24 months of experience in the IT industry. A typical candidate will have CompTIA A+ and Network+ certifications or have equivalent knowledge, but those certifications are not required to register for the exam.

The tests are administered at both Thompson Prometric and VUE testing centers. The phone number for registering with Thompson Prometric Security+ in the US is 1-800-977-3926. The phone number for registering with VUE in the US and Canada is 1-877-551-PLUS (7587). To find registration phone numbers for other countries, or to register online, visit the VUE (*http://www.vue.com*) or Thompson Prometric (*http://www.2test.com*) Web sites.

When you call, please have the following information available:

- Name and number of the exam, which is Security+ SY0-101
- Social Security number or testing ID
- Mailing address and telephone number
- Employer or organization
- Date on which you want to take the test
- Testing location (you can find this online from the test provider's Web site)
- Method of payment (credit card or check)

Payment is made at the time of registration, either by credit card or by requesting that an invoice be sent to you or your employer. Vouchers and coupons are also redeemed at that time.

Preparing for the Security+ Exam

The process of preparing for the Security+ exam is unique to every student, but there are a wide variety of resources to aid you in the process, including the following:

- **Classroom instruction.**   There are many organizations that offer instructor-led training courses for the Security+ exam. The advantages of this type of training are that you have access to a networking lab in which you can experiment and a teacher whom you can ask questions. This type of training can be quite expensive, however, often running several hundred dollars per day.

- **Computer-based training (CBT).**   CBT courses come on one or more CD-ROMs and can contain multimedia-training materials such as audio and video, in addition to graphics and text. A typical CBT includes software that you install on your computer that enables you to track the lessons you've completed and the amount of time you've spent on each one, as well as your results for any exercises and practice exams that might be included. The advantage of a CBT is that you can work with it at your own pace without having to travel to a training center. CBTs can also be expensive, but not as expensive as classroom training.

- **Online training.**   Some training companies offer Security+ courses using Web-based training, which is usually similar in format to a CBT, but delivered online instead of from a CD-ROM. One advantage of online training is that usage information and quiz scores can be maintained by the training company on its servers, making it a good solution for corporations looking for an employee-training program. Some courses also offer feedback from a live instructor, through online message boards or chat applications, which can place this medium a step above CBTs. Depending on the format of the course, however, online training might not be satisfactory for users limited to relatively low-speed dial-up Internet connections. For corporate customers, however, who usually have high-speed connections, online training could be ideal, and is generally comparable in cost to CBTs.

- **Study guides.**   Books always provide the most information for your training dollar. A student who is disciplined enough to work through a comprehensive Security+ study guide is likely to absorb more information from books than from CBTs or online training courses, and for substantially less money. There are many different Security+ books available, many with exercises and practice questions that provide feedback and progress indicators similar to those in the electronic training formats.

- **Practice exams.**   Practice exams for the Security+ Certification are available in book form, on CD-ROM, and on Web sites. The interface used for the examination by the testing centers should not present a challenge to users familiar with computers, so it should make little difference to most people whether their practice tests are in printed or electronic form. What is more important is the content of the practice exams. In addition to providing the correct answers, a good practice exam should also explain why each possible answer to a question is either right or wrong.

Taking the Security+ Exam

The Security+ exam is administered by computer, and is completely "closed book." You are not permitted to bring any written materials into the testing room with you, although you are given a pencil and a blank piece of paper or a scratch tablet on which you can write any information you want before the exam begins. Many candidates memorize a page full of crucial facts and jot them down in the testing room before the exam begins. You can then use your own notes during the exam, but you must turn them in afterward; you cannot take them out with you.

The testing room typically contains a group of computers, with cubicles or dividers to prevent any distraction or communication between candidates. In most cases, there is a window through which a proctor observes the testing process. You are given time in the testing room to make your own notes. You can then take an orientation exam on the testing computer to familiarize yourself with the format of the software.

The exam is preloaded on the computer when you arrive, and you can start the test at any time. The exam consists of 100 questions, chosen at random from a pool, so that the probability of two people taking the exact same exam is very slight. You have 90 minutes to take the exam; a clock on the computer screen keeps you informed of the time remaining. Each question appears on a separate screen, and you can move forward and backward through the questions by clicking the appropriate arrows. Instructions for using the testing software appear on each screen, although most users familiar with graphical user interfaces don't need them.

The questions are all multiple choice. Some questions require you to select a single answer; these questions have radio buttons on the answers so you can make only one choice. Some questions require more than one answer. These questions have check boxes and also indicate how many selections you can make. All questions are graded either right or wrong; there is no partial credit. If you do not select the required number of responses to a question, the software flags that question and reminds you that it is incomplete at the end of the exam. In some cases, questions include graphics, such as charts or network diagrams. You are asked a question about the graphic, and you might have to click on a particular part of the graphic to indicate your answer.

As you take the test, you can answer each question as it appears, or you can fill a check box that flags an unanswered question to review later. This feature is for user convenience only. You can return to any question at any time in the exam by clicking the forward and backward arrows. The flags only enable you to return to specific questions without having to go through all the questions you have already completed.

Candidates have different techniques for taking multiple-choice exams. Some people read all of the questions first before selecting any responses. This can be beneficial, because later questions might provide a hint or trigger your memory about the subject of an earlier question. However, don't waste too much time doing this, or you might find yourself rushing through the last few questions. Answering 100 questions in 90 minutes works out to less than one minute for each question, so you can't afford to spend too much time on any one question.

The key to taking an exam of this type is to read each question carefully. The language of the questions is chosen very carefully, and sometimes rather deviously. In many cases, questions are designed to trick you into thinking that they are easier than they actually are. If an answer seems painfully obvious, read the question over again. Chances are, the obvious answer is not the correct one. In some cases, all of the responses are correct, and you are instructed to select the one that best answers the question, so always be sure to read all of the possible responses, even when the first one seems correct.

Even if you are completely stumped about a question, you should take a guess before the exam is over. Leave yourself a few minutes at the end of the test to make any guesses you need to, so that you don't leave any questions unanswered.

At the end of the exam there is a brief delay as the computer totals your score. You then receive the results on the spot, with a printed report that breaks down your score into several topics. If you fail the test, this report can be an excellent guide to the material that requires further study. If you pass, the report contains the certification number that you can use to prove your status. Although you receive a score for the exam, the Security+ Certification exam is strictly pass/fail. You can use your high score for bragging rights among your friends and colleagues, but all candidates passing the exam receive the same certification, which is a certificate that CompTIA mails to you a few weeks after the exam.

Technical Support

Every effort has been made to ensure the accuracy of this book and the contents of the companion disc. If you have comments, questions, or ideas regarding this book or the companion disc, please send them to Microsoft Press using either of the following methods:

E-mail: TKINPUT@MICROSOFT.COM

Postal Mail: Microsoft Press
Attn: *Security+ Certification Training Kit* Editor
One Microsoft Way
Redmond, WA 98052-6399

The Microsoft Press Web site (*http://www.microsoft.com/mspress/support*) provides corrections for books. Please note that product support is not offered through this Web site. For further information regarding Microsoft software support options, please connect to *http://www.microsoft.com/support*.

For information about ordering the full version of any Microsoft software, please connect to *http://www.microsoft.com*.

C H A P T E R   1

General Networking and Security Concepts

About This Chapter

This chapter provides a general overview of security concerns. Throughout the rest of the book, you will learn more about each of these topics in greater depth. After finishing this book and passing the Security+ exam, you will be able to understand the concepts, concerns, and language of a security expert.

Note Throughout this book, you will find references to RFC (Request for Comment), NIST (National Institute for Standards and Technology), and CC (Common Criteria) documents which supplement the topic being discussed. Unless otherwise noted, these documents can be found at the following Web sites:

CC: *http://www.commoncriteria.org*

NIST: *http://www.csrc.nist.gov/publications*

RFC: *http://www.icann.rfceditor.org*

For your convenience, some key RFC, NIST, and CC documents are included on the Supplemental Course Materials CD-ROM. These documents are provided as supplemental information. However, we recommend that you go to the respective Web sites to get the most up-to-date documents if you intend to use the information to manage your security issues.

Before You Begin

The prerequisite knowledge expected for the Security+ candidate is the CompTIA A+ and Network+ certifications or equivalent knowledge, along with knowledge and experience with Transmission Control Protocol/Internet Protocol (TCP/IP). There are no prerequisites for this chapter, but this book assumes you meet the prerequisites specified by CompTIA.

Lesson 1: The Big Picture

A network is two or more machines interconnected for communications. This is a very simple view of a network, but it does help lay the groundwork for the big picture, which is today's networking and business environment.

Companies connect computers to share information and resources, providing better efficiency and productivity at a lower cost. Servers are computers that are built with a lot of computing power and data storage capacity so that they can answer requests from client computers on the network. Printers are an example of resources that can be added to the network and managed from the servers.

Client computers can connect to the servers so a company's employees can store and retrieve data, and print information to the network printers. The servers are backed up, and in the event of data loss, the information can be restored from the backup media. This provides the employees with the tools needed to do their job and provides an efficient, cost-effective, reliable work environment where the information the company generates is stored securely and is somewhat safe from equipment failure or user mishap.

To help employees be more productive, Internet access is configured. This allows a company's employees to communicate with people at other companies using instant messaging, e-mail, and many other methods. The other companies are connected to the Internet and sensitive data is transferred back and forth. The Internet provides a fast, inexpensive way to conduct business, so the company tries to conduct as much business as possible using the Internet.

When business is conducted, sensitive data is stored and transferred, and sensitive communications occur. Some opportunistic people might attempt to disrupt that business, steal or destroy the data, or exploit the communications.

As the "computer person" in a small company, a member of the Information Systems (IS) group at a larger company, or even just a regular user who enjoys surfing the Internet and e-mailing family and friends, you need to be aware of some information security basics. Even if you are not filling a high tech job, if you connect to the Internet, sensitive data you store on your system can be compromised. Your system can be used to attack or bring down other systems and your system can be infected with a virus that could harm operations.

If you are currently in or want to get a job in a high tech field, you must understand how to protect your company's assets (including the information stored on the computers), provide employees with the tools needed to perform their jobs, and provide a communications link with other companies and data sources. One of your first steps is to understand information security, its terms, and its concepts.

After this lesson, you will be able to

- Understand what is at stake
- Understand how to value your assets
- Understand the goal of information security
- Understand how to manage risk

Estimated lesson time: 20 minutes

What's at Stake

You might think that attacks are unlikely and that they do not cause too much damage. According to an article published on Newsfactor.com in February of 2001, Frank Bernhard of the University of California at Davis conducted a study of 3,000 U.S. businesses, and found that computer hackers and other security breaches cost businesses nearly 6 cents for every dollar of revenue. That is a lot of damage.

Valuing Your Assets

For every company, information has value. If every soft drink maker had the formula for Coca-Cola, everyone could make it and the Coca-Cola Company would have a harder time selling its product. For an airplane manufacturer, it might be the plans to a new jet that will revolutionize the airplane industry. Whatever the company and whatever the industry, there is information that needs to be protected and secure.

Just how important and valuable is your company's information? The following are some of the questions to ask that might help you understand the value:

- What is the loss to my company's assets if the company's data is compromised?
- What is the loss of intellectual property worth to my company?
- What is the loss in revenue or market share?
- What is the loss of privacy worth?
- What is the damage to my company's reputation worth?

For every company, the value of information is different. For most companies, information is one of the top assets, if not the top asset they have. If a piece of hardware fails or the building the company is in gets damaged, the losses can be costly, but the equipment can be replaced or the damages repaired in most cases. However, if the information is destroyed, it is gone forever and cannot be replaced. This could cause irreparable damage. You must also realize that the value of information changes over its lifetime. Also, the value might be real or perceived.

- **Real value.**   Imagine you work for a company that makes tea. If your company has a formula for a special blend of tea and the yearly sales of that tea is $5 million, then you could say that formula has a value of $5 million. Five years from now, coffee might be more popular so the yearly sales of the tea might drop to $2 million. The value of the formula would have dropped from $5 million to $2 million. The information did not change, but the value of the information changed.

- **Perceived value.**   The tea company you work for has a very smart management and marketing group. The management team has a plan for collaborating with a distribution company to increase the availability of the tea across the world. The marketing team has an idea for a marketing campaign that will make the tea more popular and could slow the rise in popularity of coffee.

Having access to the management and marketing team's information would have value, but the value is not tangible, it is perceived. Regardless of whether information has a tangible or perceived value, it is your responsibility to protect the information. The higher the real or perceived value, the larger the target for theft.

Understanding the Goal of Security

The C-I-A triad, shown in Figure 1-1, is a common term used when talking about information security. C-I-A stands for

- **Confidentiality.**   Ensures that information is accessed only by authorized personnel.
- **Integrity.**   Ensures that information is modified only by authorized personnel.
- **Availability.**   Ensures that information and systems can be accessed when needed by authorized personnel.

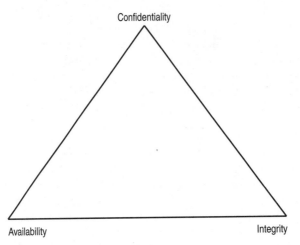

Figure 1-1.   The C-I-A triad

When you combine efforts to provide data confidentiality, data integrity, and data availability with physical security you can provide a very effective security solution.

Throughout the rest of this book, the defenses presented protect against the threats described. The job of the IS specialist, especially the security specialist, is to provide highly available, reliable data to only those who should have access when they need access.

Managing Risk

Your company's information has value and must be available where and when needed, for use by authorized personnel. As a security expert, your job is to minimize the chance that the C-I-A triad will collapse.

Risk management, shown in Figure 1-2, is the complete process used to identify, control, and mitigate the impact of uncertain events. Because it is impossible to eliminate risk completely, the goal of risk management is to reduce risk and maintain the C-I-A triad. You do this by determining what the risks are, identifying threats and vulnerabilities, and then reducing them.

Figure 1-2.   Risk management

You minimize risk by identifying the risks and creating a mitigation plan for those risks. *Mitigation* is defined as making something less harmful or less painful; therefore, you are planning to lessen your risks. For the tea company, the mitigation plan might be to limit the number of copies of the formula and number of locations in which it is stored. It might also include limiting the number of people that have access to the formula and how they can access it.

To minimize risk, you first identify the potential risks, threats, and vulnerabilities that your company faces.

- *Risk* is the exposure to loss or possible injury. With information security, the risk is that your company's information will fall prey to outside forces and cause your company losses in time, money, and reputation.

   With the tea company, the risk is that if the formula is compromised through exposure, other companies might start making a very similar tea. This would cause a loss in market share for the tea company. If the tea formula were commonly known and the value was in creating the tea inexpensively, then the risk due to loss of the formula would not be that great. The value would then be in the production process.

- A *threat*, for information security, is any activity that represents possible danger to your information. Threats can take many forms, but any threat poses a danger to the C-I-A triad. In the example of the tea company, another company could steal the formula for the tea, or an employee could sell the formula to another company.

- A *vulnerability* is a weakness in your information security that could be exploited by a threat; that is, a weakness in your systems and network security, processes, and procedures. With the tea company, the formula for the tea is the valued information. People have to have access to the formula to make the tea and the formula has to be stored somewhere.

Some of the vulnerabilities could include the location the formula is stored in, the number of people that need to have access to the formula, and where the formula is accessed.

Putting It All Together

For information security, you must protect the C-I-A triad, but you cannot protect it at any cost, and there is not always a need to protect information. For instance, if your company sells bottled water purified using the process of reverse osmosis, the process is well known, and therefore it does not make good business sense for you to protect that information. However, if your company has a revolutionary process that cuts the cost and time for water purification in half, it would make sense to secure that information. There is a limit to the value of implementing protection so you must combine your knowledge of value, threats, vulnerabilities, and risks to put together a feasible plan. To do this, follow this plan:

- Place a value on the information.
- Identify as many risks as possible and their associated threats and vulnerabilities.
- Mitigate the identified risks.
- Be aware that there are always things that you overlooked.

There is a limit to your ability to mitigate risk, and sometimes the cost or difficulty of reducing the risk is greater than the risk itself. For instance, if you work at a tea company and have a data file that contains all of the ingredients used to produce your entire line of tea products, it might not be worth the time, money, and effort to protect that information, because it is simply a laundry list of ingredients. However, if you have a recipe for your best-selling tea and your company is the only maker of that tea, it could be worth considerable time, effort, and money to protect that information. Every risk plan is different because every company has a different set of circumstances, budget, and workforce to use in minimizing risk. Some of the questions you can ask to help better identify the constraints that your company is working under include the following:

- What information needs to be secured?
- What is the value of the information?
- What are the chances that the information can be compromised?
- What is the cost to the company if the information is compromised?
- In what manner is the information accessed?
- How many people access the information?
- Is the information easily secured?

Regardless of whether you decide to mitigate a risk, you should identify as many potential risks as possible and develop a mitigation plan that encompasses each of them. Once you identify the risks and assign a cost (in time and money) to secure the information, you can compare that with the information's value to determine what security measures are reasonable. For every situation, the risk management and trade-offs will be different. Using the tea company as an example, you might identify the following:

■   The value of the tea formula is $5 million because sales of the tea are $5 million.

■   The risk is that competitors might obtain the tea formula.

■   The threats are that someone from outside will locate and gain access to the tea formula, or an employee will gain access to the formula and sell it or give it to competitors.

■   The vulnerabilities are that the formula is stored in five different locations and that a large number of people have access to the formula.

■   To mitigate the risks, the formula could be stored in one location and made accessible, no one, but this is impractical. A better mitigation plan might be to reduce the number of locations to three and limit access to 25 people.

■   Things you might not have thought of would be to limit access to the area where the formula is used to produce the tea, post a list of the people who have access, and use a method to authenticate the people accessing the formula.

There are probably several additional threats, vulnerabilities, risks, and mitigations that you can identify. Identifying as many of these as possible is required of a good security specialist.

Exercise: Creating a Risk Management Plan

You are the security specialist for a small company that makes and sells scented candles. Your company sells these candles to retail stores, but also sell the candles over the Internet. The supplies that you use to make the candles are purchased over the Internet from four different suppliers. Your company has a remote sales force that works worldwide and accesses your internal network across the Internet. You also have employees who are allowed to work from home and access the company's network through a remote access solution.

The company does $12 million each year in sales, with $3 million in sales of everyday candles to retail stores, $2 million in sales of specialty scented candles that are only available on the Internet, and $7 million in sales of candle-making supplies.

In this exercise you need to:

- Identify the value of the various parts of the business.
- Identify as many threats as you can.
- Identify as many vulnerabilities as you can.
- Identify as many risks as you can.
- Develop a risk management plan.

There are no definitive answers to this exercise. It was designed to encourage you to think about possible risks and how you might mitigate them. Throughout the book you will gain valuable information that you can use to provide a better, more detailed answer to this exercise. Record your answer now, and after completing this training kit, return to this exercise to realize the knowledge and expertise you have gained.

Lesson Review

The following questions are intended to reinforce key information presented in this lesson. If you are unable to answer a question, review the lesson and then try the question again. Answers to the questions can be found in Appendix A, "Questions and Answers."

1. Although there is a need for information security, and there is a small chance of getting hacked, there is not normally any damage done and the cost to the company that is hacked is relatively minor. (True or False?)

2. You work for a company that sells tea and tea supplies. The total annual sales for the company are $5 million. The sales of tea total $2 million and the sales of tea supplies total $3 million. The tea has a very interesting taste that cannot be duplicated. Which of the following should be considered when placing a value on the tea formula, and why?

   a. How the tea is produced
   b. What the total annual sales of the tea is
   c. Where the tea formula is stored
   d. How many people in the company have access to the tea formula

3. You work for a company that sells tea and tea supplies. The total annual sales for the company are $5 million. The sales of tea total $2 million and the sales of tea supplies total $3 million. The tea has a very interesting taste that cannot be duplicated. The marketing group for your company has a marketing plan that is expected to double the sales of the tea from $2 million to $4 million. What is the real value of the tea formula? What is the perceived value of the marketing plan?

4. When talking about information security, what are the three cornerstones of the C-I-A triad?

5. List the sequence in which you perform the following steps when creating a risk management plan.

   a. Identify the vulnerabilities to your C-I-A triad

   b. Identify the value of your C-I-A triad

   c. Identify the threats to your C-I-A triad

   d. Identify how you can mitigate the risks

Lesson Summary

In this lesson, you learned that information security revolves around ensuring that your company's information security plan provides data confidentiality, data integrity, and data availability. The key points to remember are the following:

- Confidentiality is assuring information is secure, with access limited to appropriate persons.

- Integrity is ensuring information is not accidentally or maliciously altered or destroyed.

- Availability is assuring information and communication services will be ready for use when expected.

- To assure that your information plan maintains confidentiality, integrity, and availability, security is necessary. You must identify the possible threat and intrusion points, your vulnerabilities, the risk if your security plan fails, and ways to mitigate those risks by mounting a defense. To mitigate risks, you must determine a value for the information you are protecting and what the potential liability would be if that information were in the wrong hands. In doing this, you must understand the legal ramifications of what you do and ensure that the string of evidence remains intact to allow legal authorities to gather the necessary data and prosecute those responsible.

- The C-I-A triad is a way to remember that the confidentiality, integrity, and availability of information is the concern of every IS specialist, and especially the security specialist.

Lesson 2: Identifying Threats

You can categorize threats to help make them more easily identifiable. They are not always based on someone attacking your computer systems or network. For example, imagine you are working for a tea company where people order tea over the Internet, and the employees fill the orders by accessing a database on a server you maintain. If the server is down, it does not really matter if the room the servers are in floods or if a virus infects the server and temporarily destroys all of the data. The information is still not available to those who need access to it.

After this lesson, you will be able to

- Identify the source of a threat
- Understand what an attack is
- Understand what malicious code is
- Understand who is attacking
- Understand what social engineering is

Estimated lesson time: 25 minutes

Sources of Threat

To plan for or react to a threat, you must understand the nature of the threat. For instance, if you protect your data files by installing software to block traffic from the Internet, this protects access from external sources, but does little to prevent someone inside the company from accessing the data. There are many ways to categorize threats, but the important thing is to identify as many threats as possible and create a risk management plan for each.

When identifying the source of a threat, there are several questions you can ask to help identify the type of threat, and then mitigate it. Some of the questions you might ask include these:

- Is the threat due to a disaster of some sort, or is it due to an attack?
- If it is an attack, is it the threat coming from someone that works for the company, or from someone outside of the company?
- If the threat is from attack, is it a well-known attack?
- If the threat is an attack, are you able to identify it by reviewing audit files?
- If the threat is an attack, is it a business-related attack?

The more you know about the type of threats that could occur, the better you can plan and minimize the risk. The more categories or ways you have of identifying threats, the more threats you are likely to be able to identify and plan for.

Threats from Disaster

Disaster is defined as sudden or great misfortune. Some disasters are natural disasters, whereas others are fabricated. For instance, a fire could be a natural event (such as a forest fire) or manufactured (such as a fire created by an arsonist). Some things are not considered disasters, but could certainly be disastrous to your company's C-I-A triad.

- **Natural disasters.** The C-I-A triad can be affected by natural disasters such as earthquakes or hurricanes. You need to identify those natural disasters most likely to affect your company and create a plan to mitigate potential losses.

  To plan for a natural disaster, you must identity the types of natural disaster that are most likely, determine how often those events occur (historically), and then create a mitigation plan to minimize the impact on your company. The plan might not be implemented, but it should still be identified.

- **Man-made disasters.** Man-made or fabricated disasters that could affect the C-I-A triad include fire, loss of power, or a structural collapse. Because the meaning of disaster is a sudden or great misfortune, the event would be large and affect more than just information security. The concern and priority is for the safety of the people caught in the disaster, but good planning will help a company recover from the misfortune quicker.

- **Mishap.** A *mishap* is defined as an unfortunate accident. If a server fails and the specialists who repair and restore the server are all away, then the C-I-A triad is at risk. Consider the severity and likelihood of the event, whether it is a disaster of epic proportions, or a minor mishap so you can minimize risk.

Threats from Attack

Threats from attack are a more recognized occurrence, and are typically harder to plan for than disasters or mishaps because this type of threat is constantly changing. Malicious users are always adapting methods of attacks to take advantage of different types of technologies and specific vulnerabilities that are discovered. To understand how to defend against an attack, you must understand the technology under attack. Many threats can fall into a number of categories, and the objective is not to categorize attacks; rather, the goal is to create a number of categories to help identify threats.

- **Threats based on the business.**   Some threats are directly related to the business your company is in; therefore, the attacks that are most likely to occur can be better identified. For instance, if your company has a special formula for tea, then the threat would likely come from someone trying to steal the formula. If your company maintained Web sites for other companies, then the threat would likely be to shut the Web sites down, redirect people to a different Web site, or gather any confidential data associated with that Web site.

- **Threats that can be verified.**   Verifiable threats can be identified by data that is captured. For instance, if you have a Web site that someone is trying to hack into, then you might be able to review log files or set an alert to identify the type of attack, the time it occurred, and other specific data. This might not help you minimize the risk of the intruder succeeding with this attack, but it will help you identify an attack type and prepare your security to defend against it. More important, it will enable you to better prepare for a similar attack in the future.

- **Widely known threats.**   Some threats are widely known and you can simply read about them. This type of threat is typically focused on a specific application or technology and might or might not be malicious. An example of this type of threat is the ILOVEYOU virus that infected e-mail systems. The virus sent e-mails to affected users' entire e-mail address books. Although the virus did not destroy system data, it did overload e-mail servers around the world and demonstrated that damage could be done to e-mail receivers' computers. Although no damage was done to data, e-mail service (a mission-critical service) was unavailable, thus breaking the C-I-A triad.

- **Internal threats.**   You must also be aware of internal threats that could affect the C-I-A triad. For instance, if you are using wire to connect all of the systems together on the network, there is a chance that someone could gain access to your network or record the communications that occur on your local network. If you do not use some authentication method for internal users, then the integrity of your information is at risk.

- **External threats.**   External threats originate from outside of your company. For instance, if you are connecting to a Web site on the Internet, the Web site could download an application to your computer that would access the address book in your e-mail program. Alternatively, someone could capture the communications between you and a Web site you are connecting with to buy a new car. By doing that, the malicious user could learn your name, address, and other personal information, such as a credit card number or bank account number. This type of threat would be would be an external threat.

Attacks

An *attack* is an attempt to bypass security controls on a computer. The attack could alter, release, or deny data. Attack types vary almost at the speed of light, but most have a name that describes the attack type well.

Attacks are covered in depth in later chapters, but to give you an idea of some of the current techniques in use today, a short list of attack types follows with a brief description:

- **Denial of service (DoS).**   This type of attack renders a service inoperative. For instance, a DoS attack can make a popular Web site unavailable for some length of time. A distributed denial of service (DDoS) attack has the same impact, but the attack is distributed to many attacking computers.

- **Spoofing.**   For information security, *spoofing* is pretending to be someone else by impersonating, masquerading, or mimicking that person. If you provide a user name and password, Internet Protocol (IP) address, or any other credential that is not yours to gain access to a network, system, or application, then you are spoofing that system. There are a number of spoofing techniques in use today, but one of the most common is IP spoofing, which is falsifying the information in an IP packet.

- **Man-in-the-middle.**   This is exactly what it sounds like. For networking, a computer captures the communications between two computers and impersonates them both. For instance, a client computer connects to a server to download a monthly transaction statement. The man-in-the-middle computer would impersonate the server when communicating with the client, and the client computer when communicating with the server. This allows the man-in-the-middle computer to capture all of the communications between the client and server computers.

- **Password guessing.**   This type of attack involves guessing a user name and password in an attempt to gain access to a network or system. There are password programs available that attempt to break a password using a brute force technique, and others that try passwords against a dictionary. A dictionary attack cannot only match words with a dictionary, but can use upper and lower case or switch numbers for letters in an attempt to break a password.

Malicious Code

Malicious code is software or firmware that is intentionally placed in a system for an unauthorized purpose. Examples of this are the Morris Worm and the Melissa virus. A lot of information about these attacks is available on the Internet, but they are also covered in more depth later in this book. Some of the basic types are the following:

- **Virus.**   A *virus* is a program that can replicate, but not propagate, itself. It requires an installation vector, such as an executable file attached to an e-mail message or a floppy disk. A virus infects other programs on the same system and can be transferred from machine to machine through e-mail attachments or some form of media, such as a floppy disk. A virus can destroy data, crash systems, or it can be mostly harmless.

- **Worm.**   A *worm* is a program that can replicate *and* propagate itself. It propagates itself by infecting other programs on the same system, and also spreading itself to other systems across a network, without the need for an installation vector. A worm can also destroy data, crash systems, or be mostly harmless.

- **Trojan horse.**   Generally, a *Trojan horse* program looks desirable or harmless, but actually does damage. For instance, you might download what you think is a game, but when you run it, you find that it deletes all of the executable files on your hard disk.

Who Is Attacking?

To protect against attack, you must understand who is attacking and how they are doing it. Some attacks are an attempt to gain access to your information, whereas other attacks are used as a ruse. As the military strategist and general Sun Tzu Wu said, "Know thy enemy and know thy self and you will win a hundred battles." The following are some types of attackers:

- **Hacker.**   The term *hacker* has two definitions, depending on to whom you are talking. To a programmer, a hacker can be someone who pounds out code that provides a quick solution to a difficult problem. The code might not be eloquently written, but it is functional and effective. To others, a hacker is someone who breaks security on an automated information system or a network. This type of hacker (also known as a *cracker*) is typically doing something mischievous or malicious, and although they might be trying to break into a system for what they consider a good and higher cause, they are still breaking into a system.

- **Novice.**   A *novice* is someone who aspires to be a hacker, but does not have the technical skills. Typically, a novice will go to a Web site created by a hacker and run a program that attacks a network or computer system. Although a novice attack is usually easily identified and denied, it can provide enough "white noise" to hide evidence that a hacker is attempting a more serious attack on a system or network.

Social Engineering

One of the hardest attacks to defend against is *social engineering*, the act of lever-aging politeness and gullibility in others to gain access to secure resources through deceit. For instance, someone might call and say he or she is repairing a system of yours and needs the password to log on to the system and verify that the repair is complete. Another ploy might be that someone will walk up to a secured door that requires a special card to access and ask you to hold the door open so he or she can enter.

There are several ways social engineering can undermine even the best security plan. One of the best solutions for mitigating social engineering risk is user educa-tion. User education will enable your users to understand what information should never be provided to another person, and will provide best practices for handling sensitive information, as well as setting passwords and other day-to-day tasks.

Lesson Review

The following questions are intended to reinforce key information presented in this lesson. If you are unable to answer a question, review the lesson and then try the question again. Answers to the questions can be found in Appendix A, "Questions and Answers."

1. You are responsible for creating a mitigation plan for threats to your company's information security. Which of the following should your mitigation plan iden-tify as threats from fabricated and natural disasters? (Select all that apply.)

   a. Incomplete backups

   b. Power outages

   c. Your building flooding

   d. A virus infecting the servers at your company

   e. A fire in your building

2. When determining the risk posed by a threat, external threats are more danger-ous than internal threats. (True or False?)

3. Select all the attacks that are based on using malicious code:
   a. Trojan horse
   b. Social engineering
   c. Virus
   d. Novice
   e. Worm

Lesson Summary

- Threats are anything that threaten the C-I-A triad and can come from a variety of sources. Examples of threats include the following:
  - Hackers (or crackers) trying to break into your network and computers
  - Malicious code such as a computer virus or Trojan horse
  - People who work for your company and are unhappy or are being paid to gather and sell your company's information
  - Fire, flood, hardware failure, or natural disaster
- Threats can come from external sources, such as hackers and e-mail messages, but they can also come from sources internal to the company, as is the case with a disgruntled employee or someone who gains physical access to your computers.

Lesson 3: Intrusion Points

Intrusion points are areas that provide an access point to your company's information. Some of these are obvious, but others are not. For instance, you might realize that you need to install a firewall to protect the internal network and computers from hackers, but if a hacker took a temporary job at your company, the firewall would be of little use. When identifying intrusion points, you must consider internal threats as well as external threats. Some internal and external access points are as follows:

- Internal access points
    - Systems that are not in a secured room
    - Systems that do not have any local security configured
- External access points
    - Network components that connect your company to the Internet
    - Applications that are used to communicate across the Internet
    - Communications protocols

After this lesson, you will be able to

- Identify intrusion points to your network infrastructure
- Understand how Internet-based applications threaten your C-I-A triad
- Understand how communications protocols can threaten your C-I-A triad

Estimated lesson time: 15 minutes

Network Infrastructure

Your *network infrastructure* is all of the wiring, networking devices, and networking services that provide connectivity between the computers in a network. The network infrastructure also provides a way to connect to the Internet, allows people on the Internet to connect to your network, and provides people who work remotely with methods to connect to your network.

Intrusion points provide a place for someone to penetrate your network communications and gain access to the information you have stored on your computers.

Examples of how an intruder might exploit the network infrastructure include the following:

- An external intruder would attack your connection to the Internet using an attack method, such as a DoS attack, or attempting a user name and password that allows them to authenticate.

- An internal intruder might connect to an open network jack and attempt to gain access to a server with shared resources that do not require a password.

Applications Used on the Internet

Almost anyone who has a computer connects to the Internet to visit Web sites, check e-mail, and send instant messages to friends. It is also becoming more common to check credit card accounts and bank accounts across the Internet.

Each of these tasks is accomplished using an application running on your computer that allows you to interact with other computers on the Internet. There is a risk associated with providing this additional functionality. Some of the ways an intruder could exploit the applications for less-than-altruistic reasons include the following:

- An external intruder might place a virus or worm in an e-mail message and send the message to a user on your internal network. When opened, a virus might infect the system or provide the intruder with a way to control the system the e-mail was opened on.

- An internal intruder might use native operating system utilities to connect to other systems on your internal network that do not require a user name or password to gain access. They might also use an application such as a Web browser to access confidential information with limited access security.

Communications Protocols

TCP/IP is the protocol suite used for communications on the Internet. Some attacks work by modifying the structure of the IP packet, but many successful intrusions occur at higher levels in the TCP/IP stack. For instance, an intruder can exploit a Web server using the Hypertext Transfer Protocol (HTTP). Communications protocols provide a common set of rules that computers use when communicating with each other. Some protocols offer no security, whereas others provide varying degrees of security. Intruders use their knowledge of communications protocols to compromise your C-I-A triad. The following are two examples:

- An external intruder might attack your company's presence on the Internet by using a DoS attack to disable your Web server. This would cause the information to be inaccessible to your customers.

- An internal intruder might disable an e-mail server by causing a flood of e-mail messages to be sent. This would disable the e-mail server so users could not retrieve their e-mail.

Lesson Review

The following questions are intended to reinforce key information presented in this lesson. If you are unable to answer a question, review the lesson and then try the question again. Answers to the questions can be found in Appendix A, "Questions and Answers."

1. Your company has a high-speed Internet connection that can be used to access the Internet and allows people on the Internet to access your company's Web site. Each user also has a modem that he or she can use for Internet access in case the high-speed connection fails. Users can select the Web browser they want to use and are allowed to manage their own computers. Which of the following are intrusion points for the hacker?

   a. The high-speed connection

   b. The Web browser on each of the client's computers

   c. The modem that each user has

   d. The Web server for your company's Web site

2. When accessing Web sites, an intruder might exploit a Web server using the HTTP protocol. (True or False?)

3. It is always better to have several access points to the Internet so that if a hacker takes one down your company still has access. (True or False?)

Lesson Summary

- Intrusion points are places where your company's information is accessed. Examples of these include the following:

    - Places in your network infrastructure that can be accessed internally or externally

    - Applications that interoperate with other applications remotely, especially on the Internet, such as a Web browser or mail application

    - Communications protocols that are used for communications across the Internet

- External access points connect your company's systems and network to the Internet or provide access to your company's information from external locations. For instance, if your company has a Web server accessed from the Internet, it is an external access point.

- Internal access points provide access to your company's information from internal sources. For instance, a server on your network that does not require a user name or password to access information is considered an internal access point.

Lesson 4: Defending Against Threats

When talking about information security, *vulnerability* is a weakness in your information system (network, systems, processes, and so on) that has the greatest potential of being compromised. There might be a single vulnerability, but typically there are a number of them. For instance, if you have five servers that have the latest security updates for the operating system and applications running, but have a sixth system that is not current, the sixth system would be considered a vulnerability. Although this would be a vulnerability, it would most likely not be the only one. To defend against threats, you must identify the threats to your C-I-A triad, determine what your vulnerabilities are, and minimize them.

After this lesson, you will be able to

■ Understand the main areas of a layered information security defense

■ Understand why a secure network infrastructure is important

■ Understand why user authentication is important

■ Understand why auditing is important

Estimated lesson time: 25 minutes

Building a Defense

When building a defense, you should use a layered approach that includes securing the network infrastructure, the communications protocols, servers, applications that run on the server, and the file system, and you should require some form of user authentication. This is very similar to placing family heirlooms in a safe, in a cellar, in a house with a lock on the front door, with a large fence around the house. For someone to take the heirlooms, they would have to get past the fence, through the front door, to the cellar, and into the safe. This would be more difficult than if the heirlooms were placed just inside the fence.

When you configure a strong, layered defense (Figure 1-3), an intruder has to break through several layers to reach his or her objective. For instance, to compromise a file on a server that is part of your internal network, a hacker would have to breach your network security, break the server's security, break an application's security, and break the local file system's security. The hacker has a better chance of breaking one defense than of breaking four layers of defense.

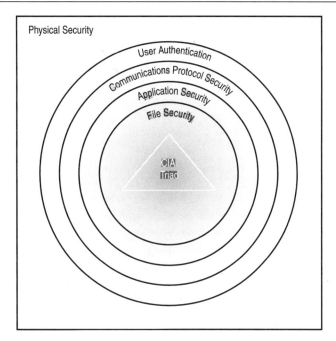

Figure 1-3.   Building a layered defense

Securing the Network Infrastructure

Securing the network is the first step to creating a strong defense. When securing a network, minimize the number of access points to the network. For instance, if Internet access is required, configure a single access point and put a firewall in place.

Using Secure Communication Protocols

Some protocols offer secure communications, whereas others offer none at all. When it makes sense, use the most secure communications protocol available. For instance, if you have a Web server that advertises your company on the Internet, then you would most likely require an unsecured protocol like HTTP, but if a customer were making a purchase, you would then require the Hypertext Transfer Protocol Secure (HTTPS) protocol, which uses the Secure Sockets Layer (SSL) protocol to secure communications. This provides a layer of security with an encryption mechanism for communications.

Securing Systems

There are entire books devoted to securing a system, and what you have to do to secure a system is based on the specific operating system that is running. The following are three areas that need attention:

- **System hardening.**   Includes removing unused services, ensuring that the latest security patches and service packs are installed, and limiting the number of people with administrative permissions. Hardening the system minimizes the risk of a security breach to the system.

- **Application hardening.**   Includes applying the latest security patches and enforcing user-level security if available. Applications on a system can be client applications, such as a Web browser, or server applications, such as a Web server application. Hardening the applications on a system minimizes the chance of a security breach using an application.

- **Enable local file security.**   Enabling local-level file security could include applying access control lists (ACLs) or an Encrypting File System (EFS); each would help ensure that only authorized people have access to the sensitive data stored in files on the hard disk.

Securing Applications

When you secure applications on a server, you ensure that the latest security patches and service packs are installed. You also enable any authentication methods available for the applications.

User Authentication

User authentication verifies that your company's information is being accessed only by authorized users. User authentication can take many forms, but typically employs a user name and password to access information.

Smart Card Authentication

Smart cards offer a two-factor authentication method. With smart cards, the system reads a chip that contains certain information, and then a password or personal identification number (PIN) must be provided to authenticate a user.

Note   The information stored on a smart card is a private key, which is covered in more depth in Chapter 3, "Certificate Basics."

Certificates

One risk associated with a person providing a user name and password is that someone might be able to capture that information and then use it to impersonate that user. To encrypt the information passing between the client and server during the user authentication process, use certificates. Certificates are used to issue public and private encryption keys.

When you use encryption keys to secure communications there are a pair of keys involved, a public key and a private key. The *public key* is used to either encrypt or sign data, and the *private key* is used to decrypt the data. The private key can also be used for authentication by encrypting a digital certificate that only the private key is able to decrypt.

You get certificates from a certification authority (CA), which can be a certificate server your company creates or another company that specializes in providing certificates.

Biometric Authentication

Biometric authentication is available when you need more exotic authentication methods. With biometric authentication, a physical characteristic and knowledge are combined to provide authentication. For instance, a user's retina or thumbprint is scanned and used for authentication in concert with a PIN or password.

Enabling Auditing

Enabling auditing does not provide a method of defense through securing a system. *Auditing* is used to capture security-related events in a log file. You then use the log file to identify possible security breaches or attempts at breaching security. In the event of a security breach, you can use the log files to help identify and prosecute the unauthorized user.

Lesson Review

The following questions are intended to reinforce key information presented in this lesson. If you are unable to answer a question, review the lesson and then try the question again. Answers to the questions can be found in Appendix A, "Questions and Answers."

1. Your company has a high-speed Internet connection that can be used to access the Internet and allows people on the Internet to access your company's Web site. Each user also has a modem that he or she can use for Internet access in case the high-speed connection fails. Users can select the Web browser they want to use and are allowed to manage their own computers. Which of the following are things you could do to defend against intrusion?

   a. Increase the number of Web browsers that can be used to make it more difficult for a hacker to identify and exploit the Web browser application.

   b. Limit the number of Web browsers that can be used to one or two so that you can better manage application updates.

   c. Have each user access the Internet using his or her modem so that hackers will be confused by the number of physical connections your company has to the Internet.

   d. Minimize the number of physical connection points to the Internet by removing the modem connections.

2. Your company wants to make sure that users with an administrator account for the network require a more stringent form of authentication than regular users. Name three methods that can be used.

3. Auditing is used to secure the network and systems on your network. (True or False?)

Lesson Summary

- Secure your network infrastructure and reduce the number of intrusion points as much as possible while still providing your company's employees with the resources and capabilities they need to be productive.

- Ensure that applications that access or communicate across the Internet have the latest security patches installed and configured to be as secure as possible and still allow your company's employees to do their jobs effectively.

- Use some form of authentication method to validate that a user attempting to access a resource should have access to that resource. Use the strongest authentication method feasible for your infrastructure.

- Enable auditing to identify when suspicious events occur and to provide a record of events that occur on your company's network and servers.

- Hardening a network, systems, and applications can be described as removing as many potential security risks as possible from the system to make it less vulnerable to attack. Harden your company's network, computer systems, and the applications running on servers and user computers.

Lesson 5: Organizational and Operational Security

Laws vary around the world, but for purposes of information security, you need to understand forensics and proper hiring and firing procedures. Without understanding the legal issues involved in these two areas, you might destroy the evidence needed to convict someone who has caused your company damage, and you might open your company up to electronic attack from a disgruntled employee.

After this lesson, you will be able to

- Understand why data preservation is important after an attack
- Understand what evidence chain of custody is
- Understand human resources concerns
- Understand employee privacy concerns

Estimated lesson time: 15 minutes

Preserving Data

Forensics is applying science to law. For information security, *forensics* is the investigation and analysis of a computer for the purpose of gathering potential legal evidence. For this to occur, data has to be preserved, and a strict chain of custody protocol must be followed. Forensics specialists (typically working for law enforcement agencies) are called in to gather evidence. You must be aware of the nature of the evidence they are gathering so that you don't inadvertently destroy it. When electronic evidence is gone, it's gone.

Chain of Custody

When you are preserving data in an attempt to prosecute someone who has breached your security, it is not only important to preserve the data, but also to identify the chain of custody for the evidence collected to ensure it is admissible and defendable in a court of law.

Chain of custody procedures ensure the integrity of the information collected by tracking its handling and storage from the point of collection to final disposition of the evidence. This procedure is used after you have been attacked and are attempting to collect data that will be used to prosecute the attacker.

For instance, if your company's Web site was hacked and the attackers downloaded an application that you sell, then you would need to collect as much data as possible to prosecute the thief. The data would have to be gathered, handled, and stored properly to be used as evidence. This includes limiting access to the evidence, documenting who handled the evidence, when it was handled, and why it was handled.

Documentation of this process must include the date and purpose each time evidence is handled or transferred, and identification of each individual in the chain of custody.

Human Resource Concerns and Privacy Issues

Managing information security also includes working with the Human Resources department of your company to ensure that when an employee leaves the company, his or her access to the company's data is terminated. You must be aware of your role in protecting the company by ensuring that you change the former employee's password and revoke his or her access rights.

Privacy issues are a sensitive subject for some employees. These employees feel that what they do with the computer they use in the office is their own business, and believe the e-mail they receive is legally viewable by only them. According to a Privacy Rights Clearinghouse fact sheet on employee monitoring, employers can do the following:

- Monitor what is on a computer screen.
- Monitor and review e-mail.
- Monitor phone calls.
- Maintain and acquire phone records.

Often, employers place logon banners on their systems advising users that monitoring activities take place and use of systems implies consent to this monitoring.

Note   Privacy regulations vary greatly from country to country. You must be cognizant of local laws when managing issues related to privacy.

Lesson Review

The following questions are intended to reinforce key information presented in this lesson. If you are unable to answer a question, review the lesson and then try the question again. Answers to the questions can be found in Appendix A, "Questions and Answers."

1. You discover that an intruder has compromised your company's C-I-A triad. Of the choices listed below, which is the most appropriate action you should take in response to this threat, and why?

    a. Attempt to identify the person that compromised the system.

    b. Preserve the log files for a forensics expert.

    c. Empty the log files so that you can try to capture specific data if another attack occurs.

    d. Leave any log files with the company's receptionist so that the forensics expert can find them.

2. If an employee is fired, what should you do as an information security specialist?

Lesson Summary

- Forensics is the investigation and analysis of a computer for the purpose of gathering and preserving evidence.

- When an employee is terminated, you must remove his or her ability to access information to minimize the chance of retaliation.

- When an attack occurs, preserve the data so that a forensics expert can attempt to gather enough information to find and eventually prosecute the attacker. When you preserve data, you do not need to collect the data; you simply need to make sure you do not destroy the data.

- Your company's employees do not own the e-mail they receive in their e-mail account at work, nor is the telephone theirs. The e-mail stored in an employee's account is subject to review by the company, as are their telephone records and calls.

- When the company dismisses an employee, you must change passwords or disable his or her accounts to prevent access to company information. A disgruntled employee can wreak havoc on the C-I-A triad.

C H A P T E R   2

TCP/IP Basics

About This Chapter

This chapter provides an overview of the Transmission Control Protocol/Internet Protocol (TCP/IP) protocol suite as it relates to information security. You are expected to already understand the basics of TCP/IP. After reviewing this chapter, you will know enough to understand how the various TCP/IP protocols are exploited to hack your network.

Important   If you are not comfortable with the construction of IP packets, read Request for Comment (RFC) 791, which can be found through the RFC Editor Website at *http://rfceditor.org*, or in the \RFC folder on the Supplemental Course Materials CD-ROM that comes with this book. For detailed information, see the *Microsoft Windows 2000 TCP/IP Protocols and Services Technical Reference* by Thomas Lee and Joseph Davis (Microsoft Press, 2000).

Before You Begin

The prerequisite knowledge expected for the Security+ candidate is the CompTIA A+ and Network+ certifications or equivalent knowledge, along with knowledge and experience with TCP/IP. There are no prerequisites for this chapter, but this book assumes you meet the prerequisites specified by CompTIA.

Lesson 1: Basic TCP/IP Principles

Computers communicate with each other to request and share information. When one computer communicates with another computer, an application running on the source computer forms a request that can be serviced by an application running on the destination computer. The two applications must be written to understand what is being requested and what is being returned.

To communicate across the same network, the two computers must be configured to form similar information packets made up of data bits that can be placed on a network, received by the correct destination computer, interpreted, and then can return the requested information.

To communicate across multiple networks, such as when communicating with another computer across the Internet, the packet must be formed in a manner that will be understood by all of the computers that will receive and forward the information packet. There must also be a unique identifier for the source computer, and a unique identifier for the destination computer to ensure that the communications reaches the correct destination computer.

When two computers communicate across the Internet (as shown in Figure 2-1), any number of computers, called *routers*, must receive the data packet, read the addressing information, and determine if the destination computer is local to that router or if the packet needs to be transmitted to another router for delivery to the destination computer.

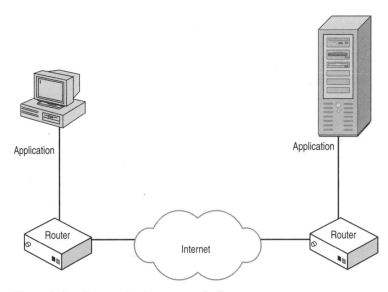

Figure 2-1.   Communications across the Internet

This routing of information requires that all computers follow the same set of rules for creating and handling packets, but have the flexibility to support a number of different transmission needs, such as different maximum frame sizes.

The information being passed from the source computer to the destination computer might also be confidential in nature. Although each router along the path must be able to read the addressing information, there must be a way to secure the data being transported so that only the destination computer can receive and interpret the information being sent by the source computer.

After this lesson, you will be able to

■ Map the TCP/IP protocol suite to the seven layer Open Systems Interconnection (OSI) communication model

■ Identify the fields of the IP header

■ Explain what packet encapsulation is

■ Explain the process of fragmentation and reassembly

Estimated lesson time: 45 minutes

What Is TCP/IP?

TCP/IP is the suite of protocols used to communicate on the Internet. Each protocol of the TCP/IP protocol suite is associated with a layer of the seven-layer OSI communications model, which is an International Organization for Standardization standard. The seven layers are the Physical layer, Data Link layer, Network layer, Transport layer, Session Layer, Presentation Layer, and the Application layer. The TCP/IP protocols are shown with their respective layers in Figure 2-2.

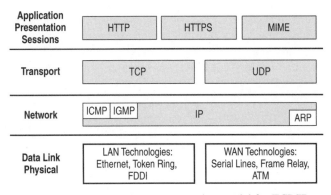

Figure 2-2.   OSI seven-layer presentation model for TCP/IP

Each layer of the protocol stack has a particular function when communications occurs between two computers:

- **Physical layer.**   The Physical layer (Layer 1) is typically implemented in hardware and is responsible for placing data bits on and receiving bits from the communications media, such as coaxial cable.

- **Data Link layer.**   The Data Link layer (Layer 2) is responsible for converting data packets that are received from the network layer and encoding them into bits. It is also responsible for accepting bits from the physical layer and converting them into data packets. The data packets that are formed into groups of bits are known as frames. This layer is divided into two sub-layers: the Media Access layer (MAC) and the Logical Link Control layer (LLC). The MAC sub-layer controls how a computer on a network gains access to the data, and permission to transmit that data on the network. The LLC sub-layer manages frame synchronization, error checking, and flow control.

- **Network layer.**   The Network layer (Layer 3) provides routing and switching capabilities, and creates logical paths between two computers to create *virtual circuits*. This layer is responsible for routing, forwarding, addressing, internetworking, error handling, congestion control, and packet sequencing. When packets are received from the Transport layer, the Network layer is responsible for ensuring that the packet is small enough to be a valid packet on the underlying network. If the packet is too large, this layer breaks the packet into several packets, and on the receiving computer, this layer places the packets in the proper sequence to reassemble the packet. If the interconnecting devices cannot handle the amount of traffic being generated, this layer also provides congestion control.

- **Transport layer.**   The Transport layer (Layer 4) transfers data between end systems or hosts, and is responsible for end-to-end error recovery and flow control between the two end systems. This layer ensures complete data transfer between the two systems.

- **Session layer.**   The Session layer (Layer 5) establishes, manages, and terminates connections between applications on two computers. The session layer sets up, coordinates, and terminates all interchanges between applications on both computers. This layer manages session and connection coordination.

- **Presentation layer.**   The Presentation layer (Layer 6) provides a heterogeneous operating environment by translating from the application's data format to the underlying network's communications format. This layer is also known as the *syntax* layer.

- **Application layer.**   The Application layer (Layer 7) support end-user and application processes. Communication partners and quality of service levels are identified, user authentication and privacy considered, and any constraints on data syntax identified.

Note   The Internet Protocol (IP) operates at the Network layer. The Internet relies on the services provided by IP to fragment and route IP datagrams from source computer to destination computer, regardless of the physical network the two computers are on. For IP networks, a *datagram* is a portion of a message transmitted over a packet-switching network. The current version of IP used on the Internet is version 4 (IPv4). A list of IP versions can be found at the Internet Assigned Numbers Authority (IANA) Web site at *http://www.iana.org/assignments/version-numbers*.

Many attacks that occur take advantage of the Internet layer to compromise your defenses and break the confidentiality-integrity-availability (C-I-A) triad, whereas others attack protocols at the Transport and Application layers. To effectively defend against attacks, you must understand what information is available at each layer of the four-layer DARPA communication model, which we discuss next, as well as how the attacks are occurring, which is discussed in Lesson 2.

Reviewing the Four-Layer DARPA Model

The four-layer DARPA model is a collection of protocols that was originally developed in 1968 by BBN Technologies, which was hired by the Defense Advanced Research Projects Agency (DARPA) to establish a packet switched network between research institutions in the United States. At the time, functionality and performance were of greater concern than security. Rather than breaking communications into seven layers, as the International Organization for Standardization (ISO) Open Systems Interconnection (OSI) model specifies, the DARPA model presents four layers. Figure 2-3 shows the general mapping between the four-layer DARPA model and the seven-layer OSI model.

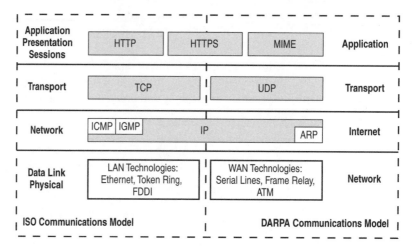

Figure 2-3. Comparing the DARPA communications model to the OSI communications model

- **Application layer.**   The Application layer is the top layer. Protocols, such as Domain Name System (DNS), File Transfer Protocol (FTP), Simple Mail Transfer Protocol (SMTP), or HTTP use the TCP/IP protocol suite to identify and communicate with other computers. The application typically has the name of the destination computer and relies on another service that operates at the Application layer to identify the IP address of the destination.

    Once the IP address of the destination is known, a request (in the form of a packet) is formed, containing detailed information. This is passed to the next lower layer in the DARPA model.

- **Transport layer.**   When a request from the Application layer is received by the Transport layer, the Application layer request includes information that determines which of these Transport layer protocols will be used.

    UDP provides connectionless, unreliable communications, whereas TCP provides connection-oriented, reliable delivery of the information to the destination.

Note   UDP communications is referred to as *unreliable*, which means that the datagrams are sent without sequencing or acknowledgment, and the Application layer is responsible for recovering or resending lost datagrams.

A request is formed and passed to the next lower layer in the DARPA model.

- **Internet layer.**   The Internet layer is responsible for routing packets between networks. IP is a routable protocol that provides the functions necessary to deliver a package of bits from a source to a destination. The request that is formed at this level is a packet of bits known as a datagram. IP provides for transmitting datagrams from sources to destinations, and for fragmentation and reassembly of long datagrams, if necessary, for transmission through "small packet" networks.

  A request is formed and passed to the next lower layer in the DARPA model.

- **Network Interface layer.**   The Network Interface layer is used for communicating with other computers. When a packet is sent from the source computer to the destination computer, the Internet layer determines whether the system is on the local network or on a remote network.

  - If the destination is local, the Network Interface layer uses the ARP protocol to determine the media access control (MAC) address of the destination computer's network interface card, creates a frame header, uses the information passed down from the Internet layer as the payload, creates a preamble, and then pushes the completed packet on to the wire. A frame header is control information added by protocols at this layer. The payload is the packet presented to this layer from the Internet layer.

  - If the destination is remote, the Network Interface layer uses the ARP protocol to determine the MAC address of the designated default gateway, creates a frame header, uses the information in the datagram as the payload, creates a preamble, and then pushes the completed packet on to the wire, where the default gateway sends the packet to an upstream router.

Reviewing the TCP/IP Communications Flow

Any time one computer needs to communicate with another, a sequence of steps is followed. For this example, we relate Web browsing to the TCP/IP communications flow.

When a user at a computer wants to access a Web page, he or she typically starts a Web browser application and types the name of the Web site he or she wishes to visit. The browser generates a request to have the Web site name resolved to an IP address. The browser then attempts to establish communications with that Web site.

The information that is passed from the upper layers of the DARPA model to the lower layers is packaged for delivery by each necessary protocol as it goes down through the TCP/IP stack. When the datagram reaches the destination, the packet is passed up the TCP/IP stack and the process is reversed. Figure 2-4 represents this communications process.

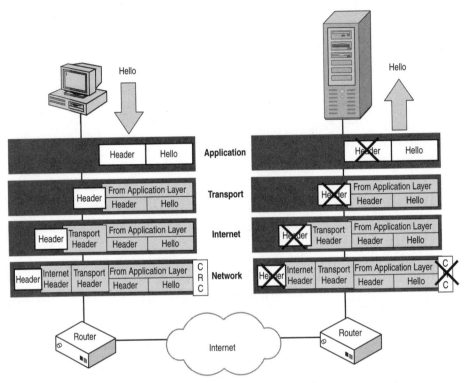

Figure 2-4.   Following communications from a source computer to a destination computer

When application data is sent from one computer to another:

1. The information is passed from the Application layer to the Transport layer.

2. The Transport layer protocols consider the Application layer information as the payload (or data) that needs to be delivered and create a header that contains information such as source and destination port, to help with delivery of the information to the destination computer. That information is passed to the Internet layer.

3. The Internet layer protocols considers the Transport layer information as the payload that needs to be delivered and create an IP header that contains information such as destination IP addresses, to help with delivery of the datagram to the destination computer. That information is passed to the Network Interface layer.

4. The Network Interface layer protocols consider the Internet layer information as the payload that needs to be delivered and creates a preamble and a frame header, which contains the source and destination MAC addresses, to help with delivery of the datagram to a destination on the local network once it arrives, and trailer information, called a checksum that contains the count of the number of bits in a transmission so that the receiver can ensure the packet did not get damaged in transit. A checksum is an error detection method that is used to determine if a single bit error occurred in transmission. The information is placed on the local network.

5. When the information reaches the destination computer, the Network Interface layer protocols strip the preamble and checksum from the packets and then pass the payload to the Internet layer.

6. The Internet layer protocols strip the IP header from the packet and pass the payload to the Transport layer.

7. The Transport layer protocol strips the TCP or UDP header and passes the payload to the Application layer.

8. The application that is specified to manage that data receives the data.

Understanding Network Interface Frames

When the Network Interface layer creates an information packet, or frame, to place on the network, there are three general components to the packet: the header, the payload, and the Frame Check Sequence (FCS).

The payload is the information provided by the Internet layer, whereas the header and FCS (also known as the *trailer*) are created by the Network Interface layer. There are a number of local area network (LAN) protocols that can be used on a network, and each has a different header and trailer structure.

Note   Knowing the LAN technology that is in use allows a hacker to identify the local source and destination addresses and determine what bits of the packet represent the payload. This information can be used to disrupt the C-I-A triad.

Header

Header information differs with different LAN technologies, but there are some things that are always contained in the header. There is always a preamble, or some other sequence of bits that identify the start of a valid frame. All Network Interface layer headers also have fields for the destination and source MAC address. For instance, Ethernet II header packets contain a series of alternating ones and zeros that is 7 bytes long, followed by the bit sequence 10101011. This signals the beginning of a valid Ethernet II packet, and the 6 bytes of data following are the destination MAC address. Figure 2-5 shows an Ethernet II header.

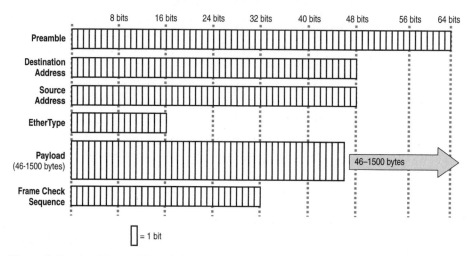

Figure 2-5. An Ethernet II header

Payload

The *payload* is the information that is passed from the application through the Transport and Internet layers to the Network Interface layer. For the Network Interface layer, the payload must be encapsulated in a packet with a header and trailer and then placed on the wire.

The maximum size of a payload varies for various LAN technologies. For instance, the maximum size of an Ethernet II payload is approximately 1500 bytes, whereas the maximum payload for an Asynchronous Transfer Mode (ATM) frame is approximately 48 bytes.

Frame Check Sequence

The FCS is also called a *cyclic redundancy check* (CRC) and provides a bit-level integrity check for the packet. This ensures that the packet arrived without transmission-related damage. The CRC is generated using an algorithm on the bits that comprise some or all of the fields at the source. When the destination computer receives the packet, the same algorithm is used to verify that the packet was not damaged in transit.

More Info   More information about the CRC used in network layer communications can be found at the International Telecommunication Union (ITU) Web site at *http://www.itu.int.*

Understanding IP Datagrams

There are two general components to the IP datagram: the header and the payload. Much like the packet created by the Network Interface layer, when IP is used to form a datagram, there is a structure to the packet that can be recognized by every implementation of TCP/IP in use. This allows any computer running any operating system to communicate with any other computer, as long as both are using the same version of the TCP/IP protocol suite.

Because TCP/IP is an industry-standard protocol and every implementation of TCP/IP can decode the header information of an IP datagram, every hacker and cracker can identify that same information and use it to compromise your C-I-A triad.

Exploring the IP Header

The header portion of an IP packet contains information that is used to determine the characteristics of the packet, the destination and source addresses, whether the datagram is one of several packets, and what protocol is in use.

Although the size of an IP header can vary, it is defined in industry standards. Therefore hackers and crackers are able to sniff a packet on networks, including the Internet, and read the information. Understanding the information that is presented in an IP packet will help you understand how the integrity of the information you send across a local network or the Internet can be compromised. Figure 2-6 shows an IP datagram header. A brief explanation of each field follows.

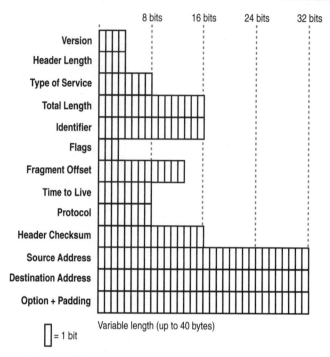

Figure 2-6.   An IP datagram header

- **Version (4 bits).**   The Version field is used to identify the IP version of the packet. IPv4 is the current version in use on the Internet, but there are IPv6 stacks available for most operating systems in use today.

- **Internet Header Length (4 bits).**   The Header Length field identifies how large the IP header is. The field specifies the length of the header in 32-bit words (4-byte blocks) and points to the beginning of the payload. The header defines the length in number of bytes, and the valid numbers range from 5 to 15. This means the header length can range from 20 bytes to 60 bytes in length.

- **Type of Service (8 bits).**   This field is used to define the parameters for the type of service desired. Service levels that can be requested as a packet travels from the source computer to the destination computer include levels of priority, delay, throughput, and reliability.

- **Total Length (16 bits).**   This is the total length of the datagram (measured in bytes), and includes both the header and payload. When you read the RFC defining the IP datagram (see RFC 791), you will notice it states that this field is measured in octets. An octet is 8 bits in length, which is a byte. The maximum size of a valid IP datagram is 65,535 bytes, although the RFC-recommended size is 576 bytes, which allows for a 64-byte header and a 512-byte payload.

- **Identifier (16 bits).** This value is set by the sender and is used for reassembly of fragmented IP datagrams at the destination.

- **Flags (3 bits).** These bits are used to indicate whether an IP datagram can be fragmented, and if so, if it is the last fragment. IP fragmentation is covered in more depth later in this chapter.

- **Fragment Offset (13 bits).** This field specifies where in the IP datagram this fragment belongs. This is measured in 8-byte (64-bit) increments, and the first fragment always has an offset of 0, because it is the first fragment in the series. The fragment and fragment offset information is extremely important because datagrams do not always reach the destination in order.

- **Time-to-Live (8 bits).** The Time-to-Live (TTL) field specifies the maximum number of links a packet can pass through to reach the destination computer. The source computer sets the maximum TTL, and then each router that handles the packet decrements the TTL by 1 and forwards the packet. If the TTL decrements to 0 before reaching the destination, the packet is discarded.

- **Protocol (8 bits).** This field specifies the protocol used at the Transport layer of the DARPA four-layer model. For instance, if the datagram is a TCP packet, then this field would be set to 6. If it were a UDP packet, this field would be set to 17. For a complete list of valid protocols, refer to *http://www.iana.org/ assignments/protocol-numbers*.

- **Header Checksum (16 bits).** This field is used to provide a bit-level integrity check of the header information. This checksum is for the IP header only and does not include the IP payload portion of the datagram. The source computer calculates the initial checksum before the packet is sent. As each router receives the packet, the checksum is verified, the TTL is decremented, a new checksum is calculated, and the packet is forwarded. If the checksum is incorrect at any router between the source and destination computer, the datagram is discarded.

- **Source IP Address (32 bits).** This is the IP address of the source computer.

- **Destination IP Address (32 bits).** This is the IP address of the destination computer.

- **IP Options and Padding (variable).** This field is optional and can vary in length. If this field is used, it must be added in increments of 32 bits. That is, if the datagram has one option (defined in 8 bits), an additional 24 bits (all zeroes) must be added as padding. Thus the added option will add 32 bits (4 bytes) to the overall length of the IP header. Each option is defined in 8 bits, and has three fields: a 1-bit copied flag, a 2-bit option class, and a 5-bit option number. More information about options can be found at *http://www.iana.org/assignments/ip*.

Payload

The payload is the packet that is provided by the Transport layer. This packet includes the Application layer data, which is added to a Transport layer packet for delivery to the destination computer.

Note   The size of the payload can vary greatly, because the IP protocol allows an overall IP datagram size of up to 65,535 bytes, but can be as small as approximately 600 bytes.

Reviewing ICMP Header Fields

The ICMP protocol reports errors and control conditions on behalf of the IP protocol. This is because the IP protocol provides end-to-end datagram delivery capabilities, but is not designed to be absolutely reliable. Figure 2-7 shows an ICMP header. A brief explanation of each field follows.

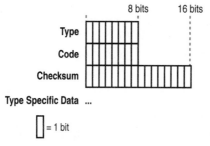

Figure 2-7.   ICMP message structure and header fields

The ICMP message is encapsulated in an IP datagram. As with the IP datagram, there is a Network Interface layer header and trailer, and an IP header. With those are the ICMP header and ICMP message data. The ICMP header fields can vary, but always have the following fields:

- **Type (8 bits).**   This field specifies the format of the ICMP message. This includes Echo Request, Echo Reply, Source Quench, Parameter Problem, and so forth.

  More Info   A complete list of ICMP parameters for the Type field is available at *http://www.iana.org/assignments/icmp-parameters*.

- **Code (8 bits).**   This field further qualifies ICMP message within an ICMP type. When combined with the ICMP type, it can identify the specific ICMP message. For instance, if the type field is 3 (destination unreachable), and the code is 1 (host unreachable), that would indicate that the network was reachable, but the host was not. The specific fields for each type field are listed in the ICMP parameters document listed in the preceding note.

- **Checksum (16 bits).**   This field provides a checksum for the ICMP message. The algorithm used for this checksum is the same algorithm used for the IP header.

- **Optional Data.**   This field is an optional data field that can be used by the ICMP type.

Reviewing IGMP Header Fields

The IGMP protocol provides *multicast* or one-to-many datagram delivery. For instance, if you want to send the same datagram to 100 computers, you would use the IGMP protocol to send the message. With IP, you would have to send 100 separate datagrams to accomplish the same task.

To receive multicast datagrams, a computer must inform the router it uses to forward multicast traffic. This is accomplished by sending a *host membership report*, an IGMP protocol message that a computer sends to the router it is configured to use requesting that multicast messages be forwarded. Once the router receives the report, it forwards multicast datagrams.

A *host membership query* is an IGMP protocol datagram that a router sends at intervals to verify that computers on a segment are still listening for multicast traffic. Figure 2-8 shows the IGMP message structure.

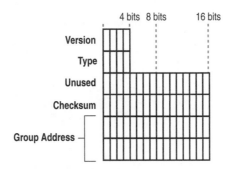

Figure 2-8.   IGMP message structure

Like ICMP, the IGMP message is encapsulated in an IP datagram. As with the IP datagram, there is a Network Interface layer header and trailer, and an IP header. With those is the IGMP message data. There are different versions of IGMP, and each has different header information.

For IGMP version 1 (IGMPv1), the header has the following fields:

- **Version (4 bits).**   This field indicates the version of IGMP that is in use.
- **Type (4 bits).**   This field indicates the type of IGMP message.
- **Unused (8 bits).**   This field is unused. The sender blanks the field and the receiver ignores the field.
- **Checksum (16 bits).**   The checksum is the 16-bit one's complement of the one's complement sum of the 8-byte IGMP message. When the checksum is computed, the checksum field should first be set to 0. When the data packet is transmitted, the checksum is computed and inserted into this field. When the data packet is received, the checksum is again computed and verified against the checksum field. If the two checksums do not match then an error has occurred.
- **Group Address (32 bits).**   In a Host Membership Query message, the group address field is zeroed when sent, ignored when received. In a Host Membership Report message, the group address field holds the IP host group address of the group being reported. For IGMP version 2 (IGMPv2), the header has the following fields:
- **Type (8 bits).**   This field indicates the type of IGMP message and is a combination of the version and type fields that IGMPv1 identifies.
- **Maximum Response Time (8 bits).**   The Max Response Time field is used only in Membership Query messages. It specifies the maximum allowed time before sending a responding report in units of 1/10 second. In all other messages, it is set to zero by the sender and ignored by receivers.

   Varying this setting allows IGMPv2 routers to tune the "leave latency" (the time between the moment the last host leaves a group and when the routing protocol is notified that there are no more members). It also allows tuning of the amount of IGMP burst traffic on a subnet.
- **Checksum (16 bits).**   The 16-bit one's complement of the one's complement sum of the IGMP message, starting with the IGMP Type field. For computing the checksum, the checksum field should first be set to 0. When the data packet is transmitted, the checksum is computed and inserted into this field. When the data packet is received, the checksum is again computed and verified against the checksum field. If the two checksums do not match then an error has occurred.
- **Group Address (32 bits).**   In a Membership Query message, this field is set to zero when sending a General Query, and set to the group address being queried when sending a Group-Specific Query. In a Membership Report or Leave Group message, this field holds the IP multicast group address of the group being reported or left.

Understanding Fragmentation

Different networks support different maximum-sized frames of information. For this reason, an IP datagram might need to be split into several datagrams for transmission and then reassembled at the destination computer. *Fragmentation* is breaking a single IP datagram into several smaller datagrams for transport across "small-packet" networks. This allows packets to travel from a source computer to a destination computer across various types of networks. Figure 2-9 shows an IP datagram being fragmented into three datagrams in the following way:

1. The TCP datagram is packaged into a frame.
2. A frame is placed on the local network.
3. An intermediary router fragments the datagram into three fragments.
4. Three fragments are received by the destination computer.
5. Destination computer reassembles the three fragments using information in the header.

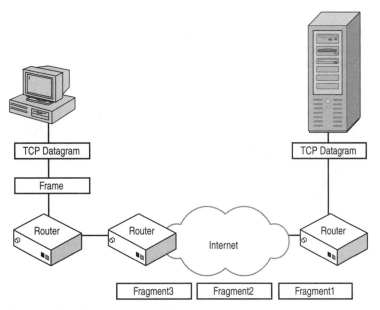

Figure 2-9.   Fragmenting an IP datagram

In Figure 2-9, an IP datagram is transmitted on a network that supports a maximum packet size of 4352 bytes to a router that connects to the destination computer's network. The maximum packet size supported on that network is 1492 bytes. The actual size of the packet is 1600 bytes, so it must be fragmented before it can be sent to the destination computer.

When the router receives the IP datagram, it divides the payload of the IP datagram into two pieces, and then adds a header to each. The header contains information that allows the destination computer to recognize the packet is fragmented and to reassemble the IP payload information when both datagrams are received.

Understanding Transport Layer Communications

The UDP and TCP protocols are used at the Transport layer of the four-layer DARPA communications model. Understanding the header information for the Transport layer protocols and how each initiates communications will help you understand how hackers and crackers take advantage of that information to compromise your C-I-A triad.

When one computer communicates with another, applications must be running on both computers to send and receive the data. The UDP and TCP protocols provide a procedure that the applications use to accomplish this communication. Two pieces of information that allow computers to communicate are the IP address and the port address. The destination IP address identifies the destination computer, and the destination port helps identify the application that will receive the information.

Reviewing User Datagram Protocol and its Header Fields

More Info   Assigned port numbers for well-known ports, registered ports, dynamic ports, and private ports can be found at *http://www.iana.org/cgi-bin/sys-port-number.pl.*

The UDP protocol is connectionless; therefore there is no handshake with the destination computer to establish communications before transmitting data to the destination computer. Examples of Application layer protocols that communicate using the UDP protocol are DNS and Trivial File Transfer Protocol (TFTP). The header fields that are defined in the UDP header are as follows:

- **Source Port (16 bits).**   This is an optional field that indicates the port of the sending process. It is optional because the sender is not establishing communication to the destination, rather it is sending a message.
- **Destination Port (16 bits).**   This field identifies the port that will receive the data on the destination computer.
- **Length (16 bits).**   This field indicates the length in octets of the datagram, including the UDP header and data.
- **Checksum (16 bits).**   This field provides a checksum for the UDP message. The algorithm used for this checksum is the same algorithm used for the IP header. The checksum is calculated including the UDP pseudo-header. The pseudo-header is created and conceptually prefixed to the UDP header and is used to help protect against misrouted datagrams. It is a pseudo-header because it is not actually sent with the datagram.

Reviewing the Transmission Control Protocol and its Header Fields

The TCP protocol is *connection-oriented*, which means that the source and destination computer establish a connection and then transfer data. This ensures reliable delivery of the data to the destination computer. TCP also supports *bytestream*, which means the data from the Application layer is segmented into datagrams that the source and destination computers will support, and then reassembled at the destination computer. The TCP header structure has the following fields:

- **Source Port (16 bits).**   This field indicates the Application layer protocol that is sending the TCP segment. It is combined with the IP address to create a *socket*, a unique identifier that acts as an endpoint in a connection because it defines the computer and Application layer protocol in the top layer of the TCP/IP stack that will manage the communications between two computers.

- **Destination Port (16 bits).**   This field indicates the Application layer protocol for the destination computer.

- **Sequence Number (32 bits).**   This field represents the first data octet of the segment. Because TCP supports bytestream communications, the Application layer is responsible for reassembling the incoming TCP segments.

- **Acknowledgement Number (32 bits).**   This field specifies the value of the next sequence number the sender of the segment is expecting to receive.

- **Data Offset (4 bits).**   This field indicates where the TCP segment data begins and is used when the segments are reassembled.

- **Reserved (6 bits).**   These are reserved for future use and must be set to 0.

- **Flags (6 bits).**   This field provides the control bits, also called TCP flags.

More Info   The TCP flags are defined in RFC 3168, and Internet Official Protocol Standards document STD0007.

- **Window (16 bits).**   This indicates the number of data octets that the sender of the segment is willing to accept, which is the available receive buffer size.

- **Checksum (16 bits).**   This field provides a checksum for the UDP message. The algorithm used for this checksum is the same algorithm used for the IP header.

- **Urgent Pointer (16 bits).**   This field indicates the location of urgent data in the segment. This field is only used if the control bits are set to Urgent Pointer field significant (URG).

- **Options and Padding (variable).**   One or more TCP options can be added to the TCP header.

The TCP Three-Way Handshake

To establish TCP communications, two computers use a *three-way handshake*, as shown in Figure 2-10. The handshake process uses the information in the header to establish a communications link between the two computers that will provide reliable data transfer.

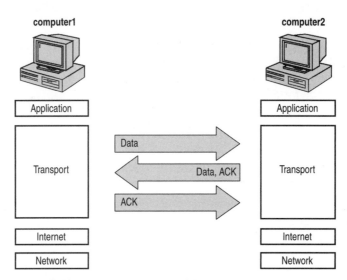

Figure 2-10.   TCP three-way handshake

With the three-way handshake the two computers that are establishing communications set a starting sequence number for the data being sent, the size of the receive buffer, the maximum segment size, and the TCP options supported. For this example, computer1 is establishing communications with computer2. The three segments that are used to establish communications are as follows:

- **SYN segment.**   This is the first segment of the three-way handshake. The information sent by computer1 includes source and destination port, starting sequence number, the receive buffer size, maximum TCP segment size, and the supported TCP options.

- **SYN-ACK segment.**   This segment is the reply that computer2 returns to computer1. The information sent includes source and destination port, starting sequence number, acknowledgment number, receive buffer size, maximum TCP segment size, and an acknowledgment that computer2 supports the options that computer1 sends. When computer2 sends this message, it reserves resources to support this connection.

- **ACK segment.**   This segment is sent by computer1 to establish the final TCP connection parameters that will be used between the two computers. The information sent includes the source and destination ports, sequence number, acknowledgment number, ACK flags, and window size.

Once the handshake is complete, both computers recognize how communications will occur, what the starting sequence number is, what limitations exist for packet size, and what TCP options are supported. They are then ready to begin data transfer.

Exercise 1:   Following a Packet from Source to Destination

In this exercise, place the steps in the order they would occur if you were connecting to a Web page from your home computer.

1. The Network Interface layer protocols consider the Internet layer information as the payload (or data) that needs to be delivered and they create header information to help with delivery of the datagram to a destination on the local network, as well as trailer information that is used to ensure the packet did not get damaged in transit. That information is placed on the local network.

2. The Transport layer protocol strips the header and trailer information and passes the payload to the Application layer.

3. The Internet layer protocols consider the Transport layer information as the payload (or data) that needs to be delivered and they create header information to help with delivery of the datagram to the destination. That information is passed to the Network Interface layer.

4. The Internet layer protocols strip the header and trailer information from the packet, and pass the payload to the Transport layer.

5. The application that is specified to manage that data receives the data.

6. An application is started that needs to connect to a server and retrieve information. A message is created and passed from the Application layer to the Transport layer.

7. The Network Interface layer protocols strip the header and trailer information from the datagram and pass the payload to the Internet layer.

8. The Transport layer protocols consider the Application layer information as the payload (or data) that needs to be delivered and they create header information to help with delivery of the information to the destination. That information is passed to the Internet layer.

Exercise 2: Identifying Information Captured Using Network Monitor

In this exercise, you will view and identify information captured using Microsoft Network Monitor on a system running the Microsoft Windows XP operating system. Figure 2-11 shows the results of a network capture when viewing the home page at *http://www.ietf.org*.

Refer to Figure 2-11 and provide the missing information in the list below.

- Ethernet frame length: _____
- IP version: _____
- Application-level protocol in use: _____
- First octet of the source IP address: _____
- First octet of the destination IP address: _____

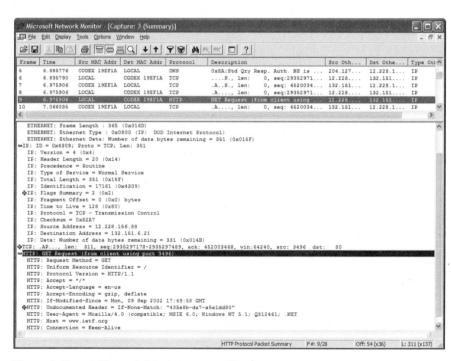

Figure 2-11. A Network Monitor capture file

If you have a system connected to the Internet, and you are either at home connecting to an ISP or have explicit, written permission to capture network traffic, you can capture network traffic and use your capture file to identify the information listed above. Follow the steps listed below to duplicate the results displayed in Figure 2-11, using your network monitor.

1. Flush the DNS look-up cache (if applicable for your operating system). For instance, if you are running Windows XP, you type **ipconfig /flushdns** at the command prompt.

2. Start a network monitor capture.

3. Open a Web browser. Go to *http://www.ietf.org* and view the home page.

4. After returning to the home page configured in your Web browser, close the Web browser.

5. Stop the network monitor capture.

6. View the captured data.

Lesson Review

The following questions are intended to reinforce key information presented in this lesson. If you are unable to answer a question, review the lesson and then try the question again. Answers to the questions can be found in Appendix A, "Questions and Answers."

1. After each layer of the DARPA communications model shown below, list the TCP/IP protocols that the particular layer uses.

   Application Layer

   Transport Layer

   Internet Layer

   Network Interface Layer

2. Place the following TCP/IP communications steps in the correct order:

   a. The IP protocol adds a header to the packet and passes the packet to the next lower layer.

   b. The Transport layer protocol adds a header to the Application layer request and passes the packet to the next lower layer.

   c. The network interface adds header and trailer information to the packet and places it on the network.

   d. An application is started that requests communications with a computer on the network. The application forms a packet and passes the request to the next lower layer.

   e. The Transport layer strips the header and passes the packet to the next higher layer.

   f. The Network Interface layer receives the packet from the network, strips the header and trailer information, and passes the packet to the next higher layer.

   g. The Internet layer strips the header and passes the packet to the next higher layer.

   h. The Application layer strips the header and passes the information to the application.

3. What protocol and field store the address of the destination computer?

   a. The source address of the Ethernet II frame

   b. The destination address of the Ethernet II frame

   c. The source address of the IP datagram

   d. The destination address of the IP datagram

4. Which header contains a field that specifies the total size of a frame?

   a. Transport layer header

   b. Internet layer header

   c. Network Interface layer header

   d. All of the above

Lesson Summary

In this lesson, you reviewed the four layers of the DARPA communications model, associated the TCP/IP protocol suite to those layers, and identified the various fields of an IP header. Specifically, you should understand the following:

- The four layers in the DARPA communications model are the Application layer, Transport layer, Internet layer, and the Network Interface layer.

- Applications operate at the Application layer and typically when two computers communicate, they both have an application that can interpret the communication packets sent by the other computer.

- The Transport layer supports the TCP and UDP protocols. UDP provides efficient communications, but TCP provides reliable, connection-oriented communications.

- The IP, ICMP, and IGMP protocols operate at the Internet layer of the DARPA communication model. The IP address header contains the source and destination computer IP addresses and identifies the Transport layer protocol of the datagram.

- The Network Interface layer is responsible for actually placing the packet on the network. The header information added at this layer provides the MAC address of the source and local network destination computer.

- The fields of the header information at the Transport, Internet, and Network Interface layers can all vary in length, but are all well-defined and the information in the header can be interpreted by any application that understands IP header information.

Lesson 2: TCP/IP Layers and Vulnerabilities

Now that you have reviewed the four communication layers used with the TCP/IP suite and can identify the information that is contained in an IP datagram, you should consider the types of attacks that might occur at each level. This is not meant to be a comprehensive list; rather it provides you with an understanding of the types of attacks that can occur at different levels.

In Chapter 11, "Incident Detection and Response," you will review attacks that have already occurred on local networks as well as on the Internet, and each provides detailed information on how the TCP/IP protocol was exploited.

After this lesson, you will be able to

- Identify the types of attacks that can occur at the Network Interface layer
- Identify the types of attacks that can occur at the Internet layer
- Identify the types of attacks that can occur at the Transport layer
- Identify the types of attacks that can occur at the Application layer

Estimated lesson time: 20 minutes

Identifying Possible Network Interface Layer Attacks

At the Network Interface layer, the packet of information that is placed on the wire is known as a *frame*. The packet is comprised of three areas: the header, the payload, and the FCS. Because the Network Interface layer is used for communications on a local network, the attacks that occur at this level would be carried out on local networks. Some of the ways the network layer can be exploited to compromise the C-I-A triad include the following:

- **MAC address spoofing.**   The header contains the MAC address of the source and destination computers and is required to successfully send a directed message from a source computer to a destination computer. Attackers can easily spoof the MAC address of another computer. Any security mechanism based on MAC addresses is vulnerable to this type of attack.

- **Denial of service (DoS).**   A DoS attack overloads a single system so that it cannot provide the service it is configured to provide. An ARP protocol attack could be launched against a computer to overwhelm it, which would make it unavailable to support the C-I-A triad.

- **ARP cache poisoning.**   The ARP cache stores MAC addresses of computers on the local network that have been contacted within a certain amount of time in memory. If incorrect, or *spoofed*, entries were added to the ARP cache, then the computer is not able to send information to the correct destination.

Identifying Possible Internet Layer Attacks

At the Internet layer, IP datagrams are formed. The packet is comprised of two areas: the header and the payload. Some of the ways the Internet layer can be exploited to compromise the C-I-A triad include the following:

- **IP address spoofing.**   If the IP header fields and lengths are known, the IP address in the IP datagram can be easily discovered and spoofed. Any security mechanism based on the source IP address is vulnerable to this attack.
- **Man-in-the-middle attacks.**   This attack occurs when a hacker places himself or herself between the source and destination computer in such a way that neither notices his or her existence. Meanwhile, the attacker can modify packets or simply view their contents.
- **DoS.**   With a DoS attack at this level, simple IP-level protocols and utilities can be exploited to overload a computer, thus breaking the C-I-A triad.
- **Incorrect reassembly of fragmented datagrams.**   For fragmented datagrams, the Offset field is used with packet reassembly. If the offset is changed, the datagram is reformed incorrectly. This could allow a datagram that would typically not pass through a firewall to gain access to your internal network, and could disrupt the C-I-A triad.
- **Corrupting packets.**   Because IP datagrams can pass through several computers between the source and destination, the information in the IP header fields is read and sometimes modified, such as when the information reaches a router. If the packet is intercepted, the information in the header can be modified, corrupting the IP datagram. This could cause the datagram to never reach the destination computer, or it could change the protocols and payload information in the datagram.

Identifying Possible Transport Layer Attacks

At the Transport layer, either a UDP header is added to the message or a TCP header is added. The application that is requesting the service determines what protocol will be used. Some of the ways the Transport layer can be exploited to compromise the C-I-A triad include the following:

- **Manipulation of the UDP or TCP ports.**   By knowing the UDP and TCP header fields and lengths, the ports that are used for communications between a source and destination computer can be identified, and that information can be corrupted or exploited.

- **DoS.** With a DoS attack at this level, simple IP-level protocols and utilities can be exploited to overload a computer, thus breaking the C-I-A triad. For instance, by knowing the steps involved in a three-way TCP handshake, a hacker or cracker might send the packets in the incorrect order and disrupt the availability of one of your servers. An example of this is a SYN flood, where a hacker sends a large number of SYN packets to a server and leaves the session half open. The server leaves these sessions half-open for a prescribed amount of time. If the hacker is successful in opening all available sessions, legitimate traffic will be unable to reach the server.

- **Session hijacking.** This kind of attack occurs after a source and destination computer have established a communications link. A third computer disables the ability of one the computers to communicate, and then imitates that computer. Because the connection has already been established, the third computer can disrupt your C-I-A triad.

Identifying Possible Application Layer Attacks

Application layer attacks can be some of the most difficult to protect against because they take advantage of vulnerabilities in applications and lack of end-user knowledge of computer security. Some of the ways the Application layer can be exploited to compromise the C-I-A triad include the following:

- **E-mail application exploits.** Attachments can be added to e-mail messages and delivered to a user's inbox. The user can open the e-mail message and run the application. The attachment might do immediate damage, or might lay dormant and be used later. Similarly, hackers often embed malicious code in Hypertext Markup Language (HTML) formatted messages. Exploits of this nature might take advantage of vulnerability in the client's e-mail application or a lack of user knowledge about e-mail security concerns.

- **Web browser exploits.** When a client computer uses a Web browser to connect to a Web server and download a Web page, the content of the Web page can be active. That is, the content is not just static information, but can be executable code. If the code is malicious, it can be used to disrupt the C-I-A triad.

- **FTP client exploits.** File Transfer Protocol (FTP) is used to transfer files from one computer to another. When a client has to provide a user name and password for authentication, that information can be sent across the Internet using plain text. The information can be captured at any point along the way. If the client uses the same user name and password as they use to attach to your corporate servers, that information could be obtained by a hacker or cracker and used to access your company's information.

Lesson Review

The following questions are intended to reinforce key information presented in this lesson. If you are unable to answer a question, review the lesson and then try the question again. Answers to the questions can be found in Appendix A, "Questions and Answers."

1. At what layer of the DARPA communication model can a DoS attack occur?

   a. Network Interface layer

   b. Internet layer

   c. Transport layer

   d. Application layer

   e. All of the above

   f. None of the above

2. An attack occurs that attempts to disrupt a computer by sending TCP hand-shake packets in the wrong order. At what communications layer would this attack occur?

   a. Network Interface layer

   b. Internet layer

   c. Transport layer

   d. Application layer

Lesson Summary

Knowing the information that is available in each field of the headers created at the Network Interface, Internet, and Transport layers of the TCP/IP protocol suite allows dissimilar computers running on dissimilar networks to communicate with each other, because the information that is passed from computer to computer can be interpreted by each computer. This provides great functionality and communications compatibility, but unfortunately, it also provides hackers and crackers with the information needed to disrupt your company's C-I-A triad. The types of attacks that can be formed at each layer include the following:

■ Attacks at the Network Interface layer involve manipulation of the header information and addressing. This layer supports communication on a local network, and therefore uses MAC addresses to communicate. Attacks at this layer are localized to a single network, and can use the MAC addressing information protocols that are used to resolve MAC addresses to deny or disrupt communications.

■ Attacks at the Internet layer also involve manipulation of the header information and addressing. The IP addresses of the source and destination computers are part of the header, as well as the Transport layer protocol that particular datagram is using. Attacks can therefore involve exploiting the IP addressing information. Other attacks at this layer could cause a denial of service, or cause fragmented datagrams to be reassembled incorrectly.

■ Attacks at the Transport layer can take advantage of the TCP and UDP protocols and the various implementations of those protocols. Examples of this type of attack would be sending the ending sequence of a TCP three-way handshake, or sending a packet that is larger that the largest supported packet size.

■ Attacks at the Application layer typically attack applications that are used to pass information between client and server computers. An example of this would be a client opening a Web browser and retrieving a Web page from a Web server. An attack might send damaging information and commands to the client computer.

C H A P T E R   3

Certificate Basics

About This Chapter

This chapter introduces the basic principles of cryptography, certificates, and symmetric and asymmetric keys. By the end of this chapter, you should be familiar with the basic terminology used to describe cryptography for information security and have an understanding of the structure that supports certificate use.

Before You Begin

There are no prerequisites for this chapter.

Lesson 1: Understanding Cryptography

Cryptography is defined as secret writing, or the enciphering and deciphering of messages in secret code or cipher. With respect to information security, cryptography is a branch of mathematics concerned with transforming or concealing data to provide information security using mathematical algorithms. Cryptography is currently one of the ways that you protect your confidentiality-integrity-availability (C-I-A) triad by providing a method to ensure the following:

- **Confidentiality.**   *Confidential* means private or secret. Confidentiality ensures that only authorized personnel access information. One way to provide confidentiality is to encrypt data.

- **Integrity.**   *Integrity* means having an unimpaired condition. Integrity ensures that information is accessed and modified only by those people who are authorized.

- **Nonrepudiation.**   *Repudiate* means to reject as unauthorized or nonbinding. Nonrepudiation prevents an individual or process from denying performing a task or sending data.

- **Identification and authentication.**   Access control allows access only to those who should have it. This is accomplished through identification and authentication, which ensures that when data is received or accessed, the sender is authorized.

To understand how cryptography helps provide confidentiality, integrity, nonrepudiation, and access control, you must first understand how cryptography works.

After this lesson, you will be able to

- Understand the basic principles of cryptography
- Understand what a key is
- Understand what an algorithm is
- Understand the difference between a secure hash function, a symmetric key, and an asymmetric key

Estimated lesson time: 20 minutes

Understanding Cryptography and Keys

Cryptography is not a new technology, as it has been around for quite a while. Egyptian hieroglyphs are a form of cryptography, and Julius Caesar used cryptography to send messages that could only be decrypted by the intended recipient. He did this by shifting the alphabet in his messages by three. Figure 3-1 demonstrates this technique using the English alphabet (which has 26 characters) and shifting by 13 rather than three.

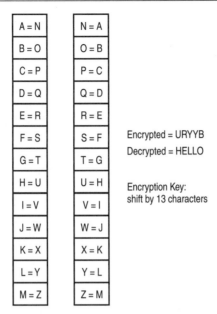

Figure 3-1.   Using cryptography to encipher and decipher a message

Use Figure 3-1 to decipher the following: FRPHEVGL. Even from this simple example, you can see how encryption can be used to "hide" information as it is transferred from one location to another. The clue to deciphering the message is in having the key. A *cryptographic key* consists of a set of instructions that govern ciphering or deciphering messages, and can include a random or pseudo-random number. In the preceding example the encryption algorithm is $C = M - K$, where C = the cipher text, M = the message to be "hidden," and K = cryptographic key. Knowing the ciphertext is FRPHEVGL, you can reverse the algorithm to decipher the message $M = C + K$. Knowing the value of the key, you can decipher FRPHEVGL by adding 13 from each letter's place in the alphabet and discover that the plaintext of the message is SECURITY.

In today's computing environment, cryptography is used to scramble or encrypt and then decrypt information. Encryption is the process of encoding plaintext information. This is accomplished by applying an algorithm to the plaintext using a key, which is kept secret. For an encryption algorithm to be considered strong a *cryptanalyst*, or code breaker, must not be able to break the code, even with complete knowledge of the algorithm and ciphertext. *Decryption* is the process of decoding the encrypted message. *Plaintext* is information that is not encrypted. *Ciphertext* is information that is encrypted. The two types of algorithms that are used today are symmetric algorithms and asymmetric algorithms.

Note   Encryption is used to scramble information so that only the intended recipient or recipients can decipher it, but it is possible to decipher any encrypted information, given enough time and computing power.

Both symmetric and asymmetric algorithms can be used to encrypt and decrypt information, but each does it differently and each is suited for different cryptographic services.

What Is an Algorithm?

An *algorithm* is a procedure for solving a mathematical problem. This can require that the same procedure be repeated several times to solve the problem, such as when determining the greatest common denominator of two numbers. Figure 3-2 shows how the alphabet shift cipher can be converted into a mathematical problem. The algorithm that is used to encipher the message could be represented as $C = M + K$, where M is the plaintext message and K is the key.

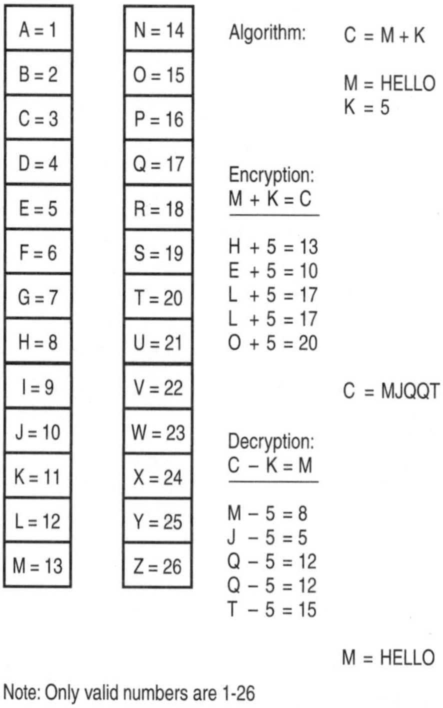

A = 1	N = 14
B = 2	O = 15
C = 3	P = 16
D = 4	Q = 17
E = 5	R = 18
F = 6	S = 19
G = 7	T = 20
H = 8	U = 21
I = 9	V = 22
J = 10	W = 23
K = 11	X = 24
L = 12	Y = 25
M = 13	Z = 26

Algorithm: $C = M + K$

M = HELLO
K = 5

Encryption:
$M + K = C$

H + 5 = 13
E + 5 = 10
L + 5 = 17
L + 5 = 17
O + 5 = 20

C = MJQQT

Decryption:
$C - K = M$

M − 5 = 8
J − 5 = 5
Q − 5 = 12
Q − 5 = 12
T − 5 = 15

M = HELLO

Note: Only valid numbers are 1-26

Figure 3-2.   Creating an algorithm to encipher and decipher a message

Use Figure 3-2 to decipher the following: XJHZWNYD. Remember that the number following 26 is 1 when deciphering this message. You must know the value of the key, which is 5. Knowing that, you can quickly decrypt these letters to read SECURITY.

Without the key, it could take quite a while to decrypt the preceding message, but with the computing power available today, even in personal computers, stronger methods of encrypting are necessary. Encryption algorithms ensure that encrypting information is easy, and the decryption process is impossible to break without knowing the key. This is one of the hallmarks of a good algorithm.

There are three types of encryption that are typically used in information security: hash algorithms, symmetric algorithms, and asymmetric algorithms. Each provides different solutions for protecting your C-I-A triad.

Using a Secure Hash

A hashing algorithm is used to provide data integrity. A *hash* is a one-way mathematical function (OWF) that creates a fixed-sized value (known as a hash or message digest) based on a variable-sized unit of data. A hashing algorithm will always produce the same hash value based on the same input data and never have two different data units produce the same hash value. Some common hash algorithms currently in use include the MD4, MD5, and SHA-1 algorithms.

Note   Knowing the common hash algorithms that are in use is very helpful information, but in-depth knowledge of these algorithms is not necessary to understand the technology. Hash algorithms involve very complex math, generally reserved for university-level math courses. More information on the MD4 and MD5 algorithms can be found at the RSA Security Web site at *http://www.rsasecurity.com*, and in RFC 1320 and RFC 1321. (RFC articles can be found at *http://www.icann.rfceditor.org*.)

A hash of data can be compared to a person's fingerprint. The fingerprint is unique to the person and of a relatively fixed size, but it is not nearly as large as the entire person. A hash is a unique identifier that is virtually unable to be reproduced with different data, and it is part of all of the data it represents. Some of the characteristics of MD4, MD5, and SHA-1 are as follows:

- **MD4.**   Produces a 128 bit message digest (hash), very fast, appropriate for medium security usage.
- **MD5.**   Produces a 128 bit message digest (hash), fast (not as fast as MD4), more secure than MD4, and widely used.
- **SHA-1.**   Produces a 160 bit message digest (hash), standard for the U.S. government, but slower than MD5.

Using Symmetric Algorithms

A *symmetric algorithm* uses the same key for encrypting and decrypting data, and everyone that is allowed to encrypt and decrypt the data has a copy of the key. This is also known as a *shared secret*. Symmetric algorithms provide confidentiality by encrypting data or messages. Some of the past and current symmetric key encryption algorithms include Data Encryption Standard (DES), Triple DES (3DES), Advanced Encryption Standard (AES), International Data Encryption Algorithm (IDEA), Blowfish, and RC4.

More Info   More information on the DES, 3DES, and AES algorithms can be found at *http://www.csrc.nist.gov/encryption/tkencryption.html*.

In the earlier alphabet example, you add 5 to each letter to encrypt, and would subtract 5 letters to decrypt; 5 is the symmetric key. If you shared that secret information with someone else, that person would also be able to encrypt and decrypt messages to and from you. There are advantages and disadvantages to using symmetric keys. Some of the advantages are as follows:

- **Speed.**   The algorithms used with symmetric encryption are relatively fast, so they impact system performance less and are good for encrypting large amounts of data (for instance, data on a hard disk or data being transmitted across a remote access link).
- **Strength.**   Symmetric algorithms are difficult to decipher without the correct algorithm; therefore they are not easy to break. Well-tested symmetric algorithms such as 3DES and AES are nearly impossible to decipher without the correct key. Also, a technique can be used in which encrypted data can be encrypted a second or even third time. This way, if someone does break the encryption, he or she will have access to only more encrypted information.

Some of the disadvantages of using symmetric keys are as follows:

- **Poor key distribution mechanism.**   There is no easy way to securely distribute a shared secret; therefore wide-scale deployment of symmetric keys is difficult.
- **Single key.**   There is a single key (single shared secret); therefore if the secret is compromised, the impact is widespread. Because there is a single key that can be shared with some or many, symmetric keys are not suited to provide integrity, authentication, or nonrepudiation.

Some of the characteristics of specific symmetric keys are as follows:

- **DES.**   56-bit key, U.S. Government standard until 1998, but not considered strong enough for today's standards, relatively slow.
- **Triple DES.**   Performs 3DES operations, equivalent of 168-bit keys, more secure than DES, widely used, relatively slow.
- **AES.**   Variable key lengths, latest standard for U.S. Government use, replacing DES.
- **IDEA.**   128-bit key, requires licensing for commercial use.
- **Blowfish.**   Variable key length, free algorithm, extremely fast.
- **RC4.**   Variable key length, stream cipher, effectively in public domain.

Asymmetric Algorithms

Asymmetric algorithms use different keys to encrypt and decrypt data. One method of asymmetric encryption is called public key cryptography. *Public key cryptography* uses two keys that form a key pair. These two keys are known as the *public key* and the *private key*. (The private key is also known as the *secret key*.) Unlike symmetric algorithms, the key that encrypts the plaintext cannot be used to decrypt the ciphertext. Instead, the public key encrypts the plaintext, and the private key decrypts the ciphertext.

- **Public key.**   Provided to everyone who needs to send you encrypted data.
- **Private key.**   This is the key that only you possess. When a plaintext message is encrypted using the public key, only the person with the private key can decrypt the ciphertext. When a plaintext message is encrypted using the private key, it can be decrypted by everyone who possesses the public key, and that person can be certain the plaintext message originated with the person who possessed the private key.

Asymmetric keys provide authentication, integrity, and nonrepudiation. They can also support confidentiality when used for key management. Some examples of asymmetric encryption algorithms are Diffie-Hellman (DH) and RSA. The RSA asymmetric algorithm is the basis for public key cryptography.

More Info   To learn more about RSA and the Diffie-Hellman key exchanges, visit the RSA Security Web site at *http://www.rsasecurity.com*.

There are advantages and disadvantages to using asymmetric keys. Some of the advantages are as follows:

- **Provide a secure way to communicate with an individual.**   Because there is a public key and a private key, the public key can be provided to anyone that you want to send you encrypted information, but only you can decrypt that information. This helps ensure data confidentiality.
- **Provide a method to validate an individual.**   You can use a private key to create a digital signature, which can be used to verify that you are who you claim to be. This helps provide an authentication method and nonrepudiation. Digital signatures are explained in Lesson 2 of this chapter.

Some of the disadvantages of using asymmetric keys include the following:

- **Asymmetric encryption is relatively slow.**   Asymmetric algorithms are generally slower than symmetric algorithms due to the increased computational complexity required to encrypt and decrypt data; therefore it is not suited to provide confidentiality for large amounts of data.

Some characteristics of specific asymmetric keys are as follows:

- **RSA.**   Variable-length key, de facto standard for public key encryption.
- **Diffie-Hellman.**   Variable-length key, used to securely establish a shared secret.
- **Elliptic curve cryptography.**   Variable-length key, currently too slow for widespread implementation.

The purpose of using cryptography is to ensure confidentiality, integrity, identification and authentication, and nonrepudiation. Given enough time, though, a hacker can decrypt the information. The strength of symmetric and asymmetric keys comes from the length of the key (the random or pseudo-random binary number) and the algorithm that is used to encrypt the data.

Standards and Protocols

For algorithms to be widely used and supported, protocols and standards are created and are maintained by various governing bodies. The National Institute of Standards and Technologies (NIST) and the National Security Agency (NSA) have available current information on cryptographic standards and specifications.

The NIST provides measurements and standards for U.S. industries and creates Federal Information Processing Standards (FIPS) that detail computer security. The Internet Engineering Task Force (IETF) documents how cryptographic mechanisms are implemented with current communications protocols.

The following is a list of some sites that have general information as well as tools that can be used to further explore cryptography. These sites also provide links to information on specific cryptographic algorithms in use today:

- *http://www.nist.gov.* This site has information security standards listed, including access to most FIPS that cover cryptography. From the site's home page you can navigate to the Standards page, and then to the Information Technology Standards page.

- *http://www.nsa.gov.* This site includes historical and informative documentation covering cryptography. It also includes security recommendation guides for currently used technologies, such as Microsoft and Cisco products. There are also links to partners, such as the NIST. To view current security recommendation guides, from the home page, navigate to the INFOSEC page and follow the links to the guides you are interested in viewing.

- *http://www.ietf.org.* This site maintains the standards used on the Internet. The RFC Web page can be used to locate details about how encryption methods and mechanisms are implemented. To locate RFCs on a specific topic, from the home page, navigate to the RFC Editor Web pages, and search the database for a specific encryption mechanism. For instance, to find the RFC that explains how the AES encryption mechanism is implemented for Transport Layer Security (TLS), you would perform a search using the RFC search engine for AES.

- *http://www.x9.org.* This is the home page for the Accredited Standards Committee X9, which was accredited by the American National Standards Institute (ANSI). This organization is an affiliation of industry leaders that identifies technical problems, identifies the best solutions, and codifies them as nationally accepted standards. The format for these standards is X9.xx, such as X9.30.1 Public Key Cryptography Using Irreversible Algorithms.

- *http://csrc.nist.gov/encryption.*   NIST cryptographic toolkit.
- *http://csrc.nist.gov/publications/fips/fips46-3/fips46-3.pdf.*   Information on DES and Triple DES.
- *http://csrc.nist.gov/publications/fips/fips197/fips-197.pdf.*   Information on AES.
- *http://csrc.nist.gov/encryption/skipjack/skipjack.pdf.*   Information on SKIP-JACK (an encryption algorithm), and Key Exchange Algorithm (KEA).
- *http://www.itl.nist.gov/fipspubs/fip180-1.htm.*   Secure Hash Standard for Secure Hash Algorithm (SHA-1), which is used to create a 160-bit message digest.
- *http://csrc.nist.gov/encryption/shs/FR_180-2.pdf.*   Draft for SHA-256, SHA-384, and SHA-512, which provides for message digest lengths of 256 bits, 384 bits, and 512 bits.

Lesson Review

The following questions are intended to reinforce key information presented in this lesson. If you are unable to answer a question, review the lesson and then try the question again. Answers to the questions can be found in Appendix A, "Questions and Answers."

1. Select the answer that best describes cryptography.
    a. Cryptography is encrypting messages with a secure hash function to provide information security.
    b. Cryptography is decrypting messages with a secure hash function to provide information security.
    c. Cryptography is encrypting and decrypting data to provide information security.
    d. Cryptography is providing information confidentiality using a shared secret, also known as an asymmetric key pair.

2. Which of the following best describes a key?
    a. A procedure for solving a mathematical problem in a fixed number of steps
    b. A set of instructions that govern ciphering or deciphering messages
    c. A one-way mathematical function that creates a fixed-sized representation of data
    d. An algebraic equation for solving a mathematical problem in a fixed number of steps

3. What is a procedure for solving a mathematical problem in a fixed number of steps?

    a. A secure hash function

    b. A symmetric key

    c. An asymmetric key

    d. An algorithm

4. Match the term to the definition:

1. Symmetric key	a. A procedure for solving a mathematical problem in a fixed number of steps
2. Asymmetric key pair	
3. Secure hash function	b. A one-way mathematical function that creates a fixed-sized representation of data
4. Algorithm	c. Two keys that form a key pair; one key is used to encrypt data, and the other key is used to decrypt data
	d. A single key is used for encrypting and decrypting data, and everyone that is allowed to encrypt and decrypt the data has a copy of the key

Lesson Summary

- Cryptography is encrypting and decrypting data to provide information security.
- The four goals of cryptography are to provide data confidentiality, data integrity, identification and authentication, and nonrepudiation.
- A key is a set of instructions that govern ciphering or deciphering messages.
- A secure hash function is a one-way mathematical function that creates a fixed-sized representation of data.
- A symmetric key is a single key used for encrypting and decrypting data, and everyone that is allowed to encrypt and decrypt the data has a copy of the key.
- An asymmetric key pair is made up of two keys that form a key pair; one key is used to encrypt data, and the other key is used to decrypt data.
- A public key is provided to many people and is used to validate that a message came from the private key holder or to encrypt data to send the private key holder.
- A private key is a secret key that only the private key holder has. It is used to decrypt information encrypted with the public key, and also to create a digital signature.

Lesson 2: Using Cryptography

Cryptography can help secure your company's C-I-A triad by providing confidentiality, integrity, identification and authentication, and nonrepudiation. Now that you understand the basics of cryptography, you must understand how it can be applied to information security to create a solution. By combining the abilities of secure hash functions, symmetric key encryption, and asymmetric key encryption, you can create a solution that provides confidentiality, integrity, authentication, and nonrepudiation.

After this lesson, you will be able to

- Understand how cryptography provides confidentiality
- Understand how cryptography provides integrity
- Understand how cryptography provides authentication
- Understand how cryptography provides nonrepudiation

Estimated lesson time: 15 minutes

Confidentiality

You provide information confidentiality by using symmetric algorithms. Because symmetric key encryption relies on a shared secret, everyone that needs access to a particular file need only have a copy of the encryption key that was used for encryption. Symmetric encryption is also a relatively fast encryption method, so it is suited for encrypting large amounts of data, such as files on a computer.

 Note   Asymmetric key pairs can be used to provide confidentiality by encrypting data, but this is not a viable solution. Asymmetric encryption is relatively slow, and therefore not practical for encrypting large amounts of data, such as data files.

How It Works

You are the network administrator for your company, responsible for providing secure access to files. You must also secure the files so that if an unauthorized person gains access to them, he or she cannot access the data in the files.

The solution is to identify all of the files that require encryption and all of the people that should have access to those files. You then choose a symmetric algorithm to encrypt and decrypt a file. After you have generated the symmetric key that will be used, you provide the symmetric encryption key to everyone who requires access. Finally, you encrypt all the files requiring encryption using the key.

Additional Considerations

The solution just given will work, but there are several issues that need to be addressed to make the solution workable. Issues with this solution include the following:

- Distributing the symmetric key to the users who need access
- Securing the symmetric key against loss, theft, or distribution to unauthorized people
- Maintaining a list of people authorized to use the symmetric key and retrieving the key from people and computers no longer authorized to access the data
- Replacing the symmetric key in the event that it is compromised

Important   To obtain the Security+ certification, you are expected to have a functional understanding of how cryptography works, the terminology, and the standards. To fully understand how to implement a symmetric key encryption solution however, you must gain a deeper knowledge of symmetric key encryption and the available solutions.

Integrity

Integrity means something is unimpaired and complete. Symmetric key encryption, secure hash functions, and asymmetric cryptography all provide different types of information integrity. Using cryptography does not protect the information from intentional or unintentional damage, but does assure that the information being delivered has not been tampered with or modified. The primary type of information integrity that can be provided by each solution is as follows:

- **Communications integrity with secure hash functions.**   When secure hash functions are used to create a message digest, the message digest can be saved and later compared to another message digest from the same data to ensure the data has not been tampered with. For instance, if you run a hash function on a file and then a few weeks later rerun the hash function and the two message digests do not match, the file has been modified.
- **Encrypted data integrity with keyed hash functions.**   Keyed hash functions provide data integrity. When data is hashed, a key is used in the hashing algorithm. The recipient must use this key to validate the message. The hash value produced with the keyed hashing algorithm is called a message authentication code (MAC). The key operates much like a symmetric key in that it becomes a shared secret. This key is sometimes referred to as a magic number. When using this type of algorithm, the receiving application must also possess the session

key to recompute the hash value so it can verify that the base data has not changed. This provides a mechanism to ensure that the encrypted data has not been tampered with.

- **Communications integrity using an asymmetric algorithm.**   Asymmetric algorithms can provide integrity by being combined with hash functions to produce digital signatures. You create a digital signature by creating a message digest of a plaintext message using a hash algorithm. You then encrypt the hash value with your private key. The receiver decrypts the encrypted hash value using your public key and then generates a hash of the message. If the decrypted hash value from you matches the hash value the receiver generates, the message could only have originated from you and could not have been tampered with in transit.

Identification and Authentication

You can use symmetric and asymmetric keys for identification and authentication. The primary type of identification and authentication that can be provided by each solution is as follows:

- **Authentication with asymmetric algorithms.**   Asymmetric algorithms can provide authentication using a challenge-response protocol. When you want to access a system, the system sends a random number (called a nonce) that you encrypt with your private key. The system then verifies your credentials by decrypting the encrypted nonce using your public key. This type of authentication is ideally suited for use with remote access and physical access to restricted areas, such as the room where your servers are located.

- **Authenticating users with symmetric algorithms.**   Symmetric algorithms can authenticate users. When you want to access a system, the system sends a nonce that you use as the key to use a symmetric algorithm to encrypt your password. The system then uses the nonce to decrypt your password. You are successfully validated if the decrypted password matches the password the system has for you.

How It Works

As the network administrator for your company, you are responsible for providing a way to identify and authenticate users from other companies who are accessing your business-to-business (B2B) server remotely.

You deploy an asymmetric public key algorithm for each of the users requiring remote access. Configure your server so that a challenge-response protocol is used to access the B2B information. When users attempt to access the system, the server issues a challenge and decrypts the challenge the user returns (using that user's public key). If the challenges match, the user is granted access.

Providing Nonrepudiation

You can provide a means of nonrepudiation using public key asymmetric algorithms. There are two keys (a public key and a private key), and only you possess your private key. The private key can be used to create a digital signature, and anyone with a copy of your public key can verify that the message is from you and has not been altered. This also provides proof that you sent the message.

Note   For nonrepudiation you must use a trusted third party (TTP) to bind your public key to a user or system. More information about TTPs is provided in Lesson 3.

How It Works

You are the security specialist of a company that conducts business over the Internet and requires a method that proves that the party placing the order sent the order message. This proof is used in the event of a billing dispute, so the mechanism must provide nonrepudiation.

You should require people wishing to do business with you to acquire a digital identification and configure their e-mail service to use that digital signature. Configure your server so that a digital signature is required when submitting all orders.

Lesson Review

The following questions are intended to reinforce key information presented in this lesson. If you are unable to answer a question, review the lesson and then try the question again. Answers to the questions can be found in Appendix A, "Questions and Answers."

1. Which is the best mechanism for providing confidentiality?

   a. Secure hash function

   b. Symmetric key

   c. Asymmetric key

   d. Algorithm

2. You need to send an e-mail message to someone and ensure that the integrity is verifiable when it arrives. Which would best provide that capability?

   a. Using a secure hash function to create a message digest

   b. Using an asymmetric public key to create a digital signature

   c. Using a symmetric key to create a digital signature

   d. Using an algorithm to create a message digest

3. You need to provide a method to allow the receiver of an e-mail to be able to authenticate that a message came from a specific person. Which would best provide that capability?

   a. Using a secure hash function to create a message digest

   b. Using an asymmetric key pair to create and validate a message digest

   c. Using a symmetric key to create and validate a message digest

   d. Using an algorithm to create a message digest

4. You need to provide a mechanism that can establish nonrepudiation when sending e-mail to a business partner. Which would best provide that capability?

   a. Using a secure hash function to create and validate a digital signature

   b. Using an asymmetric key pair to create and validate a digital signature

   c. Using a symmetric key to create and validate a digital signature

   d. Using an algorithm to create and validate a digital signature

Lesson Summary

- By combining the abilities of secure hash functions, symmetric key encryption, and asymmetric key encryption, you can create a solution that provides confidentiality, integrity, authentication, and nonrepudiation.

- Using a symmetric key or shared secret to encrypt and decrypt large amounts of data is the best way to provide confidentiality.

- You can provide message integrity using a secure hash function to create a message digest, although symmetric keys and asymmetric key pairs provide data integrity in other ways.

- Asymmetric encryption can be used to create a digital signature, which can be attached to an e-mail. This authenticates who sent the message.

- You can establish nonrepudiation by using an asymmetric key to create a digital signature and attaching it to an e-mail. This can verify the sender's identity.

Lesson 3: Identifying the Components of a Public Key Infrastructure

Using asymmetric key pairs is simple enough to implement, but when scaled beyond a small community using a few applications, it becomes difficult to distribute the public keys and hard to track and manage private keys. When a private key is compromised, it is difficult to locate and remove that key.

The security infrastructure created to solve these problems is known as a *public key infrastructure* (PKI). PKI uses asymmetric key pairs and combines software, encryption technologies, and services to provide a means of protecting the security of communications and business transactions. RFC 2459 defines the X.509 PKI, which is the PKI defined for use on the Internet. It is comprised of certificates, certification authorities (CAs), certificate management tools, and certificate-enabled applications.

More Info   RFC 2459, "Internet X.509 Public Key Infrastructure Certificate and CRL Profile," provides detailed information on PKI standards for Internet use.

After this lesson, you will be able to

- Understand what a PKI is
- Understand what certificates are
- Understand what a certification authority is
- Understand how certificates are used

Estimated lesson time: 20 minutes

Components of a PKI

A PKI uses public key encryption technologies to bind public keys to their owners and to help with reliable distribution of keys across multiple heterogeneous networks. Figure 3-3 shows the major components of a PKI.

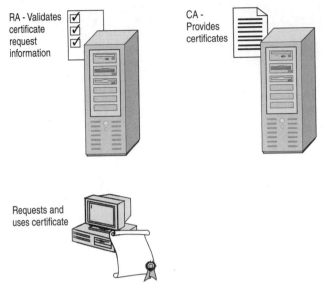

Figure 3-3.   Major components of a PKI

The PKI provides a framework of services, technologies, protocols, and standards that enable you to deploy and manage a strong and scalable information security system. With the PKI in place, companies can conduct business electronically and be assured of the following:

- The person or process sending a transaction is the actual originator.
- The person or process receiving a transaction is the actual receiver.
- The integrity of the data has not been compromised.

The basic components that make up a PKI are as follows:

- **Digital certificates.**   An electronic credential used to authenticate users.
- **Certification Authority (CA).**   A computer that issues digital certificates, maintains a list of invalid certificates, and maintains a list of invalid CAs.
- **Registration authority (RA).**   An entity that is designed to verify certificate contents for a CA.
- **Key and certification management tools.**   Tools for auditing and administering digital certificates.
- **Certificate publication point.**   A location where certificates are stored and published.
- **Public key-enabled applications and services.**   Applications and services that support using certificates.

What Are Certificates?

Certificates are a digital representation of information that identifies you and are issued by CAs, which are often a TTP. A TTP is an entity trusted by other entities with respect to security-related services and activities. The certificate (Figure 3-4) includes the TTP, subscriber, subscriber's public key, its operational period, and the digital signature of the TTP issuing it. The TTP is vouching that the person or process with the certificate can be trusted.

Figure 3-4.   Certificate contents

A TTP creates and issues a certificate that is valid for a specific amount of time, much like a credit card, which is issued by a credit card company and is valid for a specific amount of time. Just as a credit card can be canceled at any time, so can a certificate.

Certificates can be used with a variety of applications and security services to provide authentication, data integrity, and security. Uses for certificates include the following:

- **Secure mail.**   Configure the Secure Multipurpose Internet Mail Extensions (S/MIME) protocol to ensure the integrity, origin, and confidentiality of e-mail messages.

- **Secure Web communications.**   Use certificates with Secure Sockets Layer (SSL) or TLS protocols for authenticating and encrypting communications between servers and clients.

- **Secure Web sites.**   Use certificates to authenticate access to secure Web sites.

- **Custom security solutions.**   Use certificates to provide confidentiality, integrity, authentication, and nonrepudiation for custom applications.

- **Smart card logon process.**   Use certificates to authenticate users with smart card devices attached to their computers.

What Are CAs?

A CA is a computer that is recognized as an authority trusted by one or more users or processes to issue and manage X.509 public key certificates, a revocation list of CAs that are no longer valid, and a revocation list of certificates that have been revoked.

Each CA creates and maintains a list of the certificates that it has issued, as well as a list of certificates that have been revoked. A CA can revoke a certificate for many reasons, for example:

- When the certificate owner's private key is lost
- When the owner leaves the company he or she works for
- When the owner changes names

A CA must also maintain a list of CAs that are no longer valid. A certificate revocation list (CRL) is a signed, time-stamped list of server serial numbers of CA public key certificates that have been revoked. The CRL is necessary to allow CAs to accept and reject certificates that were issued by a different CA.

There are two types of CAs that can be used by a company, a commercial CA, and a private CA:

- A commercial CA is operated by a certificate-issuing company and provides certificates to the general public, or for use when communicating with other entities.
- A private CA is used to issue certificates for your company's private use, such as when an employee attempts to gain access to an internal server or gain access remotely.

How It Works

A PKI can be compared to performing credit card transactions remotely. Refer to Figure 3-5 and compare a generic PKI and credit card transaction.

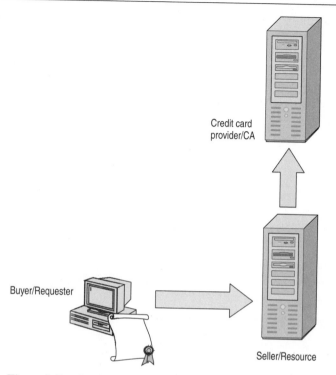

Figure 3-5.   Comparing a credit card transaction with a PKI transaction

For comparison, if you order a product over the telephone using a credit card:

- You provide your credit card information along with information that can prove that you are the actual holder of the card.
- The seller of the product cannot view your signature and cannot view any additional identification. They trust that because you had the credit card information and proper billing information you are the holder of the card.
- They send you the product you are purchasing.

If you do not receive the product, you can cancel the transaction. If your credit card information is not correct, the seller does not have to send you the product. Both parties rely on the credit card company as the TTP.

Now, when you make a purchase and use a certificate and PKI for validation:

- You provide your certificate.
- The seller of the product still cannot view your signature and cannot view any additional identification. They trust that because you have a valid certificate, you are the owner of the certificate.
- They send you the product you are purchasing.

This is a simplified version of how PKI is implemented, what the major components do, and the function it provides.

Lesson Review

The following questions are intended to reinforce key information presented in this lesson. If you are unable to answer a question, review the lesson and then try the question again. Answers to the questions can be found in Appendix A, "Questions and Answers."

1. Which best describes a PKI?
   a. A digital representation of information that identifies you as a relevant entity by a TTP
   b. An entity that is recognized as an authority trusted by one or more users or processes to issue and manage a certificate
   c. Uses asymmetric key pairs and combines software, encryption technologies, and services to provide a means of protecting the security of communications and business transactions
   d. A list of certificates issued by a CA that are no longer valid

2. Which best describes a certificate?
   a. A digital representation of information that identifies you as a relevant entity by a TTP
   b. An entity that is recognized as an authority trusted by one or more users or processes to issue and manage a certificate
   c. Uses asymmetric key pairs and combines software, encryption technologies, and services to provide a means of protecting the security of communications and business transactions
   d. A list of certificates issued by a CA that are no longer valid

3. Which best describes a CA?

    a. A digital representation of information that identifies you as a relevant entity by a TTP

    b. An entity that is recognized as an authority trusted by one or more users or processes to issue and manage a certificate

    c. Uses asymmetric key pairs and combines software, encryption technologies, and services to provide a means of protecting the security of communications and business transactions

    d. A list of certificates issued by a CA that are no longer valid

4. What are some reasons a certificate might be placed on a CRL? Select all correct answers.

    a. The certificate owner lost the private key.

    b. The certificate owner is going on a business trip and wants the certificate expiration refreshed so it does not expire.

    c. The certificate owner left the company.

    d. The certificate owner changed names.

    e. The certificate owner lost the public key.

Lesson Summary

- Using asymmetric keys without a supporting infrastructure is not scalable to a large environment. A public key infrastructure (PKI) uses asymmetric key pairs and combines software, encryption technologies, and services to provide a means of protecting the security of communications and business transactions.

- A certificate is a digital representation of information that identifies you as a relevant entity by a trusted third party (TTP).

- A certification authority (CA) is an entity that is recognized as an authority trusted by one or more users or processes to issue and manage certificates.

- A certificate revocation list (CRL) is a list of certificates issued by a CA that are no longer valid.

Lesson 4: Understanding CA Trust Models

For a CA solution to scale to support any size enterprise, there must be a structure in place to allow the CAs to validate certificates provided by other CAs. Trusts and trust models allow this to happen.

After this lesson, you will be able to
■ Understand what a trust is between CAs

■ Understand what a mesh trust model is

■ Understand what a hierarchical trust model is

■ Understand what a bridge CA is used for

Estimated lesson time: 15 minutes

Trust Models

When multiple CAs are implemented in an infrastructure, there must be a way for one CA to accept the certificates issued by another CA. They must be able to rely on each other's certificates for the CA structure to scale to any size deployment. For a PKI, a *trust* is a relationship that allows a CA to trust a certificate issued by another CA. A *trust path* links several CAs together so that the trust relationship can extend beyond the two CAs that have formed a trust.

For a CA to form a trust relationship with another CA, each issues a certificate for the other CA. For instance, if CA1 and CA2 want to trust the certificates that each has issued, both CAs would issue a certificate for each other. When a user or process issued a certificate by CA1 authenticates with CA2, CA2 validates that it issued a certificate to CA1. If it does have a valid certificate, CA2 trusts the certificate issued by CA1. Two common ways to configure trust paths that provide a scalable solution involve using a mesh architecture or a hierarchical architecture.

Mesh Architecture

With a mesh architecture, multiple peer CAs issue certificates to each other. To certify, they create certificates for each other. Figure 3-6 shows a peer CA arrangement with users and computers on two different CAs. Use this figure to follow the example given here.

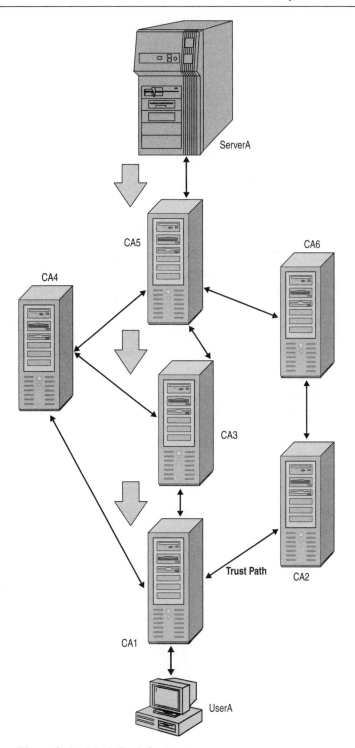

Figure 3-6.   Mesh CA infrastructure

UserA has a certificate issued by CA1 and needs access to data on ServerA. ServerA has a certificate issued by CA5.

The process follows like this:

1. UserA presents its certificate to ServerA.
2. ServerA verifies UserA certificate with CA1.
3. ServerA verifies CA1 certificate with CA3.
4. ServerA verifies CA3 certificate with CA5.

Because ServerA relies on CA5 and CA5 trusts CA3, CA3 trusts CA1, and CA1 issued the certificate for UserA, the certificate is valid with ServerA.

Hierarchical Architecture

With a hierarchical architecture, there is a top-level CA known as a root CA, which issues certificates to subordinate CAs. Those CAs can then issue certificates to other CAs, and so on. The CAs at each level can issue certificates to subordinate CAs or users. All certificate holders in the hierarchy know the root CA; therefore the certification path need only be from subordinate CAs to the CA directly up the hierarchy. Figure 3-7 shows a hierarchical CA arrangement with users and computers on two different CAs. Use this figure to follow the example given here.

UserA has a certificate issued by CA1 and needs access to data on ServerA. ServerA has a certificate issued by CA5.

The process follows like this:

1. UserA presents its certificate to ServerA.
2. ServerA verifies UserA certificate with CA1.
3. ServerA verifies CA1 certificate with CA3.
4. ServerA verifies CA3 certificate with RootCA.

Because all certificate holders know the root CA, ServerA relies on RootCA, RootCA trusts CA3, CA3 trusts CA1, and CA1 issued the certificate for UserA, the certificate is valid with ServerA.

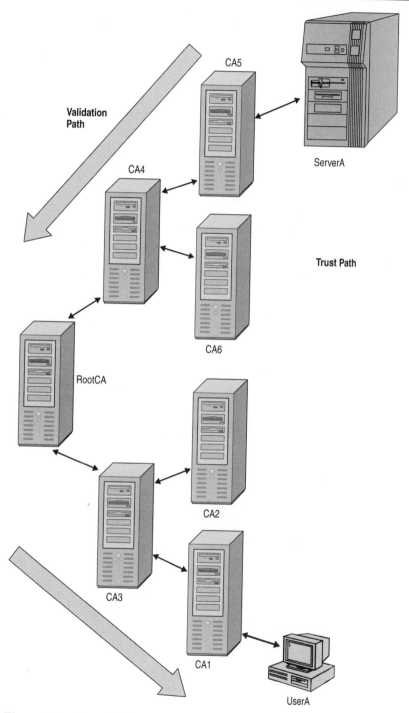

Figure 3-7. Hierarchical CA infrastructure

Bridge CA Architecture

A bridge CA connects mesh and hierarchical architectures together. This allows different companies to have their own trust architecture, and then have a single connection using a bridge CA. If the trust relationship needs to be broken, there is only a single point to manage.

- If the bridge is connecting to a hierarchical structure, then the trust is with the root CA.
- If the bridge is connecting with a mesh structure, then the trust is with a single CA.

The CA that connects with a bridge CA is known as a *principal CA*. Figure 3-8 shows a bridge CA arrangement with users and computers on two different CA architectures. Use this figure to follow the example given here.

UserA has a certificate issued by CA1 and needs access to data on ServerA. ServerA has a certificate issued by CA5.

The process follows like this:

1. UserA presents its certificate to ServerA.
2. ServerA verifies UserA certificate with CA1.
3. ServerA verifies CA1 certificate with RootCA.
4. ServerA verifies RootCA with BridgeCA.
5. ServerA verifies BridgeCA with CA3.
6. ServerA verifies CA3 with CA5.

A bridge CA does not issue certificates to end users, but does issue certificates to other CAs.

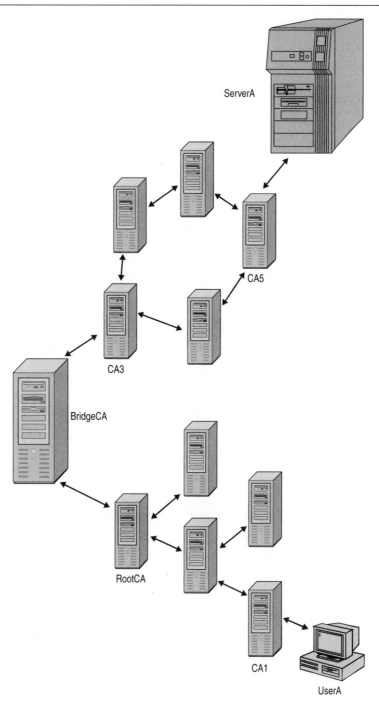

Figure 3-8. Bridge CA

Lesson Review

The following questions are intended to reinforce key information presented in this lesson. If you are unable to answer a question, review the lesson and then try the question again. Answers to the questions can be found in Appendix A, "Questions and Answers."

1. You are the security specialist for your company and you have just installed a third CA. Each CA supports three different geographical locations. You are attempting to access a server that was issued a certificate by the new CA, but your certificate is not being accepted. Which is the best way to solve the problem?

   a. Have the new CA issue you a certificate

   b. Have the new CA and each of the old CAs issue a certificate to each other

   c. Reinstall the software on the new CA

   d. Make the new CA a bridge CA

2. Which statements are true of a mesh architecture? Select all that apply.

   a. Connects mesh and hierarchical architectures together.

   b. There is a top-level CA known as a root CA.

   c. Multiple peer CAs issue certificates to each other.

   d. Does not issue certificates to end users.

3. Which statements are true of a hierarchical architecture? Select all that apply.

   a. Connects mesh and hierarchical architectures together.

   b. There is a top-level CA known as a root CA.

   c. Multiple peer CAs issue certificates to each other.

   d. Does not issue certificates to end users.

4. Which statements are true of a bridge CA? Select all that apply.

   a. Connects mesh and hierarchical architectures together.

   b. There is a top-level CA known as a root CA.

   c. Multiple peer CAs issue certificates to each other.

   d. Does not issue certificates to end users.

Lesson Summary

- To create a scalable solution, you have to design a CA architecture so that CAs can validate certificates issued by other CAs by establishing trusts between CAs.

- Trusts are established between CAs by having each CA issue a certificate to the other CA.

- With mesh trust architectures, all CAs issue certificates for all other CAs. This provides multiple trust paths that can be used for certificate validation.

- Hierarchical trusts establish a top-level CA known as a root CA. Subordinate CAs can be created below that. All users issued certificates in the hierarchy know the root CA, so certificate validation across multiple arms of the hierarchical structure validate through the root CA.

- Bridge CAs connect mesh and hierarchical architectures together. They do not issue certificates to end users, only to other CAs.

Lesson 5: Understanding Certificate Life Cycle and Key Management

The certificate life cycle defines the processes by which a CA requests, issues, revokes, renews, and audits certificates. The CA that issues a certificate defines what the certificate life cycle is. Key management involves determining how keys are stored and whether key management is centralized or distributed.

After this lesson, you will be able to
- Explain what a key life cycle is
- Identify the stages of a key life cycle
- Explain what key management is

Estimated lesson time: 10 minutes

Key Life Cycle

For keys to be effective there must be a mechanism in place to track and manage keys, remove keys when necessary, and validate that a key is still viable. You must secure keys throughout the key life cycle. The key life cycle of a certificate can be broken into five distinct stages, as discussed in the following sections.

Certificate Enrollment

Certificate enrollment procedures vary, but typically users requesting certificates from a CA initiate a request. This is a cooperative process between a user (or a user's PKI software, such as an e-mail or Web browser application) and the CA. The enrollment request contains the public key and enrollment information. Once a user requests a certificate, the CA verifies information based on its established policy rules, creates the certificate, posts the certificate, and then sends an identifying certificate to the user.

Certificate Distribution

Certificate distribution occurs when the CA distributes the certificate to the user. This is considered a separate process because it might require management intervention from the CA. During this stage, the CA sets policies that affect the use of the certificate.

Certificate Validation

When a certificate is used, the certificate status is checked to verify that the certificate is still operationally valid. (Certificate validation is also know as status checking.) During the validation process, the CA checks the status of the certificate and verifies that the certificate is not on a CRL. Applications can also check on the status of certificates before they are used, if configured to do so. Currently, few applications automatically check for certificate revocation status due to the overhead involved in contacting the CRL distribution point.

Certificate Revocation

A certificate issued by a CA includes an expiration date that defines how long the certificate is valid. If a certificate needs to be revoked before that date, the CA can be instructed to add the certificate to its CRL. Reasons a certificate might need to be revoked include the certificate being lost or compromised, or the person the certificate was issued to leaving the company. When a certificate is revoked, the CA administrator must supply a reason code. The revocation codes are as follows:

- Unspecified reason (0)
- Private key compromise (1)
- CA compromise (2)
- Certificate user's affiliation changed (3)
- Certificate or private key has been superseded by a new certificate or private key (4)
- The issuing CA is no longer in operation (5)
- The certificate has been placed on hold (6)
- CA has withdrawn the certificate user's privileges to use the certificate or private key (9)
- AIA compromise (10)

PKI-enabled applications are configured to check CAs for their current CRL, and do not operate if they cannot verify that the certificate has not been added to the CRL.

Note   M of N control can be used to manage certificate revocation. Using M of N, you can specify that two different managers are needed to perform certificate revocation. This is very similar to the safeguard added to firing a nuclear missile, which requires two different keys (held by two different people) to activate and fire a missile.

Certificate Renewal

When a certificate reaches its expiration date, if the certificate is allowed to be renewed, a user can ask the CA to renew the certificate. This might happen automatically, or it might require user intervention. When renewing a certificate you must choose whether or not to generate new public and private keys.

Certificate Destruction

When a certificate is no longer in use, the certificate and any backup copies or archived copies of the certificate should be destroyed, along with the private key associated with the certificate. This helps ensure that the certificate is not compromised and used.

Certificate Auditing

The CA performs certificate auditing, and the process varies depending on the CA and the management tools available to it. Certificate auditing involves tracking the creation, expiration, and revocation of certificates. In certain instances, it can also track each successful use of a certificate.

Key Management

One of the concerns with keys is that someone will break the encryption and compromise a key. Unless you are using an encryption algorithm that is known to be weak, chances are much better that the attack will come from the key being compromised due to poor key management rather than the encryption being compromised. To make sure that your encryption solution is not compromised, you must make sure the encryption used is strong, but also ensure the key management is done in a secure manner.

More Info   Read more about preferred key management techniques in, "Key Management Guidelines (Workshop Document)" which can be found on the NIST Web site at *http://csrc.nist.gov/encryption*.

Before a key is created and distributed, you must determine whether the key will be stored with a software solution or hardware solution, and whether centralized or distributed key management will be used.

Software Storage

With software storage of an archived key, the key can be stored on a floppy disk or other type of removable media and placed in a safe or electronic vault. When you need to provide a user with a key, you can copy the key to a floppy disk and use the copy of the key to perform the operation. When the key is in use, it is loaded into active memory on the computer. To ensure the integrity of the key, it can be stored in an approved cryptographic module, an approved and properly configured operating system, a secured, limited-access environment, or split into multiple components. When you are finished using the copy of the private key, you must destroy the media it was copied to in a secure manner. With this type of storage, distribution is relatively simple and cost effective, but it is also somewhat easier to compromise than a hardware solution.

Hardware Storage

With hardware storage of a key, the key is placed on a hardware storage medium, such as a smart card or hardware security module (HSM). Additionally, HSMs also generate the keys on the hardware device to prevent the need to transmit the private key over a network connection or other medium. When you need to provide a user with a key, you program the smart card with the key and give the key to the user. With this type of storage, distribution requires you to distribute the smart card to the user and requires that the computers that are used be equipped with smart card readers. This is a secure way to store keys and is difficult to compromise, but it requires specialized equipment and is more costly than the software storage solution.

Centralized Key Management

With centralized key management, one group controls all of the CAs in the organization. This has many advantages when it comes to security, both physical and logical, because you can provide a single CA management infrastructure and a reliable key distribution system that can be used by the entire organization, rather than maintaining many such points. Using a centralized key management solution can be less efficient than a decentralized key management solution, but will be more secure.

Decentralized Key Management

With decentralized key management, you create your own key management and distribution solution. It is your responsibility to maintain secure keys that are not compromised and maintain a CRL on your CAs. For a large number of certificates that are used only by your company, this might be a cost-effective key management solution. In a decentralized key management model, there is a root CA, several subordinate CAs, and several issuing CAs. Collectively, they are called a CA hierarchy. The root CA is the top of the hierarchy and is only used to issue certificates for the subordinate CAs. The subordinate CAs are created for each area of the organization. For example, you might have a subordinate CA for the finance department, IT department, and research department. Each subordinate CA creates certificates used to create issuing CAs, which are usually created for use with a specific application, such as the e-mail CA and the Web server CA. Thus each group in the organization is responsible for managing its own certificates. Because many groups will use management CAs, decentralized management is less secure than centralized management, but more efficient.

Key Recovery

When a key is lost or corrupted, the data that is encrypted is no longer accessible. To recover access to that data, a key recovery technique must be used. Your organization should have a key recovery process in place to recover lost keys.

Key Escrow

One way to perform key recovery is known as *key escrow*. With key escrow, you split a decryption key into one or several parts and distribute these parts to escrow agents or trustees. To recover, the trustees can use their portion of the key to either to reconstruct the missing key or decrypt the communications. Key escrow is rarely implemented because of the privacy concerns that the key escrow agent will use the escrowed key.

Key Encapsulation

With key encapsulation, you encrypt data in a communication with a session key and encrypt that session key with a trustee's public key. The encrypted session key is sent with the encrypted communication, and the trustee is able to decrypt the communication when necessary.

Lesson Review

The following questions are intended to reinforce key information presented in this lesson. If you are unable to answer a question, review the lesson and then try the question again. Answers to the questions can be found in Appendix A, "Questions and Answers."

1. Match each portion of the certificate life cycle with the answer that best describes it.

1. Enrollment	a. CA distributes the CA to the user
2. Distribution	b. Involves tracking the creation, expiration, and revocation of certificates
3. Validation	
4. Revocation	c. A request is initiated by users requesting certificates from a CA
5. Renewal	d. Occurs when a certificate reaches the expiration date
6. Destruction	e. CA adds the certificate to its certificate revocation list
7. Auditing	f. Verifying that the signature is valid, that a trusted CA has issued the certificate, that the certificate can be used for its intended purpose, and determining if the certificate has been revoked
	g. The process of deleting the certificate after it has been published on the CRL

Lesson Summary

- The key life cycle of a certificate is broken into seven distinct stages: certificate enrollment, certificate distribution, certificate validation, certificate revocation, certificate renewal, certificate destruction, and certificate auditing.
- During certificate enrollment, a user requests a certificate from a CA.
- Once the CA is satisfied with the credentials presented by the user requesting the certificate, the CA distributes the certificate to the user.
- If anything occurs before the expiration of the certificate that warrants the cancellation of the certificate, it is added to the CA's certificate revocation list (CRL).
- If the certificate is not revoked and reaches the expiration date, it can be renewed.
- To better manage and control certificates, CAs track various events, such as creations, revocations, renewals, and in some cases, successful usage.

C H A P T E R   4

Network Infrastructure Security

About This Chapter

The term *infrastructure* means underlying foundation. On a computer network, the network infrastructure includes the cables, connectivity devices, hosts, and connection points of the network. In this chapter you learn ways in which network infrastructure equipment might be exploited or attacked. This chapter also presents strategies and devices that can increase the security of your network.

Before You Begin

You should understand the concepts presented in Chapter 2, "TCP/IP Basics."

Lesson 1: Understanding Network Infrastructure Security

This lesson is an introduction to common network infrastructure security concerns. Just as the human skeletal system is the framework of your body, the network infrastructure is the framework of your network. One successful attack on your network infrastructure can cripple your network or even open it to different types of attacks. To properly defend your network infrastructure, you must understand the common security concerns that apply to the network infrastructure.

After this lesson you will be able to

- Discuss general security concerns for your network infrastructure
- Explain how the physical network infrastructure could be at risk
- Document potential exploitations of network infrastructure device configurations

Estimated lesson time: 10 minutes

Infrastructure Security Overview

Organizations and individuals are concerned about protecting their data, equipment, trade secrets, and the privacy of their associates. Successful attacks against a network infrastructure could result in a compromise or loss of any or all of those items. To protect your network infrastructure from attack, you must first be aware of the types of attacks that could be launched against it, which include any of the following:

- Physical sabotage; equipment destruction
- Packet sniffing; eavesdropping
- Network mapping and port scanning to identify targets for attack
- Reconfiguration or disabling of connectivity or security devices
- Use of your network devices to launch an attack on another network
- Use of your network devices to host unauthorized, illegal, or destructive services
- Erasing data

To protect your network from such attacks, you must control access to critical resources, protocols, and network access points. This includes protecting the physical security of equipment and the configuration of devices.

Securing Physical Equipment

The equipment that forms your network infrastructure should be as physically secure as possible. If an attacker can gain access to your router, switch, or even server, your network infrastructure could be easily compromised. Attacks need not be sophisticated to be effective. A person with a knife or hammer in the wiring closet or server room could potentially cause more damage than a computer virus.

Scott Culp of the Microsoft Security Response Center compiled a list called "Ten Immutable Laws of Security." The third law states, "If a bad guy has unrestricted physical access to your computer, it's not your computer anymore." This is also true if the attacker is able to gain unrestricted physical access to any of the equipment that is part of your network infrastructure. Any system to which an attacker is able to gain unrestricted physical access should be considered fully compromised.

More Info   To learn more about "The Ten Immutable Laws of Security" visit *http://www.microsoft.com/technet* and search for that title.

The solution is preventing attackers from ever gaining access to your network infrastructure. Unfortunately, protecting every hub, switch, PC, router, cable, and other component from every type of physical attack is difficult. In addition to protecting your network from attackers, you should be concerned with other forces that could compromise the integrity of your network. For example, fires, floods, tornadoes, and earthquakes could destroy your network infrastructure.

Some ways in which you might physically secure your network infrastructure include the following:

- Hire security guards.
- Install sensors, alarms, and closed-circuit TV cameras and monitoring equipment.
- Use physical access badges and security cards.
- Install backup electrical power.
- Bury network cables (or enclose them in walls).
- Lock wiring closets and server rooms.
- Encase equipment in protective housings.
- Use tamper-proof seals on equipment casing.
- Install fences and parking lot gates.
- Maintain fire-extinguishing and detection systems appropriate for your equipment and facility.
- Ensure your facilities meet appropriate construction standards.

Physically securing your network infrastructure first involves prioritization. You must decide what equipment is most critical and in the greatest need of securing. For example, the loss of a central server, router, switch, or hub is probably a bigger problem than the loss of a cable connecting a public terminal to your network.

You should use a cost-benefit analysis to determine how much of your network infrastructure you should secure. When performing such an analysis, consider the cost of securing the equipment against the costs that could be incurred if the equipment were compromised. Also, consider the likelihood that the equipment would be compromised or lost. Such consideration is called *risk assessment* and is explored further in Chapter 10, "Organizational Security."

Securing Equipment Configuration

Equipment configuration is another area in which your network infrastructure might be vulnerable to an attack. Attacks on device configuration can be physical, such as rerouting cables in a wiring closet, or logical, such as changing the routing table of a router.

Physical security, as discussed previously, is required to protect equipment from physical configuration attacks. Logical security is required to secure your network infrastructure from attacks on device configuration that can take place remotely. For example, routers and switches maintain logical routing or switching tables, which allow them to correctly transfer network packets to their proper destination. An attacker might try to modify or corrupt those tables to redirect or stop normal network communication. To protect your routers, switches, and central servers, you can assign complex passwords to management consoles to help prevent someone from gaining unauthorized administrative access. *Complex passwords* have mixed case, alphanumeric, multiple characters, and special characters that are difficult to guess or crack with a password-cracking program. Secure passwords should be at least six characters in length, which is defined as a minimum by many operating system vendors and organizations. However, some are moving to seven—or even eight—character password minimums.

Note   To protect your device configurations, restrict remote access wherever possible. To protect passwords from compromise through packet sniffing, use the strongest authentication and encryption methods available to each device you must configure remotely. Authentication and encryption are covered briefly later in this chapter. For more in-depth coverage of authentication, see Chapter 7, "User Security." Encryption is covered in more detail in Chapter 3, "Certificate Basics" and Chapter 6, "Application Security." The focus of this text is on security issues concerning network infrastructure equipment. In many cases, only brief descriptions of infrastructure devices are provided. If you require a more thorough description of devices discussed in this chapter, please read the *Network+ Certification Training Kit, Second Edition* (Microsoft Press, 2001), and the *A+ Certification Training Kit, Third Edition* (Microsoft Press, 2001).

Lesson Review

The following questions are intended to reinforce key information presented in this lesson. If you are unable to answer a question, review the lesson and then try the question again. Answers to the questions can be found in Appendix A, "Questions and Answers."

1. List three or more items that are considered part of a network infrastructure.

2. What are some of the actions you might take to secure your physical network infrastructure?

3. In addition to physical attacks, what other types of attacks might be directed against your network infrastructure?

4. Name other security threats that are not related to people attacking your network.

Lesson Summary

- You must control access to critical resources, protocols, and network access points. This includes protecting the physical security of equipment and the configuration of devices.

- Attacks against your network infrastructure can include physical attacks, such as destruction or theft of equipment, and the physical modification of equipment configurations. Attacks can also involve the logical modification of network infrastructure device configurations, such as changing a routing or switching table.

- You can protect your physical network infrastructure with security personnel, closed-circuit TV, alarms, access cards, locks, tamper-proof seals, backup electrical power, and similar measures.

- Restrict remote administration of network infrastructure equipment whenever possible. When you must allow remote administration, be sure to use the most secure authentication and encryption possible.

Lesson 2: Securing Network Cabling

Most networks utilize network cable in some form. In this lesson you learn ways in which network cable can be compromised and methods for securing it. This lesson investigates three major types of cabling: coaxial, twisted-pair, and fiber optic.

Note Although wireless networks are increasing in popularity, network cabling is still used in most organizations. Physical cable currently provides a more secure, reliable, high-speed network connection than wireless. Wireless networking is discussed in Lesson 3.

After this lesson, you will be able to

- Document ways in which network cabling can be compromised
- Secure network cabling

Estimated lesson time: 15 minutes

Coaxial Cable

There are several different types and grades of coaxial (coax) cable, but the same basic structure applies to all of them. All coaxial cable has a center conductor, an outer conductor, and an outer sheath. Electronic transmissions (representing data) travel through the center conductor. The remainder of this section focuses on how coaxial cable can be compromised and ways to protect it.

Sabotaging Coaxial Cable

Coaxial cable is more difficult to cut than the other types of cable discussed in this lesson, but a pair of wire cutters can quickly cut through it nevertheless. Cutting coaxial cable isn't necessary to disrupt communications on a coaxial network. A heat or energy source placed near coaxial cabling can also impede communications. Because coaxial cable is typically used in bus topologies, a cut wire or severe electromagnetic interference (EMI) or radio frequency interference (RFI) could bring down the entire network. EMI and RFI are types of noise that can affect the reception of electronic transmissions, including those carrying data on a network. EMI and RFI can lead to the malfunctioning of other sensitive electrical and electronic equipment. Physically removing a terminator, which can be found at each end of a coaxial bus network, is yet another way to disrupt communication on the network.

To protect your coaxial network segments from sabotage, you should be sure to protect the physical cable. Any point along the network is vulnerable to compromise and sabotage due to the bus nature of a coaxial network segment.

Eavesdropping on Coaxial Networks

Because coaxial networks utilize a bus topology, signals traverse the entire segment on their way to the destination host. Any connection along the coaxial network is susceptible to eavesdropping, which can also be achieved by tapping into the coaxial cable at almost any point on the network. However, eavesdropping usually involves disruption of service because the bus network must be temporarily disconnected to insert a new station.

To help prevent eavesdropping, protect your network cable as much as possible by burying it underground, placing it inside walls, and protecting it with tamper-proof containers. For maximum protection, you should do the following:

- Document your cable infrastructure.
- Investigate all outages on your coaxial network.
- Physically inspect your cable infrastructure on a routine basis.
- Investigate all undocumented hosts and connections.

Twisted-Pair Cables

You should already be familiar with twisted-pair cabling standards. All twisted-pair cables have one or more pairs of wires that are twisted together inside a cable sheath. The wires themselves are made of copper and covered by a plastic coating to prevent them from making an electrical connection to each other. The cable sheath itself is typically a plastic tube containing the wires. The individual wire pairs are twisted inside the cable sheath to help prevent the loss of electrical signals traversing the cable pairs. The remainder of this section focuses on ways in which twisted-pair cable can be compromised and methods for securing it.

Sabotaging Twisted-Pair Networks and Countermeasures

Twisted-pair networks can also be sabotaged. The cables can be easily cut with a pair of wire cutters or regular office scissors, or a heat or energy source could disrupt communications. However, twisted-pair networks typically utilize a star configuration, so the loss of a single cable should not disrupt the entire network, unless the cable that was cut provided connectivity to the central server or gateway router. In a mesh configuration, cutting a single network cable might not even interrupt network communications.

To protect your twisted-pair network segments from sabotage, you should be sure to protect the physical cables. Protecting central connectivity devices such as hubs and patch panels is more important than protecting individual twisted-pair segments. The next priority is to protect crucial segments, such as those going to central servers, routers, or connecting hubs and switches. Finally, you should physically inspect your network cable infrastructure routinely.

Eavesdropping on Twisted-Pair Networks and Countermeasures

Electronic signals traverse the twisted-pair cable. Someone spying on your network could listen to these passing signals. There are three main ways in which a twisted-pair network might be compromised by eavesdropping:

- Physically attaching a *protocol analyzer* to a twisted-pair connection point. A protocol analyzer is a device or computer software program that allows its user to capture and decode network traffic. Other names for it are data sniffer, network sniffer, or packet sniffer.
- Splicing into the twisted-pair cable.
- Using escaping electromagnetic signals to eavesdrop on signals passing through the wire.

Physical security is the main method of protecting twisted-pair networks from eavesdropping, and you should protect your central network devices before focusing on individual hosts. Using switches instead of hubs can make eavesdropping more difficult because switches direct network traffic bound for a specific host directly to that host, whereas hubs direct traffic bound for a specific host to any host attached to the hub. However, there are tools that attackers can use to compromise switches, as discussed in the next lesson.

Managed devices (such as hubs, switches, and routers) can alert you when a cable is unplugged or a new connection is created. Such warnings can also alert you to the presence of an eavesdropper.

Fiber Optic Cable

You should already be familiar with fiber optic cabling standards. Fiber optic cable utilizes a glass or plastic filament that conducts light pulses to transfer data. Outside of the fiber optic core, there is a glass cladding, a plastic spacer, protective Kevlar fibers, and then a protective outer sheath.

Fiber optic cable is the most secure cable because it cannot be affected by electromagnetic interference and does not leak electrical signals. However, of the cable types discussed in this lesson, fiber optic cable is the most expensive and most difficult to install. The remainder of this section focuses on ways in which fiber optic cable can be compromised and secured.

Sabotaging a Fiber Optic Cable

Sabotage of a fiber cable is easier than sabotage of any other cable type. Fiber cables can be crushed, bent, snapped, and often inadvertently damaged. Any damage to the fiber cable disrupts the signal between the two points to which the cable is attached.

To protect your fiber optic cable from sabotage or the possibility of eavesdropping, protect the physical cable. If there is an outage between two points on the fiber cable, you must determine why that outage occurred to ensure that it was not due to sabotage.

Note   A power outage could also be used to insert rogue devices. Consider that an attacker might create a situation to insert a device. After a power outage, you should ensure that your network cables are still properly routed and that no rogue devices are present.

Eavesdropping on a Fiber Optic Connection

Electronic eavesdropping is virtually impossible on fiber optic cables because they emit light pulses. To eavesdrop on a fiber network you must disrupt the communications between two hosts. The fiber cable must be cut, the ends polished, and a fiber optic card inserted between the connection. During the insertion, the connection between the two hosts is unavailable. The difficulties involved and possibilities for detection make such an exploitation highly unlikely.

Exercise: Identifying Cable Vulnerabilities

Match the cable type in the left column with the compromise it's susceptible to in the right column. More than one compromise might apply to any given cable type.

1. Fiber optic   a. EMI and RFI
2. Twisted-pair   b. Breaking or cutting
3. Coaxial   c. Eavesdropping

Lesson Review

The following questions are intended to reinforce key information presented in this lesson. If you are unable to answer a question, review the lesson and then try the question again. Answers to the questions can be found in Appendix A, "Questions and Answers."

1. What techniques can be used to sabotage coaxial and twisted-pair networks?

2. Which coaxial and twisted-pair sabotage methods do not work on fiber optic cable?

3. List eavesdropping methods for each type of cable: twisted-pair, coaxial, and fiber optic.

4. What methods can you use to help protect your network from eavesdropping?

Lesson Summary

- Network cabling is a vulnerable part of your network infrastructure. However, an attacker or spy must have physical access to your cable (or at least be able to get close to the cable) to exploit or attack your network cable infrastructure.

- Sabotage is a simple matter for a saboteur who is able to gain physical access to your network cable infrastructure. The saboteur could cut a coaxial or twisted-pair cable to disrupt network communications. Also, coaxial and twisted-pair cable are susceptible to EMI and RFI, so a source of EMI/RFI placed near a cable or wire bundle could be enough to disrupt communications. Fiber optic cable is impervious to EMI and RFI, but is easily broken.

- Use the following techniques to protect your cable infrastructure:

  - Document your entire cable infrastructure. Keep that documentation current.

  - Investigate all hosts and connectivity devices that are not documented.

  - Protect your network cable as much as possible by burying it underground, placing it inside walls, and protecting it with tamper-proof containers.

  - Check the physical integrity of your network infrastructure cabling on a regular basis. Verify your network infrastructure after power outages.

  - Enable managed devices to alert you of the presence of disconnected cables or unauthorized connections. Investigate all alerts and outages.

Lesson 3: Securing Connectivity Devices

Many connectivity devices on your network have both physical components and logical configurations. A spy or an attacker might compromise both the physical components and the logical configuration of your network devices. In this lesson, specific network devices are examined with emphasis on ways in which these devices might be compromised, attacked, or in other ways exploited. Methods for increasing the security of these devices are also discussed in this lesson.

After this lesson, you will be able to

- Describe exploitation and choose appropriate security measures for hubs, bridges or switches, and routers
- Document ways in which a firewall could be compromised and select related security solutions
- List the potential for private branch exchange (PBX) exploitations and choose appropriate methods for securing a PBX
- Describe modem exploitations and select appropriate security measures
- Explain the risks and choose the appropriate security measures for wireless networks

Estimated lesson time: 40 minutes

Hubs

You should already be familiar with hubs as connectivity devices on Ethernet networks. As you know, hubs can be active or passive. Active hubs repeat network signals and are sometimes referred to as multiport repeaters. Because hubs are central connectivity devices, they could be targets for attack. The remainder of this section focuses on how hubs can be compromised and secured.

Compromising Hubs

Hubs are simple to sabotage if the saboteur has physical access to the device. A hub can be disconnected or destroyed, or simply turned off, if it is an active hub. When a hub is disabled, the devices attached to it are unable to communicate.

Eavesdropping through a hub is also possible. If there is an open hub port or one of the legitimately connected devices can be disconnected, an attacker or spy could use the port to gain information or attack another device on the network. The open or disconnected port could be used to place a hacking device (or another computer to which the hacker has full control) to gather information from the network or to attack other devices.

Securing Hubs

Because hubs are physical devices, they should be physically protected. Try to lock hubs in wiring closets. If the hub cannot be locked in a room or closet, try to secure it in some other type of protective encasement. At a minimum, you should periodically check hubs to be sure that all cables are connected properly and that no rogue connections exist.

Managed hubs can be used to detect physical configuration changes. Managed hubs report hub statistics and connection information to management software. You can configure a managed hub to send an alert when a configuration is modified. Of course, because a managed hub has a (software) configuration, an attacker could compromise the hub's configuration to disrupt network communication or mask evidence of another attack.

Switches and Bridges

Switches and bridges communicate at the Data Link layer (Layer 2) of the Open Systems Interconnection (OSI) model. They make switching and bridging decisions based on the media access control (MAC) address of each network interface. Switches and bridges maintain tables that allow them to transfer packets to the appropriate network segment. Bridges are typically used to divide a network segment in half. Switches typically divide a network segment into many smaller segments, one segment for each port on the switch. These devices typically only separate unicast traffic; broadcast and multicast traffic is often allowed to pass through the bridge or switch (because these types of traffic are destined for multiple hosts). The remainder of this section covers compromising and securing switches and bridges.

Note   You might see the terms Layer 3 and Layer 4 switching in marketing and technical documents from some networking vendors. If you carefully analyze descriptions of these devices, you should see that they are hybrid technologies that incorporate the functions of traditional switches and traditional routers. These devices are also called high-performance routers.

Compromising Switches and Bridges

As previously mentioned, switches and bridges maintain a table that contains MAC address mappings to each of their connection points. The table allows the switch or bridge to direct Layer 2 communications to the correct network segment or port, making it a potential target for attack. A central switch could also be the target of a saboteur. Destroying a central switch, disconnecting power, or disconnecting all of the network cables would disrupt all communications passing through the device.

Along the lines of disrupting communication, there are scripts such as macof that can be used to flood bridges and switches with random MAC addresses. Assuming the switch or bridge is able to learn new addresses, such an attack could reduce the performance of the switching or bridging device and slow network traffic.

Gaining Administrative Access

If an attacker can gain administrative access to the switch or bridge, he or she can reroute network communications. These communications can be redirected to a host on the network under the control of the attacker, which could be the attacker's system or a system the attacker was able to gain control over using some other technique. If the attacker decides to sabotage communications on the network, he or she can do so at any time once administrative access is obtained. Of course, the attacker must gain administrative access to the bridge or switch first. A skilled attacker can do this by trying default administrative passwords or running a password attack against the device. Switches in particular often have a function called *port mirroring*, which allows an administrator to map the input and output from one or more ports on the switch to a single port. This is meant to help in troubleshooting communication problems on a network. However, if an attacker is configuring port mirroring, he or she could watch all network traffic that passes through the switch. The attacker might do this to gather information about other systems on the network or in hopes of decoding a password or other valuable information, such as trade secrets.

Occasionally, connectivity devices might have software configuration problems or security vulnerabilities. For example, someone might discover that a switching table can be updated without any administrative authorization, meaning anyone could compromise your switch, if they had access to your network. Vendors usually resolve problems like these quickly once they are discovered. To protect your connectivity devices, be sure to keep track of vendor patches and install them when they are available.

ARP Cache Poisoning

Although switches and bridges segment the network, it might be possible for an attacker to use Address Resolution Protocol (ARP) cache poisoning (also known as ARP spoofing) to propagate traffic through a switch. ARP cache poisoning was introduced in Chapter 2 as a method for placing incorrect information in computers' ARP caches to misroute packets. The ARP cache is used to store Internet Protocol (IP) to MAC address mappings.

For an attacker to conduct ARP cache poisoning, he or she must typically gain physical connectivity to the local segment. The attacker must then compromise the ARP caches of the hosts on that segment. ARP cache poisoning involves overwriting entries in the ARP cache to cause a computer to send all network traffic directly to the attacker's computer. If an attacker is able to do this to all the computers on the segment, he or she could effectively listen to (and forward) data packets without network users realizing it. The attacker would then be able to listen to the network traffic sent on that network, most likely to steal trade secrets or obtain unencrypted passwords.

Note   Attackers might use arpspoof (part of the dsniff toolset) to poison an ARP cache.

Securing Switches and Bridges

There are several measures you can take to prevent attacks against your switches and bridges. As with other network devices, you should physically secure them so they cannot be tampered with or destroyed. Here are other suggestions that can help to secure your switches and bridges:

- Secure all physical connections on your network segments. Be sure that no unauthorized connections can be made. Also, limit physical access to your switch locations and use security personnel and monitoring devices to ensure connectivity devices are secure.

- Set complex passwords for administrative consoles. Restrict device administration to as few people as possible from as few locations as possible. Also, be sure to change administrative passwords routinely and whenever an administrator leaves the company.

- Manually enter ARP mappings on critical devices, such as central servers, switches, bridges, and so on. If you manually enter all necessary MAC addresses, prevent the switch or bridge from learning new addresses.

- Keep your switches and bridges current with the latest vendor security patches.

- Document your device configurations so you know for sure what is normal and authorized.

- Monitor your network with management tools that alert you to unauthorized connections. Tools such as ARPWATCH can monitor activity on your network and keep a database of MAC-to-IP address mappings. The tool can also alert you to changes in these ARP mappings.

Routers

As you know, routers communicate at the Network layer (Layer 3) of the OSI reference model. Routers also maintain ARP caches and routing tables to perform their task of routing network packets. The remainder of this section focuses on ways in which routers can be compromised and secured.

Compromising Routers

As previously mentioned, routers maintain both ARP caches and routing tables. These tables allow the router to transfer and route communications appropriately on the network, and they are also potential points of attack. A central router might also be the target of a saboteur. Destroying a central router, disconnecting power, or disconnecting its network cables would disrupt all communications passing through the device.

Because routers maintain ARP caches, they could be susceptible to ARP cache poisoning. In addition to ARP caches, routers maintain routing tables that can be modified by a remote connection or a physical connection through a console cable to the router. Routing tables can also be updated automatically using a routing protocol. If an attacker is able to modify a routing table, network traffic could be misrouted to a host chosen by the attacker. If the host is under the attacker's control, it could be used to decode network packets (to steal or modify data). As stated earlier, you should secure and monitor physical connection points to your network to prevent ARP cache poisoning.

If an attacker can gain administrative access to the router, he or she can reroute communications on the network. These communications can be redirected to a host on the network under the control of the attacker, which could be the attacker's system or a system the attacker was able to gain control over using some other technique. If the attacker decides to sabotage communications on the network, he or she can do so at any time once administrative access is obtained. Of course, the attacker must gain administrative access to the router first. A skilled attacker can do this by trying default administrative passwords or running a password attack against the device.

Attackers could also utilize routing protocols such as the Routing Information Protocol (RIP) to update routing tables with bogus information. This is called *RIP spoofing*, and it is a problem for devices that utilize RIP version 1 (RIPv1). However, RIP version 2 (RIPv2) allows for passwords to be set at the routers. Therefore, on a RIPv2-enabled router an attacker would have to compromise the router's password to submit bogus routes.

As stated previously, connectivity devices might have software configuration problems or security vulnerabilities. For example, someone might discover that a router can be updated or disabled without any administrative authorization (meaning anyone could compromise your router, if they had access to your network). Vendors usually resolve problems like these quickly once they are discovered. To protect your connectivity devices, be sure to keep track of vendor patches and install them when they are available.

Securing Routers

A central router could also be the target of a saboteur. Destroying a central router, disconnecting power, or disconnecting all of the network cables would disrupt all communications passing through the device. To increase the security of your routers, consider the following suggestions:

- Ensure the routers are kept in locked rooms or containers.
- Check the security of all incoming and outgoing connections.
- Limit physical access to your network cable infrastructure, wiring closets, and server rooms.
- Use security personnel and monitoring equipment to protect connection points and devices.
- Utilize complex passwords for administrative consoles. Be sure to change administrative passwords routinely and whenever an administrator leaves your organization.
- Set access list entries to prevent inappropriate connections and routing of traffic. For example, packets with the IP address of your internal network should not be coming from the external interface on the router. If this happens, it is usually an indication that someone is trying to perform IP address spoofing as described in Chapter 2.
- Keep your routers current with the latest vendor security patches.
- Be sure to document and regularly review your network configuration.
- Disable RIPv1 and utilize only RIPv2 or other routing protocols that allow you to secure router updates with passwords.

Firewalls

The term *firewall* is used generically to describe any device that protects an internal network (or host) from malicious hackers or software on an external network (or network to which the host is connected). Firewalls perform a variety of tasks to filter out potentially harmful incoming or outgoing traffic or connections. They are often implemented between an organization's internal network and the Internet. However, this is not always the case. Some firewalls are used to subdivide internal networks or even to protect individual computers.

The five main services that firewalls provide are packet filtering, application filtering, proxy server, circuit-level, and stateful inspection. These services are described in more detail in the following sections.

Packet Filtering

A *packet filtering firewall* or gateway checks each packet traversing the device. The firewall inspects the packet headers of all network packets going through the firewall.

Packets are passed or rejected based on a set of predefined or administrator-defined rules. Packet filter rules can accept or reject network packets based on whether they are inbound or outbound, or due to the information contained in any of the following network data packet fields:

- **Source IP Address.**   This field is used to identify the host that is sending the packet. Attackers could modify this field in an attempt to conduct IP spoofing. Firewalls are typically configured to reject packets that arrive at the external interface bearing a source address of the internal network because that is either an erroneous host configuration or an attempt at IP spoofing.

- **Destination IP Address.**   This is the IP address that the packet is trying to reach.

- **IP Protocol ID.**   Each IP header has a protocol ID that follows. For example, Transmission Control Protocol (TCP) is ID 6, User Datagram Protocol (UDP) is ID 17, and Internet Control Message Protocol (ICMP) is ID 1.

More Info   A table listing common Protocol IDs can be found in Appendix B, "Ports and Protocol IDs."

- **TCP or UDP Port Number.**   The port number that indicates the service this packet is destined for, such as TCP port 80 for Web services.

More Info   A table listing common TCP and UDP ports can be found in Appendix B, "Ports and Protocol IDs."

- **ICMP Message Type.**   ICMP supports several different functions that help to control and manage IP traffic. Some of these messages can be used to attack networks, so they are frequently blocked at the firewall. For example, ICMP echo requests can be exploited to cause a broadcast storm.You can read more about ICMP message types in Request for Comments (RFC) 793. (RFC articles can be found at *http://www.rfc-editor.org*.)

- **Fragmentation Flags.**   IP fragmentation was described in detail in Chapter 2. Firewalls can examine and forward or reject fragmented packets. Some flawed implementations of TCP/IP allow for the reassembly of fragmented packets as whole packets (without receipt of the first packet, which contains the full header information). A successful fragmentation attack can allow an attacker to send packets that could compromise an internal host.

- **IP Options Setting.**   This field is used for diagnostics. The firewall should be configured to drop network packets that use this field. Attackers could potentially use this field in conjunction with IP spoofing to redirect network packets to their systems.

Application Filtering

An *application filtering firewall* intercepts connections and performs security inspections. The firewall must be equipped with the appropriate applications to perform this task. In this way, the firewall acts as a proxy for connections between the internal and external network. The firewall can check and enforce access control rules specific to the application. Application filtering firewalls are used to check incoming e-mails for virus attachments; these firewalls are often called *e-mail gateways*.

Proxy Server

Like an application filtering firewall, a *proxy server* takes on responsibility for providing services between the internal and external network. However, the proxy server can actually be the server providing the services or it can create a separate connection to the requested server. In this way, a proxy server can be used to hide the addressing scheme of the internal network. Proxy servers can also be used to filter requests based on the protocol and address requested. For example, the proxy server could be configured to reject incoming connections to http://www.internal.local or outgoing connections to http://www.external.net.

Circuit-Level

A *circuit-level firewall* controls TCP and UDP ports, but doesn't watch the data transferred over them. Therefore, if a connection is established, the traffic is transferred without any further checking.

Stateful Inspection

A *stateful inspection firewall* works at the Network layer. The firewall evaluates the IP header information and monitors the state of each connection. Connections are rejected if they attempt any actions that are not standard for the given protocol.

Any of these listed firewall features can be implemented in combination by a given firewall implementation. Placing multiple firewalls in series is a common practice to increase security at the network perimeter. If an attacker is able to breach the first firewall, the second offers additional protection. Using multiple firewalls in series (back-to-back) is one example of creating a *defense-in-depth*, as shown in Figure 4-1, which means that you are using multiple layers of protection to keep your network secure.

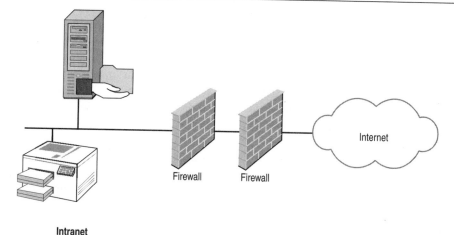

Intranet

Figure 4-1.   Defense-in-depth using multiple firewalls back-to-back

Another type of network infrastructure defense method is called *defense-in-breadth*, which refers to using multiple layers of protection with different configuration mechanisms. This means than an attacker requires a breadth of knowledge to exploit your layers of protection. For example, you could create a defense-in-breadth by using multiple firewalls in series from different manufacturers. The idea is that two firewall products from different manufacturers are less likely to be exploited than two firewall products from the same manufacturer.

Note   Defense-in-depth and defense-in-breadth configurations go beyond placing multiple firewalls in series. Defense of the network can involve a combination of virus scanners, e-mail gateways, firewalls, secure host configurations, and routine security inspections.

Exploiting Firewalls

Poorly implemented firewall configuration is a common reason firewalls are compromised. For example, firewalls can be configured with a *default-allow rule* or a *default-deny rule*. The default-allow rule (also known as allow-all) means that a firewall permits all inbound network packets except those that are specifically prohibited. Network administrators and security personnel usually view this setting as too permissive. The other option is the default-deny rule, which rejects all inbound packets except those that are specifically permitted. This is the standard configuration of a secure firewall.

Flaws in firewall software are another reason firewalls are compromised. Usually, vendors release software patches or temporary solutions quickly after they are made publicly known. The following list describes other ways in which firewalls might be compromised:

- **Compromising the firewall management console or password.**   Firewalls can be configured through a management console. Management of the firewall might be restricted to a connection through a serial cable or it could be open to remote network connections. An attacker might try to gain access to the firewall through these administrative connections. If successful, the attacker could take control of the firewall.

- **Circumventing the firewall.**   If there is another way into the network, or another path can be created, then compromising the firewall would be as simple as using a different path. A dial-up connection from a server on your internal network, for example, could provide another path to your network.

- **Physically tampering with the firewall.**   If attackers can gain physical access to your firewall, they might attempt to disconnect it, reroute network cables to avoid it, or sabotage it in some other way.

Securing Firewalls

As described in the previous section, there are several ways an attacker might attempt to neutralize your firewall, so protecting it requires vigilance. To protect your firewall, follow this advice:

- Keep track of security bulletins concerning your firewall product. Apply all software patches as they are made available.

- Update virus definition files routinely.

- Physically protect the firewall.

- Document the firewall configuration and review that configuration regularly.

- Limit the methods for managing the firewall. If remote management is allowed, use the most secure authentication available.

- Use complex passwords. Be sure to change administrative passwords routinely, and always change them when an administrator leaves your organization.

- Know and test the firewall rules by trying to make connections to unauthorized ports or services from outside the firewall.

- Ensure that there are no network paths or connections that can be used to circumvent the firewall.

Remote Access

Remote Access Service (RAS) servers allow clients to use dial-up connections to access servers and internal networks. The RAS server typically has a modem (or bank of modems) that allows incoming connections from clients that might be compromised by an attacker. Compromises of RAS servers typically involve exploitation of the RAS software itself. These are usually the result of an oversight in the software programming by the RAS server vendor. The RAS server vendor should provide software patches to correct these programming flaws. Check for software patches from your RAS server and apply them as they are made available.

Note   This section and the two that follow present a brief introduction to RAS as it relates to your network infrastructure. More in-depth coverage of these concepts is presented in Chapter 5, "Communications Security."

Attackers might also try to make unauthorized connections by guessing passwords. To protect against this, some RAS servers allow for password policies. When possible you should configure a password policy to lock out accounts after several incorrect logon attempts. Lockout settings are typically configured for three to five incorrect logon attempts, and the lockout period is often about 30 minutes. Such a policy helps prevent someone from successfully guessing a password. (You must ensure that user passwords are complex enough to prevent an attacker from guessing them with a limited number of guesses, however.)

Some RAS server implementations allow you to implement security measures that require some physical component or card (such as a smart card) that uses a digital certificate to grant access. Further, the access card itself typically requires a personal identification number (PIN) that is required to allow access. This is called *two-factor authentication* because the user must have the card (first factor) and know a PIN (second factor) to access the system.

Attackers might also attempt to decode passwords by packet sniffing connections from legitimate users. To do this, the attacker would have to eavesdrop on the dial-up circuit through which the user is connecting to your RAS server. This means the hacker must connect to the physical telephone line that is used to make the connection (or compromise a telephone switching device to propagate that information to the attacker). This is difficult and requires a highly skilled attacker. The best protection against such an exploitation would be to use strong authentication and data encryption between the client and RAS server.

TACACS+

Terminal Access Controller Access Control System Plus (TACACS+) is an authentication protocol that provides a method for a remote access client to authenticate with an RAS server. Authentication is used to determine whether a remote user should be allowed to access the network. The TACACS+ server can be configured with an access control list or it can contact a central server, such as a UNIX Network File Service (NFS) server running Network Information Service (NIS). NFS is the standard file sharing mechanism used by UNIX servers. An NIS server provides a master accounts database for users on a UNIX-based network.

Note   Previous versions of TACACS+ were TACACS and XTACACS. Although they share similar names and have the same goals, the older versions are not compatible with the newer TACACS+ protocol.

The TACACS authentication system started with UNIX. Today it is used in both UNIX and non-UNIX network devices (such as routers) that provide remote access. Users authenticate with a TACACS+ server by providing a user name and password. TACACS+ allows for Challenge Handshake Authentication Protocol (CHAP) encrypted passwords. CHAP is an algorithm that is used to encrypt passwords that are passed between two points, protecting them from eavesdropping attacks. TACACS+ encrypts the entire authentication packet between the TACACS+ client and server.

RADIUS

Remote Authentication and Dial-In User Service (RADIUS) is a protocol similar to TACACS that provides authentication to RAS connection attempts. RADIUS is a widely supported protocol standardized by the Internet Engineering Task Force (IETF). RADIUS servers can provide authentication to remote access connections using their own internal user database. RADIUS servers can also be configured as RADIUS proxy servers, which are able to authenticate against another RADIUS server or RADIUS-enabled directory service. RADIUS servers and clients are also capable of supporting CHAP to encrypt password exchanges.

Figure 4-2 illustrates possible RADIUS and RADIUS proxy server authentication. The RADIUS server can grant remote access from its own local database or be configured to contact another directory service, such as UNIX NIS, Novell NetWare e-Directory, or Microsoft's Active Directory service. Users dial in remotely to the appropriate dial-in location. Authentication is relayed to the RADIUS server. If the RADIUS server is a RADIUS proxy server, it consults the appropriate directory service accounts database.

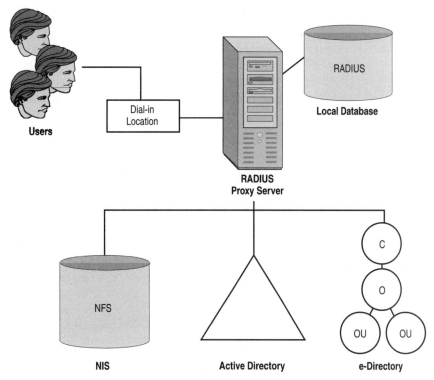

Figure 4-2. RADIUS and RADIUS proxy authentication services

Note   Shiva Access Manager and Cisco Secure ACS are examples of products that support both the RADIUS and TACACS+ protocols.

Telecommunications Hacking

Telecommunications systems provide internal phone services for many organizations. These private telecommunications systems are known as PBX systems. They usually offer a variety of features such as voice mail, multiple-party calling, long-distance access restrictions, and call tracking. PBX systems are potential targets for attackers. Attackers who gain unauthorized access to the PBX system could potentially use it to do the following:

- Make free long-distance calls by changing billing records.
- Compromise or shut down the organization's voice mail system.
- Reroute incoming, transferred, or outgoing calls.
- Compromise the rest of your organization's network, as PBX systems are part of your network infrastructure. For example, locate a modem-equipped PC. Use that PC to create an analog connection to the internal network, and then use the analog connection to access the internal network.

Hacking PBX Systems

PBX systems are frequently an organization's most valuable communication asset. If the PBX system is compromised, the organization could lose business. There are relatively few brands of PBX systems available, so an attacker could use knowledge of a few select systems to compromise a wide variety of businesses. Although PBX systems are complex, a skilled attacker could use the system to compromise your network infrastructure. There are a variety of methods that an attacker might use to compromise the PBX system:

- PBX systems come with default passwords for system maintenance. Attackers could run password attacks to guess these PBX maintenance passwords. Once an attacker acquires a management password, he or she can reconfigure the PBX system.

- PBX systems are often expensive and upgrades are difficult. Therefore, many businesses use older PBX systems that might have unencrypted databases with obvious data structures that could be manipulated.

- PBX security is not as popular a topic as computer security. Many businesses don't think to protect their PBX systems or know how to do so. Users might be tricked into giving up passwords for the telephone system because awareness of exploitation is not as high as it is with computer systems.

- Remote management and upgrades of PBX systems are commonplace. Remote connections could be used to install malicious software or reconfigure the PBX system.

- Many people use and have access to the PBX-connected telephones. These terminals could be used to attack or reconfigure the PBX system.

- Telecommunications infrastructure might extend into unused floors and offices, making it easier for someone to hide an unauthorized connection (or conceal hacking attempts).

Protecting Your PBX

Physically securing PBX equipment should be a high priority. Ensure that access to the main PBX wiring room and switching equipment is controlled. The telecommunications infrastructure should be carefully documented and routinely checked for unauthorized connections. Other items to consider when protecting your PBX system are as follows:

- Shut down or secure off-site transfers with passwords. Off-site transfers are typically enabled so that the vendor or a contracted service provider can update your PBX automatically. Attackers could exploit this system to reconfigure your PBX.

- Program system exclusion lists to limit long-distance calling. Consider blocking 900 numbers and other toll numbers.

- Program system schedules to shut down services that are not required during off hours and days.

- Educate users about PBX security. Ask users not to write down passwords or program their phones with passwords in auto-dial. Tell users to clear phones that display dialed numbers after resetting passwords (so their password is not stored in the redial feature of the phone).

- Enforce a PBX password change and audit policy. Ensure that passwords are not left at default values and that they are routinely changed.

- Audit PBX access to ensure that former employees, partners, and contractors who no longer need access are removed from the system.

- Secure maintenance ports and limit the number of entry points. Disable unnecessary remote management features. Implement the highest available security features for maintenance and remote management.

- Routinely check for vendor software and hardware updates, and verify all software updates to the PBX system.

- Log maintenance, software updates, remote management, and all other system access.

- Consider implementing a dynamic telemanagement system that tracks system access, checks for fraud, and performs audits. It can also alert you to unauthorized usage and log suspicious usage.

More Info   The National Institute of Standards and Technology (NIST) has written SP 800-24, "PBX Vulnerability Analysis" which describes PBX hacking and security measures. (NIST articles can be found at *http://csrc.nist.gov/publications*.)

Modems

Modems connect computers to the Internet and to private networks, but those connections could be susceptible to compromise or attack. As explained earlier, modems can be used to circumvent the security provided by your organization's firewall and other security devices. Modems can provide direct access to a system on a network and potentially be used to access other systems on that network. Exploited modem dialing software can be used to erase hard drives or cause the modem to dial emergency services, for example.

To protect your network from modem exploits, follow these procedures:

- Remove all unnecessary modems from computers on your network.

- Check for software updates for all computers that must have modems.

- Monitor security bulletins from modem vendors for newly discovered security gaps and apply software patches as soon as they are available.

- Isolate computers configured with modems to limit the damage that can be caused by those systems should the modem be compromised.

- Monitor computers with modems regularly to ensure they have not been compromised.

Wireless

Many different manufacturers have released wireless access points (APs) that can be used with wireless network cards. The communication between the AP and the network card travels as radio or infrared signals through the air. Attackers who are as far as more than a mile away from the AP could potentially intercept these signals. There is no need for the attacker to splice into wires or add connectivity devices to gain access to a wireless network in this way. APs can also function as hubs, switches, and routers and are therefore vulnerable to the same exploits mentioned earlier concerning those devices.

Note   There is a growing trend of people driving around neighborhoods and business areas with wireless network identification equipment to locate APs. These people then mark and map places where they can gain free Internet access. This trend makes the implementation of wireless networks even more dangerous because it could open your network up to individuals and equipment beyond your control. For this reason, the United States Federal Bureau of Investigation (FBI) and the Computer Emergency Response Team (CERT) urge individuals and businesses to use the most secure authentication and encryption on their wireless networks.

There are numerous exploits that compromise wireless networks. Many wireless network devices allow you to enable strong authentication and encryption mechanisms to prevent unauthorized network access and packet sniffing. However, additional "hacker tools" are available that could allow attackers to compromise data encryption, steal passwords, and even hijack (or take over) sessions between clients and servers. To keep a wireless network reasonably secure you must stay current on the latest security bulletins and vendor patches. You should also implement the most secure authentication and encryption methods available.

IEEE 802.11b defines a method for user authentication called Extensible Authentication Protocol over LANs (EAPOL). EAPOL allows vendors to provide a standard method for granting access to authorized wireless users. Most APs allow you to secure authentication by allowing you to set a specific access code on the wireless network interface card (NIC) and AP. Most wireless vendors also support Wired Equivalent Privacy (WEP) encryption, which allows you to configure a shared key to encrypt communications between the wireless NIC and the AP. Specifications for authentication and access are evolving quickly, so you should check the wireless vendors (such as Linksys, NetGear, Cisco, and Dlink) for the latest security improvements before implementing a wireless network. Another potential method for increasing wireless security is to implement your wireless networks in a location that is designed to reduce signal leakage, such as an underground facility with thick walls.

Wireless networks can also be interrupted by EMI and RFI and the only real counter-measure to that is a stronger signal. This is something the wireless user or administrator can typically only control by purchasing an AP that offers a stronger signal. When laying out a wireless network you should ensure that you don't place workstations or APs near any obvious sources of EMI and RFI, such as elevators, copier machines, radio transmitters, or industrial equipment.

Exercise: Identifying Network Infrastructure Exploits

Match the equipment exploits in the left column with the appropriate devices in the right column. Some exploits can be used on multiple device types.

1. Physical sabotage
2. Overwriting MAC-to-IP address mappings
3. Rerouting cables
4. Packet sniffing
5. EMI and RFI

a. Routers
b. Switches and bridges
c. Hubs
d. Hosts on the network
e. Wireless AP
f. ARP cache

Lesson Review

The following questions are intended to reinforce key information presented in this lesson. If you are unable to answer a question, review the lesson and then try the question again. Answers to the questions can be found in Appendix A, "Questions and Answers."

1. List security issues that are common to managed hubs, switches, and routers.

2. Describe security issues that are common to switches and routers.

3. How might an attacker compromise a firewall implementation?

4. List ways in which a PBX can be compromised.

5. What are the security implementations available for wireless networks?

Lesson Summary

- Physically secure as much of your network infrastructure as possible. This includes locking central connectivity devices in rooms or protective enclosures.

- Managed devices on your network infrastructure can be vulnerable to password guessing attacks. Any device that can be managed locally and especially remotely should be configured with the most secure authentication and encryption available.

- Monitor software and hardware vendor Web sites and bulletins for information on security exploits. You should apply all available security fixes as soon as possible.

- Configure managed devices such as hubs, switches, routers, PBX systems, and firewalls to alert you of unauthorized connections.

- Configure the most secure authentication and encryption on all wireless devices.

- Ensure that your firewall virus definition files are routinely updated.

- Document your network infrastructure, including the configuration of all connectivity devices, computers with modems, PBX system configuration, and all network cable attachments.

- Routinely audit your network infrastructure to ensure there are no unauthorized connections, configurations, or devices.

Lesson 4: Exploring Secure Topologies

This lesson focuses on network designs that enhance security. Many networks today are in some way connected to the Internet. The presence of malicious software and hackers makes the Internet a potentially dangerous network. Organizations that provide their internal users and clients with Internet access expose their networks to potential attacks. Organizations that provide services to Internet users also open their resources to attack. Organizations providing connections or services to the Internet must realize the need for protective equipment, software, and secure topologies.

After this lesson, you will be able to

- List different types of security zones
- Explain the purpose of a perimeter network
- Describe the function of network address translation (NAT)
- Identify uses for virtual private networks (VPNs)
- Explain the use of virtual local area networks (VLANs)

Estimated lesson time: 20 minutes

Security Zones

Organizations often create security zones by placing firewalls between internal and external networks. Multiple firewalls are often used to create multiple layers of protection between the internal and external networks, as previously discussed. Some network designs place a network segment between two firewalls. This network segment between the firewalls is called a *perimeter network* (also known as a DMZ, demilitarized zone, or screened subnet). The creation of a perimeter network creates a division of the network infrastructure into three separate subordinate network structures called *security zones*. Security zones help organizations classify, prioritize, and focus on security issues based on the services that are required in each zone. These security zones are as follows:

- **Intranet.**   The organization's private network; this is used by employees and those internal to the organization (such as contractors and on-site partners).
- **Perimeter network.**   Used to provide services to users on the Internet and sometimes those inside the organization.
- **Extranet.**   Depending on the security devices used and the network layout, the external network might be called a wide area network (WAN), Internet, public network, or untrusted network. For example, some three-pronged firewalls label the external network connection as a WAN, and others as the Internet.

The following three sections of this lesson discuss intranet, perimeter network, and external security zones in greater detail.

Intranet

The security zone closest to the company is called the intranet. This is also known as the internal network, private network, local area network (LAN), trusted network, protected network, and company or organizational network. The intranet is typically the network (or networks) that contains most of the organization's private resources, including computers, users, data, printers, and other network infrastructure equipment.

Organizations typically don't expect malicious attacks from their own intranets. This is why this security zone is often considered the trusted network. However, former and current employees and contractors might attack resources on the intranet. Intranet users could wittingly or unwittingly install viruses, and they could also try to access or spy on confidential resources. Additionally, internal users probably have access to some part of or possibly the entire physical network. Physical access could enable users to unplug equipment, destroy equipment, or attach unauthorized devices to the network. Security for the intranet security zone typically includes the following measures:

- Firewall protection from the external network and the perimeter network
- Installing and updating virus-scanning software
- Observing and auditing confidential resources
- Using host-based firewalls for computers that maintain confidential data
- Documenting and auditing the physical infrastructure and critical systems configurations to ensure there are no unauthorized devices or connections
- Restricting and monitoring access to critical systems, services, and confidential information
- Removing unnecessary services from mission-critical servers

---

Note   VLANs and VPNs can also be used to further secure the intranet. These concepts are introduced separately later in this lesson.

Perimeter Network

The *perimeter network* provides a semisafe zone in which a private organization can provide limited services to an external network. Typically, the external network is the public Internet, and a perimeter network could be set up between any two networks.

Note   A perimeter network is sometimes referred to as a demilitarized zone, or DMZ. DMZ is a military term for an area in which two warring groups are not allowed to bring weapons. Such an area is established to allow peaceful negotiation and create a buffer between the militaries of each opposing force. In network security terms, DMZ is a metaphor for a buffer zone between two networks.

An example implementation of a perimeter network follows. Assume you are the network administrator for your company. You wish to provide Web services to users on the Internet, but want to prevent those users from accessing your company's intranet. Additionally, you want to protect your company's Web server as much as possible. You decide to use a configuration similar to the one shown in Figure 4-3. Using this configuration, the Web server is protected by a firewall that allows access to the Hypertext Transfer Protocol (HTTP) for Web services, but all other protocols are restricted. A separate firewall is used to protect the intranet from all Internet access (including HTTP access).

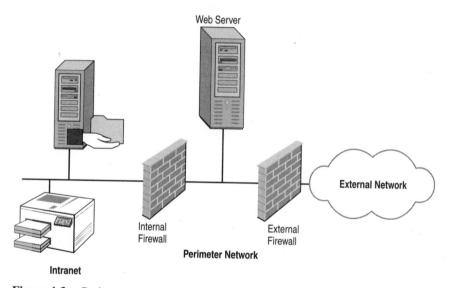

Figure 4-3.   Perimeter network configuration example

Some firewalls, called *three-pronged firewalls*, are able to separate the intranet and external networks while also creating a perimeter network. In this case, the firewall has three separate network interfaces: one for the external network, one for the intranet, and another for the perimeter network. This type of perimeter network configuration is not as secure as the previously illustrated one using two separate firewalls. In a perimeter network created by a three-pronged firewall, there is a single device protecting both the perimeter network and intranet. A failure or compromise of the three-pronged firewall could lead to the compromise of the perimeter network and intranet simultaneously. Figure 4-4 shows an example of a three-pronged firewall.

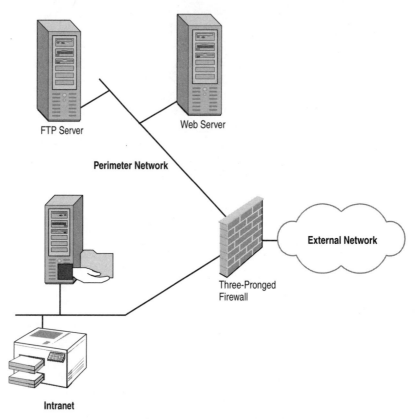

FTP Server

Web Server

Perimeter Network

External Network

Three-Pronged
Firewall

Intranet

Figure 4-4.   Perimeter network created by a three-pronged firewall

Note   Firewall manufacturers often label the ports of a three-pronged firewall as LAN, DMZ, and WAN.

In cases in which only a single host is required to provide services to the Internet, the three-pronged firewall can be pointed directly to that host. In this case the host is called a *bastion host* or *screened host* (see Figure 4-5). The host itself should be as secure as possible to protect it from attack. Such a configuration doesn't necessarily require a three-pronged firewall. The bastion host could be placed on a network segment before the firewall. In any configuration, the security of the bastion host is provided on the host itself.

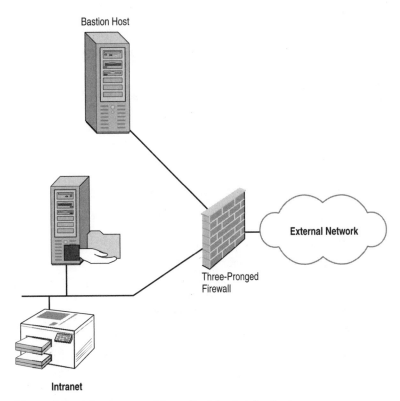

Figure 4-5.   Three-pronged firewall with a bastion host

Other firewalls create a perimeter network without a physically separate third connection for the perimeter network. Instead, these firewalls have two physical connections: internal and external network. However, they have a software configuration that enables the routing of additional protocols to one or more hosts, which are considered perimeter network hosts. Although this type of configuration also creates a perimeter network, it is less secure than the previous two methods described. The lack of a third physical connection in this configuration means that the separation between the perimeter network and intranet is entirely programmatic and not based on any type of physical connection. Just as with a three-pronged firewall, a compromise of this firewall could lead to a compromise of the perimeter network and intranet simultaneously. Security for the perimeter network security zone typically includes the following components:

- Firewall protection from the external network
- Limiting the services provided and removing all unnecessary services
- Auditing of all services
- Name resolution services that are separate from the internal network
- Removal or restriction of remote management services
- Careful documentation and auditing of all physical and logical configurations
- Frequent data and configuration backups

Note   Web and File Transfer Protocol (FTP) servers are commonly placed in a perimeter network.

Extranet

Another security zone that is optionally created by an organization is known as an *extranet*. The extranet is typically used for partner access to resources. For example, the United Nations has an extranet that provides secure access to shared resources for the various member nations.

Extranets are similar to perimeter networks in that they are semisecure zones. The purpose of an extranet is to share information and technology between members of multiple organizations. Extranets are typically created using VPN connections, which are encrypted connections that can be used on a private or public network. Two VPN servers or a VPN client and a VPN server can create a VPN connection. The two devices utilize an agreed-on encryption method to implement a secure encrypted connection with one another. If two servers implement the VPN, they can encrypt communication between two points. Figure 4-6 shows an example of two partner networks connected by two VPN servers.

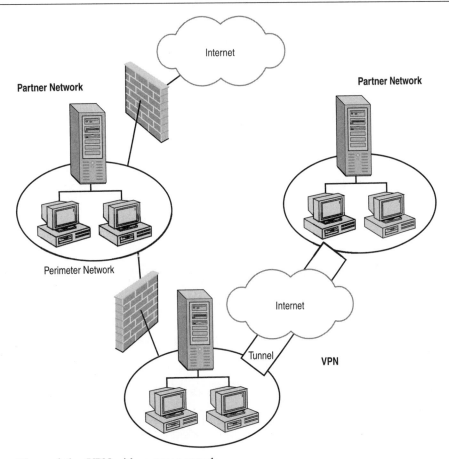

Figure 4-6.   VPN with partner network

Two intranets, two perimeter networks, or one of each can be used to create the extranet. The idea is that the two connected networks are used to share resources between the partner organizations. Some organizations implement multiple perimeter networks to handle such configurations. The first perimeter network is used to provide services to Internet users and the second is used to provide extranet services to partner organizations, as shown in Figure 4-7. Security for the extranet security zone typically includes the following components:

- Firewall protection from the external network
- Limiting the services provided and removing all unnecessary services
- Auditing of all services
- Use of VPN connections

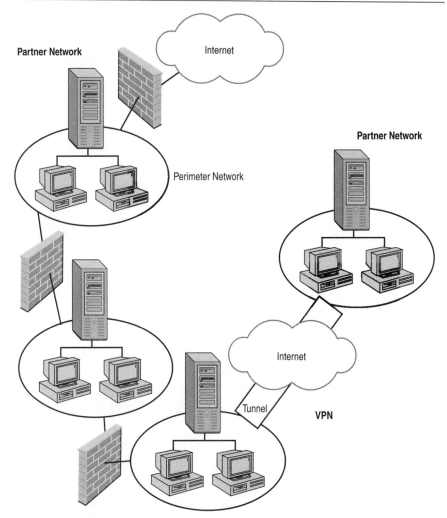

Figure 4-7. VPN with separate perimeter network

Implementing NAT

NAT is a Network and Transport layer translation technique that allows an organization's publicly assigned IP addresses to be different from its private IP addresses. NAT translates the internal IP address range to an external IP address or address range. NAT can be implemented in a firewall, a router, or a workstation or server computer. A device running NAT is placed between an internal network and an external network.

More Info   NAT is described in more detail in RFC 3022.

NAT can be used to solve a few different issues. The type of NAT in use depends on the configuration and purpose for which it is being used. Here are the different types of NAT configurations you might encounter:

- **Static NAT.**   Static NAT maps an internal IP address to an external IP address on a one-to-one basis. For example, if you have an internal IP address of 192.168.1.1, you could map that to a single public IP address. The security benefit to using this type of NAT is that external clients do not have direct access to your internal clients (nor can they obtain the actual IP address of the internal client). Further, your firewall could be configured to block the private IP range from traversing it. This prevents IP spoofing attacks from the external network.

- **Dynamic NAT.**   Dynamic NAT maps a range of internal IP addresses to a range of external IP addresses. For example, a range of five internal addresses might be mapped to a range of five external IP addresses. The security benefits of this type of NAT are similar to static NAT. One additional benefit is that the external-to-internal address mappings can change, which might further complicate attacks focused on an individual network host.

- **Overloading NAT.**   Overloading NAT is also known as port address translation (PAT). This is a possibly the most poplar form of NAT because a single Internet address can provide Internet access to multiple private clients. Overloading can be implemented with a single or multiple Internet addresses. The NAT server keeps track of the IP addresses in use. Different TCP and UDP ports are used to keep track of different connections, as shown in Table 4-1. Security benefits of this type of NAT go beyond static and dynamic NAT. The external IP structure can be completely different from the internal network structure with PAT. For example, hundreds of internal hosts might be communicating with hundreds of different Internet hosts using a single IP address.

Tip   As a reminder, private IP ranges are 10.x.x.x, 172.16.x.x–172.31.x.x, and 192.168.x.x. Also, the range for Automatic Private Internet Protocol Addressing (APIPA) is 169.254.x.x. You should already be familiar with the difference between private, public, and APIPA addresses.

To illustrate how NAT works, assume you are a network administrator who must connect three computers to the Internet simultaneously. One problem is that you only have a single Internet address: 131.107.1.1. To connect all three hosts, you create an internal address range using 192.168.1.1–192.168.1.3. Then you use a NAT device to share the Internet address (131.107.1.1) with all three internal hosts.

The three internal clients are Host A (IP address 192.168.1.1), Host B (IP address 192.168.1.2), and Host C (IP address 192.168.1.3). To illustrate how NAT devices can keep track of multiple simultaneous connections to the Internet, look at Table 4.1 and consider the following:

- Hosts A and B are communicating with an Internet Web server with IP address 131.107.178.205.
- Host C is communicating with an FTP server with IP address 131.107.37.221 over TCP ports 21 and 20.

Table 4-1.   NAT Port-Mapping Table

Local Socket	Translated Socket	Remote Socket
192.168.1.1:1025	131.107.1.1:1025	131.107.178.205:80
192.168.1.2:1027	131.107.1.1:1026	131.107.178.205:80
192.168.1.3:1025	131.107.1.1:1027	131.107.37.221:20
192.168.1.3:1026	131.107.1.1:1028	131.107.37.221:21

The NAT device keeps track of each connection by mapping a unique port to each connection. Notice that all IP address and port combinations (IP sockets) are unique in the table. The NAT device uses the official IP address 131.107.1.1 repeatedly, assigning a unique TCP port each time.

NAT obscures and protects the internal network (also known as the stub network). The NAT server could still be a target for attack from the external network. If the NAT server is compromised, the organization's Internet access could be lost. Further, hosts inside the private network might also be compromised. The NAT server needs protection, such as a virus scanner, firewall, and intrusion-detection software (discussed in the next lesson). If the NAT server allows remote administration, disable this feature or configure the most secure methods for authentication and encryption available.

Using VLANs

Intranet switches can be used to create VLANs on the intranet. VLANs are essentially virtual subnets that are created by switches and supported by routers that are VLAN enabled. Switches create VLANs by tagging the data frames that they receive from hosts. Each port on the switch can be associated with a VLAN, which behaves like an IP subnet and might require routing to communicate with hosts on other VLANs. Although the physical connections on the network might not change, VLANs can change the network infrastructure. For example, you can use VLANs to segment all of the servers on your network into one subnet.

Note   Frame tagging is not the only method for creating a VLAN, but it is the generally accepted method standardized by IEEE 802.1q. You can locate this specification on the Institute of Electrical and Electronics Engineers, Inc. Web site at *http://ieee.org*.

VLANs control broadcast traffic and each VLAN is considered a *broadcast domain* because all hosts on a VLAN are able to send broadcast traffic to all hosts on a VLAN. Broadcast traffic is not allowed to pass beyond the logical confines of the VLAN. Routers are typically used to connect VLANs, so that hosts on separate VLANs are able to communicate.

As a security benefit, VLANs can hide the true physical configuration of your network. They can also be used to isolate certain hosts without costly reconfiguration of your physical network infrastructure.

Because switches create VLANs, compromising a switch could compromise the VLAN. If an attacker takes control of (or sabotages) a switch hosting one or more VLANs, VLAN hosts might also be vulnerable to compromise. At a minimum, communications traversing the switch might be exploited or disrupted in such an attack.

To protect your VLANs, you must ensure that your switches, VLAN-enabled devices, and the segments between them are secure. Keep up with security bulletins concerning your VLAN-enabled devices and apply all software patches as soon as they are available.

Exercise: Selecting Infrastructure Security Measures

Each of the statements in the left column describes a technology discussed in this chapter. Match the terms in the right column with the descriptions in the left column.

1. Used to secure and encrypt network data transmitted between partner networks

2. The area between the internal and external network typically used to provide semisecure services to the external network

3. A device that can be used to create screened subnets and separate the internal network from the external network

4. Can mask your internal IP address range and allow multiple hosts to share a single IP address

a. Perimeter network

b. NAT

c. VPN

d. Firewall

Lesson Review

The following questions are intended to reinforce key information presented in this lesson. If you are unable to answer a question, review the lesson and then try the question again. Answers to the questions can be found in Appendix A, "Questions and Answers."

1. What is the purpose of dividing a network into security zones?

2. What are the major benefits of a perimeter network?

3. How can NAT be used to protect your network?

4. How are VPNs used?

5. What are the benefits of VLANs?

Lesson Summary

- Security zones help organizations classify, prioritize, and focus on security issues based on the services that are required in each zone. When a perimeter network is present there are at least three security zones: intranet, perimeter network, and extranet. The perimeter network is a semisecure network used to provide services to clients on the external network. The internal network is the most secure network (at least two firewalls separate it from the external network). The external network is the least trusted network and the location from which the organization can most expect to be attacked.

- Some organizations require a separate security zone called an extranet, which is an extension of the private network (or a portion of that network) to provide services to trusted partners.

- NAT can be used to protect your internal network-addressing scheme from discovery by hosts on the external network. This helps prevent attacks against individual hosts and obscure the number of hosts and services provided by the internal network. NAT can also allow multiple internal hosts to share one or more IP addresses and connections to the Internet.

- VLANs can combine or subdivide internal physical network segments logically using switches and frame tagging. VLANs can change the logical structure of your network without the need for physical reconfiguration. VLANs can be used to isolate hosts and segments and control broadcast traffic.

Lesson 5: Securing and Monitoring Network Resources

This lesson wraps up the information on protecting your network infrastructure by focusing on network resource security and monitoring. The first part of the lesson focuses on monitoring and securing workstations, mobile devices, servers, and connectivity devices. Next, you learn about software and hardware that can be used to detect attacks. Finally, the lesson discusses ways to learn from attackers without risking your production equipment.

After this lesson, you will be able to

- Document methods to monitor and secure workstations, mobile devices, and servers
- Select appropriate methods for monitoring network infrastructure connectivity devices
- List how intrusion detection systems can help to protect networks
- Describe the purpose of honeypots and honeynets and select appropriate uses for them

Estimated lesson time: 20 minutes

Securing and Monitoring Workstations

The workstations on your network are tools for productivity, but they could also be vulnerable to attack. Workstation attacks can cause your organization's employees to lose time and valuable data. If an attacker compromises a workstation it can be used to attack other systems on your network as well. Here is a list of ways to protect your workstations:

- Install virus-scanning software and keep virus definition files up to date.
- Monitor system logs for errors.
- Configure logging or auditing for critical system resources and data.
- Limit access to workstations to a specific user or set of users.
- Control access to local and shared resources.
- Remove unnecessary applications and services.
- Configure automated or centralized backup systems.
- Ensure the latest operating system and application security fixes are applied and kept current.

Network monitoring systems and some intrusion detection systems (discussed later) can help you monitor the workstations on your network. These systems can send alerts when certain thresholds are exceeded (for example, if the system has less than 5 percent free hard disk space). Here are some items to monitor on your workstations:

- **System logs.**   Look for error messages about file system changes, permission changes, services that no longer start, or other system modifications and critical error messages.

- **Audit logs.**   Audit logs are typically activated to track specific resources, such as access to a secure folder, file, or printer.

- **Hard disk space.**   Workstations might fail to log errors, fail to detect attacks, or fail to function properly at all if they run out of hard disk space.

- **Network counters.**   If a system is under attack, network counters could indicate that an attack is underway.

- **Access denied errors.**   When an attacker is attempting to guess a password, the server component that shares files on the workstation might record a high number of errors by which access is denied.

Protecting Mobile Devices

Laptops, notebooks, and personal digital assistants (PDAs), among other electronic devices, are widely used on many networks. These devices, just like workstations, are important to secure, protect, and monitor, but monitoring these devices is often more difficult than monitoring workstations due to their mobile nature.

All of the precautions you take to protect your organization's workstations should be used (wherever possible) to protect your organization's mobile devices. Additional items to consider for protecting mobile devices include the following:

- **Antitheft devices.**   Consider using motion alarms, locking cables, and tracking equipment to protect your mobile devices.

- **Additional identifying marks or colors.**   If a laptop is stolen from an environment in which many people are carrying laptops, it might be difficult to spot. If your company logo or your name appears prominently on the laptop or mobile device, you might be able to recognize it more easily. Further, if your devices have identifying marks, a thief might be less likely to steal it in the first place, knowing the theft would be more difficult to conceal.

- **Data encryption.**   If your mobile devices are used to transport sensitive data (such as trade secrets or competitive information), you might consider using data encryption, which can prevent sensitive files from being easily decrypted.

When mobile devices are on the network, you should monitor them as if they are workstations. Of course, PDAs and similar devices might not have the same components to monitor, so monitoring must be adjusted on a product-by-product basis.

Securing and Monitoring Servers

You should perform the same tasks on your organization's servers to secure and monitor them as you do on your organization's workstations. Network servers require even more attention than individual workstations, however, because the loss of a server affects more people. In some ways, network servers are easier to protect than individual workstations, because they need not be physically touched or logged on to by normal users. Here are some additional protections that you should perform on your network servers:

- Physically secure servers in a locked room.
- Prevent users from logging on interactively (at the console).
- Carefully control and monitor access to resources, such as the file system, shared data, and printers.
- Carefully control and monitor access to all services. Additional services such as user databases, account directory services, Web services, and other services provided by servers should be logged. You should track service access errors (access denied), failures of services to load, and any changes in running services (either additional services or services that are disabled or stopped).
- Frequent backups of server configurations, shared data, and service data are critical to protecting your server. Be sure to test backups by actually restoring data to an alternate location to be sure that your backups are working. Also, you should keep your backup media physically secure. Password protect backup media, encrypt it, and store it in fireproof safes if possible.

You must also be sure to monitor access and availability of the resources the server provides. For example, you should monitor the availability of the HTTP service and Web site files of the Web server. Most services allow for additional logging and this feature should be utilized. On the file server, be sure to appropriately secure files and monitor inappropriate access to those files. Most network operating systems allow you to configure auditing on critical system and data files.

Monitoring Connectivity Devices

Network management systems are available from many vendors that collect information from connectivity devices. For example, if a router or switch is dropping frames because too much data is incoming, an alert can be sent to the network management system's console and potentially other locations, such as the network manager's pager.

Many network management systems use the Simple Network Management Protocol (SNMP) to gather information from a variety of systems, including individual hosts on the network. Cisco, IBM, and Hewlett-Packard all offer network management systems that can monitor network devices.

Implementing Intrusion Detection

An *intrusion detection system* (IDS) is a hardware device with software that is used to detect unauthorized activity on your network. An IDS is usually configured to log and alert you to unauthorized activity on your network. IDSs can be implemented on individual hosts, servers, at the network perimeter, or throughout the entire network. Some IDS solutions are designed as distributed systems, with agents on all hosts on the network. There are several different ways in which IDSs might be implemented. Here is a general list of how they are implemented and used:

- A network intrusion detection system (NIDS) is used to discover attackers on your network. A NIDS monitors network traffic and traffic patterns that can be used to discover someone attempting a denial-of-service attack, port scans, or attempts to guess the password to a secured resource. Snort is one of the most popular examples of a NIDS.

- A system integrity verifier (SIV) monitors a single system's file structure to determine if (and when) an attacker modifies, deletes, or changes a system file. Tripwire is one of the most popular examples of an SIV.

- A log file monitor (LFM) parses system log entries to identify possible system attacks or compromises. LFMs can protect a single computer or multiple computers. SWATCH (The Simple WATCHer and filter) is a popular example of an LFM for UNIX operating systems.

Although IDSs are designed to protect your network, attackers might attempt to attack, bypass, disable, or fool those systems. During heavy network traffic, an NDIS could be overwhelmed and might have to drop some packets. Those packets could be evidence of a network attack. Because many IDSs are configured to recognize attack patterns, it is important that you keep attack definition files current. Support agreements and frequent updates are usually available from IDS vendors.

More Info   Chapter 11, "Incident Detection and Response," covers intrusion detection in greater detail.

Using Honeypots and Honeynets

Honeypots are systems that have no production value and are designed to be targets for attackers. *Honeynets* are networks of honeypot systems or a single honeypot system that simulates a network of vulnerable devices. Honeypots do not solve security issues or protect hosts from direct attacks, however, as do firewalls and IDSs.

Note   For the sake of efficiency, the word *honeypot* is used to represent both honeypots and honeynets in the remainder of this text.

Following are some of the potential benefits of using honeypots:

- When compared to IDSs and system logs, honeypots are more likely to give you valuable information about an attack. IDSs and system logs track large amounts of information that might not be related to any specific attacks. Connections to honeypots are likely to be actual attacks. Someone scanning, probing, or attempting to access a honeypot is probably not looking for his or her home directory (or anything else that he or she is supposed to be able to access).

- Honeypots are designed to track access, so they are not likely to run out of system resources when under attack. Production systems and firewalls are not usually able to operate optimally when they are under attack during heavy traffic periods. They might even fail to log an attack. The same is true for IDSs: When network traffic is coming at gigabit speeds, they might drop packets. Some of those packets could be attempted system attacks.

- Honeypots are often easier to configure and monitor than IDSs and firewalls. They are simply targets for attack. When someone connects to the honeypot, it is probably worth checking out.

Honeypots are usually more interesting and visible than other security devices. Firewalls might be good at preventing attacks, but they rarely capture actual attempts to compromise a system. Attacks on a honeypot illustrate that there are attackers on the network. Honeypots can also give you an idea of how sophisticated an attacker's skills are and how well that attacker knows the network. The honeypot's logs can even be used to make a case against a network attacker, if you are able to identify that person. There are potential drawbacks to placing honeypots on your network, however:

- Honeypots require extra resources. Typically, the honeypot is a software component installed on a separate computer (or maybe multiple computers). Some honeypots are separate hardware appliances.

- If honeypots are never attacked, they won't provide any information.

- Some attackers might be able to identify (fingerprint) a honeypot. If an attacker is able to determine that a system is a honeypot, he or she is likely to move on to another target.

- If a honeypot is compromised, it could be used to attack other systems. When you configure additional services or hosts on your network, you increase the number of potential targets for attackers.

More Info   For more information on honeypots, visit the following Web site: *http://www.tracking-hackers.com.*

Exercise: Identifying Security Devices

Match the term in the right column with the most appropriate statement in the left column:

1. Can help to secure your data if your laptop is stolen

2. Helps you to learn attacker techniques and potential future exploits

3. Alerts you when a recognized attack is underway

4. Helps you to keep your laptop from being stolen

a. Honeypot

b. IDS

c. Motion-sensing alarm

d. Data encryption

Lesson Review

The following questions are intended to reinforce key information presented in this lesson. If you are unable to answer a question, review the lesson and then try the question again. Answers to the questions can be found in Appendix A, "Questions and Answers."

1. What security methods are common to workstations and servers?

2. What security steps are typically implemented on mobile devices that aren't usually necessary on workstations and servers?

3. What tools can you use to monitor your network infrastructure devices?

4. What security benefits does an intrusion detection system provide?

5. How can you use a honeypot to help protect your network?

Lesson Summary

- Workstations, mobile devices, and servers can be targets of network attack. To protect your workstations, you should configure virus-scanning software, perform frequent backups, and monitor workstation logs.
- Wireless devices usually require additional security, such as antitheft devices and file encryption.
- Servers require all of the security that workstations on the network require. In addition, servers can be physically secured inside locked rooms. Additional monitoring should be configured on servers based on the services they provide.
- Network monitoring systems can be used to monitor routers, switches, hubs, and hosts. Network monitoring systems can alert you when problems arise on your network, such as when a connectivity device is not responding or can no longer keep up with the amount of incoming network traffic.
- IDSs help protect your network from attackers by alerting you to the presence of potential attacks. IDSs can also log activity so that you can track down points of attack and compromise.
- Honeypots and honeynets are used to help you detect and learn from attackers. Honeypots are attractive targets for attackers because they are often exposed directly to the Internet without the protection of a firewall. The devices are configured to track the activities of attackers so that you can learn about security weaknesses that might exist on your internal network before an attacker has a chance to exploit them.

C H A P T E R   5

Communications Security

About This Chapter

This chapter provides an introduction to providing remote connectivity and some of the general best practices that should be followed. It then provides a deeper discussion of remote access protocols and security issues, followed by wireless access concepts, standards, and security issues.

Before You Begin

The prerequisites for this chapter are Chapter 2, " TCP/IP Basics," and Chapter 4, "Network Infrastructure Security."

Lesson 1: Understanding Remote Access Connectivity

One of your responsibilities as a network administrator is to provide connectivity to your network for users from remote locations. This might include remote offices as well as individual users who are connecting to the network from their homes or while traveling.

After this lesson, you will be able to

- Understand the security implications of providing users remote access over telephone lines
- Understand the security implications of providing users remote access across the Internet

Estimated lesson time: 15 minutes

Two security concerns to consider when providing these connectivity solutions are how to manage devices not physically connected to your network and how to secure the communications link between the remote computer and your network. Because the remote computer might be a user's personal computer or device, and you might not have physical access to the system, the system might not be as secure as the computers directly attached to your network. Viruses can infect the remote system and spread to systems on your network, and possibly open an access point for hackers to exploit. You should be aware of the following when providing remote access:

- Remote access computers with sensitive documents might be exposed.
- The remote user could lack awareness of security concerns.
- The remote computer can be an avenue for unauthorized access to critical systems.
- Modems are vulnerable to dial-in attacks.
- The remote access computer might harbor malicious code.
- Remote access computers typically lack proper backups.

Remote Connections

Telephone lines and the Internet are public communications mediums that hackers can exploit to take advantage of any weaknesses in your remote access or wireless access solution. There are several ways to provide remote connectivity to your network, but the communications medium choices for remote users are typically limited to access over telephone lines or across the Internet. Examples of remote connections include the following:

- Public Switched Telephone Network (PSTN) connections use modems and standard telephone lines to transmit data. They are relatively slow, but also flexible and universal.

- Integrated Services Digital Network (ISDN) is a digital dial-up service provided by telephone companies that offers greater speeds than PSTN, but this service is also more expensive.

- Digital Subscriber Line (DSL) is a point-to-point connection that also uses standard telephone lines to carry digital signals at much higher speeds than PSTN connections.

- Community antenna television (CATV) networks use cable television technology to provide users with economical high-speed Internet access. However, CATV is a shared service, which can mean that bandwidth diminishes as more local users concurrently access the Internet.

Once a remote user is connected, there are several ways to limit the resources he or she can access. In deciding what resources to provide access to, you need to balance the capabilities the remote users require, how secure the connection must be, and the cost of providing the secure solution. For instance, if all your remote users require only access to their corporate e-mail, you can configure a Web server to provide access to the e-mail using a Web browser. By configuring e-mail access through the Web browser, you don't have to open more ports through your firewall, and you can control how the users gain access. This also limits the access they have to other networked resources and allows you to provide a relatively inexpensive solution and mitigate many of the security risks.

To implement a cost-effective solution that provides the services your remote users require while maintaining security, you must understand the connectivity technology available along with the protocols and standards used. You also need to be aware of the security risks you must minimize.

Remote Connection Mediums

Telephone lines and the Internet are two communications mediums that are used by businesses to provide remote access capabilities. As shown in Figure 5-1, the remote access server can be made accessible by connecting telephone lines to modems, which are then managed by the remote access server, or the remote access server can be connected to the Internet in some manner. With both types of connections the user is required to form a connection, but the connection can be directly to a remote access server, or to the Internet (through a service provider) and then to the remote access server. Each type of connection is explained in greater detail in the following sections.

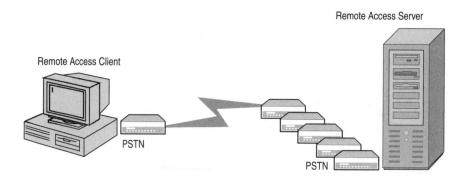

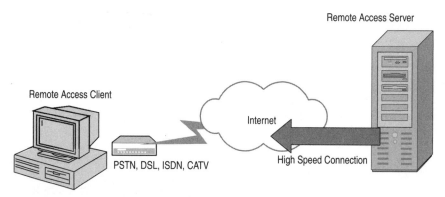

Figure 5-1. Two types of remote access server connectivity

The connection type depends on the high-speed connectivity solutions available, the cost of the service, and the reliability of the service. Each has strengths and weaknesses, costs and vulnerabilities, and security concerns that must be mitigated.

Telephone Connections

With telephone lines, modems are installed in a remote access server, telephone lines are connected, users are provided a telephone number, and they use a notebook computer, their home computer, or other dial-capable devices to gain access to the corporate network and its resources. Examples of protocols used with this type of connection include Serial Line Internet Protocol (SLIP) and Point-to-Point Protocol (PPP). PPP is the predominant protocol in use and it supports TCP/IP communications, authentication mechanisms, and several encryption methods.

When modems are used to connect to a remote access server, you can configure some additional features to provide connection-level security for your remote access clients. The Callback Control Protocol (CBCP) allows your remote access servers or clients to negotiate a callback with the other end. When CBCP is enabled, either the client or the server can request that the server call the client back either at a number supplied by the client or a prearranged number stored on the server. By configuring the server with a prearranged number to call back, you can ensure that the remote access users can call only from a specific location. The remote access server can also be configured to accept or reject calls based on the Caller ID or Automatic Number Identification (ANI) information transmitted by the phone company.

The advantages of using dial-up remote access instead of providing access across the Internet include the following:

- **Limited hacker access.**   The Internet spans the entire world and the number of users is astounding. Many of the computers connected to the Internet have modems, and they typically dial a local number to gain access to the Internet. By providing access to your network through a dial-up solution, you will likely curb the number of hackers that attempt to hack your network, and they will probably be localized to a smaller geographic location, namely where the number is a local telephone call.

- **Less likelihood of being sniffed.**   Although it is possible to sniff communications across telephone lines, it requires that the hacker gain access to the telephone lines between the remote user and the remote access server. All telephone calls are routed through telephone switching equipment and the hacker can intercept the communication there, but the chances of that are less likely. You should still encrypt communication over public telephone lines to be safe.

Disadvantages of using dial-up lines to provide a remote access solution include the following:

- **Costs for long-distance connections.**   If all of the remote access users are within the local calling area, there will be no toll charge for long-distance calling, but if you are supporting users that travel or those based in different geographical locations, the cost of providing the solution is greatly increased.

- **Lower productivity.**   Because the connection speed is limited, remote users might not be as efficient and productive as they would be using a higher speed solution.

- **War dialing.**   A technique known as *war dialing* can be used to dial all of the telephone numbers in a specified range and record those that have a modem connected. Once the phone numbers that have modems are identified, a hacker can redial the system and attempt to break into the computer system. Because the telephone prefix exchange for most organizations is easy to discover, modems that allow users to dial in present a risk.

Internet Connections

When accessing your company's network across the Internet, you connect a remote access server to the Internet, typically through a secure interface such as a firewall. Users connect to the Internet through an Internet service provider (ISP), and a virtual private network (VPN) connection is established between the remote user's computer and the remote access server.

The remote access user can connect to the Internet using a number of different connection devices, including a telephone modem, ISDN modem, DSL modem, or cable modem. Regardless of how the remote user connects to the Internet and how your server is connected to the Internet, the communications link is established across the Internet. Some of the advantages of using Internet-based remote access include the following:

- **Lower costs.**   If remote access users are based in a widespread geographical area or if they travel, providing access through the Internet can be less costly because long-distance charges can be minimized. Because most areas have Internet access without incurring toll charges, using an ISP that supports your remote user base can be a cost-effective solution.

- **Fewer external connection points.**   Because most companies require access to the Internet, using a single Internet connection that is secured for access to your company's internal network as well as access to the Internet from the internal network provides a single connection point. This limits the number of connection points a hacker can attempt to exploit and requires you to maintain and monitor fewer access points.

Disadvantages of using the Internet to provide access to your internal network include the following:

- **More attacks.**   Because you are connecting your internal network to the Internet through a secured communications link, hackers from around the world can attempt to break into your network. Similarly, because connections over cable modems and DSL are much faster than dial-up connections, hackers can carry out more attacks, and more sophisticated attacks, in a shorter period of time than they can over dial-up connections.

- **More accessibility to sniffing.**   The traffic generated between your remote users and your remote access server is more susceptible to sniffing. A hacker can intercept the communications traffic and, even if it is encrypted, attempt to decrypt the information.

- **Increased exposure to attackers.**   Before a user makes a VPN connection to the company network, he or she must first connect his or her computer to the Internet securely. If the user's computer is not secured, his or her computer and the company's network are susceptible to any attacker on the Internet.

Exercise: Configuring a Remote Access Connection

In the following exercise, you learn how to configure a remote access connection on a computer running Microsoft Windows 2000. (This exercise should work similarly on Windows ME, Windows 98, and Windows XP, although the steps may vary slightly.)

1. From the Start menu, click Settings, then Control Panel.

2. Open Network And Dial-up Connections.

3. Create a new connection by running the Make New Connection Wizard.

4. Complete the Create a New Network Connection Wizard to create a dial-up connection using the following information:

   a. Dial-up to private network

   b. Use a modem for the dial-up connection

   c. Any phone number

   d. Allow only yourself to use the connection

   e. Use the default name for your new connection

5. Start the Create a Connection Wizard by following steps 1-3 and then create another connection using the following information:

   a. Connect to a private network through the Internet

   b. Do not dial the initial connection

   c. IP Address of 192.168.0.1

   d. Allow only yourself to use the connection

   e. Use the default name for your new connection

6. Compare the two connections that you created and review the information necessary to create each and answer the following questions:

   a. Did you need to provide a telephone number for each type of connection? If not, which did you have to provide the telephone number for?

   b. Did you have to dial an initial connection for both of them?

   c. Did you have to provide an IP address for both connection types?

Lesson Review

The following questions are intended to reinforce key information presented in this lesson. If you are unable to answer a question, review the lesson and then try the question again. Answers to the questions can be found in Appendix A, "Questions and Answers."

1. What are two types of remote access connectivity solutions?

2. What security concerns must you consider when providing remote access connectivity solutions?

3. A technique used to identify modems connected to telephone lines is known as
   a. Callback Control Protocol
   b. War dialing
   c. War driving
   d. War walking

Lesson Summary

As a network administrator, you will most likely be required to provide remote access to your network, and with wireless communications becoming common, you must understand both technologies. In this lesson you learned the following:

- When you provide remote access to your network, the computers used by remote users might not be as secure as the computers on your local network.

- Dial-up connections can be used to provide users remote access to your network. If this is the only link used to provide external access to your network, the number of hackers that attempt to break into your network might be reduced. The cost associated with providing this type of connectivity might be higher than providing access across the Internet due to higher long-distance charges.

- War dialing is a programmatic technique used to dial every possible telephone number in a specified range. Therefore, keeping your remote access telephone numbers unpublished cannot be considered a reliable method of securing your remote access telephone number against hackers.

- The Internet can be used to provide remote access to your network. This can be a more cost-effective way to provide access, especially if your company requires Internet connectivity for day-to-day operations. This can also increase the number of hackers that attempt to gain access to your network.

Lesson 2: Providing Secure Remote Access

From the network layer up, a remote connection is no different than a direct local area network (LAN) connection, but the data-link and physical layers can take several different forms. To understand how to provide secure access to your remote access users, you must understand the standards and protocols associated with remote access and the security configurations that can be used.

After this lesson you will be able to

- Understand the authentication protocols that can be used to secure a remote access connection
- Understand how RADIUS can be used to provide centralized remote access authentication
- Understand how TACACS can be used to provide centralized remote access authentication

Estimated lesson time: 25 minutes

Remote Connection Requirements

For a remote computer to communicate with a server, both computers must have common protocols at the physical and data-link layers. They must also be configured to provide secure communications, and the server should be configured to require the remote user to authenticate. Figure 5-2 displays required elements for a remote connection and gives a brief explanation of each.

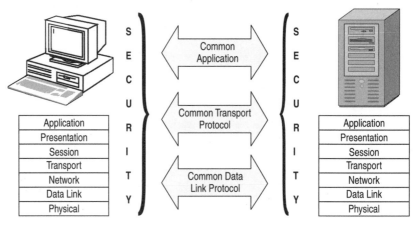

Figure 5-2.   Remote connection requirements

When remote users are authenticated and gain access to networked resources, you should limit the access they have to only those resources required to complete necessary tasks. For instance, if the remote access users at your company require only the ability to access e-mail, then only provide them access to e-mail. The protocols used at the different layers include the following:

- **Common data-link layer protocols.**   The two computers to be connected must share common protocols at the data-link layer and above. This means that you must configure both computers to use a data-link layer protocol suitable for point-to-point connections, such as PPP or SLIP. There must also be network and transport layer protocols in common, such as Transmission Control Protocol/Internet Protocol (TCP/IP), Internetwork Packet Exchange (IPX), Network Basic Input/Output System (NetBIOS), or NetBIOS Enhanced User Interface (NetBEUI).

- **TCP/IP configuration.**   If your remote computer will be using TCP/IP to communicate with the host network, the computer must be assigned an IP address and other configuration parameters appropriate for that network. You can configure the TCP/IP settings if someone familiar with the host network supplies them to you, but most remote networking solutions enable the network server to assign configuration parameters automatically using Dynamic Host Configuration Protocol (DHCP) or some other mechanism.

- **Host and remote software.**   Each of the computers to be connected must be running an application appropriate to its role. The remote (or client) computer needs a client program that can use the physical layer medium to establish a connection (by instructing the modem to dial a number, for example). The host (or server) computer must have a program that can respond to a connection request from the remote computer and provide access to the network.

- **Security.**   The host computer and the other systems on the network to which it is attached must have security mechanisms in place that control access to network resources to ensure that only authorized users are permitted access and to restrict the access of those authorized users to only the resources they need.

Using Authentication Mechanisms

The PPP protocol used with remote access is combined with one of several authentication mechanisms that provide varying degrees of security and support differing levels of encryption. Each remote access server can be configured to authenticate remote users, or centralized authentication and access control can be used. The following are examples of remote access authentication methods:

- **Password Authentication Protocol (PAP).**   PAP requires a password, but the password is sent in cleartext, so PAP is not a very secure authentication mechanism. All 32-bit Windows operating systems include remote access client support for PAP.

- **Shiva Password Authentication Protocol (SPAP).**   SPAP incorporates a reversible encryption mechanism. SPAP is more secure than PAP, but does not provide protection against remote server impersonation. All 32-bit Windows operating systems include remote access client support for SPAP.

- **Challenge Handshake Authentication Protocol (CHAP).**   Defined in Request for Comments (RFC) 1994, CHAP uses the Message Digest 5 (MD5) hashing algorithm to hash the password. (RFC articles can be found at *http:// www.icann.rfceditor.org*.) The hash is then sent from client to server. Only the remote access server can send the password challenge. Because the password is never sent from the client to the server, this is more secure than PAP or SPAP. All 32-bit Windows operating systems include remote access client support for CHAP.

- **Microsoft Challenge Handshake Authentication Protocol (MS-CHAP).** Microsoft's implementation of the CHAP protocol provides greater security than CHAP, in addition to Microsoft networking domain login support capabilities. MS-CHAP uses the Message Digest 4 (MD4) hash made up of the challenge string, session ID, and the MD-4 hashed password. All 32-bit Windows operating systems include remote access client support for MS-CHAP.

- **Microsoft Challenge Handshake Authentication Protocol version 2 (MS-CHAPv2).**   MS-CHAPv2 introduces larger initial encryption key size and support for bidirectional challenge. This allows the client to send a challenge to the remote access server. MS-CHAPv2 also uses MD4 for hashing of the password. All 32-bit Windows operating systems include remote access client support for MS-CHAPv2.

Centralized Authentication

Authentication can be provided by each of the remote access servers used, or it can be provided through centralized authentication and access control. Figure 5-3 shows a centralized authentication server validating the authentication requests that the remote access servers are receiving from the remote access clients. Enabling centralized authentication is done by configuring a server to support Remote Authentication Dial-In User Service (RADIUS), or Terminal Access Controller

Access Control Service (TACACS) or TACACS+, and then configuring the remote access server to use the RADIUS or TACACS server to authenticate the remote access clients.

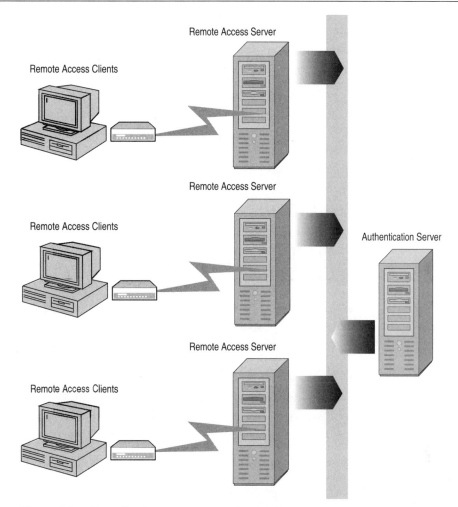

Figure 5-3.   Centralized remote access authentication

In Chapter 4, you were introduced to the RADIUS and TACACS authentication protocols as they relate to your network infrastructure. In this section you learn the part they play in centralized authentication.

RADIUS

RADIUS is used for providing authentication, authorization, and accounting services for remote access services and separates the remote access server functions from the user authentication server functions. The communication between the computer that provides remote access support and the computer that provides user authentication is established using RADIUS. The separation of remote access and user authentication allows the following:

- The RADIUS client and server to support different operating systems and hardware architectures.
- The RADIUS client and server to be geographically separated.
- User accounts to be secure by ensuring that the accounts are located on servers within the private network and not directly exposed to the Internet.
- Encryption of authentication traffic between the RADIUS client and the RADIUS server using Internet Protocol Security (IPSec) or VPN tunnels.
- Outsourcing of dial-up remote access to third-party organizations.

The remote access client connectivity feature provided by the RADIUS client determines how remote users access the private network. The remote access client connectivity provided by the RADIUS client allows the remote access users to do the following:

- Use a variety of authentication protocols, such as CHAP, MS-CHAP, or cleartext to get authenticated.
- Encrypt data using a variety of encryption algorithms, such as Microsoft Point-to-Point Encryption (MPPE) or Data Encryption Standard (DES).
- Connect using a variety of protocols, such as TCP/IP or Internetwork Packet Exchange/Sequenced Packet Exchange (IPX/SPX).
- Connect using a variety of technologies, such as dial-up modems, DSL, or ISDN.

Remote user authentication provided by the RADIUS server determines the user accounts that are authenticated, and the accounting provided by the RADIUS server creates a historical record of RADIUS transactions that occur between the client and RADIUS server. Remote user accounting records the following information:

- The length of time the remote user is connected
- Remote user authentication success or failure
- Situations when the RADIUS server is unable to authenticate a RADIUS client

The purpose of having RADIUS clients and servers is to centralize and secure the authentication of remote users. Instead of allowing all remote clients to send a RADIUS request to a RADIUS server, only a small number of RADIUS clients are authorized. However, even this reduced number of RADIUS clients allows the possibility of someone attempting to impersonate a RADIUS client when communicating with a RADIUS server.

To thwart such an attempt, the administrator sets a password, called a *shared secret*, during the configuration of RADIUS. Both the RADIUS client and server know the shared secret, but it is never sent over the network. Instead, the service uses a hashing system to verify the shared secret. The location of each RADIUS client that will be sending authentication packets is specified to the RADIUS server, and only these specified RADIUS clients can forward authentication packets to a RADIUS server.

The shared secret is not used between just the RADIUS client and server. The shared secret is also used during the encryption process for a remote access client's password. This means that a shared secret needs to always be included in a RADIUS solution, and it needs to be a password that is difficult to guess. Like any password, a shared secret is case-sensitive and must match exactly on RADIUS clients and servers.

RADIUS Authentication and Accounting

Now that you understand what RADIUS does, refer to Figure 5-4 while reviewing the RADIUS authentication process that follows.

1. Access servers, such as dial-up network access servers, VPN servers, and wireless access points, receive connection requests from access clients.

2. The access server, configured to use RADIUS as the authentication, authorization, and accounting protocol creates an Access-Request message and sends it to the RADIUS server.

   - The RADIUS server evaluates the Access-Request message.

   - If required (as is the case when Extensible Authentication Protocol [EAP] is used), the RADIUS server sends an Access-Challenge message to the access server. The access server or access client processes the challenge and sends a new Access-Request to the RADIUS server.

   - The user credentials and the authorization of the connection attempt are verified.

3. If the connection attempt is both authenticated and authorized, the RADIUS server sends an Access-Accept message to the access server.

   - If the connection attempt is either not authenticated or not authorized, the RADIUS server sends an Access-Reject message to the access server.

4. On receipt of the Access-Accept message, the access server completes the connection process with the access client and sends an Accounting-Request message to the RADIUS server.

5. After the Accounting-Request message is processed, the RADIUS server sends an Accounting-Response message to the access server.

6. The client connection request is completed.

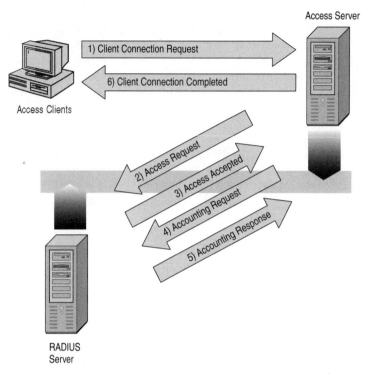

Figure 5-4.   RADIUS authentication process

TACACS and TACACS+

TACACS provides a way to centrally validate users attempting to gain access to a router or access server. TACACS+ was designed by Cisco Systems, Inc., and it provides a standard method for managing dissimilar network access servers (NASs) from a single set of management services. An NAS provides connections to a single user, to a network or subnetwork, and to interconnected networks. TACACS+ has three major components:

- The protocol support within the access servers and routers
- The protocol specification
- The centralized security database

Similar to an internal security database, TACACS+ supports the following three required features of a good security system:

- **Authentication.**   The TACACS+ protocol forwards many types of user name and password information. This information is encrypted over the network with MD5. TACACS+ can forward the password types for Apple Remote Access (ARA), SLIP, PAP, CHAP, and standard Telnet. This allows clients to use the same user name and password for different protocols. TACACS+ is extensible to support new password types such as Kerberos CHAP (KCHAP).

TACACS+ authentication supports multiple challenge and response demands from the TACACS+ server. This allows token card vendors to provide advanced features such as sending back a second token-generated number after the first one is manipulated by a security server.

- **Authorization.**   TACACS+ provides a mechanism to tell an access server which access list a user connected to port 1 uses. The TACACS+ server and location of the user name and password information identify the access list through which the user is filtered. The access list resides on the access server. The TACACS server responds to a user name with an Accept message and an access list number that causes that list to be applied.

- **Accounting.**   TACACS+ provides accounting information to a database through TCP to ensure a more secure and complete accounting log. The accounting portion of the TACACS+ protocol contains the network address of the user, the user name, the service attempted, protocol used, time and date, and the packet-filter module originating the log. The billing information includes connect time, user ID, location connected from, start time, and stop time. It identifies the protocol that the user is using and might contain commands being run if the users are connected through Telnet. The auditing information includes which commands and arguments were used and the connection the command came from. The protocol provides enough information so that a server can produce intruder detection routines, reporting statistics, number of packets, and number of bytes.

RADIUS and TACACS+ Differences

There are many differences between RADIUS and TACACS+, but some of the key differences are the following:

- RADIUS runs over User Datagram Protocol (UDP), whereas TACACS+ runs over TCP. As a result, the transport is more reliable and less sensitive to disruption of the lower layers.

- RADIUS provides a user profile with authentication that defines all the user-specific parameters, whereas TACACS+ separates authentication and authorization.

- TACACS is typically used only for network devices, such as routers and switches, whereas RADIUS is used by computers and network devices.

Virtual Private Networks

Authentication methods provide a mechanism to authenticate a remote user, but do not provide protection for data that is traveling across a public communication medium. A VPN, as shown in Figure 5-5, is a secure connection between a remote computer and a server on a private network that uses the Internet as its network medium. The network is permanently connected to the Internet and has a server that is configured to receive incoming connections through the Internet. The remote user connects to the Internet by using a modem to dial in to an ISP located nearby. Many ISPs offer national and even international service, so users can connect to the Internet with a local telephone call.

The remote computer and the network server then establish a secured connection that protects the data exchanged between them as it travels over the Internet. This technique is called *tunneling*, because the connection runs across the Internet inside a secure conduit, protecting the data in the way that a tunnel under a river protects cars from the water above it.

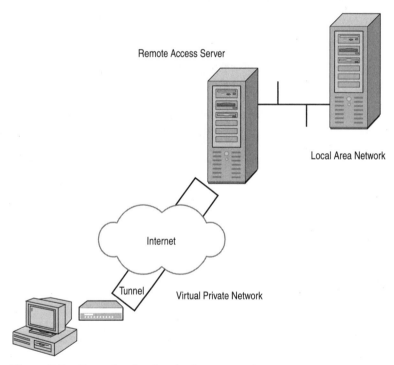

Figure 5-5.   Example of a virtual private network

In general, security is not a single product or technology, but an integration of several technologies combined with management policy that provides protection balanced with acceptable risks. Security services should include confidentiality, integrity protection, authentication, authorization, and replay protection. Some protocols that are used in association with VPNs include the following:

■ **Point-to-Point Tunneling Protocol (PPTP).**   Created by the PPTP Industry Forum (US Robotics [now 3Com], 3Com/Primary Access, Ascend, Microsoft, and ECI Telematics).

- **Layer 2 Tunneling Protocol (L2TP).**   A combination of PPTP and L2F (designed by Cisco Systems), which evolved through the Internet Engineering Task Force (IETF) standards process.

- **Internet Protocol Security (IPSec).**   An architecture, protocol, and related Internet Key Exchange (IKE) protocol, which are described in RFCs 2401 through 2409.

Point-to-Point Tunneling Protocol

One protocol that makes VPN tunneling possible is PPTP. PPTP works with PPP to establish a connection between the client computer and a server on the target network, both of which are connected to the Internet. The connection process begins with the client computer dialing up and connecting to a local ISP, using the standard PPP connection establishment process. When the computer is connected to the Internet, it establishes a *control connection* to the server using TCP. This control connection is the PPTP tunnel through which the computers transmit and receive all subsequent data. The following are some characteristics of PPTP:

- It is a Layer 2 protocol that encapsulates PPP frames in IP datagrams for transmission over an unsecured public IP network, such as the Internet.
- It accomplishes authentication through the same methods as PPP, including PAP, CHAP, and MS-CHAP.
- It requires an IP-based network and header compression is not supported. PPTP does not support IPSec, and encryption is provided using standard PPP methods.

When the tunnel is in place, the computers send their data through it by encapsulating the PPP data that they would normally transmit over a dial-up connection within IP datagrams. The computer then sends the datagrams through the tunnel to the other computer. Although it violates the rules of the Open Systems Interconnection (OSI) model, the data-link layer frame is carried within a network layer datagram.

The PPP frames are encapsulated by IP, and they can also contain other IP datagrams, which contain the actual user data that one computer is sending to the other. Thus, the messages transmitted through the TCP connection that forms the tunnel are IP datagrams that contain PPP frames, and the PPP frames can contain messages generated by any network layer protocol. Therefore the data can be:

- Another IP datagram
- An IPX message
- A NetBEUI message

Because the tunnel is encrypted and secured using an authentication protocol, the data is protected from interception. After the IP datagrams pass through the tunnel to the other computer, the PPP frames are extracted and processed by the receiver in the normal manner. Most Network Address Translation (NAT) implementations include protocol editors for the Generic Routing Encapsulation (GRE) protocol, which is used by PPTP for control packets and TCP 1723 traffic, which uses the PPTP tunnel. PPTP also supports many protocols and multicast environments, and it combines standard user password authentication with strong encryption, without the complexity and expense of a Public Key Infrastructure (PKI).

Layer 2 Tunneling Protocol

L2TP is a mature, widely implemented IETF standards track protocol. L2TP encapsulates PPP frames to be sent over IP, X.25, Frame Relay, or Asynchronous Transfer Mode (ATM) networks. When configured to use IP as its transport, L2TP can be used as a VPN tunneling protocol over the Internet. L2TP over IP uses UDP port 1701 and includes a series of L2TP control messages for tunnel maintenance.

L2TP also uses UDP to send L2TP-encapsulated PPP frames as tunneled data. These encapsulated PPP frames can be encrypted or compressed. When L2TP tunnels appear as IP packets, they take advantage of standard IPSec security using IPSec transport mode for strong integrity, replay, authenticity, and privacy protection. L2TP was specifically designed for client connections to network access servers and gateway-to-gateway connections.

PPP also provides a wide range of user authentication options, including CHAP, MS-CHAP, MS-CHAPv2, and EAP, which supports token card and smart card authentication mechanisms. L2TP/IPSec therefore provides well-defined, interoperable tunneling, with the strong and interoperable security of IPSec.

Tip   When possible, use multifactor authentication. The three factors are Type 1, which is something you know, such as a password; Type 2, which is something you have, such as a smart card; and Type 3, which is something you are, such as a fingerprint. For instance, you could require remote users to have a smart card for authenticating with the remote server. When authenticating, the user could be required to provide a personal identification number (PIN) as part of the authentication process. For something you are, a retinal scanner or thumbprint reader could be used. The most common and most secure method is combining something you have with something you know.

By placing L2TP as a payload within an IPSec packet, communications benefit from the standards-based encryption and authenticity of IPSec, while also having a highly interoperable way to accomplish user authentication, tunnel address assignment, multiprotocol support, and multicast support using PPP. This combination is commonly referred to as L2TP/IPSec.

Note   Due to incompatibilities between the IKE protocol and NAT, it is not possible to use L2TP/IPSec or IPSec tunnel mode through an NAT while taking advantage of automated key exchange with most current NAT implementations. NAT traversal (NAT-T) technologies should be available in early 2003 that will allow IPSec to work through NAT connections by encapsulating the IPSec packets in UDP packets.

Internet Protocol Security

With IPSec, you can provide privacy, integrity, and authenticity for network traffic in the following situations:

- End-to-end security for IP unicast traffic, from client to server, server to server, and client to client using IPSec transport mode.
- Remote access VPN client and gateway functions using L2TP secured by IPSec transport mode.
- Site-to-site VPN connections, across outsourced private wide area network (WAN) or Internet-based connections using L2TP/IPSec or IPSec tunnel mode.

An automatic security negotiation and key management service is also provided using the IETF-defined IKE protocol. Implementing IKE provides three authentication methods to establish trust between computers:

- IKE uses only the authentication properties of Kerberos v5 authentication. (For more information, go to *http://www.ietf.org/proceedings/99mar*, click the link to Section 2.6.2, and then click the Internet draft titled "A GSS-API Authentication Mode for IKE.")
- Public/private key signatures using certificates are compatible with several certificate systems, including Microsoft, Entrust, VeriSign, and Netscape.
- Passwords, termed *preshared authentication keys*, are used strictly for establishing trust between computers.

IPSec provides integrity protection, authentication, and (optional) privacy and replay protection services for IP traffic. IPSec packets are of two types:

- IP protocol 50 called the *Encapsulating Security Payload* (ESP) format, which provides confidentiality, authenticity, and integrity.
- IP protocol 51 called the *Authentication Header* (AH) format, which provides integrity and authenticity for packets, but not confidentiality.

IPSec can be used in two modes: *transport mode*, which secures an existing IP packet from source to destination, and *tunnel mode*, which puts an existing IP packet inside a new IP packet that is sent to a tunnel endpoint in the IPSec format. Both transport and tunnel mode can be encapsulated in ESP or AH headers.

IPSec transport mode was designed to provide security for IP traffic end to end between two communicating systems (for example, to secure a TCP connection or a UDP datagram). IPSec tunnel mode was designed primarily for network midpoints, routers, or gateways, to secure other IP traffic inside an IPSec tunnel that connects one private IP network to another private IP network over a public or untrusted IP network (for example, the Internet). In both cases, a complex security negotiation is performed between the two computers through the IKE, normally using PKI certificates for mutual authentication.

The IETF RFC IPSec tunnel protocol specifications did not include mechanisms suitable for remote access VPN clients. Omitted features include user authentication options or client IP address configuration. To use IPSec tunnel mode for remote access, some vendors chose to extend the protocol in proprietary ways to solve these issues. Although a few of these extensions are documented as Internet drafts, they lack standards status and are not generally interoperable.

Note   A limitation of IPSec is that it only supports unicast IP datagrams. No support for multicasts or broadcasts is currently provided.

IPSec can have an impact on network performance, dependent on the network configuration. Ensuring that the routers and firewalls have sufficient memory and processor capacity helps minimize performance degradation.

Comparing VPN Solutions

Although L2TP/IPSec is an excellent solution for multivendor interoperability in both client-to-gateway and gateway-to-gateway scenarios, its usage of IPSec does require a PKI to be scalable. Also, because of incompatibilities between IKE and NAT, neither L2TP/IPSec, IPSec pure tunnel mode, nor IPSec transport can pass through typical NATs. Table 5-1 summarizes some of the key technical differences among these three security protocols.

Table 5-1.   VPN Solution Comparisons

Capability	PPTP/PPP	L2TP/PPP	L2TP/IPSec	IPSec/Transport	IPSec/Tunnel
User authentication	Yes	Yes	Yes	Yes	Yes
Machine authentication	Yes	Yes	Yes	Yes	Yes
Interoperates with NAT	Yes	Yes	No	No	No
Can carry non-IP packets	Yes	Yes	Yes	No	Yes
Supports encryption	Yes	Yes	Yes	Yes	Yes

Table 5-1.   VPN Solution Comparisons   *(continued)*

Capability	PPTP/PPP	L2TP/PPP	L2TP/IPSec	IPSec/Transport	IPSec/Tunnel
Supports PKI	Yes	Yes	Yes	Yes	Yes
Packet authentication	No	No	Yes	Yes	Yes
Supports multicast	Yes	Yes	Yes	No	Yes

Secure Shell Protocol

The Secure Shell (SSH) protocol and software package was originally developed at the Helsinki University of Technology as a secure, low-level transport protocol. SSH allows users to log on to a remote computer over the network, execute commands on it, and move files from one computer to another while providing strong authentication and secure communications over unsecured channels.

SSH is intended as a replacement for Telnet, rlogin, rsh, and rcp on UNIX-based computers. To provide secure file transfer, SSH2 has been introduced as a replacement for FTP: SFTP.

More Info   Visit the IETF Web site at *http://www.ietf.org* for more information on SSH and SSH2.

This technology secures connections over the Internet by encrypting passwords and other data. Once launched, SSH transparently provides strong authentication and secure communication over unsecured networks.

SSH provides host and user authentication, data compression, protection for data confidentiality, strong encryption, cryptographic host authentication, and integrity protection. However, SSH is not designed to protect against flaws inherent in the operating system, such as poorly developed IP stacks and insecure password storage. The SSH protocol consists of three major components:

- The transport layer protocol (SSH-TRANS) provides secure authentication, confidentiality, and network integrity. The possibility of SSH-TRANS providing encryption is also available. Transport is typically run over a TCP/IP connection, but it can also be used on top of another reliable data stream.

- The user authentication protocol (SSH-USERAUTH) authenticates the client-side user to the server. It runs over the transport layer protocol.

- The connection protocol (SSH-CONN) multiplexes the encrypted tunnel into several logical channels. It runs over the user authentication protocol.

SSH uses public key encryption as the main method for user authentication, but rhosts/shosts authentication can be used as well. Through these methods of authentication, SSH provides secure access to a specific account over a network. You can verify that the public key the server sends is the same as the previous one by using strict host key checking. This also prevents users from accessing a host for which they do not have a public key. SSH also provides protections from the following:

- **Packet spoofing.**   An IP packet appears to be yours, but it is actually someone else's.
- **IP/Host spoofing.**   An IP address or host name is yours, and someone else is using it.
- **Password sniffing.**   The network packets that contain your password are read.
- **Eavesdropping.**   The network packets are read and someone sees what you are typing.

SSH provides a UNIX administrator with the ability to run secure sessions through an untrusted network. Because of the way SSH is written, it is designed to be a drop-in replacement for remote connections like the Berkeley services, such as rlogin, rsh, and rcp. In addition to authenticating, SSH provides an encrypted session to protect against spoofed packets and password sniffing. This enables you to use your account over an unsecured channel and still not pass data in the clear.

Exercise: Configuring the Authentication Method for a Dial-Up Connection

In the following exercise, you learn how to configure the authentication method for a dial-up connection on a computer running Microsoft Windows 2000. (This exercise should work similarly on Windows ME, Windows 98, and Windows XP, although the steps may vary slightly.)

1. From the Start menu, open Control Panel.
2. Open Network Connections.
   a. Open Network and Dial-up Connections
   b. Create a new connection by running the Make New Connection Wizard
3. Complete the Create a Network Connection Wizard to create a dial-up connection using the following information:
   a. Dial-up to a private network
   b. Select the device you wish to use for this dial-up connection
   c. Any phone number
   d. Allow only yourself to use the connection
   e. Use the default name for the new connection

4. Open the Properties dialog box for the connection you just created by right-clicking the connection and selecting Properties.

5. In the Security tab, click Advanced (Custom Settings) and then click Settings.

6. Click Allow These Protocols, and then select each of the check boxes.

7. Right-click on the protocols that can be selected and select What's This? from the shortcut menu.

8. Review the information for each of the protocols and answer the following questions:

   a. For PAP, is the password encrypted?

   b. For CHAP, is MD4 or MD5 used?

   c. Does MS-CHAPv2 offer one-way or mutual authentication?

9. Click Cancel to close the Advanced Security Settings dialog box without saving any changes.

10. Click Cancel again to close the Dial-Up Connection Properties dialog box.

Lesson Review

The following questions are intended to reinforce key information presented in this lesson. If you are unable to answer a question, review the lesson and then try the question again. Answers to the questions can be found in Appendix A, "Questions and Answers."

1. During port-based access control interaction, an authenticator

   a. Enforces authentication before it allows user access to the services

   b. Requests access to the services

   c. Checks the supplicant's credentials

   d. Allows data exchange between two ports

2. Which protocols support VPN tunneling?

   a. PPP

   b. PPTP

   c. TCP

   d. SLIP

3. A RADIUS server can only provide authentication for one remote access server. (True or False?)

4. Select all of the following that are advantages of TACACS+:
   a. Provides a standard method for managing dissimilar networks
   b. Provides distributed user validation for users attempting to gain access to a router or access server
   c. Provides centralized validation for users attempting to gain access to a router or access server
   d. Runs over UDP for more efficient communications

5. The L2TP protocol uses which port?
   a. 443
   b. 80
   c. 1701
   d. 29

6. Which do SSH protect against?
   a. NFS mounting
   b. Packet spoofing
   c. Password sniffing
   d. Internet attacks

Lesson Summary

Providing remote access to your network introduces security risks that must be mitigated by implementing strong user authentication and authorization methods.

- A VPN is a connection between a remote computer and a server on a private network that uses the Internet as its network medium.

- PPTP is a tunneling protocol that helps provide a secure, encrypted communications link between a remote client and a remote access server. Other protocols that are associated with VPNs include IPSec, IKE, L2F, and L2TP.

- RADIUS provides centralized authentication, authorization, and accounting services for remote access connectivity.

- TACACS+ provides a way to centrally validate users attempting to access a router or access server.

- SSH provides strong authentication and secure communications over unsecured channels and protects against packet spoofing, IP spoofing, host spoofing, password sniffing, and eavesdropping.

Lesson 3: Understanding Wireless Standards and Protocols

Wireless networking provides the opportunity for greater freedom of movement in the home or workplace. For home users, wireless networking can provide a solution to the complex job of stringing new Ethernet Category 5 cabling to multiple rooms. For corporate users, the ability to move throughout the workplace and continue to have access to networked resources is important. With the convenience of wireless access, however, comes the need to secure it.

Imagine yourself as the security manager for your company's network. You have just helped with the installation of wireless technology. You notice someone working with a notebook computer in the parking lot outside your building, but think nothing of it. You imagine it is probably just someone waiting to pick up a spouse or friend. Later you walk by and the same person is still there, so you ask that person what he or she is doing and find that the person is connected to your wireless network and accessing your network resources.

There is a technique very similar to war dialing that is known as *war driving*. War driving is when a person drives around businesses and neighborhoods attempting to locate a wireless access point (AP) by using a portable device running a utility that sniffs out and catalogs wireless APs.

To help secure your company's wireless access capability, you must understand the terminology, standards, and protocols that govern wireless technology development and implementation.

After this lesson, you will be able to

- Explain how a wireless network operates in ad hoc or infrastructure mode
- Understand the 802.11x standards and specifications
- Understand the Wireless Access Protocol suite of protocols
- Understand the security provided by the 802.1x standard

Estimated lesson time: 20 minutes

How Wireless Networking Works

Wireless networking is not unlike networking on cable. Computers can form a peer-to-peer network, or can be connected to form a client/server network. Hubs and switches can be used to connect network segments and allow communications over a broader area. Standards and protocols are employed so that the devices on the network operate in a common manner. If the computers that form the wireless network are running in ad hoc mode, however, they can communicate directly with one another without the need for an access point, as shown in Figure 5-6.

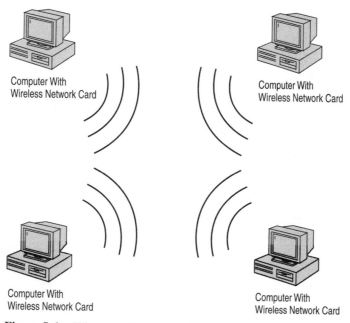

Computer With
Wireless Network Card

Computer With
Wireless Network Card

Computer With
Wireless Network Card

Computer With
Wireless Network Card

Figure 5-6.   Wireless ad hoc networking

Ad hoc networking is not very scalable and offers little control over communications, but does provide the ability to form a peer-to-peer network with other wireless-enabled computers near you. To scale and provide some control over the communications, an access point (AP) can be introduced. This is a device that controls the communications flow between the wireless computers accessing it, and can forward communications to wired networks or other APs. This type of wireless networking is said to be running in *infrastructure mode*, as shown in Figure 5-7.

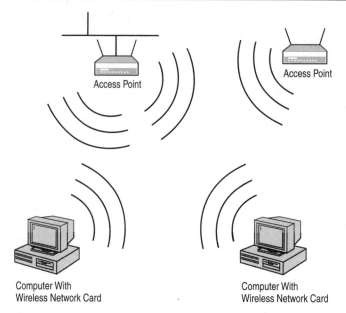

Figure 5-7.   Wireless networking with an AP

Wireless Standards

Standards that govern the speeds and operation of wireless technology are governed by International Electrical and Electronics Engineers (IEEE) standards. The IEEE 802.11 standards cover wireless networking. Since being introduced, wireless speeds have increased dramatically. The following list provides some of the standards and their speeds:

- **802.11a.**   Maximum speed 54 Mbps
- **802.11b.**   Maximum speed 11 Mbps; fallback speeds 5, 2, and 1 Mbps
- **802.11g.**   Maximum speed 22 Mbps; fallback speeds 11, 5, 2, and 1 Mbps

IEEE 802.11b devices are commonly used today and can transmit in the 2.4 GHz range at speeds of up to 11 Mbps and a range of up to 1500 feet outdoors. The standard requires the use of Direct Sequence Spread Spectrum (DSSS), which means that devices must synchronize with one another to use a pattern of frequency switching.

IEEE 802.11b networks, like their wired Ethernet counterparts, must also have some mechanism for data flow control to ensure that data does not get lost as a result of many computers trying to communicate with one another simultaneously. To this end, IEEE 802.11b uses Carrier Sense Multiple Access (CSMA) like typical Ethernet networks; however, it uses collision avoidance (CA), rather than collision detection. With CSMA/CA networks, devices wait until the channel is clear before sending the data. The receiving station sends an acknowledgment back to the sending system when it receives the frame. If the sending device does not receive an acknowledgment within a particular time, it retransmits the frame.

Communicating Across Multiple APs

Wireless networking allows a user to travel from room to room or building to building and stay connected to the network at all times. There are two different modes of communications that can be configured with wireless APs: basic service sets (BSS) and extended service sets (ESS).

BSS

When an AP exists, the wireless devices (notebooks and handhelds) no longer communicate in ad hoc mode. Instead, all traffic from one device destined for another device is relayed through the AP. Even though it seems like this would double the amount of traffic on the wireless local area network (WLAN), this also provides for traffic buffering on the AP when a device is operating in a low-power mode. With this model, the computers can only communicate through the AP they are close to and have selected.

ESS

The compelling force behind a WLAN deployment is the fact that with IEEE 802.11, users are free to move about without switching network connections manually. With a single infrastructure BSS, this moving about would be limited to the signal range of one AP. Through the ESS, the IEEE 802.11 architecture allows users to move among multiple infrastructure BSSs. In an ESS, the APs talk among themselves, forwarding traffic from one BSS to another, as well as switching the roaming devices from one BSS to another. They do this using a medium called the distribution system (DS). The DS forms the spine of the WLAN, making the decisions whether to forward traffic from one BSS to the wired network or back out to another AP or BSS.

Wireless Application Protocol

Wireless Application Protocol (WAP) provides a suite of protocols used for securing communications in layers 3 through 7 of the OSI model. The WAP communications model can be compared to the seven-layer OSI model; communication is broken into logical layers, and protocols are written to operate at those layers, as shown in Table 5-2. Understanding how some of these protocols provide support and security for your network will help you better secure your wireless network solution.

More Info   More information on WAP can be found at the Open Mobile Alliance Web site at *http://www.wapforum.org*.

Table 5-2. Layers and Protocols of the WAP Communications Model

Layer	Protocol	Description
Application	Wireless Application Environment (WAE)	Wireless Markup Language (WML) protocol operates at this layer.
Session	Wireless Session Protocol (WSP)	Uses a token-based version of Hypertext Transfer Protocol (HTTP) to support operations over limited bandwidth.
Transaction	Wireless Transaction Protocol (WTP)	Supports multiple message types and limits the overhead of packaging sequencing.
Transport	Wireless Transport Layer Security (WTLS)	Security layer, based on standard Transport Layer Security (TLS)
Bearer	Wireless Datagram Protocol (WDP)	Provides a consistent interface between over-the-air protocols.

Wired Equivalent Privacy

Wired Equivalent Privacy (WEP) is the mechanism created in the IEEE 802.11b standard that utilizes a cryptographic security countermeasure to provide confidentiality, and has the added benefit of becoming an authentication mechanism. This benefit is realized through a shared key authentication that allows the encryption and decryption of the wireless transmissions. When high security is needed, other mechanisms, such as IEEE 802.1x, should be employed.

Most APs advertise that they support WEP in at least 40-bit encryption, but often the 128-bit option is also supported. For corporate networks, 128-bit encryption-capable devices should be considered as a minimum. With data security enabled in a closed network, the settings on the client for the Service Set Identifier (SSID) and the encryption keys have to match the AP when attempting to associate with the network, or it will fail.

WEP uses the RC4 encryption algorithm, where both the sender and receiver use the *stream cipher* to create identical pseudo-random strings from a known shared key. The sender logically performs the binary exclusive OR operation (XOR) on the plaintext transmission with the stream cipher to produce the ciphertext. The receiver takes the shared key and identical stream and reverses the process to gain the plaintext transmission.

For this process, a 24-bit *initialization vector* (IV) is used to create the identical cipher streams. The IV is a nonsecret binary vector used as the initializing input algorithm for the encryption of plaintext. The IV is produced by the sender, and is included in the transmission of each frame. A new IV is used for each frame to prevent the reuse of the key, weakening the encryption. This means that for each string generated, a different value for the RC4 key is used. Although a secure policy, consideration of the components of WEP bear out one of the flaws in WEP. Because the 24-bit space is so small with respect to the potential set of IVs, in a short period of time, all keys are eventually reused. This weakness exists for both the 40- and 128-bit encryption levels.

To protect against some rudimentary attacks that insert known text into the stream to attempt to reveal the key stream, WEP incorporates a checksum in each frame. Any frame not found to be valid through the checksum is discarded. This sounds secure, but WEP has well-documented flaws, which are covered in later sections.

The WEP Authentication Process

Shared key authentication is a four-step process that begins when the AP receives the validated request for association. After the AP receives the request, a series of management frames are transmitted between the stations to produce the authentication. This includes the use of the cryptographic mechanisms employed by WEP as a validation. Strictly with respect to WEP, in the authorization phase, the four steps break down in the following manner:

1. The requestor (the client) sends a request for association.
2. The authenticator (the AP) receives the request, and responds by producing a random challenge text and transmitting it back to the requestor.
3. The requestor receives the transmission, ciphers the challenge with the shared key stream, and returns it.
4. The authenticator decrypts the challenge text and compares the values against the original. If they match, the requestor is authenticated.

WEP Advantages and Disadvantages

WEP provides some security and privacy in transmissions to prevent curious or casual browsers from viewing the contents of the transmissions held between the AP and the clients. To gain access, the degree of sophistication of the intruder has to improve, and specific intent to gain access is required. Additional benefits of implementing WEP include the following:

- All messages are encrypted using a checksum to provide some degree of tamper resistance.
- Privacy is maintained through the encryption. If you do not have the key, you cannot decrypt the message.
- WEP is easy to implement. Set the encryption key on the AP and repeat the process on each client.
- WEP provides a very basic level of security for WLAN applications.
- WEP keys are user definable and unlimited. You do not have to use predefined keys, and you can and should change them often.

As with any standard or protocol, WEP has some inherent disadvantages. The focus of security is to allow a balance of access and control while juggling the advantages and disadvantages of each implemented countermeasure for security gaps. The following are some of the disadvantages of WEP:

- The RC4 encryption algorithm is a known stream cipher. This means it takes a finite key and attempts to make an infinite pseudo-random key stream to generate the encryption.

- Once you alter the key you have to tell everyone so they can adjust their settings. The more people you tell, the more public the information becomes.

- Used on its own, WEP does not provide adequate WLAN security.

- WEP must be implemented on every client as well as every AP to be effective.

Security Implications of Using WEP

From a security perspective, WEP can be used to deter curious hackers, but used alone, it will not stop determined hackers. Because WEP relies on a known stream cipher, it is vulnerable to certain attacks. By no means is it the final authority, and it should not be the only security countermeasure in place to protect your network. Some of the security challenges faced with wireless networks include the following:

- With wireless communication, it would be a relatively easy matter to put together the hardware to allow an eavesdropper to pick up signals in open, unsecured areas without having physical access to the interior of a building. Therefore, physical security is more challenging.

- Users might have the need to move between wireless zones without having to reconfigure components. In situations in which the wireless zone is in a different administrative domain, users should be able to contact the appropriate domain controller, even if that zone is, for example, located in an airport or another office that provides wireless connectivity.

Security of 64-Bit versus 128-Bit Keys

It might seem obvious to a nontechnical person that something protected with a 128-bit encryption scheme would be more secure than something protected with a 64-bit encryption scheme. This, however, is not the case with WEP. Because the same vulnerability exists with both encryption levels, they can be equally broken within similar time limits.

With 64-bit WEP, the network administrator specifies a 40-bit key, typically 10 hexadecimal digits (0–9, a–f, or A–F). A 24-bit IV is appended to this 40-bit key, and the RC4 key scheme is built from these 64 bits of data. This same process is followed in the 128-bit scheme. The administrator specifies a 104-bit key—this time 26 hexadecimal digits (0–9, a–f, or A–F). The 24-bit IV is added to the beginning of the key, and the RC4 key schedule is built.

Acquiring a WEP Key

As mentioned previously, programs exist that allow an authenticated or unassociated device within the listening area of the AP to capture and recover the WEP key. Depending on the speed of the machine listening to the wireless conversations, the number of wireless hosts transmitting on the WLAN, and the number of IV retransmissions due to 802.11 frame collisions, the WEP key could be cracked within a couple of hours. If an attacker attempts to listen to a WEP-protected network when there is very little network traffic, it would take much longer to obtain the data necessary to crack WEP.

Armed with a valid WEP key, an intruder can successfully negotiate association with an AP and gain entry onto the target network. Unless other mechanisms such as media access control (MAC) filtering are in place, this intruder is now able to roam across the network and potentially break into servers or other network machines. If MAC filtering is occurring, another procedure must be attempted to get around this.

Wireless Transaction Layer Security

WTLS is the security layer of the WAP, providing privacy, data integrity, and authentication for WAP services. WTLS, designed specifically for the wireless environment, is required because the client and the server must be authenticated for wireless transactions to remain secure and because the connection needs to be encrypted. For example, a user making a bank transaction over a wireless device needs to know that the connection is secure and private and not subject to a security breach during transfer (sometimes referred to as a man-in-the-middle attack). WTLS is necessary because mobile networks do not provide complete end-to-end security.

WTLS is based on the widely used TLS v1.0 security layer used in Internet communication. Because of the nature of wireless transmissions, modifications were made to TLS v1.0 to accommodate for the low bandwidth, datagram connection, limited processing power and memory capacity, and cryptography exporting restrictions of wireless transmissions. The WTLS classes of security are as follows:

- Class 1: Anonymous authentication
- Class 2: Server authentication
- Class 3: Two-way client and server authentication

Security in the WLAN

Data security is one of the biggest concerns facing network administrators when implementing a WLAN. In a wired environment, the lack of access to the physical wire can prevent someone from wandering into your building and connecting to your internal network. In a WLAN scenario, it is impossible for the AP to know if the person operating the wireless device is sitting inside your building, passing time in your lobby, or sitting in a parked car just outside your office. Acknowledging that passing data across an unreliable radio link could lead to possible snooping, the IEEE 802.11 standard provides three ways to ensure a greater amount of security for the data that travels over the WLAN. Adopting any (or all three) of these mechanisms decreases the likelihood of an accidental security exposure.

The first method makes use of the 802.11 SSID. This SSID can be associated with one or more APs to create multiple WLAN segments within the infrastructure BSS. These segments can be related to floors of a building, business units, or other data-definition sets. Because the SSID is presented during the authentication process, it acts as a crude password. Because most end users set up their wireless devices, these SSIDs could be shared among users, thus limiting their effectiveness. Another disadvantage to using SSIDs as a sole form of authentication is that if an SSID were to be changed (due to an employee termination or other event, for example), all wireless devices and APs would have to reflect this change. On a medium-sized WLAN, rotating SSIDs on even a biannual basis could prove to be a daunting and time-consuming task.

As mentioned earlier, the AP also can authenticate a wireless device against a list of MAC addresses. This list could reside locally on the AP, or the authentication could be checked against a database of allowed MACs located on the wired network. This typically provides a good level of security, and is best used with small WLAN networks. With larger WLAN networks, administering the list of allowable MAC addresses requires some back-end services to reduce the amount of time needed to make an addition or subtraction from the list.

The third mechanism IEEE 802.11 offers to protect data traversing the WLAN was also mentioned earlier. The privacy service uses an RC4 based encryption scheme, or WEP, to encapsulate the payload of the 802.11 data frames. WEP specifies a 40-bit encryption key, although some vendors have implemented a 104-bit key. As mentioned previously, WEP is not meant to be an end-to-end encryption solution. WEP keys on the APs and wireless devices can be rotated, but because the 802.11 standard does not specify a key-management protocol, all key rotation must be done manually. Like the SSID, rotating the WEP key would affect all APs and wireless users and take significant effort from the network administrator.

Understanding 802.1x

IEEE 802.1x is a standard for port-based network access control that provides authenticated network access to 802.11 wireless networks and wired Ethernet networks. That is, these standards allow for additional authentication methods. Port-based network access control uses the physical characteristics of a switched LAN infrastructure to authenticate devices that are attached to a LAN port and to prevent access to that port when the authentication process fails.

During a port-based network access control interaction, as shown in Figure 5-8, a LAN port adopts one of two roles: authenticator or supplicant. In the role of *authenticator*, a LAN port enforces authentication before it allows user access to the services that can be accessed through that port. In the role of *supplicant*, a LAN port requests access to the services that can be accessed through the authenticator's port. An *authentication server*, which can either be a separate entity or colocated with the authenticator, checks the supplicant's credentials on behalf of the authenticator. The authentication server then responds to the authenticator, indicating whether the supplicant is authorized to access the authenticator's services.

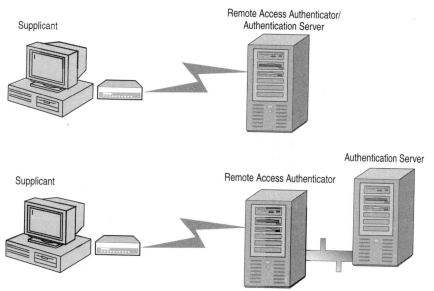

Figure 5-8. Remote access authentication roles

The authenticator's port-based network access control defines two logical access points to the LAN through one physical LAN port. The first logical access point, the *uncontrolled port*, allows data exchange between the authenticator and other computers on the LAN, regardless of the computer's authorization state. The second logical access point, the *controlled port*, allows data exchange between an authenticated LAN user and the authenticator.

IEEE 802.1x uses standard security protocols, such as RADIUS, to provide centralized user identification, authentication, dynamic key management, and accounting. When a client device connects to a port on an 802.1x switch and AP, the switch port can determine the authenticity of the devices. Due to this, and according to the protocol specified by 802.1x, the services offered by the switch can be made available on that port. Only Extensible Authentication Protocol over LAN (EAPOL) frames can be sent and received on that port until the authentication is complete.

When the device is properly authenticated, the port switches traffic as though it were a regular port. Some terminology for the 802.1x standard that you should familiarize yourself with includes the following:

- **Port.** A port is a single point of connection to the network.
- **Port Access Entity (PAE).** The PAE controls the algorithms and protocols that are associated with the authentication mechanisms for a port.
- **Authenticator PAE.** The authenticator PAE enforces authentication before it allows access resources located off that port.
- **Supplicant PAE.** The supplicant PAE tries to access the services that are allowed by the authenticator.
- **Authentication Server.** The Authentication Server is used to verify the supplicant PAE. It decides whether the supplicant is authorized to access the authenticator.
- **Extensible Authentication Protocol over LAN (EAPOL).** The 802.1x standard defines a standard for encapsulating EAP messages so that they can be handled directly by a LAN MAC service. 802.1x tries to make authentication more encompassing, rather than enforcing specific mechanisms on the devices. Because of this, 802.1x uses EAP to receive authentication information.
- **Extensible Authentication Protocol over Wireless (EAPOW).** When EAPOL messages are encapsulated over 802.11 wireless frames, they are known as EAPOW.

With the addition of the 802.1x standard, clients are identified by user names, not the MAC address of the devices. This facet was designed not only to enhance security, but also to streamline the process for authentication, authorization, and accountability for your network. 802.1x was designed so that it could support extended forms of authentication, using password (that is, one-time password or Kerberos) and nonpassword (that is, biometrics, IKE, smart card) methods.

Exercise 1: Identifying Maximum Wireless Speeds

In this exercise, you match the wireless standard with the maximum speed it supports.

1. 802.11a
2. 802.11b
3. 802.11c

a. 22 Mbps transmitting at 2.4 GHz
b. 22 GHz transmitting at 2.4 GHz
c. 54 Mbps transmitting at 2.4 GHz
d. 54 GHz transmitting at 2.4 Mbps
e. 11 Mbps transmitting at 2.4 GHz
f. 11 GHz transmitting at 2.4 Mbps

Exercise 2: Identifying Key Wireless Access Terms

Match the term in the left column with the most appropriate statement in the right column.

1. ESS
2. WTLS
3. 802.1x
4. BSS
5. WEP
6. WAP

a. The mechanism created in the 802.11 standard that utilizes a cryptographic security countermeasure to provide confidentiality, and has the added benefit of becoming an authentication mechanism.

b. Security layer is based on standard Transport Layer Security (TLS).

c. A suite of protocols used for securing communications in layers 3 through 7. The communications model can be compared to the seven-layer OSI model.

d. The APs talk amongst themselves forwarding traffic from one BSS to another, as well as switch the roaming devices from one BSS to another.

e. Wireless devices (notebooks and handhelds) no longer communicate in ad hoc mode. Instead, all traffic from one device destined for another device is relayed through the AP.

f. A standard for port-based network access control that provides authenticated network access to 802.11 wireless networks and wired Ethernet networks.

Lesson Review

The following questions are intended to reinforce key information presented in this lesson. If you are unable to answer a question, review the lesson and then try the question again. Answers to the questions can be found in Appendix A, "Questions and Answers."

1. What is the maximum transport speed supported by the 802.11b standard?

   a. 2.4 GHz

   b. 2 Mbps

   c. 11 Mbps

   d. 10 Mbps

2. What is the encryption method employed by WEP? What is the maximum bit encryption supported?

   a. RC4

   b. RC5

   c. 64-bit encryption

   d. 128-bit encryption

Lesson Summary

- IEEE 802.11b devices can transmit in the 2.4 GHz range at speeds of up to 11 Mbps and a range of up to 1500 feet outdoors.

- The IEEE 802.11 standard provides three ways to provide a greater amount of security for the data that travels over the WLAN: using SSIDs, providing a mechanism to authenticate wireless users, and employing encryption capabilities.

- WEP utilizes the RC4 encryption algorithm to provide up to 128-bit encryption and also provides the added benefit of becoming an authentication mechanism.

- WAP is a transport protocol used with wireless networking, and most application development for wireless applications uses WML.

- WTLS is the security layer of the WAP, providing privacy, data integrity, and authentication for WAP services.

- IEEE 802.1x is a standard for port-based network access control that provides authenticated network access to 802.11 wireless networks and wired Ethernet networks.

- During a port-based network access control interaction, a LAN port adopts one of two roles: authenticator or supplicant. In the role of authenticator, a LAN port enforces authentication before it allows user access to the services that can be accessed through that port. In the role of supplicant, a LAN port requests access to the services that can be accessed through the authenticator's port.

C H A P T E R   6

Application Security

About This Chapter

As you have seen in earlier chapters, there are many different ways in which an attacker might attempt to compromise your network. In this chapter you learn how attackers might try to exploit applications on your network. The focus is placed primarily on client applications, as securing servers is covered in Chapter 8, "Security Baselines."

Before You Begin

This chapter assumes the basic knowledge of TCP/IP as presented in Chapter 2, "TCP/IP Basics." You should also understand certificates as presented in Chapter 3, "Certificate Basics."

Note   In this chapter you will find references to software programs that have been developed to help manage security issues. These software programs are provided as examples of what is available in the industry. We strongly recommend that you research these products fully before attempting to use them.

Lesson 1: E-Mail Security

A connection between any client and server on the Internet is routed through potentially dozens of independent systems. At any point along that connection, network traffic can be monitored. Transmitting unencrypted communications over the Internet is about as private as sending a postcard through the mail because anyone with access to the infrastructure along the way can read the message.

E-mail is one of the most popular forms of communication today. Unfortunately, many security issues plague e-mail communications. In this lesson, we address several of these e-mail security concerns. The main topics discussed in this lesson are encrypting e-mail, e-mail application vulnerabilities, unsolicited e-mail, and e-mail hoaxes and scams.

After this lesson, you will be able to

- Install and appropriately apply secure electronic messaging
- Take steps to prevent the exploitation of e-mail application vulnerabilities
- Implement antispam measures
- Take steps to reduce the exposure of your organization to e-mail scams
- Reduce the propagation of e-mail hoaxes

Estimated lesson time: 60 minutes

Secure Electronic Messaging

Just like a postcard traveling through the mail, standard e-mail offers little privacy from individuals who want to read other people's mail. E-mail can literally be collected and read by almost anyone with a *protocol analyzer* (also called a data sniffer, network sniffer, packet sniffer, and other derivatives of these terms). As you should know from your previous experience, a protocol analyzer is a device (or computer software program) that allows its user to capture and decode network traffic. The Computer Emergency Response Team (CERT) reported in 1994 that tens of thousands of Internet hosts were compromised by sniffing e-mail message packets (with a protocol analyzer) for user names and passwords.

Note   Mailsnarf is an example of an automated program for collecting information from e-mail messages. Mailsnarf is included with a group of programs packaged as *dsniff*. You can find out more about these programs on the Packet Storm Web site.

In addition to a lack of privacy, e-mail can easily be forged. An attacker can modify the sender field of an e-mail message so that it can appear to come from anyone. The attacker can just as easily modify the reply field so that replies to the messages are sent to an address under her or his control. Many people today receive e-mail messages with unsolicited advertisements that seem to come from their own e-mail addresses. If someone used your name or e-mail address to send a message to one of your colleagues, would he or she know the difference? Worse yet, would your colleague reply to the attacker, thinking that you sent the message?

Secure electronic messaging addresses these security concerns. It allows you to encrypt messages, so that only the intended recipients can decrypt them. Secure electronic messaging also allows you to digitally sign messages, so that your message recipients can be sure that the message is really from you.

Note   General Dynamics has a secure electronic messaging product named Secure Electronic Messaging System (SEMS). That product is not discussed further in this text. The term *secure electronic messaging* in this chapter and in many other technical documents refers generically to methods for encrypting and digitally signing e-mail.

PGP

Pretty Good Privacy (PGP) is a set of software tools that allows you to encrypt, decrypt, and digitally sign computer data and e-mail. PGP's encryption and decryption services are asymmetric, as described in Chapter 3. This encryption can be applied to e-mail, stored files, some forms of instant messaging, and virtual private networking. This chapter limits the discussion to e-mail encryption. PGP performs these functions to allow you to sign and encrypt e-mail:

- **Create keys.**   PGP creates your key pair, which is your public and private key.
- **Manage keys.**   PGP allows you to store other users' public keys on a local key ring.
- **Encrypt/decrypt e-mail.**   Colleagues use your public key to encrypt messages to you. You use your private key (or secret key) to decrypt those messages.
- **Sign/authenticate e-mail.**   You use your private key to digitally sign messages to your colleagues. Your colleagues use your public key to decrypt your signature and verify that the message actually came from you.

You must send your public key to anyone who you would like to be able to encrypt messages to you and verify your digital signature on messages from you. Your private key is maintained on your local computer by default. You can also store your private key on removable media, such as a floppy disk. The private key is protected by a pass phrase (password) that you configure during PGP installation and configuration. This pass phrase is requested every time you decrypt or digitally sign a message.

Note   PGP integrates with the following e-mail applications: Qualcomm Eudora, Microsoft Exchange, Microsoft Outlook, Microsoft Outlook Express, and Lotus Notes.

S/MIME

The Secure Multipurpose Internet Mail Extensions (S/MIME) specification is similar to PGP in that it seeks to enable the encryption and digital signing of e-mail messages. S/MIME is designed for integration into e-mail and messaging products. S/MIME, like PGP, utilizes asymmetric encryption techniques. However, S/MIME clients rely on certificates generated by a public key infrastructure (PKI), as described in Chapter 3.

More Info   S/MIME version 3 is documented in RFC 2633 and S/MIME version 2 is documented in RFC 2311. (RFC articles can be found at *http://www.icann.rfceditor.org*)

To utilize S/MIME, you must have an S/MIME-enabled application and access to a PKI certificate. This certificate can come from an internal PKI provided by your organization or an external infrastructure. Two popular external PKI service providers are Verisign (*http://www.verisign.com*) and Thwate (*http://www.thwate.com*).

More Info   RSA Security, Inc. maintains a list of S/MIME-enabled products on its Web site at *http://www.rsasecurity.com/standards/smime/products.html*. Three of the most popular S/MIME-enabled applications are Netscape Communicator and Microsoft Outlook and Outlook Express.

Once you have installed and configured your key pair, you can begin using S/MIME. When you are utilizing an external PKI, you might have to send your public key in the form of a digital signature to people you would like to allow to encrypt messages to you. If your PKI is internal, other users should be able to automatically enroll your e-mail signing and encryption certificate and public key from the internal PKI.

Note   Client e-mail settings for digital signatures and encryption are often independently configurable. For example, Microsoft's Outlook e-mail client allows you to digitally sign all (or selected) messages and separately digitally encrypt all (or selected) messages.

E-Mail Vulnerabilities

Vulnerabilities are often found in software, and e-mail software is no exception. Beyond product vulnerabilities, e-mail is often used to exploit other vulnerabilities. Such attacks can damage e-mail servers, erase e-mail or other data, or run other malicious software, resulting in loss of data, time, and money.

One of the most widespread attacks launched through e-mail was the Melissa macro virus, which did two harmful things to users of Microsoft Outlook and Microsoft Word for Windows. First, it infected Word files stored on the victim's local system and garbled the documents. Second, the virus opened the victim's Microsoft Outlook address book and e-mailed itself to the first 50 addresses using the victim's e-mail address and account. This virus is estimated to have caused $80 million in damages. The creator of the virus was eventually caught and sentenced to 20 months in prison and a $5,000 fine. Numerous other exploits and vulnerabilities for a wide array of e-mail programs exist on networks around the world.

To protect your network and your organization from e-mail vulnerabilities, you must vigilantly monitor security alerts and update virus-scanning software. E-mail gateway servers can scan incoming messages and isolate or remove virus attachments. This is a common line of defense in many organizations. Individual computers can also be configured with virus scanners, creating a defense-in-depth. This helps to prevent internal users from infecting other internal users and provides a backup in case the e-mail gateway is unable to stop an infected message.

More Info   CERT sends out confirmed reports of software exploits on a variety of software free of charge. Visit *http://www.cert.org* for more information and to sign up for their security alerts.

You should also educate your organization's users about how to spot a potential threat. For example, many exploits arrive in the form of e-mail attachments, so users should be trained not to open attachments that appear suspicious or that were unsolicited, even if they came from a colleague. Many organizations train users never to open attachments and prohibit them from being sent or received through the e-mail gateway.

As exploits are discovered in e-mail client and server programs, vendors typically provide software patches. Be sure to monitor vendor security updates. Test and apply security patches for your applications as they are made available.

Spam

Spam is a term used to describe unsolicited e-mail (typically commercial advertisements) sent to a large number of addresses. On February 18 and 19, 2002, a major Internet service provider (ISP) found out that spam is dangerous for business.

Legitimate e-mails were taking as long as 24 hours to deliver because the ISP's e-mail servers were processing so much spam. Antispam organizations, such as Brightmail, report that the volume of spam is rising much more quickly than the volume of normal e-mail. In a March 1, 2002, article titled "The High Price of Spam," Business Week Online reported, "For some ISPs and corporations, spam makes up more than 50% of total e-mail."

To protect your organization from the debilitating effects of spam, you should install filtering software at your Internet gateway and client desktops. Many products are available to help prevent spam. Examples include SpamAssassin, Brightmail, Cloudmark, DigiPortal's ChoiceMail, and Mailshell. You should also educate your network users on how to help avoid spam. Spam.org has compiled the following list of tips to help reduce spam:

- **Never respond to spam.**   This helps spammers confirm that they have a live e-mail address. They can then sell your address to other spammers.

- **Don't post your address on your Web site.**   Addresses on Web sites can be "harvested" by automatic software that scans Web sites for e-mail addresses.

- **Use a second e-mail address in newsgroups.**   Newsgroups are another location where spammers collect e-mail addresses. The address that you use for posting messages is likely to be used for spam. However, if you create a second address (called your public address) and use that for posting to newsgroups, you can expect spam on that account. This prevents spam from clogging your normal inbox.

- **Don't provide your e-mail address without knowing how it will be used.** Many Web sites ask you to log in with your e-mail address and a password. Be sure to look for a privacy statement regarding the information requested. Also, consider whether you trust the organization not to sell your information. If you can't find a privacy policy or you don't trust the organization not to sell your information, don't log in, sign up, or in any other way give them your address.

- **Use a spam filter.**   Spam filters can help to reduce spam. Many products refer to spam filters as junk mail filters. Some let you create rules based on the subject, sender, or message body, allowing you to keep messages out of your inbox by moving or even deleting them.

- **Never buy anything advertised in spam.**   Companies use spam because people respond to the advertisements.

The U.S. Federal Trade Commission (FTC) would like to know if you receive spam. They ask you to send a copy of unwanted or deceptive messages to uce@ftc.gov. The FTC stores these messages in a database and pursues law enforcement actions against the people who send them. You can also file online complaints about spam messages, including problems with unsubscribe functions, to the FTC through their Web site at *http://www.ftc.gov.*

More Info   You can learn more about fighting and preventing junk mail from *http://www.spam.org* and *http://www.junkbusters.org*.

SMTP Relay

Simple Mail Transfer Protocol (SMTP) relaying is what an e-mail server does when it transfers e-mail. Some spammers attempt to funnel their junk mail through other e-mail servers that permit SMTP relay. If spammers can forward mail from a server not normally linked to spam, they can get more spam to more people. When someone else's e-mail server is used for spam without permission, the act of spamming becomes an attack. Why? The victim's server is likely to slow down and will not be able to service e-mail as efficiently as before. More important, many ISPs are likely to block mail from the victim's e-mail server. This means the victim must discover the problem and then contact each ISP to explain that the mail server was attacked and convince them to unblock mail from their mail server.

To protect your organization's servers from becoming a spammer's junk mail relay station, you must restrict access to SMTP relay. For example, most major ISPs typically protect themselves from being used for spamming attacks by restricting the use of SMTP servers to customers only. That way, if a customer account is used for spam, it can be locked out, stopping the spam. The spammer might even be tracked down and legally prosecuted. Noncustomer accounts are prevented from using the SMTP server at all.

Note   SMTP relay should be disabled (if it is available) on any device that the organization does not intend to use for mail transfer.

Scams

Like spam, an e-mail scam is a solicitation. The real difference between the two is that a scam is not offering a legitimate product or service. E-mail scams are typically an attempt to steal money, products, or services. Usually they ask the intended victim to transfer money or provide bank account or credit card information.

One of the most notorious e-mail scams is known as the Nigerian money laundering scam. This scam appears to have started sometime in the 1980s. The scam invitation is delivered through faxes, letters, and most recently e-mails. It can involve the following situations: overinvoiced or double-invoiced oil or other supply and service contracts; a bequest left to you in a will; and money cleaning where money must be chemically cleaned before it can be used (because embezzled money must be moved to an established account outside the country). The perpetrator of the scam either asks for a deposit up front or information about the victim's bank account. If the victim provides bank account information, money from the victim's account is transferred out (instead of in). The July 2000 Business Link online newsletter from the Better Business Bureau (BBB) reported that Americans lose $100 million per year to this scam. Worldwide, the scam was estimated to be worth $5 billion as of 1996.

Note Although this scam is known as the Nigerian money laundering scam, it is not a direct reflection on the government or people of Nigeria. This scam is also conducted outside of Nigeria and might not even include "Nigeria" in the subject or body.

To protect your organization, its employees, and its clients from scams like this, create a policy prohibiting the release of sensitive information through inappropriate channels. You must define what should be considered sensitive information, such as bank account numbers, social security numbers, and so on. Also, you must define appropriate and inappropriate channels, which vary by organization. In most organizations, account information, personal information, and company funds are controlled and monitored, yet organizations and individuals continue to be defrauded by scams.

Educating your organization's network users to the existence and prevalence of e-mail scams is the best defense. To assist with your organization's education program concerning e-mail scams, the FTC has compiled a list of common e-mail scams. The FTC published the list in a consumer alert article titled "FTC Names Its Dirty Dozen: 12 Scams Most Likely to Arrive Via Bulk Email." Those top 12 scams are the following:

- Business opportunity scams
- Make money by sending bulk e-mail
- Chain letters
- Work-at-home schemes
- Health and diet scams
- Effortless income
- Free goods
- Investment opportunities
- Cable descrambler kits
- Guaranteed loans or credit, or easy terms scams
- Credit repair scams
- Vacation prize promotions

The full FTC article can be found on their Web site at *http://www.ftc.gov.*

More Info   In addition to the FTC, you can learn more about Internet scams from these Web sites: Cyber Criminals Most Wanted (*http://www.ccmostwanted.com*) and Scambusters (*http://www.scambusters.com*).

Hoaxes

E-mail hoaxes and scams continue to be a problem for network users. An e-mail hoax is often spread like a chain letter or rumor. Hoaxes contain false information that is believable. Hoax e-mails are often forwarded from one person to many others, making it possible for an idea in a single e-mail to spread exponentially.

Hoax e-mails request that the e-mail be forwarded to colleagues. One of the most infamous hoax messages was the Good Times virus hoax that has been widely propagated on the Internet several times. The gist of the original message is that there is a virus sent through e-mail that is able to erase your computer's hard disk if you open the message. The message is said to be propagated by a user named "Good Times" or the message subject is "Good Times," thus the name of the hoax.

Other hoaxes indicate that people might have been given a virus by one of their colleagues. People are asked to search their computers for files that are said to be viruses, when the files are actually part of popular operating systems. For example, the files Sulfnbk.exe, Jdbgmgr.exe, and Cleanmgr.exe, which are common to Microsoft Windows operating systems, have been called viruses by e-mail hoaxes. The hoaxes tell users to delete these files and forward this information to everyone in their address book.

To protect your organization from hoaxes, you should create a written policy that prohibits the forwarding of known hoaxes. The policy should also be posted to help users identify potential hoaxes. Be sure to educate your network users on the existence of these hoaxes and the damage and loss of productivity they can cause. For example, here are five tell-tale signs (compiled by *http://www.hoaxbusters.org*) that an e-mail is a hoax:

- **Urgent.**   Words of urgency, importance, warnings, or specifically "virus alert" often appear in the subject line.
- **Tell all your friends.**   There is always some request to forward the information to others.
- **This isn't a hoax.**   The message usually contains some type of corroboration from someone specific or generic who might seem to be trustworthy. For example, the original sender might write something like, "I verified this by calling the number" or "This alert was reported by some official-sounding person, news station, or other authority."

- **Dire consequences.**   Hoaxes often tell you to act immediately or risk losing something, such as all the data on your hard disk.

- **History.**   If the message has "FW" in the subject line, or many angle brackets (such as >>>>>>) in the subject body, the message has probably been forwarded several times, a good indication that it is probably a hoax.

Be sure to communicate that users should not delete any files that an e-mail instructs them to delete. Instead, they should forward such messages to technical support personnel for an official response and action plan. An existing and up-to-date virus scanner can be used verify the actual existence of a virus. You can cross-check reported file names with organizations that can alert you to hoaxes, such as hoaxbusters.org, cert.org, vmyths.com, icsalabs.com, and the major virus scanner providers.

Exercise 1: Downloading and Installing PGP Freeware

In this exercise you install PGP Freeware. The exercise is accurate step by step if you are using a computer running Microsoft Windows 2000 Professional.

Note   PGP Freeware is available for other operating systems, such as Amiga, Atari, BeOS, EPOC (Psion), MacOS, MS-DOS, Newton, OS/2, PalmOS, and UNIX. However, the installation steps can be quite different for these operating systems. (Newer versions of PGP are available for Windows XP and Macintosh OSX. Search for PGP 8.0 through your favorite Web search engine for more information.)

The steps should be quite similar for earlier versions of the Microsoft Windows operating system. You need a Web browser and a program that allows you to decompress software, such as WINZIP or PowerZip. Both PowerZip and WINZIP allow you to download demo versions that work for this exercise.

1. Log on as a user with administrator permissions to the local Windows 2000 system.

2. Open your Web browser and navigate to your favorite Web search engine. Type **PGP Freeware 7.03** as the search criteria. This should bring up a list of locations from which you can download PGP Freeware 7.03. Choose a site from which to download.

3. Most Web sites organize PGP Freeware versions by operating system. For Microsoft Windows 2000 Professional, choose the Windows 2000 link. If you are using a different operating system, choose the appropriate link.

4. Most Web sites organize PGP Freeware by version. Choose PGP version 7.0.3, if available (steps might vary slightly if you choose a version other than 7.0.3).

5. You should see a link to download PGP Freeware 7.03. Choose the Download PGP 7.0.3 link as well as any hotfixes. (You'll probably have to download the program and each hotfix separately.) You should see a list of download locations. Notice that you are offered either HTTP or FTP downloads. You can choose any type that your software supports, but File Transport Protocol (FTP) downloads are typically faster. If you are not sure what your software supports, try FTP. If that doesn't work, use Hypertext Transfer Protocol (HTTP).

6. Your browser program should ask you where you would like to save the zipped program. Save the program and hotfixes to the location of your choice.

7. Navigate to the location where you saved the files and use your file decompression program to extract the installation files to the location of your choice.

8. Navigate to the location where you decompressed the installation files. You should find a PGP FW folder. Open that folder and double-click the PGPfreeware 7.0.3.exe file.

9. The PGPfreeware 7.0.3 Installer first displays a Welcome page. Click Next to proceed with the installation.

10. Read and accept the license agreement by clicking Yes. The Read Me page appears.

Note If you do not agree to the terms of the license agreement, click No. If you click No, the installation terminates and you are unable to complete the exercise.

---

11. Click Next. The User Type page appears.

12. Assuming that you have never used PGP before, you should select No, I Am A New User and click Next. The Install Directory page appears.

13. Click Next if you want to install PGP Freeware in the default location. Otherwise, use the Browse feature to change the location of the installation.

14. When you have chosen the location, click Next. The Software Components page appears. For this exercise you can clear the PGPnet Personal Firewall/IDS/VPN check box.

Note If you choose to install PGPnet Personal Firewall/IDS/VPN, the installation steps vary slightly, as you have to configure the PGPnet component.

---

15. Click Next. The Start Copying Files page appears.

16. Confirm your settings and click Next to copy the files. An advertisement for PGP Personal Security might appear. If so, click Next again to begin copying the files.

17. Once the files are copied, you are asked to restart your computer. Click Finish to continue. Your computer restarts.

After the installation of PGP, you can install the hot fixes. To do so, navigate to the location where you downloaded the PGP hot fixes and extract the hot fix files from the compressed files you downloaded. Navigate to the executable files that are the hot fixes and run them. Each file asks you to restart your system. Restart after you've installed both hot fixes.

After you restart your system and log on, you should see that PGP Freeware is available on your system. You should be able to access PGP documentation and utilities by clicking Start, Programs, and PGP. At this point you should read Part 1: Overview including Chapter 1, "PGP Basics" and Chapter 2, "A Quick Tour of PGP."

Exercise 2: Creating PGP Keys

To start working with PGP, you must first create a PGP Key pair. This exercise works step-by-step on any Windows 2000 operating system.

1. Click Start, Programs, PGP, PGPKeys. The PGPKeys window opens.
2. Click the Keys menu and then click New Key menu option. The Key Generation Wizard opens.
3. Click Next to proceed. The Name and Email Assignment page opens.
4. Enter your name and e-mail address in the locations provided. Click Next. The Passphrase Assignment page appears.
5. In the Passphrase text box, enter a pass phrase that is difficult to guess. Confirm your pass phrase by typing it again in the Confirmation text box.

Important   For stronger pass phrase security, you should use at least eight characters with a combination of uppercase and lowercase letters, numbers, and nonalphabetic characters.

---

6. Click Next to continue. The Key Generation Progress page appears.
7. Click Next when the key generation process is finished. The Completing The PGP Key Generation Wizard page appears.
8. Click Finish. The PGPKeys window is updated with your new key pair.

At this point, if you want to allow others to encrypt messages to you, they must install PGP and create a key pair. Then you and your colleagues can exchange key pairs as described in Chapter 3, "Making and Exchanging Keys" of the PGP documentation. You should also review Chapter 4, "Managing Keys" to learn how to appropriately utilize the keys you exchange.

If you want to learn how to secure your e-mail, review Chapter 5, "Securing Email" of the PGP documentation to learn how to send encrypted messages and digitally sign e-mail. You can also use PGP to encrypt the data on your hard disk, which is explained in Chapter 6, "Securing Files" of the PGP documentation. You can also use PGP to encrypt and sign communications over ICQ (I Seek You) as described in Chapter 7, "Securing Instant Messages" of the PGP documentation.

Note   You can download Adobe Acrobat Reader free from Adobe's Web site at *http://www.adobe.com.*

Lesson Review

The following questions are intended to reinforce key information presented in this lesson. If you are unable to answer a question, review the lesson and then try the question again. Answers to the questions can be found in Appendix A, "Questions and Answers."

1. Name two ways in which you can increase the privacy of e-mail.

2. What are some steps you should take to protect your organization from the exploitation of e-mail vulnerabilities?

3. What can you do to help your organization combat spam?

4. What steps can you take to reduce your organization's exposure to e-mail scams?

5. How can you reduce the propagation of e-mail hoaxes?

Lesson Summary

- You can protect e-mail by using secure electronic messaging programs. PGP-enabled and S/MIME-enabled applications are able to encrypt, decrypt, and digitally sign e-mail. When implemented properly, only the intended recipient can read encrypted e-mail. Further, the recipient can verify the authenticity of the message by checking the sender's digital signature.

- E-mail vulnerabilities plague almost all e-mail systems. It is very likely that the discovery and exploitation of vulnerabilities will never end. Therefore, it is imperative that you pay attention to security alerts from vendors concerning their applications, in addition to generic alerts provided by organizations such as cert.org. Further, you should test and apply security fixes as soon as they are made available.

- You can protect your organization from spam by implementing e-mail filters at the Internet gateway and on client desktops. You can also educate network users on how to avoid being targeted by spam. A list of six steps to help people reduce their exposure to spam is available on the Spam.org Web site.

- E-mail scams are not new. Many scams that are carried out today over e-mail were propagated through letters and faxes before e-mail became popular. Awareness of the existence of most scams is the best defense against them. To that end, the FTC has compiled a list of 12 common e-mail scams. To protect your organization from these scams, educate network users about them and create policies that help to prevent people in your organization from being caught in a scam.

- You can help reduce the propagation of e-mail hoaxes by educating users about how to recognize these hoaxes. Hoaxbusters.org has compiled a list of five tell-tale signs of an e-mail hoax. Ask users to review the list. Your organization's technical support personnel should verify all alerts to be sure that they are not hoaxes before communicating them to network users.

Lesson 2: Web Security

As mentioned in Lesson 1, unencrypted communications on the Internet should not be considered safe. Almost anyone with a protocol analyzer and the inclination to use it could compromise unencrypted data exchanges.

Beyond packet sniffing, attackers can utilize several other methods to exploit an organization's network and computers. Often, these attacks focus on application vulnerabilities that are a result of programming errors. Attackers might also trick your users into downloading software that can be used to compromise your organization's systems.

After this lesson, you will be able to

- Select appropriate encryption technologies for Web communications
- Identify and select corrective action for active content vulnerabilities, buffer overflows, cookie vulnerabilities, and Common Gateway Interface (CGI) program vulnerabilities

Estimated lesson time: 60 minutes

SSL/TLS

The Secure Sockets Layer (SSL) and Transport Layer Security (TLS) protocols were developed to help secure client/server exchanges on the Internet. Most people wouldn't write their credit card number, expiration date, and billing address on a postcard to make a purchase through the mail because they know anyone who saw their postcard could use this information to make fraudulent purchases against their accounts. The same considerations apply to personal or confidential information such as medical records. If you wouldn't want to write something down on a postcard, you probably shouldn't send it across the Internet unencrypted.

In December of 1994, Netscape Communications Corporation released the SSL protocol. SSL is based on the asymmetric PKI encryption methods developed by RSA Corporation. In January 1999, the Internet Engineering Task Force (IETF) established RFC 2246, which documented a new protocol based on SSL version 3 called TLS protocol version 1. SSL and TLS gained wide acceptance in the late 1990s. TLS is different enough that it does not interoperate with SSL, but TLS does include a mechanism that allows it to back down to SSL 3. Today, many different software vendors' products support versions of SSL and TLS.

Note Because SSL and TLS were derived from the same protocol and supported by many of the same applications, the two protocols are often referred to simultaneously as SSL/TLS.

SSL/TLS provides protection against eavesdropping, tampering, and forgery of communications on the Internet. Clients and servers can authenticate one another over SSL connections and establish an encrypted communications link across the Internet. SSL/TLS is an application-independent layer that works between the Transport and Application Layers of the Transmission Control Protocol/Internet Protocol (TCP/IP) protocol stack, as shown in Figure 6-1. Consequently, any network application that can use TCP/IP can also use SSL/TLS. However, the application must be specifically programmed to include SSL/TLS compatibility.

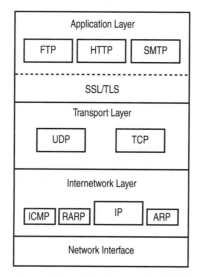

Figure 6-1.   SSL/TLS in the TCP/IP protocol stack

SSL/TLS can provide the following services for client/server applications:

- **Authentication of the server to the client.**   When a customer wants to buy a product from a merchant's Web site, the customer wants to know that he or she is actually communicating with a server owned by that merchant. SSL/TLS allows the customer's computer to verify that the server is indeed the merchant's server (and not a rogue server set up by a thief to steal credit card information). For this to work, the server must have a valid certificate from a certification authority (CA) trusted by the client.

- **Negotiation of a common cryptographic algorithm or cipher.**   The client and the server can negotiate the type of encryption used for the connection. This enables the client and server to agree on an encryption technique that they both support.

- **Authentication of the client to the server (optional).**   When there is a desire to limit access to the server, client computers can be installed with certificates that confirm their identity. Such authentication isn't always desirable or necessary. For example, in most e-commerce transactions, merchants do not verify their customer's identity using SSL/TLS or certificates because many potential customers would not have certificates. Therefore, vendors frequently choose to identify their customers by credit card number, expiration date, and billing address.

- **Use of asymmetric encryption to transfer shared secrets.**   Asymmetric (or public key) encryption is difficult to break, but is also computationally intensive. Symmetric encryption is much more efficient for transferring data. SSL/TLS utilizes asymmetric encryption to transfer a shared secret (symmetric key) so that the actual data encryption is faster, but the method of establishing the encrypted communication is still highly secure.

- **Establish an encrypted connection.**   Finally, and most important, all communication between the client and server is encrypted. SSL/TLS is also protected by a mechanism to detect connection tampering, such as data being altered during transit.

Almost all Internet-based online purchases today are protected by SSL/TLS. SSL/TLS encryption gives consumers, merchants, and financial institutions confidence in the privacy of Internet transactions.

HTTPS

Web communications are conducted using HTTP. Web communications that are secured by SSL/TLS are referred to as HTTPS communications. Client Web browsers often indicate HTTPS connections by showing https:// (instead of http://) in the protocol field of the Web address.

Note   Another less popular method for transmitting data securely over HTTP is Secure HTTP (S-HTTP or S/HTTP), which is documented in RFC 2660. Most vendors do not implement support for S/HTTP in their products.

Although HTTPS encrypts communication between the client and server, it doesn't guarantee that the merchant is trustworthy or that the merchant's server is secure.

SSL/TLS is designed to positively identify the merchant's server and encrypt communication between the client and server. SSL/TLS cannot stop the merchant from doing something unethical with the credit card information once it is collected. SSL/TLS does not protect information stored on the merchant's server. Unfortunately, many merchants' Web servers have been compromised (and customer credit card information has been stolen). Consequently, many merchants do not store credit card information on their servers.

Buffer Overflows

A *buffer* is a data area that is shared by either hardware devices or program processes. In this section the focus is on program buffers, which allow programs to operate with different priorities. Each buffer has a defined area and boundary.

Buffer overflows occur when a program tries to store more data in the buffer than it was designed to hold. The data that does not fit into the designated buffer can overflow into an adjacent buffer. The overflowed data can overwrite and corrupt valid data of another program. Buffer overflows can be caused by a programming error or a specific attack against an application. An attacker can use a buffer overflow on the target system to exercise some type of control over that system. In an attack, the buffer overflow condition can be used to damage files, change data, acquire confidential information, or execute code on the target computer. The attacker might even be able to gain full control over the target system.

Note   Buffer overflows have been exploited in almost every type of application, including Web applications. Web servers and clients from many different software vendors have been exploited by buffer overflows.

The best defense against buffer overflow attacks is having software developers follow secure coding practices. If you or people in your organization develop programs, these practices should be applied. Applying secure coding practices means designing programs with security in mind. Think about ways in which the application could be compromised or used to compromise another application, device, or the operating system. Some specific best practices for secure code development are as follows:

- Run programs as the least privileged account possible. If your application doesn't have to be equivalent to root or administrator, don't make it run as such.
- Use safe compilers to help minimize the impact of buffer overflows (for example, Stack Guard).
- Design the program to check all user input for validity. If done properly and thoroughly, users won't be able to send invalid or out-of-bound strings that can overflow the buffer to your program.

Note   More specific recommendations for secure code development can be found in software development kits (SDKs). SDKs are programming guides that explain the structures, functions, and methods for developing programs for specific platforms.

The best protection against buffer overflow conditions after a program is released is for the program vendor to produce a security patch. To protect existing systems, security administrators should test and apply all security patches as they are made available.

Active Content

In an effort to make browsing more exciting, functional, and useful, software vendors and Web developers created and enabled *active content*. Active content materials are small executables or script code that is rendered within the client's Web browser. For example, some banks offer mortgage calculators on their Web sites. These mortgage calculators are considered active content. Two of the most popular types of active content are JavaScript and ActiveX components. Active content (or *dynamic content*) is designed to run a script on a client system. Unfortunately, with this added capability comes an added security risk: some scripts could be used to perform harmful actions on a client machine.

Note   Active content that is intended to cause harm, but is disguised as something valuable or desirable, is called a *Trojan horse*. This term is borrowed from the ancient Greek story about the large wooden horse that was presented as a gift to the city of Troy, yet secretly contained an army of Greek soldiers. The Trojan horse was used to get the soldiers inside the city to compromise its defenses. To a computer user, a Trojan horse is a seemingly useful program that when activated performs a malicious or illicit action, such as destroying files.

In this section the focus is on threats to, and protection of, Web clients. In Chapter 8 we provide recommendations for protecting Web servers from script exploits.

Java Applets

Java is a programming language developed by Sun Microsystems that has a number of features that make it well suited for use on the Web. Small self-contained Java programs, called *Java applets*, can be run on most client Web browsers. For example, Netscape Navigator and many versions of Microsoft's Internet Explorer support Java applets.

Java applets are referenced inside a Web page from an APPLET tag. The tag is used to load Java source code files. The Java source code is run through a client-side engine or *Java Virtual Machine* (VM). Java VMs exist for most operating systems, including UNIX, Macintosh, and Windows.

Note   The Microsoft Windows XP operating system does not ship with a Java VM, which means it doesn't support Java applets. You need to download a Java VM before you can see Java applets in Windows XP.

Unfortunately, an attacker could use a Java applet to compromise client systems. To protect yourself and your organization from Java applet exploits, you can disable Java support on your system. Most widely used Web browsers (including Netscape and Internet Explorer) allow you to disable Java.

JavaScript

Netscape Corporation created JavaScript, a scripting language that shares many of the same structures and features of Java. However, Java and JavaScript were developed separately and are treated as two independent languages.

Most Web browsers, including Netscape and Internet Explorer, support JavaScript. JavaScript is typically embedded inside a Hypertext Markup Language (HTML) page and read by a client browser. A SCRIPT tag inside HTML coding is used to note the use of JavaScript. JavaScript is commonly used to communicate with other components (such as CGI programs, described later) or to accept user input.

Note   JavaScript can be used to open Java applets. For example, JavaScript and Java applets might be used to create mortgage calculators, interactive maps, surveys, and much more.

An attacker could use JavaScript to compromise client systems. For example, there is a JavaScript exploit for Internet Explorer that can open up a command prompt window on a computer running Windows 2000 or Microsoft Windows Me. Such a script could be used in conjunction with additional code to send commands to the command prompt window that could potentially delete files, download viruses, or cause some other harm.

To protect yourself and your organization from malicious JavaScripts, you can disable JavaScript on your client Web browsers, as shown in Figure 6-2. Although disabling JavaScript can protect you from malicious code, it also disables useful active content. However, you can selectively enable JavaScript when visiting Web sites with useful applets that you trust. If you choose to enable JavaScript, you should keep up with the latest software patches for your client Web browser.

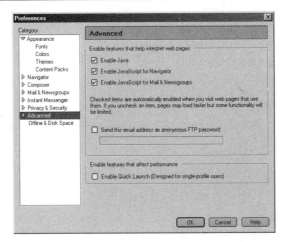

Figure 6-2.   Java and JavaScript settings in Netscape Navigator

ActiveX

As previously mentioned, ActiveX components also provide dynamic content. ActiveX is a Microsoft technology targeted for Internet Explorer. Many versions of Internet Explorer support both ActiveX and JavaScript. Like JavaScript, ActiveX components (or controls) can communicate with other applications, receive user input, and provide useful application services to users. Also like JavaScript, ActiveX controls can be used to exploit a client system.

Internet Explorer is the only browser that currently supports ActiveX. To help protect systems from ActiveX exploits, Internet Explorer allows you to selectively control downloading and running of ActiveX controls, as shown in Figure 6-3. You can configure Internet Explorer to automatically download, prompt you for downloading, or disable the downloading of ActiveX components.

If you allow and use ActiveX controls, you should monitor vendor Web sites and security alert services for information about possible exploits. If you find out that a certain ActiveX control is vulnerable to an exploit, you should consider uninstalling it until a security patch is provided.

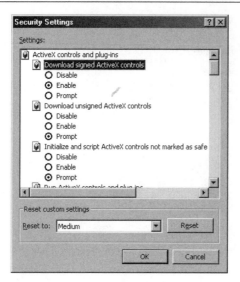

Figure 6-3.   ActiveX settings in Internet Explorer

More Info   For information on how to remove an ActiveX control, see Microsoft Knowledge Base article Q154850, "How to Remove an ActiveX Control in Windows." Use the search feature at *http://support.microsoft.com* to locate the article by searching for Q154850.

Signing Active Content

In an effort to increase the security of dynamic content, some vendors have implemented processes to check for digital signatures before active content is installed. Active content creators are expected to digitally sign their active content before posting it for download. Content developers can obtain digital certificates for signing their applications from a third-party certificate authority such as Verisign or Thawte. The digital signature helps to ensure that the content is authentic and comes from a trustworthy vendor.

Microsoft employs a technology called *Authenticode* in Internet Explorer to check for digital signatures before downloading ActiveX components. Sun Microsystems has created a Java plug-in that works in Internet Explorer and Netscape to check for digital signatures before downloading Java applets. Signing active content increases security in several ways, including the following:

- Users are notified in a pop-up dialog box that an applet or control is about to be installed.

- The digital signature of the component is matched to the service provider, so that clients can verify they are downloading the control from the correct service provider (and not an attacker-modified control that could do terrible things to their systems).
- The user is given a chance to cancel the installation of the ActiveX control through a pop-up dialog box.

Although the signed active content increases security in the ways mentioned earlier, it does not protect the user from what the actual component or applet can do or new security holes it might introduce. Therefore, it's important that you keep up with security alerts and security patches from the vendors from which you download active content.

Cookies

A *cookie* is a small amount of data that a Web server stores about a user on the user's own computer. For example, a cookie might be used to record different advertisements that a client browser has loaded. This enables the Web server to display different advertisements (instead of showing the same advertisement repeatedly).

Client browsers must allow servers to store cookies on them. Most client browsers do allow this because cookies are so widely used and many sites do not function properly if cookie support is disabled. Cookies are stored in different locations, depending on the Web browser. For example, Netscape stores cookies in a file named Cookies.txt, Opera stores them in a Cookies.dat file, and Internet Explorer stores each cookie as a separate file in the *%windir%*\Temporary Internet Files directory by default.

Cookies can be used for many different reasons. For example, some cookies are used simply to store user preferences when they connect to a Web site. Other cookies are used to maintain state information (status of the connection between client and server, described in RFC 2965). Some servers also use cookies for client authentication purposes. Unfortunately, cookies can also be used to compromise Web clients and servers in the following ways:

- An attacker could use a program such as Telnet to send a client browser any type of cookie the hacker wants. If a Web server relies on the information in the cookie to control access or services, the attacker could potentially formulate a cookie that bypasses that access control.

- Cookies can be manipulated or stolen. An attacker can use cookies to acquire inappropriate information about network users, the organization, or the security of the internal network.

- Attackers could use *script injection* (placing a script on the client's computer) to redirect cookies to the attacker's system. Hackers might also just eavesdrop on the connection reading cookies.

More Info   To learn more about cookie exploitation and management tools visit the following Web sites: *http://www.codeproject.com*, *http://www.kburra.com*, *http://www.peacefire.org*, and *http://www.digizen-security.com.*

To protect your organization and clients from cookie exploits consider the following advice:

- Do not configure a Web server to rely on information stored in a client's cookie to control access to resources or provide any additional services that could be used to exploit your Web server.

- Try not to store sensitive information, such as authentication credentials or bank account codes, in cookies.

- If you must store sensitive information in a cookie, use SSL/TLS to protect the information inside the cookie. This should help prevent the information from being intercepted and exploited by an attacker.

CGI

CGI programs are commonly used on Web servers to produce dynamic content. CGI is a specification for transferring information between an application and a Web server. For example, CGIs are frequently used to perform data input, search, and retrieval functions on databases. CGI programs can be written in any programming language or format, such as C, C++, Visual Basic, Fortran, PERL, TCL, UNIX shell script, or AppleScript.

CGI programs can be targets of attack and avenues for exploiting your Web server. Unlike JavaScript or ActiveX controls, which run on client browsers, CGI programs run on the Web server. Just like any other program, a CGI program might contain security holes that allow an attacker to access your network or its systems. CGIs are typically a target for attackers because they are frequently used on public (Internet-facing) Web servers. Here are some exploits an attacker might try against your CGI applications:

- Running the CGI program over and over again from multiple Web browsers. Each time a CGI program runs, a new process (executing program) is started. This can tie up the Web server's system resources, causing it to slow down considerably.

- Exploiting default CGI programs that ship with Web servers. Many Web server products come with sample programs. If a sample program wasn't written with security in mind, an attacker could use it to exploit your Web server.

- Exploiting free or popularly available CGI programs. Attackers often study popular programs for security holes.

- Sending bogus data to CGI programs in an attempt to compromise the applications.

- Exploiting *hidden fields* within your CGI programs. Hidden fields are sometimes used to pass data between CGI applications through the client browser. The browser itself never displays the data (hence the name hidden field). However, the client could potentially read the hidden field as it is passed and modify the information as it is returned to the server.

- Using *server-side includes* (SSIs) to compromise scripts. SSIs can allow one document to be inserted into another. In addition, data can be fed into or out of another program if SSI is enabled where programs are stored. Attackers might be able to use SSI to compromise your scripts.

More Info   Check The World Wide Web Security FAQ maintained by the World Wide Web Consortium (W3C) at *http://www.w3.org/Security/Faq* for more information on potential Web server exploits.

For your Web server to be able to run CGI programs, you must allow the Web server read and execute permissions to your CGI directory. Be sure not to allow write permissions to this directory, because an attacker could use that permission to load a malicious CGI program to that directory and run it to compromise your Web server.

To protect your Web server and network from compromise from an attack involving CGI programs, consider implementing the following tips:

- Limit the use of CGI programs. CGI programs increase the workload of your Web server, which can cause it to respond slowly. Wherever possible, limit the use of CGI programs.

- Limit CGI programs to specific directories. This way you can control security permissions on those directories. Restrict access to those directories by configuring the fewest permissions possible for the fewest user accounts.

- Configure CGI programs to run as the least privileged user possible.

- Remove all default and sample programs from your Web server.

- Check all CGI applications for security holes, especially if they are free or popularly available. Only use CGI applications that are thoroughly tested and quality checked.

- Don't trust client applications to submit properly formatted data or the correct amount of data. Attackers might try to transmit bogus data or more data than you expect to exploit your CGI application. The CGI application must check the data returned and reject the data if it is invalid, too long, or improperly formatted.

- Don't trust a client-side script (JavaScript, for example) to protect CGI applications from improperly formatted data. If you allow a client-side application to preprocess data for your CGI program, an attacker might find a way around the preprocessor. For instance, the attacker might try sending data directly to the CGI application through another client application like Telnet. Don't trust preprocessing; ensure that the CGI application checks its own received data.

- Disable SSI. If your Web server must support SSI, turn them off on your script directories.

More Info   For additional tips on securing CGI applications, visit the National Center for Supercomputing Applications (NCSA) Web site at *http://hoohoo.ncsa. uiuc.edu* and read about writing secure CGI scripts.

Instant Messaging

Instant messaging (IM) is a popular method by which people communicate today. IM allows people to send pop-up messages, files, audio, and video between computers. IM programs are easy to download and install, but many IM applications present a significant security risk to users, networks, and organizations. Common problems with many IM applications include the following:

- Unencrypted data transfer. People often send what they consider confidential or private information using IM, such as user names, passwords, or trade secrets. However, many popular IM applications transfer unencrypted data that can be easily collected and read by attackers with protocol analyzers. Msgsnarf (included with dsniff) allows for the interception of IM messages.

- Transferred files might bypass virus scanners. Many IM applications allow users to transfer files directly. This often prevents virus scanners configured on the e-mail gateway from detecting viruses because the virus is in a file that was not transferred through e-mail.

- Attackers could exploit IM vulnerabilities, such as buffer overflows. Like other applications, IM applications could have security holes, but these security holes are potentially more dangerous than those in other applications because connections are made directly from user to user through IM. If one of the IM users is an attacker, a security hole in IM can be exploited immediately. Problems were found in at least one IM application that allowed attackers to gain remote control of other IM users' computers.

- Attackers could attempt to trick people into divulging private information or running malicious programs. A persuasive attacker might convince a user to perform an unsafe action during a chat session. This type of attack is called *social engineering* because the attacker uses a social situation (human interaction) to compromise your network or organizational security.

Some organizations protect themselves from potential IM application exploits by prohibiting the use of IM. Other organizations allow the use of IM, but define an IM application that they can support and secure. If removing IM completely from your organization's network is not an option, consider taking the following actions to secure IM:

- Restrict the types of IM that are authorized for use. This prevents you from having to support, secure, and stay abreast of the security exploits of multiple types of IM applications.

- If the data transmitted between IM clients should be private, obtain an IM application that encrypts communication. Some IM products allow you to implement PKI encryption, audit usage, and configure security settings centrally.

- Create a written policy regarding the acceptable use of IM applications. Consider prohibiting the downloading of files over IM to protect your network users from potentially unsafe content.

- Educate users on the dangers of IM. Explain that dangerous files might be transferred over IM. Also, tell them that attackers could try to get them to divulge confidential information.

- Ensure that all IM users have updated virus scanners and that they use them.

- Monitor IM vendor alerts and general security alerts for the discovery of security holes. Test and apply all vendor security patches immediately.

- Internally (and between systems on trusted partner networks), you could use virtual private network (VPN) solutions to encrypt network traffic between hosts.

- Install and configure an IM server, such as Microsoft Exchange Server 2000, for internal-only IM.

Note   Top Secret Messenger and Message Inspector are two products that address IM security issues.

Exercise 1: Application Security Solutions

Match the security issues in the left column with the products or specifications that address those issues in the right column:

1. E-mail forgery
2. Clear text e-mail
3. Sniffing Web connection packets
4. Clear text IM
5. Buffer overflows
6. Cleartext cookie transmission

a. PKI-enabled IM applications
b. Secure coding practices
c. PGP
d. SSL/TLS
e. S/MIME
f. Security patches

Lesson Review

The following questions are intended to reinforce key information presented in this lesson. If you are unable to answer a question, review the lesson and then try the question again. Answers to the questions can be found in Appendix A, "Questions and Answers."

1. How might you secure communications between a Web browser and client?

2. What is a software developer's defense against buffer overflows? How should a security administrator handle buffer overflows?

3. What type of CGI exploits do attackers look for?

4. What types of security issues can arise from cookies?

5. What problems does signing active content seek to solve? What security issues might still exist in signed content?

Lesson Summary

- SSL/TLS can be used to protect Web communications by encrypting them. SSL/TLS can also be used to identify and authenticate clients securely and protect the transfer of passwords across the Internet.

- Active content is frequently used on the Internet to provide value-added services. Unfortunately, active content might be used to exploit systems. Users who interact with malicious active content might run programs that harm their systems and others on the network. To protect your organization from active content exploits, consider disabling the processing of active content. You should also warn network users of the potential for exploits.

- Buffer overflows occur when an application receives more data than it was designed to handle in its buffer. A buffer that overflows could negatively affect other applications. Buffer overflows are frequently found and exploited by attackers. To protect your organization from buffer overflows, ensure that your developers use secure coding practices. As a security administrator, apply all security fixes as they are made available.

- Cookies are sometimes used to store authentication information or other private data. Cookies can be stolen and packet sniffed during transfers. To improve the security of cookie data, use SSL/TLS encryption. Limit or prevent the use of cookies for authentication or private information.

- CGI programs that are not created using secure coding practices are likely to have vulnerabilities. Buffer overflows are one of the most commonly exploited vulnerabilities of CGI applications. To secure CGI applications, ensure that they are developed using secure coding practices. On your Web server, you should remove all unused CGI applications. Also, inspect all CGI applications for security flaws.

- Instant messaging (IM) programs typically transfer messages in cleartext between hosts. These communications can easily be intercepted and read by attackers with protocol analyzers. Further, buffer overflow security exploits have been discovered in several popular IM applications. Be sure to test and apply all security patches as soon as they are made available by software vendors.

Lesson 3: File Transfer

There are many different protocols and utilities for transferring information over computer networks. In this lesson you learn about several file transfer and sharing methods and how to secure them. In some cases, the answer to securing these file sharing methods is to completely disable or remove them. In other cases, you'll learn specific actions to take to make file sharing more secure. In most of this lesson the focus is placed on securing file transfer programs for client operating systems. In Chapter 8, specific recommendations for securing file servers are covered.

After this lesson, you will be able to

- Protect file transfers from packet sniffing
- Protect your network from security issues related to file-sharing software

Estimated lesson time: 15 minutes

FTP Client Security Issues

FTP, described in RFC 959, is one of the first protocols used for sharing information on the Internet. Most operating systems that include the TCP/IP protocol also include FTP client software. FTP is client/server software that allows clients to download and upload files. The FTP server is used to store files and control access to those files.

There are two basic types of FTP servers: those that require authentication and those that allow *anonymous FTP*. FTP servers that use authentication require users to supply user names and passwords. Anonymous FTP servers do not require authentication and instead have users log on as "anonymous" and then enter their e-mail address as the password.

One of the major security issues with FTP client/server communications is that it is typically unencrypted. This means that a protocol analyzer, as shown in Figure 6-4, could easily capture passwords.

Figure 6-4. FTP packet captures

Figure 6-4 illustrates an anonymous FTP logon exchange. However, a simple packet capture utility can be used to compromise a standard FTP password transmission. However, FTP password transmissions typically transmit using multiple network packets, one character at a time. Further, the files transferred over FTP can also be decoded packet-by-packet and reassembled by attackers with protocol analyzers.

To protect your FTP client/server communications from password sniffing, consider using some type of encryption between them. One solution is to implement a VPN connection between the FTP client and server. Another option is to implement an FTP client and server that support encryption. The following sections cover Secure FTP and Kerberized FTP.

Secure FTP

Secure FTP (SFTP, S/FTP, or S-FTP) supports SSL/TLS encryption for FTP communications. SSL/TLS encryption protects the transfer of the password and all data between the client and server. Both the FTP client and FTP server must have SFTP software to enable encrypted authentication and file transfers. Further, because SSL is used, a CA is required to issue a certificate to the client and server.

SFTP software is available for all major operating systems. Many versions of SFTP are part of secure shell (SSH) software. In addition to SFTP, SSH provides encrypted versions of many remote administration utilities typically associated with administering UNIX systems. Many versions of the UNIX and Linux operating systems come with SSH and SFTP; other operating systems, such as those from Microsoft and Apple, might require additional client software.

More Info   More information and examples of SFTP software are available from Glub Tech at *http://www.glub.com/products*. For more information on SSH, see SSH Communications Security Corporation's Web site at *http://www.ssh.com* and the OpenSSH Web site at *http://www.openssh.com*.

Kerberized FTP

Kerberized FTP is based on the Kerberos protocol developed by the Massachusetts Institute of Technology (MIT). Kerberos is a secure asymmetric encryption method that is used to encrypt client/server authentication. Kerberized FTP provides secure authentication between the FTP client and server and it also encrypts file transfers. To use Kerberized FTP, both the FTP client and FTP server must be Kerberized.

More Info   To learn more about Kerberized FTP, visit the MIT Web site Help section on Kerberized FTP at *http://web.mit.edu*.

File Sharing

Many client operating systems are capable of sharing files on the network. The *Server Message Block* (SMB) and *Network File System* (NFS) are two of the most popular file-sharing protocols. These protocols often ship as part of popular operating systems such as Microsoft Windows, UNIX, and Linux. Unfortunately many client systems are compromised because users are often unaware that these protocols are enabled. In the following sections you'll learn how to disable SMB and NFS file sharing if it was inadvertently enabled on a client system.

More Info   For information on securing an NFS or SMB file server, see Chapter 8.

File sharing is not limited only to preinstalled protocols. Some users intentionally download and install file-sharing software that is often used to trade copyrighted software. Often, this file-sharing software can provide a method for users to download potentially harmful software. Such software is typically categorized as file-trading software. In the following section you'll learn more about the many different types of file-trading software that can pose security risks to your network.

SMB File Sharing

SMB is a file-sharing protocol often used for sharing resources in Microsoft networks. The revised version of SMB is called Common Internet File System (CIFS). Although SMB and CIFS are convenient ways for people to share files on a network, these shares are often exploitable targets for attackers. Network users might enable SMB file sharing and not realize the potential security consequences of doing so. There are many tools available for exploiting these file shares that are not properly secured.

In Microsoft operating systems, SMB/CIFS is enabled and disabled through a service called Microsoft File and Printer Sharing, as shown in Figure 6-5.

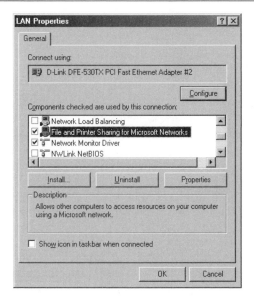

Figure 6-5.   SMB file sharing in Microsoft Windows 2000

Other operating systems such as UNIX, NetWare, and Linux can also use SMB and CIFS for file sharing. These non-Microsoft operating systems typically require an additional SMB file-sharing program, such as Samba. Samba is free software that is often included in distributions of UNIX and Linux operating systems. To disable SMB file sharing on non-Microsoft clients, disable the Samba service. The directions for doing so vary greatly depending on the operating system you are using, so consult the operating system's documentation for specific details.

Note   You can find out more about SMB/CIFS auditing and attack utilities at *http://www.atstake.com* and *http://www.nai.com*. Examples of these utilities are SMBCapture, SMBRelay, and SMB Grind.

NFS File Sharing

NFS is a file-sharing protocol developed by Sun Microsystems for UNIX-based operating systems. There are versions of NFS for non-UNIX operating systems, such as those from Novell and Microsoft. NFS allows network users to share files and access files shared on other NFS systems. Unfortunately, there are many possible security exploits that can be used to attack systems using NFS. Many users are unaware that they are sharing files over NFS.

To disable NFS file sharing on UNIX-based operating systems, look for the /Etc/ Exports file, where NFS shared directories are listed. If you clear out all entries in that file, all sharing is disabled. Further, you can disable the NFS daemon. Steps to disable NFS file sharing in other operating systems vary, so check the software vendor's documentation for specific directions.

File-Trading Programs

There are many file-trading programs available, many of which are used to illegally trade copyrighted software, which is a concern of many organizations. The file-trading programs can also be used to spread Trojan horse software. For example, the file-trading user might think he or she is downloading a screen-saver program for Windows, but instead the software is a virus.

In most cases there is no legitimate use for file-trading programs on organizational networks. Often, such programs increase network utilization and decrease productivity. To protect your organization from exploits that might arise from file-trading programs (in addition to potential liabilities that might come from copyright violations) you should create a policy restricting or prohibiting the use of file-trading utilities. Further, you should remove all unnecessary file-trading programs from the computers in your organization and prevent them from being installed. Many centralized software management systems and individual operating systems allow you to prevent users from installing software.

Lesson Review

The following questions are intended to reinforce key information presented in this lesson. If you are unable to answer a question, review the lesson and then try the question again. Answers to the questions can be found in Appendix A, "Questions and Answers."

1. What are the main security concerns of client/server FTP communications?

2. How can you mitigate the security concerns regarding FTP?

3. What are some of the dangers of using file-trading utilities?

Lesson Summary

- Standard FTP is not encrypted and consequently authentication and file transfers are not encrypted. This means that anyone with a protocol analyzer could potentially read user names, passwords, and the files transferred over this protocol.

- To protect your FTP client/server communications from packet sniffing, you can implement Secure FTP or Kerberized FTP, which encrypt FTP communications.

- File-trading utilities could pose a significant security risk to many organizations. They are often used to transfer copyrighted material from user to user. Further, these utilities can be used to circulate Trojan horse software.

- The best protection against security issues related to file-trading utilities is to prohibit their use and remove them from all systems on the network.

C H A P T E R   7

User Security

About This Chapter

In this chapter, you apply the information covered in previous chapters to create a user security strategy that provides a way to authenticate users and manage their access to files, folders, and services.

Before You Begin

The prerequisites for this chapter are Chapter 1, "General Networking and Security Concepts," Chapter 3, "Certificate Basics," and Chapter 4, "Network Infrastructure Security."

Lesson 1: Understanding Authentication

For the security specialist of a company, authenticating users is a significant challenge. For example, you might have to manage multiple users accessing resources from the same computer, or users accessing networked resources. Every time a user gains access to your company's computers, network, or resources, you must ensure that the user is permitted to access those resources. To do this, you must incorporate an authentication method into the process of providing access to resources.

After this lesson, you will be able to
- Describe different types of authentication
- Describe Kerberos authentication
- Discuss implications of combining authentication methods

Estimated lesson time: 35 minutes

Authentication requires a user to provide some proof or credential that represents something they know, something they have, or something they are before allowing access to your company's resources. Examples of each of these categories include the following:

- **Something you know.**   A password or personal identification number (PIN)
- **Something you have.**   A smart card or other physical object
- **Something you are.**   A thumbprint or other biometrics

The authentication process can be a one-way process, where only the user's credentials are authenticated, or a mutual authentication process, in which both the user and the resource authenticate to each other. To require strong authentication, you must understand what authentication methods are available, their strengths and weaknesses, and how to combine those methods to provide strong authentication.

User Name and Password Authentication

User name and password authentication are common methods used to validate that people are who they say they are. With this, a user is typically presented with a dialog box and must provide his or her user name and password. The user name is typically visible on the screen and is handled as cleartext, whereas the password is typically masked on the screen and is encrypted.

- If the authentication is performed locally, for instance when a user logs on to a stand-alone computer, there could be a process running that intercepts or records the user name and password. This could provide a hacker with the information needed to gain access to a single computer or your entire network.

■ If the authentication process is centralized, for instance when a user logs on to a network, then the user name and password are sent to a different computer that is responsible for authenticating users and providing them credentials that can be used to access networked resources available on that network.

When possible, you should require the user to have a user name and complex password rather than a simple password, and it should be enforced by the operating system or network operating system in use. Examples of a simple password include a person's first name, last name, birthday, phone number, or a common word. Although these might appear to be difficult to guess, using today's computing technology, they can be broken quickly. As described in Chapter 4, a complex password includes uppercase, lowercase, and numeric characters, symbols, and punctuation. Even when numbers are used to replace letters, there are modified dictionary password-cracking programs available that can replace standard characters with common symbols and numbers and then run against a password. For example, if you want to use a password like football and choose footba11, a password-cracking program may quickly decipher your password because it involves a simple replacement. However, the password Pho0tB@!1 is much more difficult for a password-cracking program to decipher.

Caution   Because example passwords are often added to password-cracking programs, you should not use any passwords you see printed in this or any other publication.

Although you can force a user to set a difficult password and require the user to memorize the password (as opposed to writing it down), the user might feel the password is too difficult to remember and will write it down on a piece of paper located near his or her desk or under the keyboard. Some best practices to enforce with passwords include the following:

■ Force the users to have passwords that include uppercase and lowercase letters, symbols, and punctuation. Do not allow passwords that are all alphabetic or numeric characters.

■ Force the users to change passwords every 30 to 42 days. If it appears that a password has been compromised, force the user to change the password immediately. For example, if a single user account is used to log on to multiple workstations simultaneously or within a short time interval, you might suspect that the account is compromised. Other potential indications that a user account is compromised include logons at unusual hours, attempts to access restricted resources, and multiple connections to resources that a user would not typically utilize.

- Do not allow users to use the same password again. If available, enable the histories function for passwords and do not allow the user to use the same password for at least five times. The longer the history the better. This, in concert with not allowing the user to change passwords too often, deters a user from quickly cycling through passwords to use the same one.

- Create a policy that does not allow users to write their passwords down. This is a written policy and cannot be enforced programmatically, but, if tied to disciplinary actions, it can deter users from recording their passwords.

- Create a policy that does not allow users to share their passwords with anyone, including help desk personnel. This policy cannot be enforced programmatically, but, if tied to disciplinary actions, it can also deter users.

- Provide user education on social engineering (discussed in Chapter 11, "Incident Detection and Response"), strong password creation, and the network security breaches that can occur if written policies are not followed.

- Create and follow well-defined policies for verifying the identity of a user before resetting his or her password. To prevent a hacker from pretending to be a user and getting the password reset to attack the network with the user's account, use a process to validate the identity of the user. For example, you might call the user's manager to verify the request before changing the password.

Kerberos Authentication

Kerberos is a network authentication protocol that provides strong authentication for client/server applications by using symmetric key cryptography. Kerberos is designed to provide a single sign-on to a heterogeneous environment. Because most operating systems are capable of communicating across a network and support Kerberos authentication, and Kerberos is scalable enough to operate on the Internet, it can be used as an authentication mechanism on the Internet and in other heterogeneous environments. Kerberos allows mutual authentication and encrypted communication between users and services; therefore, it can be used over public communications mediums.

The Kerberos authentication process is more stringent than using a user name and password for authentication. When a user signs onto the local operating system, a local agent (process) sends an authentication request to the Kerberos server. The server responds by sending the encrypted credentials for the user attempting to sign onto the system. The local agent then tries to decrypt the credentials using the user-supplied password. If the correct password has been supplied, the user is validated and given authentication tickets, which allow the user to access other Kerberos-authenticated services. In addition to the tickets, the user is also given a set of cipher keys that can be used to encrypt all data sessions. The following are some definitions that are used in subsequent explanations:

- **Realm.**   An organizational boundary that is formed to provide authentication boundaries. Each realm has an authentication server (AS) and a ticket-granting server (TGS). Together the AS and TGS form a Key Distribution Center (KDC). All services and users in the realm receive tickets from the TGS and are authenticated with the AS. This provides a single source of authority to register and authenticate with. Realms can trust one another, providing the capability to scale Kerberos authentication.

- **Authentication server (AS).**   In a Kerberos realm, the AS is the server that registers all valid users (clients) and services in the realm. The AS provides each client a ticket-granting ticket (TGT) that is used to request a ticket from a TGS.

- **Ticket-granting server (TGS).**   To minimize the workload of the AS in a Kerberos realm, the TGS grants the session tickets used by clients to start a session with a service. The client must use the TGT issued by the AS to request a session ticket from a TGS.

- **Cross-realm authentication.**   Cross-realm authentication is the capability of users in one realm to be authenticated and access services in another realm. This is accomplished by the user's realm registering a remote ticket-granting server (RTGS) on the realm of the service. Rather than having each realm authenticate with each other, cross-realm authentication can be configured in a hierarchical fashion. This eases authentication for the AS and TGS, but might force the client to contact several RTGSs to access a service.

- **Remote ticket-granting server (RTGS).**   An RTGS performs the same tasks as a TGS, but for a remote realm (a realm the user is not associated with). To do this, the TGS in the realm the user is in must register with the TGS of the realm of the service the user is accessing (the RTGS).

- **Ticket.**   A ticket is a block of data that allows users to prove their identity to a service. Each ticket is stored in a ticket cache on the user's local computer and is time stamped, so after a given amount of time (typically 10 hours), the ticket expires and is no longer valid. Limiting the length of time a ticket is valid reduces the chances of a hacker obtaining a ticket and being able to use it for unauthorized access.

- **Ticket cache.**   A ticket cache is a portion of memory that stores all of a user's Kerberos tickets. This cache is separate from the cache of the application that is using the ticket. With the tickets in their own cache, users need only provide their credentials once per session, even if several applications are using that ticket to access a service.

- **Ticket-granting ticket (TGT).**   A TGT is a ticket that is granted as part of the Kerberos authentication process and is stored in the ticket cache. The TGT is used to obtain other tickets that are specific to a service. For instance, if a user wanted to gain access to a specific service, his or her TGT would be used in a negotiation process to get the additional ticket. Each service requires its own ticket.

- **Authenticators.**   A series of bits, a symbol, or a group of symbols that are inserted into a transmission or message in a predetermined manner and are then used for validation. Authenticators are typically valid for five minutes. This is similar to the use of a cookie for being authenticated on a Web site. An authenticator can only be used once. This help prevents someone from intercepting an authenticator and then reusing it.

- **Principal.**   A principal is any unique entity to which Kerberos can assign tickets.

Because Kerberos is a single sign-on environment, the tickets issued by the Kerberos server provide the credentials required to access additional network resources. This means that although the user is still required to remember his or her password, he or she only needs one password to access all systems on the network to which he or she has been granted access.

In addition to using Kerberos for authentication, it is possible to configure Kerberos to encrypt, thereby ensuring communication between authenticated hosts. Kerberos is implemented by a KDC, which contains the information that allows Kerberos clients to authenticate. The information is contained in a database that makes single sign-on possible. The KDC's database does not work in the same manner as many other databases.

In Kerberos, all network information (data about users, services, and hosts) is stored in the Kerberos database. This database contains the public keys of all principles. Any sensitive information, such as passwords, always stays on the KDC and the client. The KDC and the client establish trust relationships using public key cryptography. The trust relationship allows the KDC to then determine exactly which services a host and user can access.

Figures 7-1 and 7-2 show a simplified view of the Kerberos authentication process. As shown in figure 7-1,

1. When the user logs on to a system, the client (user) sends a registration request to an AS.

2. The AS authenticates the client and provides the client with a TGT, which is valid for a fixed amount of time.

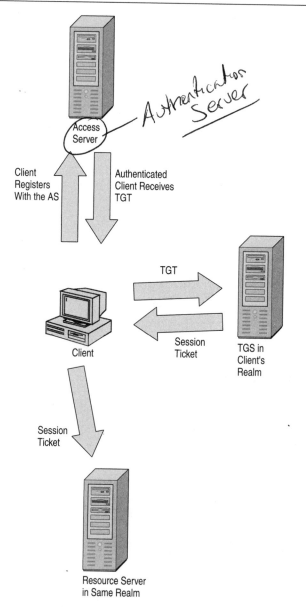

Figure 7-1.   Kerberos authentication process in the same realm

When accessing services in the same realm (Figure 7-1), the following takes place:

1. The client contacts a TGS and requests a session ticket to access the service using its TGT.

2. The client then accesses the service using the ticket the TGS provided.

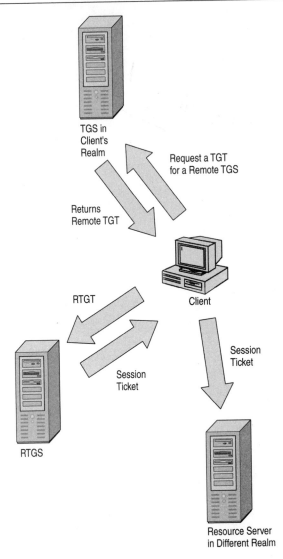

Figure 7-2. Kerberos authentication process in a different realm

When accessing services in a different realm (Figure 7-2), the following takes place:

1. The client contacts a TGS and requests a TGT for the remote realm.
2. The client contacts the RTGS and requests a session ticket to access the remote service. The client uses the remote TGT to request a session ticket to access the remote service.

Note   The client computer clock and clocks on the other servers must be somewhat accurate. The tickets that are granted are only valid for a certain amount of time, so if the clocks on the various computers are off by too much, the client tickets might not be able to be validated.

When a Kerberos client first obtains a ticket from the KDC, the token does not provide access to any particular process or network service. It is simply a token that informs other hosts that the KDC has authenticated this host, so this host and user can request services from other hosts. If the ticket and password match, then a session key is established and a credential cache is created. After the credential cache file is populated with the ticket, the host and user can use it to actually log on to hosts and request services. However, the service or host name must be contained in the Kerberos database, or access is denied.

Mutual Authentication

The term *mutual authentication* refers to the need for both the recipient and provider of a service to authenticate themselves to each other. Mutual authentication must be completed before the service can be provided. This assures the service that the user is who he or she claims to be and assures the user that he or she is connecting to the expected service. Kerberos allows a service to authenticate a recipient so that access to the service is protected. It also allows a service recipient to authenticate the service provider so that there is protection against rogue services.

In addition to a server authenticating a user and a user authenticating a client, there is the mutual authentication option of a client and a server trusting a third party, such as a certificate authority.

Certificates

Certificates provide the third-party trust in a mutual authentication scheme. A certificate is simply a block of data containing information used to identify a user. Information in the certificate includes the user's public key, information about the user, dates for which the certificate is valid, information about the issuer of a certificate, and a signature generated by the certificate issuer.

A signature can be generated using a private key over a block of data to produce another block of data known as the signature. The generator of this signature using the private key is referred to as the signer. This signature can only be decrypted using the public key of the signer, thus providing assurance in the identity of the signer.

A certificate is signed by a third-party certification authority (CA) so that if that CA says that the associated public key in the certificate is yours, any service you request can be assured that the public key is indeed yours and not from a hacker.

Certificates are typically requested from a certificate server at the site of a CA. To request a certificate, you send a certificate signing request (CSR) to the CA's certificate server, along with some other information to identify yourself. The information required is determined by the CA, and it varies from CA to CA. The CA staff then processes your CSR and generates a public and private key pair for you if they grant your request. They will most likely send you a public key over e-mail, but they should require that you retrieve your private key from them using some secure means, such as a secure Web connection download.

Remote Authentication with CHAP

Challenge Handshake Authentication Protocol (CHAP) is a protocol that can be used when a remote client needs to authenticate itself to a network server or when two routers need to authenticate themselves to each other to begin a Point-to-Point Protocol (PPP) session. CHAP avoids transmission of the actual password on the established connection. The authentication process used by CHAP involves a three-way handshake in which the network access server (NAS) sends a challenge to the client consisting of the session ID and a random string of data to the remote client.

The remote client uses a Message Digest 5 (MD5) function hash to return the following information:

- The user name
- An encrypted challenge
- A session ID
- A password

Note   As discussed in Chapter 3, MD5 takes the variable-length string of data (the information just listed), and produces a 128-bit message digest that is used for validation.

CHAP protects against replay attacks by using an arbitrary challenge string for each authentication attempt and protects against remote client impersonation by sending repeated challenges at unpredictable intervals to the remote client throughout the duration of the connection.

Tokens

A *token* is a device that can be issued to a user for use in the authentication process. For example, there are token devices that, when enabled, synchronize with a server. Each minute the numbers in the server and on the device change to a predetermined number, as long as the battery in the device is working. For a user to authenticate, he or she must type in the number on the display, which must match the number in the server for the user to be authenticated.

Tokens are often small handheld devices, with or without keypads, that can range in size from a credit card to a small pocket calculator. Among other forms, they can be smart cards with small computer chips in them, requiring a reader when used with a PC. One type of authentication process used with hardware tokens involves a challenge-response process:

1. Enter your user name at a workstation and send it to the authentication server.
2. The server responds with a challenge to the token.
3. You reply using the token (or information provided by the token).
4. The server validates the information you provided and authenticates you.

Tokens are difficult to duplicate and are generally tamper resistant. Some can be carried with you for use on any workstation, although others require appropriate hardware peripherals and software on a workstation. Although tokens offer reliable security, they can be costly and difficult to deploy in an enterprise environment.

Tokens can either provide a one-time-use password or store information about the user. The user information can be a certificate and a password, as with smart cards. Smart card technologies provide strong security through encryption as well as access control. Smart cards require a reader that is used when the authentication is required.

Biometrics

Biometric authentication is an automated method of identifying a person based on a physical characteristic, such as a thumbprint or the retina of his or her eye. Using this type of authentication requires comparing a registered sample against a new captured biometric sample, for example, a fingerprint captured during a logon. The biometric authentication mechanism typically has two modes, enrolling and verifying.

Enrolling

For initial use of the biometric, a system administrator must enroll each user to verify that each individual being enrolled is authorized. The enrolling process includes storing the user's biological feature that will be used later to verify the user's identity. This is typically acquired by using a sensor (hardware device) that can record the particular feature, such as a thumbprint scanner.

Verifying

For the verification process, the user has a sensor on his or her computer that can capture the same biological information that was used for enrollment and then transmit that information to the authenticating server. The server can then compare the information presented by the user with the stored information to validate the user.

Some considerations when selecting a biometric authentication method include the following:

- **Performance and reliability.**   This is not how fast the biometric device can perform the scan, but how well it performs the authentication process. Although device manufacturers provide information on the performance of their devices, the number of people used for the test and the assumptions for what environment the sensor will be used in vary. Reliability is typically determined by calculating the crossover error rate (CER), which is the point at which the false rejection rate (FRR) and false acceptance rate (FAR) are equal. The lower the CER the better. The FRR represents the percentage of authorized users who are incorrectly rejected, also called type 1 errors. The FAR represents the percentage of unauthorized users who are incorrectly identified as valid users, also called type 2 errors.

- **Difficulty.**   User education should be a consideration when selecting a biometric authentication device. If the device is too difficult to use, the user might have trouble using it for authentication. Also, it can easily take a user a few weeks to adjust to using the device, and during that time the FRR rate will be higher.

- **User capability.**   Some users might have an impairment that will not allow them to use a particular biometric device for authentication. You must provide a device that can be used by the majority of your users, and then provide an alternative device or authentication mechanism for those who cannot use the primary method.

- **Acceptance.**   You users might consider some devices too invasive. Select a solution that will be palatable to your users, preferably a noninvasive biometric with continuous authentication, such as iris recognition.

- **Cost.**   Some biometrics cost more to implement due to their complexity. Additionally, the cost of the individual scanning devices can vary greatly. For example, fingerprint-scanning devices are relatively inexpensive compared to iris scanning devices.

Note   You'll learn more about how biometric technology operates in Chapter 9, "Operational Security."

Combining Authentication Methods

To make authentication stronger, you can combine methods, often referred to as *multifactor* or *strong authentication*. The most common type is two-factor authentication, such as using a PIN code and a SecurID token to log on to your network. A good example of two-factor authentication with which you are probably familiar is an automatic teller machine (ATM) card for getting money out of a bank. You insert your card (something you have) into the ATM and enter your PIN (something you know) to access your account number and perform transactions.

Combining more than one authentication method greatly increases the difficulty a hacker will have overcoming your security. For instance, if you require only a user name and password, a hacker might be able to programmatically "guess" the correct password. If only a smart card is used and the card is lost or stolen, a hacker would be able to use that card for access.

Individually, any one of these approaches has its limitations. Something you have can be stolen, whereas something you know can be guessed, shared, or forgotten. Although something you are can be considered the strongest approach, hackers are able to spoof that information as well, and it can be costly to implement.

Some general areas of concern you should consider when determining what authentication methods you will implement include the following:

- **Risk analysis.**   Ensure that you know what the data that you are protecting is worth, what cost associated with the loss of the data will be, and what the chances are that the data will be compromised.

- **Solution evaluation.**   Make sure that before you purchase and implement an authentication solution, you evaluate the products you are considering to determine their ease of use, cost, reliability, integrity, and capabilities.

- **Resources.**   Consider the budget you have to perform the initial implementation and user education, as well as the continued costs of support.

- **Integration.**   Ensure that the solution you propose will work in your existing environment and can be supported with the current staff you have available.

- **Ability to customize.**   The products available might not solve the business problems and technical difficulties you face. Ensure that the solution you are implementing can be customized to suit your environment.

- **Cost.**   The cost of implementing the solution is only part of the total cost. Make sure to consider the additional costs of training your users and performing ongoing maintenance for the methods you are proposing.

- **Performance.**   Make sure the performance meets your expectations or that you realign the expectations of your users to match the performance your solution can deliver.

- **Accuracy.**   Ensure that the authentication solution you propose can be used to accurately authenticate authorized users. Although manufacturers provide CER, FAR, and FRR information, you might have differing results in your environment.

- **Reliability.**   Make sure that the solution you are proposing will operate for a reasonable amount of time in your environment. For instance, if the environment you work in is dirty, a thumbprint sensor might not be the best solution.

- **Maintainability.**   Before selecting a solution, determine what is required to maintain the solution. This includes product costs and the amount of time it takes to perform the maintenance.

- **Availability.**   Ensure that the solution you are implementing is available commercially. If the product is not fully developed or widely available, it might be harder and more costly to maintain your solution.

- **Upgradability.**   Technology changes quickly. Make sure the solution you implement can be upgraded as technology changes.

- **Interoperability.**   Make sure the authentication solution you provide is able to interoperate in your environment, and be aware of any environments in which the solution might not work.

- **Manufacturer reputation.**   Verify that the manufacturer is reputable and stands behind its product. Verify that the manufacturer will provide support after you purchase its products.

Most authentication systems employ cryptography; therefore a cryptographic key management system will be necessary. The vendor you purchase your solution from might provide the key management component, but the process of maintaining and distributing keys will most likely require that you maintain that system.

Because the security of a cryptographic system is directly related to the level of protection provided for the cryptographic keys, it is essential for you and the vendor to develop a system for managing these keys effectively. The host computer system will probably evolve over time through the addition of new software and hardware, and these changes might require corresponding modifications or upgrades to the authentication system to maintain compatibility.

Exercise 1: Following a Cross-Realm Authentication

In this exercise, place the steps in order as they would occur in the following scenario.

Scenario: You are a user who has authenticated in one realm and you wish to access a service registered in another realm.

1. The client contacts the RTGS and requests a session ticket to access the remote service.
2. The client contacts a TGS and requests a TGT for the remote realm.
3. The client accesses the service.
4. The AS authenticates the client and provides the client with a TGT.
5. The client (user) sends a registration request to an AS.

Exercise 2: Reviewing Kerberos Terminology

In this exercise, match the terms in the left column with the correct definitions in the right column.

a. Realm

b. Authentication server (AS)

c. Ticket-granting ticket (TGT)

d. Ticket-granting service (TGS)

e. Kerberos Distribution Center (KDC)

1. What a AS and TGS form together

2. The ticket a client receives that allows them to request session tickets

3. The service that a client requests a session ticket from

4. The service that registers a client and provides them with a TGT

5. The logical boundary that is formed by an AS and TGS

Lesson Review

1. What type of authentication does Kerberos provide?
   a. One-way authentication
   b. Mutual authentication
   c. Direct authentication
   d. Indirect authentication

2. With CHAP authentication, what information does a client return in response to a challenge? (Select all that apply)
   a. Session ID
   b. Random string of data
   c. User name
   d. Encrypted challenge
   e. Password

3. Select the answer that best describes token authentication:
   a. Something you have
   b. Something you know
   c. Something you are

4. Select the answer that best describes user name and password authentication:
   a. Something you have
   b. Something you know
   c. Something you are

5. Select the answer that best describes biometric authentication:

   a. Something you have

   b. Something you know

   c. Something you are

Lesson Summary

- Kerberos provides a method of mutual authentication that is scalable enough to support authentication across the Internet.

- A Kerberos realm is a boundary that is comprised of an AS and TGS. Together these form a KDC.

- Once a principal in a realm is granted a TGT, it is able to obtain session tickets for other realm principals.

- To access services in other realms, the TGS in each realm must form a relationship. When the principal in one realm needs access to a principal in another realm, the principal requests an RTGT from its TGS and then contacts the TGS for the other realm to request a session ticket for the remote service.

- With user name and password authentication, the user provides his or her user name and password to authenticate. This information is typically encrypted for transport to the authentication server, but if it is intercepted, it can be cracked programmatically. This type of authentication relies on something you know.

- With token-based authentication, the user is issued a device that is used for authentication. The device can be synchronized with a server with a number that changes at predetermined intervals, or it can contain user information and a certificate. This type of authentication relies on something you have.

- With biometric authentication, the user is issued a sensor that scans some physical attribute of the user and sends that information to the authenticating server. The server compares a stored sample to the sample provided by the user to validate the user's identity. This type of authentication relies on something you are.

- There are multiple authentication methods available, and the security offered by combining methods to form a multifactor authentication process is much greater than using any single authentication method.

Lesson 2: Understanding Access Control Models

Once users are authenticated on your network and the computers connected to your network, you must provide them with access to resources so they can accomplish the tasks of their job, but limit their access to provide them only access rights to what they need. This also applies to any other object that needs access to another, as when an application or process needs to interact with another. Administration of this access control requires you understand the access control models currently in use.

After this lesson, you will be able to

- Understand what discretionary access control is
- Understand what mandatory access control is
- Understand what role-based authentication is
- Understand the difference between a secure hash function, symmetric key, and asymmetric key

Estimated lesson time: 20 minutes

This lesson covers three concepts of access control:

- **Discretionary access control (DAC).**   The owner of an object (such as a process, file, or folder) manages access control at his or her own discretion.
- **Mandatory access control (MAC).**   Access to an object is restricted based on the sensitivity of the object (defined by the label that is assigned), and granted through authorization (clearance) to access that level of data.
- **Role-based access control (RBAC).**   Access is based on the role a user plays in the organization. For instance, a human resources manager would need access to information that a department manager would not need access to, and both would need access to some common information.

With DAC, the owner of an object sets the access permissions at his or her discretion, whereas with MAC and RBAC, access to the information is regulated by a formal set of rules. You need to utilize access control concepts when you are setting access to all computerized processes and files.

You apply access control in every state that information is found in your enterprise. This includes computerized data as well as hard-copy files, photographs, displays, and communication packets. You also must consider that employees travel carrying information with them. Information can be revealed through drawings, notes made while waiting for a plane, casual conversations that can be overheard, viewing the information on the employee's laptop while working in a public place. It is important that you know what is protected, as well as what is not protected. In addition, you should consider what can be protected and what is out of your control.

DAC

Discretionary access control is used by the owner of a file to restrict a user's access to that file. With DAC, an access control list (ACL) is maintained that lists the users with access and what type of access they have. ACLs can be stored as part of the file, in a file, or in a database.

You need to be aware of the many risks associated with DAC. These risks are inherent because there is no centralized administration, as each file owner controls the access level to his or her personal files. Some owners might not be security conscious, and as a result, they might either inadvertently or intentionally allow all users to modify any file they own. Some of the risks that you must be aware of and will have to mitigate include the following:

- Software might be executed or updated by unauthorized personnel.
- Confidential information might be accidentally or deliberately compromised by users who are not intended to have access.
- Auditing of file and resource accesses might be difficult.

The assumption of DAC is that the owner or administrator of the information has the knowledge, skill, and ability to limit access appropriately and control who can see or work with the information.

Managing Users with Groups

On a large network or a small one, one of your tasks when managing a secure environment is to provide users with access to the resources they need. With the number of computers on a corporate network, and the number of users that need access to networked resources, managing access control can be a challenge. To manage users in this environment, you must manage groups of users as opposed to individual users by grouping users together and assigning permissions to groups rather than individuals.

With discretionary authentication, the ACL can become quite large if individual users are added. This can become difficult to manage and can impact the overall system performance as well. In addition, as users leave or change positions, their access capabilities change. Using groups with intuitive names to populate ACLs and adding users to the groups is a better, more secure management technique.

MAC

Mandatory access control is a nondiscretionary control also known as multilevel security. You classify all users and resources and assign a security label to the classification. Access requests are denied if the requestor's security label does not match the security label of the resource. MAC is typically used only by organizations with high security requirements and clear policies and procedures, such as the military.

A classification level specifies the level of trust associated with the resource, and there are three major classification levels: top secret, confidential, and unclassified. Classification levels have an implicit level of trust with higher classifications. For example, confidential classification has an implicit trust with top secret; therefore a person with top secret access also has access to resources that are labeled as confidential.

Access is granted to the user if his or her classification is equal to or higher than the classification of the resource he or she wishes to access. MAC techniques reduce the need for you to maintain ACLs because the access decision logic is built into the classification hierarchy.

Although MAC and RBAC assume a set of formal rules, they differ in the management approach. With MAC, information is categorized according to sensitivity and not subject matter. Data about the same general subject matter can have multiple sensitivity ratings. People and processes within this type of management structure are determined by the kinds of sensitivity levels they are allowed to access.

RBAC

In role-based access control, information is categorized according to subject matter, which might reflect some sensitivity criteria inherent in the environment. Persons and processes are identified for access to the information by the role they play within the enterprise. For example, people in the budget department could access and use sensitive budget data, whereas people in other parts of the enterprise would be denied access to such information.

RBAC is an alternative to DAC and MAC, giving you the ability to specify and enforce enterprise-specific security policies in a way that maps naturally to an organization's structure. Each user is assigned one or more roles, and each role is assigned one or more privileges that are given to users in that role. You can assign a collection of users to a single role. For example, you might assign an administrative role to one or more system administrators responsible for maintaining your enterprise server.

Roles are mapped to a particular resource or a particular user group. When roles are mapped to a resource, the resource name defined in the role is verified and then it is determined if access is permitted to proceed. When roles are mapped to a group, the role group is compared with the group associated with a resource to determine whether the operation is permitted to proceed. Such role-based access control requires that a list of roles be maintained and that mappings from role to user or user group be established.

Exercise: Identifying Authentication Methods

In this exercise, match the authentication methods in the left column with the correct definitions in the right column.

a. RBAC

b. DAC

c. MAC

1. Permits the owner of an object (such as a process, file, or folder) to manage access control at his or her own discretion.

2. Access to an object is restricted based on the sensitivity of the object (defined by the label that is assigned), and granted through authorization (clearance) to access that level of data.

3. Access is based on the role a user plays in the organization.

Lesson Review

1. With discretionary access control (DAC), there is no mechanism for creating and enforcing rules regarding access control. Access is configured at the discretion of the owner of the object. (True or False?)

2. Which description best fits role-based access control (RBAC)?

   a. Access control is configured at the discretion of the object's owner.

   b. Access to an object is restricted based on the sensitivity of the object and is granted through authorization.

   c. Access is granted based on the user's role.

3. Which description best fits discretionary access control (DAC)?

   a. Access control is configured at the discretion of the object's owner.

   b. Access to an object is restricted based on the sensitivity of the object and is granted through authorization.

   c. Access is granted based on the user's role.

4. Which description best fits mandatory access control (MAC)?

   a. Access control is configured at the discretion of the object's owner.

   b. Access to an object is restricted based on the sensitivity of the object and is granted through authorization.

   c. Access is granted based on the user's role.

Lesson Summary

- Access control is the process of limiting access to systems and resources to those who require access. That access is limited to just the access permissions needed by the user to perform the tasks he or she needs to perform.

- DAC permits the owner of an object (such as a process, file, or folder) to manage access control at his or her own discretion. A security limitation with this model is that there is no mechanism for creating and enforcing rules regarding access control. The access controls are configured at the discretion of the owner of an object.

- With MAC, access to an object is restricted based on the sensitivity of the object (defined by the label that is assigned), and granted through authorization (clearance) to access that level of data.

- With RBAC, access is based on the role a user plays in the organization. For instance, a human resources manager would need access to information that a department manager would not need access to, and both would need access to some common information.

C H A P T E R   8

Security Baselines

About This Chapter

A security baseline is a set of rules or recommendations that establish a minimum acceptable security configuration. Security baselines, which are also called security benchmarks or checklists, are often presented as printed or electronic documents, but they can also be programs that evaluate system configuration. For example, the *Center for Internet Security* (CIS) has a large set of documents called security benchmarks for a variety of popular operating systems, routers, and Web servers. These documents and related tools serve as security baselines for the equipment in many organizations. This chapter examines security baselines for network devices, operating systems, applications, and different types of server configurations.

Before You Begin

This chapter assumes basic knowledge of Transmission Control Protocol/Internet Protocol (TCP/IP), as presented in Chapter 2, "TCP/IP Basics." You should also understand certificates as presented in Chapter 3, "Certificate Basics." Further, this chapter assumes that you know how to secure the network infrastructure and individual client applications as presented in Chapter 4, "Network Infrastructure Security," and Chapter 6, "Application Security." You should also understand virtual private networks (VPNs) as presented in Chapter 5, "Communications Security." Finally, you should have read about authentication, which was covered in Chapter 7, "User Security."

Lesson 1: Network Device and Operating System Hardening

Network device and operating system exploits are common and numerous. From a security standpoint, maintaining secure configurations, updating devices and operating systems, and monitoring for alerts is a continuous process. Many security professionals say that there is no such thing as a device or operating system that is 100 percent secure. If you don't already agree with that statement, you probably will after reading this book. However, you do already know that there are many steps that you can take to increase the security of your network and the devices that are part of it. In this section, you learn steps you can take to secure and maintain the security of your network devices and operating systems.

After this lesson, you will be able to

- Explain the importance of applying network device, operating system, and application updates
- Verify the integrity of security updates
- Locate and download security baseline information for various platforms
- Locate sources for security vulnerability alerts

Estimated lesson time: 60 minutes

There are many specific recommendations and guidelines available for a variety of operating systems. You can review and download security baseline information and related software tools from the following sources:

- Computer Emergency Response Team (CERT) Web site at *http://www.cert.org/tech_tips*
- CIS Web site at *http://www.cisecurity.com*
- United States National Security Agency (NSA) Web site at *http://www.nsa.gov* (see Security Recommendation Guides)
- National Information Assurance Partnership (NIAP) Web site at *http://niap.nist.gov*
- Computer Security Resource Center (CRSC) of the National Institute of Standards and Technology (NIST) Web site at *http://csrc.nist.gov*
- National Computer Security Center (NCSC) Trusted Product Evaluation Program (TPEP) at *http://www.radium.ncsc.mil/tpep*
- Microsoft Web site at *http://www.microsoft.com/technet/security/tools/Tools*

Network Device Updates

The processing logic of network devices such as routers, switches, and firewalls is typically maintained through *firmware updates*, programs that update the current processing logic (or operating system) of the device. Manufacturers often produce firmware updates to correct security issues.

Note   Basic input/output systems (BIOS) updates are also frequently available for a variety of computer hardware. Although many BIOS updates are aimed at increasing hardware support, some BIOS updates might be related to security issues.

To protect your network devices, be sure to monitor communications from the vendors of those devices for information on new security patches. You should also monitor security newsletters and alerts for information on new exploits. The CERT is probably the most well-known security alert system. In addition, CERT publishes a list of other information sources on its Web site at *http://www.cert.org/other_sources*.

Note   Different vulnerability reporting services have different names and codes for the vulnerabilities they discover. For example, the CERT alert codes differ from alert codes produced by the U.S. Department of Energy's Computer Incident Advisory Capability (CIAC) system. In an effort to help coordinate the naming and coding of security alerts, NIST recommends the use of the Common Vulnerabilities and Exposures (CVE) naming format. You can learn more about CVE from *http://cve.mitre.org* or by reviewing NIST Special Publication 800-51. (NIST articles can be found at *http://www.csrc.nist.gov/publications*.)

Verifying Updates

Before you install a security update, you should verify that it is authentic and not corrupted. Verification usually involves checking a digital signature or checksum to verify the authenticity of the patch. A *checksum* (or *hash*) is a computation applied to a file that results in a string that can be used to check the integrity of a downloaded file. Figure 8-1 illustrates an example of a Message Digest (MD5) checksum. Three files, all named Code.txt, exist in three different directories—test1, test2, and test3, as shown in the directory listing. All the files have the same date, time, file size, and name. However, they don't all have the same MD5 hash value because they are not all the same. The Code.txt file in the test2 directory is different than the other two files, as shown in the MD5 command hash values.

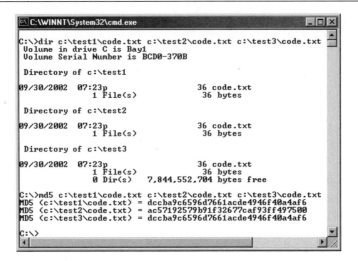

Figure 8-1. MD5 signature verification

Pretty Good Privacy (PGP) can also be used to verify file downloads. Figure 8-2 illustrates signature verification with PGP. The first Code.txt file was modified after the signature file was created and therefore shows up as a bad signature. The second file in the list is intact and therefore shows up with a proper time and date.

Figure 8-2. PGP signature verification

If an attacker compromises a vendor Web site, the attacker could feasibly post a Trojan horse in place of a security patch. Many vendors now digitally sign or compute a hash value for security updates, so that you can ensure the update's integrity. Be sure to check that signature or security hash before you install security updates.

Maintaining an Archive of Updates

No matter how you receive updates for your applications, network devices, and operating systems, you should consider building an archive of update files. Maintain all of the updates that you must apply for each type of software and hardware your organization uses. This allows you to quickly reapply updates when new systems are brought in or existing systems require reinstallation.

Testing Updates

Always test updates on nonproduction systems, if possible. This allows you to determine if the update performs properly before you load it onto your production devices, because software vendors can rarely guarantee that updates won't break other applications that you might be using on a production computer. If you don't have a test system for trying out patches, make sure you have an action plan for restoring your production systems if the security patch causes a problem.

Applying Updates

After you verify and test updates, apply them as soon as possible. The actual process for applying firmware updates varies depending on the product and vendor, but typically it is not much more involved than downloading and running a file from the vendor's Web site.

If an exploit is discovered and an update is not available, you might have to follow a workaround. For example, if an exploit for Dynamic Host Configuration Protocol (DHCP) is discovered on a router that supports DHCP, you might consider disabling DHCP on the router and enabling it on a device that doesn't have the same vulnerability. Once the security patch is available, you can decide whether you want to return to the original configuration.

Operating System and Application Updates

The SANS Institute has created a list of the top 20 security exploits (*http://www.sans.org/top20.htm*). The list shows that buffer overflows are the most common security problem. As you read earlier in Chapter 6, buffer overflows are related to programming errors. Consequently, when they are discovered, software vendors usually fix them by issuing security updates. These updates might be called upgrades, patches, service packs, or hotfixes, depending on the product and the vendor. No matter what they are called, these updates fix programming errors that might be exploited by an attacker.

Note   Software updates aren't always related to security updates. Sometimes they add new features or fix other programming issues that are related to ease of use or functionality and not necessarily a security exploit. Be sure you review what the update is fixing before installing it because you might decide that you don't need or want the update.

Checking for Updates

Almost every piece of software and hardware that your organization has is likely to be updated at some point. As with firmware updates, you must stay attuned to appropriate information sources (such as your software vendor's Web site or an alert list) so that you know about exploits when they are discovered and fixed.

More Info   The Computer Security Division of NIST maintains a searchable index of information on computer vulnerabilities called ICAT located at *http://icat.nist.gov*. (ICAT originally stood for Internet Categorization of Attacks Toolkit. However, it is not an acronym today because the focus of the toolset has changed.)

Operating systems in particular are likely to be updated routinely. Updates are so frequent that many software vendors have worked to simplify the process of finding and installing updates. For example, CERT lists scanning tools on their Web site list of security tools under the heading "Tools to Scan Hosts for Known Vulnerabilities," located at *http://www.cert.org/tech_tips/security_tools.html#D*. Two of those scanning tools are Internet Security Scanner (ISS) and Security Administrator Tool for Analyzing Networks (SATAN). Other examples of scanning tools include the Microsoft Baseline Security Analyzer (MBSA) and the Microsoft Network Security Hot Fix Checker (HFNetChk).

More Info   For more information concerning MBSA and HFNetChk, visit *http://www.microsoft.com/technet/security/tools/Tools*.

Automated Updates

Many software vendors are providing methods for receiving and applying updates automatically. Many virus scanner vendors offer automated programs for updating virus definition files. Microsoft offers an automatic updates program called Software Update Services for many of its operating systems. These automated updates can be configured to automatically download updates from the vendor's Web site on a regular schedule or whenever they are available.

More Info   For more information about Software Update Services visit *http://www.microsoft.com/windows2000/windowsupdate/sus/default.asp*.

Securing Networking Components

As you have seen thus far, there are many potential avenues that an attacker can use to exploit your network. In this section, you learn some additional avenues that attackers might take to exploit your network. More important, you learn steps that you can take to help protect your network and reduce the possible ways in which attackers might exploit it.

Disabling Unnecessary Network Services and Protocols

People often speak of disabling unnecessary "services" and "protocols" inter-changeably. This is because services and protocols often have the same name. For example, the Simple Network Management Protocol (SNMP) is by name a proto-col, but it is also a service. SNMP is typically used for remote management of hosts on a TCP/IP network. As a service, SNMP communications occur by default over User Datagram Protocol (UDP) ports 161 and 162. As a protocol, SNMP commu-nicates according to standards documented in Request for Comments (RFC) 1643. (RFC articles can be found at *http://www.icann.rfceditor.org.*)

Important   CERT Advisory CA-2002-03, titled "Multiple Vulnerabilities in Many Implementations of the Simple Network Management Protocol (SNMP)," issued February 12, 2002, warned that more than 140 hardware and software vendors had vulnerable SNMP services. Many organizations were advised to disable SNMP until their vendors were able to distribute patches. You can review the advisory at *http://www.cert.org/advisories/CA-2002-03.html.*

A *network service* is a program used to provide some function for another com-puter or device on the network. Network services are often generically referred to as *services*. Many operating systems install and enable services by default that might not be necessary or appropriate on your network. Of course, the necessity and appropriateness of a service depends on the role that the computer is perform-ing. For example, CERT Advisory CA-1996-01, "UDP Port Denial-of-Service Attack," (also CVE-1999-0103) warns of a denial of service (DoS) attack directed against two UDP services: chargen and echo.

More Info   Chargen and echo are used for testing networked computers. Chargen responds with random characters to packets sent to its UDP port 19. Echo sends a response for each packet it receives on its UDP port 7. Both services are not required for typical network communications. You can read the CERT advisory on the potential for attack on the chargen and echo services at *http://www.cert.org/advisories/CA-1996-01.html.*

Most network operating systems allow network administrators to list the services that are active on the system. In Microsoft Windows, UNIX, and Linux systems the netstat command can be used to provide a list of network connections and listening ports over which services are provided. Figure 8-3 shows the netstat command and appropriate command-line switches to show all listening TCP and UDP ports in numerical order.

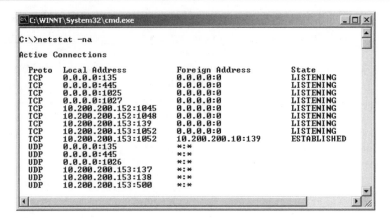

Figure 8-3. Netstat on Windows 2000 Professional

You can usually find a list of services and ports in the Services file. This file is located in different places on different operating systems. On UNIX and Linux operating systems, the file is commonly stored as the services file in the /Etc directory. Microsoft Windows 2000 and Microsoft Windows XP operating systems store the services file in the %systemroot%\System32\Drivers\Etc folder. You can view and edit the Services file in any text editor program such as vi, Emacs, or pico in UNIX/Linux operating systems or Notepad in Microsoft Windows operating systems.

Note   Recent Microsoft operating systems use the term folder instead of directory. For example, documentation refers to file and folder-level security instead of directory-level security. The Microsoft Services file is only used to map friendly names to services; you cannot actually disable services by removing entries from that file.

Once you figure out what services are running on your system, you should disable all unnecessary services. In UNIX and Linux operating systems, disabling services is typically done by editing the /Etc/Inetd.conf or /Etc/Xinetd.conf files. To disable a service in Inetd.conf, you add a pound sign (#) in front of the line referencing the service. An excerpt of an Inetd.conf file is shown here with the echo and chargen services disabled:

```
#echo       stream      tcp      nowait      root      internal
#echo       dgram       udp      wait        root      internal
discard     stream      tcp      nowait      root      internal
discard     dgram       udp      wait        root      internal
daytime     stream      tcp      nowait      root      internal
daytime     dgram       udp      wait        root      internal
#chargen    stream      tcp      nowait      root      internal
#chargen    dgram       udp      wait        root      internal
```

Once you have disabled all the unnecessary services, you must restart the inetd program so that it reads the edited Inetd.conf file. Depending on the specific distribution of UNIX or Linux, you might do this by typing **killall –HUP inetd**. The preferred technique for accomplishing a restart of inetd might be different in your specific operating system, so consult your documentation.

Note   All of the services listed in the preceding excerpt of the Inetd.conf file are typically used for testing only, and most security guidelines recommend disabling them.

In Microsoft Windows operating systems, disabling specific services can be a bit more complex because you need to know which software applications are providing which services. For example, consider the following list (excerpted from Figure 8-3):

```
Proto     Local Address
TCP       10.200.200.153:139
UDP       10.200.200.153:137
UDP       10.200.200.153:138
```

All entries in this list are associated with NetBIOS over TCP/IP services. If you have no need for NetBIOS over TCP/IP services, you can disable them through the Advanced TCP/IP Settings dialog box by clicking the WINS tab, and then choosing the option to disable NetBIOS over TCP/IP, as shown in Figure 8-4.

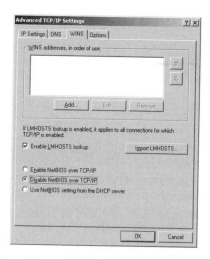

Figure 8-4.   Disabling NetBIOS over TCP/IP in Windows 2000

In addition to disabling unnecessary services on the clients and server operating systems on your network, you should filter unneeded services at the firewall. As mentioned in Chapter 4, you'd be wise to use a default-deny rule on the firewall and enable only needed services.

Removing Unnecessary Programs

The Melissa virus (described in Chapter 6) was targeted at systems running Microsoft Word and Microsoft Outlook. The Melissa virus would not have affected someone who didn't have Word and Outlook installed. The more programs you have installed and running on your system, the greater the likelihood that someone can create or find an exploit for one of your programs.

To reduce the risk of compromise on your network, you should remove all unnecessary programs from every device on your network. Most operating systems provide a method for you to determine which processes and applications are running. UNIX and Linux systems have the ps command that can be used to list running processes. In Microsoft Windows operating systems released after 1995 (including Microsoft Windows 95, Microsoft Windows 98, Microsoft Windows Me, Windows 2000, and Windows XP) you can hold the Ctrl, Alt, and Delete keys simultaneously to activate the Task Manager. In Windows XP, you can also use the tasklist.exe command to view processes on local and remote computers from the command line.

Note   A generic description for a process is a *running program*. Services, as described previously, are also running programs. In many conversations and documents there is no distinction made between a service and a process. However, in this text and others, network services are often generically referred to as services. A process therefore is any running program, whether it is involved with network communications or not. Applications are programs, too, but when many people refer to an application they are talking about a program (or group of programs) that accomplishes a specific task, which might involve one or more running processes. For example, Microsoft Windows games Minesweeper and Solitaire are applications. Here again, the lines are not perfectly clear because when Minesweeper and Solitaire are running on the system they run as single processes. In Microsoft Windows operating systems, you can review installed applications through the Add/Remove Programs icon in the Control Panel.

Once you have listed all of the running processes, you can determine if they are necessary. Determining which processes are actually necessary depends on many different factors. Later in this lesson and in the following lesson we cover some of the guidelines that help you determine which processes are necessary. However, beyond all of the recommendations, in many cases, the decision on whether a process is necessary varies depending on what the individual or organization needs to accomplish or provide.

Disabling Unnecessary Protocol Stacks

As you saw in Chapter 2, TCP/IP is a suite of protocols. TCP/IP is often referred to as a protocol stack. Other types of protocol stacks include IPX/SPX and NetBEUI.

Many operating systems and network devices are capable of running more than one protocol stack. As with removing an unnecessary service or protocol, you should also remove any unnecessary protocol stacks. For example, the IPX/SPX protocol stack is only used on Novell NetWare networks. However, recent versions of Net-Ware frequently use TCP/IP. If you convert your network to TCP/IP completely, you can remove IPX/SPX from hosts and routers on your network. The fewer protocols, protocol stacks, and services that your systems support, the less likely it is that newly discovered vulnerabilities will affect them. At a minimum, removing unnecessary services, protocols, and protocol stacks improves performance and makes systems less complex to troubleshoot.

Disabling Promiscuous Mode

Attackers who are able to compromise one of the systems on your network might use that compromised system to gather information and possibly exploit other systems. One way in which an attacker might gather information is to install a protocol analyzer program on the compromised system. The attacker then uses the protocol analyzer to monitor data packets, hoping to find passwords, user names, or additional information that might help to compromise other systems.

To protect your systems from this type of attack, you must do all you can to ensure that a system is not compromised in the first place. However, if a system is compromised, one method for stopping the attacker from gathering additional information is to disable the promiscuous mode of the network card. *Promiscuous mode* is a condition that a network adapter can be placed in to gather all passing information. Normally, network adapters do not gather information that is not specifically destined for the adapter or broadcast to all adapters. Certain programs (such as protocol analyzer programs) place adapters into promiscuous mode.

Many network card manufacturers provide directions for disabling promiscuous mode through various operating systems. Unfortunately, if the attacker is savvy enough to compromise the system and gain full control (root, superuser, or administrative access), then he or she can probably re-enable promiscuous mode on the adapter through the operating system. Some network card manufacturers make network cards on which promiscuous mode can be permanently disabled. If you can permanently disable promiscuous mode on the network adapter, even if an attacker does compromise the system, installing a protocol analyzer would not provide any additional advantages to the attacker.

Note   Some network security tools, such as vulnerability scanners and network monitors, depend on enabling promiscuous mode on your network adapter. Consequently, you should not disable promiscuous mode on systems that you must use to conduct network monitoring or run certain vulnerability scanning tools.

Disabling Unnecessary Systems

Computer systems that are not in use on your network should be disabled. Network attacks are often launched against test systems that were never properly secured and then forgotten about. Even a test system that has no legitimate user accounts locally could be quite useful to an attacker. As previously mentioned, if an attacker compromises an unsecured system, she or he could install a protocol analyzer and other tools that could lead to further exploits.

To protect your network from exploits launched against systems that are not in use, you must routinely audit your systems. You can use vulnerability scanners on your own network to scan for unsecured systems, and you can also physically inspect your network to see if there are any computers or other network devices that are no longer in use.

Note   Virtual Machines from VMWare or Virtual PCs from Connectix can be susceptible to the same attacks and viruses as the physical workstations and servers on your network. Be sure to maintain or disable these virtual machines or PCs as you would other systems on your network.

Access Control Lists

Packet filtering, as described in Chapter 4, is typically accomplished with an *access control list* (ACL). An ACL is a rule list that tells the router or firewall how to deal with network packets the router receives, so routers and firewalls use ACLs to determine which packets to forward and which to drop. As you learned in Chapter 4, packet filters can be used to restrict packets based on source address, destination address, protocol ID, TCP or UDP port number, Internet Control Message Protocol (ICMP) message type, fragmentation flags, and options.

One common problem with router and firewall configurations is that packet filters are not stringent enough. As an example, assume you work for an organization that handles name resolution for all internal client systems. In addition, you want to allow Domain Name System (DNS) zone transfers from your Internet service provider's (ISP's) DNS server (named IspDNS) to your local DNS server (named CorpDNS). Because the ISP's DNS server sends zone transfers over the standard port (TCP port 53) to your organization, you know you must enable that port on the firewall. You can configure an ACL that looks like the one shown in Table 8-1.

Table 8-1.   Sample Access Control List

Rule	Direction	Destination	Source	Protocol	Source Port	Destination Port
Zone XFR1	OUT	Any	CorpDNS	TCP	>1023	53
Zone XFR2	IN	CorpDNS	Any	TCP	53	>1023

However, if you do this, an attacker could potentially use port 53 to scan your entire network. Further, an attacker could send a bogus zone transfer right through your firewall to your DNS server. The problem is the use of "any" instead of listing the actual DNS server of the ISP. A more secure solution would be to restrict zone transfers to only the IP address of your ISP's DNS server, as shown in Table 8-2.

Table 8-2.   A More Secure Access Control List

Rule	Direction	Destination	Source	Protocol	Source Port	Destination Port
Zone XFR1	OUT	IspDNS	CorpDNS	TCP	>1023	53
Zone XFR2	IN	CorpDNS	IspDNS	TCP	53	>1023

Configuring a secure ACL is an important way to help protect your network from attack. Make sure that your firewall and router rules limit the connections that can be made and from where.

File System Security

A file system (or file management system) is a program for organizing, storing, and even sharing data. To increase the security of your network and individual systems, you should secure the file systems in use on your network. There are three main areas to consider related to file system security:

- File and directory permissions
- Data encryption
- Shared or exported data

File and Directory Permissions

File and directory permissions are used to identify who can access a file or directory. Many operating systems use file systems that allow you to set file and directory permissions. Typical permissions you can configure include read, write, and execute.

Some operating systems allow you to choose to install a file system that supports file- and directory-level security and one that does not. For example, Microsoft Windows NT, Windows 2000, and Windows XP allow you to choose between the *file allocation table* (FAT) file system and the *NTFS file system* (NTFS). FAT does not support file and directory security, whereas NTFS does. To better secure your operating system, you should select the file system that supports file- and directory-level security.

To best protect your operating systems from compromise, configure security on files and directories according to the *rule of least privilege*. This means giving each person or group only the required amount of access and nothing more. For example, if all the users in the marketing department need access to read, but not change, a file you should give them read access only, and nothing more. By limiting permissions you can protect files from being accessed or deleted by attackers who are able to compromise a trusted user account. Further, you help to prevent accidental deletions by legitimate users.

Data Encryption

Some file systems, such as NTFS in Windows 2000 and Windows XP, enable you to encrypt data. You should encrypt all files that you are concerned about keeping private. Although file system permissions should protect your files, encryption adds an additional layer of protection. For more information on data encryption, see Chapter 3, Chapter 4, and Chapter 6.

Shared or Exploited Data

Sharing files and folders is common and so is the exploitation of those shares. To secure your shared files and folders, you can typically configure access controls on them, commonly referred to as *share permissions* or *export permissions*. Be sure to follow the rule of least privilege when granting access to shared files and directories.

Note   Tips for securing file and print servers are covered in Lesson 2. The items mentioned here also apply to that lesson and vice versa.

Operating System Hardening

Operating system hardening means securing the operating system. Many of the security tips already covered in this lesson can be applied directly to hardening the operating system, including the following:

- Disable unnecessary programs and processes.
- Disable unnecessary services.
- Disable unnecessary protocols.
- Verify, test, and install all vendor patches.
- Use vulnerability scanners to identify potential security weaknesses.
- Disable promiscuous mode.
- Configure file system security according to the rule of least privilege.

In addition to taking those precautions, you should consider the following to better protect your operating system:

- **Set complex passwords for all user accounts and change them frequently.**   Setting complex passwords was discussed in Chapter 4. Be sure to routinely change passwords to keep them secure.

- **Set account lockout policies.**   If someone is trying to guess a password, they'll probably take a few guesses. If you have an account lockout policy that locks someone out after three to five attempts, the chances of that person guessing a password successfully are greatly reduced.

- **Remove or disable all unnecessary modems.**   Modems (or dial-up adapters) can become a way to circumvent the security of your network, as explained in Chapter 4.

- **Enable monitoring, logging, auditing, and detection.**   You should monitor your hosts and connectivity devices. Many operating systems allow you to log user access, file system access, and other security-related events. You can also configure a host-based intrusion detection system. Monitoring was covered in Chapter 4. Intrusion detection is covered in greater detail in Chapter 11, "Intrusion Detection."

- **Maintain backups and images.**   One of the most important ways to protect your operating systems is by backing them up. You can also use disk-imaging software to maintain a complete image of the operating system and its data.

There are many specific recommendations and guidelines available for a variety of operating systems available on the Internet. Here are some links to recommendations for specific operating systems:

- The UNIX Security Checklist v2.0 from CERT is available at *http:// www.cert.org/tech_tips/unix_security_checklist2.0.html.*

- The CIS Web site at *http://www.cisecurity.com* includes information for securing Solaris, Linux, HP-UX, Cisco IOS, Windows 2000, Windows NT, and more.

- The U.S. NSA Web site at *http://www.nsa.gov* has security guides for Windows 2000, Windows NT, and Cisco routers. Also, the NSA has published a security-enhanced version of the Linux operating system (see Security Enhanced Linux on the NSA Web site).

- The Information Systems and Technology Department of the University of Waterloo Web site at *http://ist.uwaterloo.ca/security/howto* includes information on securing Windows NT, Windows 2000, Windows XP, AIX, Solaris, and Linux.

- Windows NT Configuration Guidelines from CERT are available at *http:// www.cert.org/tech_tips/win_configuration_guidelines.html.*

- Windows 95 and Windows 98 Computer Security Information from CERT is available at *http://www.cert.org/tech_tips/win-95-info.html.*

Lesson 2 discusses securing specific types of servers. Servers present specific challenges because they must often run additional protocols and provide additional services that can potentially be exploited by attacks.

Exercise: Using MD5

MD5 can be used to verify the integrity of files, and you can download and use it with a wide variety of operating systems. Many Web sites and vendors post MD5 checksums so that you can verify that the file they post is the file you downloaded. In this exercise you locate the MD5.exe file and learn how to use it. You create three files and see the effect on the MD5 hash when you change one of those files.

Note   This exercise, as written, works on Windows 95, Windows 98, Windows Me, and Windows 2000 operating systems.

---

1. Download the MD5.exe file from the Internet. You can use any Internet search engine. Copy the MD5.exe file to your C drive.
2. Create a text file named Code.txt, type some text into the file using a text editor such as Notepad, and then save the file somewhere on your C drive.
3. Create three folders on the C drive named test1, test2, and test3.
4. Copy Code.txt to each of the folders (test1, test2, and test3).
5. Modify the contents of the Code.txt file in the test2 folder and save it.
6. From the Start menu, click Run and then type **CMD** or **command** (depending on your version of Windows) and press Enter. A command prompt appears.
7. At the command prompt, type **CD** and press Enter.
8. Type **MD5 C:\test1\code.txt**, and press Enter.
9. Type **C:\test2\code.txt** and press Enter.
10. Type **C:\test3\code.txt** and press Enter.

You should see that the first and third files have the same hash value, but the value of the second is different.

Lesson Review

The following questions are intended to reinforce key information presented in this lesson. If you are unable to answer a question, review the lesson and then try the question again. Answers to the questions can be found in Appendix A, "Questions and Answers."

1. How can you stop certain protocols from traversing your routers?

2. What can you do to make it more difficult for an attacker to sniff your network?

3. What can you do to secure your computer's file system?

4. What is the purpose of disabling unnecessary systems, programs, processes, protocols, and services?

5. Why is it imperative that you monitor security alerts?

Lesson Summary

- Vulnerabilities are often discovered in network devices, operating systems, and applications. You should monitor for security alerts to ensure that you know about exploits that could affect your equipment. Be sure to verify, test, and apply all security updates as soon as possible.

- To better protect your network devices and hosts, you should do the following:
  - Disable unnecessary programs and processes.
  - Disable unnecessary services.
  - Disable unnecessary protocols.
  - Verify, test, and install all vendor patches.
  - Use vulnerability scanners to identify potential security weaknesses.
  - Disable promiscuous mode.

- Choose secure file systems that allow you to set file- and folder-level permissions. Configure file system permissions according to the rule of least privilege.

- In addition to removing all unnecessary components and applying security updates, additional steps to secure operating systems, beyond those already discussed, include the following:
  - Set complex passwords for all user accounts and change them frequently.
  - Set account lockout policies.
  - Remove or disable all unnecessary modems.
  - Enable monitoring, logging, auditing, and detection.
  - Maintain backups and disk images.

Lesson 2: Server Application Hardening

Techniques for protecting client applications were presented in Chapter 6. This lesson focuses on securing network servers, and specifically the services they provide to network clients. Before you secure a network server, you should secure its operating system. All sections in this lesson assume that you have already secured the operating system, as discussed in Lesson 1.

After this lesson, you will be able to

- Identify methods that attackers use to exploit Web, File Transfer Protocol (FTP), e-mail, DNS, Network News Transfer Protocol (NNTP), file and printer sharing, DHCP, directory services, and database servers.
- Select methods to secure Web, FTP, e-mail, DNS, NNTP, file and printer sharing, DHCP, directory services, and database servers.

Estimated lesson time: 60 minutes

In this lesson the focus is on general security tips for specific types of servers. Beyond securing the host operating system, there are some additional security tips, presented here, that apply to all types of servers:

- **Watch out for buffer overflow vulnerabilities.**   Buffer overflows are historically the most frequent type of exploit discovered. Tracking and applying the latest security updates, as mentioned in Lesson 1, is the appropriate method for handling buffer overflows.

- **Research issues specific to your server and its applications.**   Learn about the discovered vulnerabilities concerning the applications and services you are making available.

- **Keep informed of security alerts.**   Subscribe to one or more vulnerability alert services that notify people of discovered exploits and solutions for your specific server application. Test, verify, and apply security updates as soon as they are made available.

- **Enable logging mechanisms on your server.**   You should keep a record of people who visit your server and what they do on it. Review the log to see what is happening and investigate anything that is inappropriate, such as entries that show someone is trying to access operating system files through one of your services or applications.

- **Use encryption appropriately.**   To protect the transfer of sensitive or private information, ensure that encryption is enabled between the server and client.

- **Maintain a backup.**   Keep an up-to-date backup copy of your server and the applications and services it is providing so that you can quickly recover from successful attacks.

- **Use vulnerability scanning tools.**   Some software vendors and security-related organizations produce vulnerability scanning tools designed for specific types of servers. For example, Microsoft Corporation has the IISLockDown Wizard, which is a utility that fixes common security issues with Microsoft Internet Information Services (IIS) servers.

More Info   In this lesson, several TCP and UDP ports are mentioned in the areas in which services are introduced. In Appendix B, "Ports and Protocol IDs," you can study a larger list of important TCP and UDP ports. If you want an even more comprehensive and current list of all TCP and UDP ports, check the Internet Assigned Numbers Authority (IANA) database "Protocol Numbers and Assignment Services" at *http://www.iana.org*.

Web Servers

Many organizations use Web servers to provide information and services to the public and internally on their private networks. Web servers that provide services to the public are typically referred to as Internet Web servers or *public Web servers*; those providing services to the private network are called *intranet Web servers* or *private Web servers*. Internet Web servers are typically considered to be at greater risk because they are exposed to a larger number of anonymous users. For this reason, Internet Web servers are typically located in a perimeter networks (also known as a DMZ, demilitarized zone, or screened subnet), whereas intranet Web servers are typically located on the internal network. All of the security considerations mentioned in this section can be applied equally to either type of Web server.

There are many different software vendors that provide Web servers today. In addition, many applications come with the added ability to share documents or information over a Web protocol [Hypertext Transfer Protocol (HTTP)], effectively making them Web servers. So many exploits exist for Web servers that entire books are dedicated to securing Web services. The text that follows includes a brief discussion of three potential Web server exploits: packet sniffing, directory listing, and 8.3 compatible file names. After the discussion of exploits, we review some general guidelines on how to secure a Web server.

More Info   For detailed information on securing Web servers, see NIST Special Publication 800-44, titled "Guidelines on Securing Public Web Servers."

Packet Sniffing

Web clients typically contact Web servers over the well-known TCP port 80. The port the Web server sends information to is dynamically negotiated during the TCP handshake. Normal HTTP communications are not encrypted and can be easily captured and decoded by a protocol analyzer. Methods for encrypting Web communications were covered in Chapter 6.

Directory Listing

Automatic directory listings, enabled by some Web servers, allow a client browser to see the contents of a directory when no default document is specified or available. A default document is the page that is loaded when a client navigates to a specific directory. For example, many Web servers specify a default document of index.html. When a client browser makes a connection to the Web server, the default document is loaded. However, if the client connects directly to a subdirectory without a default document, the client sees a listing of files and folders that is in the subdirectory. Attackers might use this feature to browse your Web server's directory structure and available files, which is called *directory enumeration.* To help prevent directory enumeration, disable automatic directory listings. Once this is done, your Web server posts an error message when the default document cannot be found.

More Info Attackers might attempt to use other methods to browse a Web server's directory structure. CERT warns about an exploit involving the use of Web publishing tools as a means to enumerate directories in their Vulnerability Note VU#32794, which is located at *http://www.kb.cert.org/vuls/id/32794.*

8.3 Compatible File Names

Microsoft Windows 32-bit operating systems support two types of file names. The first type is called a *long file name* (LFN), which allows for file names of up to 255 characters. The second is the *8.3 compatible file name*, which allows for eight-character file names plus a three-character file extension. Figure 8-5 illustrates a file named Longfilename.txt and its 8.3 compatible file name Longfi~1.txt.

Figure 8-5. Example 8.3 compatible name

The 8.3 compatible names are created to allow older 16-bit programs to work appropriately with files in the newer 32-bit Windows operating systems. Unfortunately, if you use the Web server application only to control access to files, an attacker can open a file using the 8.3 compatible file names without restrictions.

Web servers that run on Windows 32-bit platforms might be vulnerable to this exploit. Some software vendors have released updates to correct this problem and others advise you to disable 8.3 compatible file name support.

More Info   For more information on the 8.3 compatible file name issue, see CERT advisory CA-1998-04 at *http://www.cert.org/advisories/CA-1998-04.html.*

General Tips for Securing a Web Server

Instead of reviewing the multitude of potential Web server exploits and corrective actions, this section lists some general steps that you can take to secure a Web server. First, Web servers are most secure when you configure them as *bastion hosts*, meaning that you secure them as much as possible by removing as many services and programs from them as possible. The job of the Web server should be to serve Web pages and nothing more. Don't configure a Web server as a printer server or file server because that opens up additional avenues for exploitation. In addition to the items mentioned previously, here are some further items to consider when securing Web servers:

- **Reduce features.**   Although you might want to provide a highly engaging and interactive Web site, you must consider that every additional feature is another potential point for compromise. Remove all unnecessary plug-ins, scripts, programs, and other features that are not required on the Web server.

- **Secure available features.**   For the scripts, programs, and plug-ins that you do decide to use on your Web site, be sure to follow all appropriate cautions. Use the appropriate security for all directories, files, and objects. For example, Common Gateway Interface (CGI) scripts should be placed in their own directory and should not be run by the system account. Only read and execute permissions should be enabled for the least privileged user account possible for running CGI programs.

- **Place public Web servers in your perimeter network.**   Isolate your public Web servers from the rest of your internal network by placing them in a perimeter network. If someone compromises your Web server, you want to protect the rest of the network from being compromised through that Web server.

- **Protect your internal network by restricting or denying access to intranet Web servers.**   Web services are offered over the standard HTTP TCP port 80 or HTTPS TCP port 443. If you want to block standard Web communications, you should be sure that these ports are blocked on the firewall.

- **Carefully choose your Web directories.**   You should make your Web root directory (the directory location where users connect by default) a directory that does not include files or folders that contain operating system files or sensitive data. If possible, don't put your Web server files and your operating system files on the same physical volume. Also, don't store sensitive or private data on your Web server.

More Info   The CERT module titled "Securing Public Web Servers" is a good source for additional Web security tips, available at *http://www.cert.org/security-improvement/modules/m11.html.*

FTP Servers

Like Web servers, FTP servers can be used to serve internal or external users. *Public FTP servers* are typically open to everyone on the Internet, whereas private FTP servers are typically secured for internal use only. In Chapter 6, you learned about client-side exploits for FTP communications. In this section you learn about FTP server exploits. In addition to the general issues discussed at the beginning of this lesson, FTP servers can be exploited in the following ways:

- **Incorrectly configured FTP directory structure.**   Some administrators incorrectly configure their FTP server's structure to include files that they did not intend to be available over FTP, such as operating system files or private data.

- **Allowing write permissions.**   Some organizations allow users write permission to their servers intentionally, and others do so by mistake. Attackers search for directories on FTP servers that allow write access. Software traders utilize improperly configured FTP directories to exchange software with others.

- **Sniffing password exchanges between FTP server and client.**   FTP clients contact FTP servers over TCP port 21 to begin communications. By default, FTP communications are not encrypted and this can be easily decoded by a protocol analyzer. FTP servers that require authentication could allow for the compromise of user names and passwords, as attackers can sniff the network and capture user names and passwords. This exploit was discussed in Chapter 6.

- **FTP bounce.**   There is an FTP exploit that allows attackers to run scans against other computers through your FTP server, called an *FTP bounce*. This makes it look like your FTP server is scanning client computers. Although this attack is related to the proper functioning of FTP, many vendors have found solutions for preventing it in the form of security updates or configuration changes.

More Info   CERT Advisory CA-1997-27, "FTP Bounce" (also CVE-1999-0017), further explains the issue and shows specific vendor solutions at *http://www.cert.org/advisories/CA-1997-27.html*.

When setting up an FTP server for private or public access, you should consider the security implications of doing so. Here are some items to consider when setting up and securing an FTP server:

- **Place public FTP servers in your perimeter network.**   Isolate your public FTP servers from the rest of your internal network by placing them in a perimeter network. If someone compromises your FTP server, you want to protect the rest of the network from being compromised through that FTP server.

- **Protect your internal network by restricting or denying access to intranet FTP servers.**   FTP services are typically offered over TCP ports 21 and 20. If you want to block standard FTP communications, you should be sure to block these ports on the firewall.

- **Carefully choose your FTP directories.**   You should make your FTP root directory (the directory location where users connect by default) a directory that includes files or folders that do not contain operating system files or sensitive data.

- **Don't allow unauthenticated write access.**   Some organizations allow write access to their FTP servers. Some organizations configure *blind FTP* servers or directories, which allow write access, but not file listings (read access). This is a way for an organization to collect files anonymously or share files with people who know the exact names of those files. However, blind FTP areas can also be used for trading software. Software traders do not need to see file listings to share files, because they can only see the file names and locations. Typically software traders post these names and locations on other Web sites or share them through newsgroups, bulletin boards, or chat programs.

- **Configure encrypted authentication for your FTP servers.**   You can use S/FTP or Kerberized FTP to secure the user name and password exchanges. You can also configure a VPN to secure communications between any client and server.

- **Check your FTP directories.**   You should routinely check or scan your FTP file structure for unusual or unexpected files and folders.

E-Mail Servers

E-mail servers and clients are vulnerable to many different exploits. In Chapter 6, you learned about ways in which e-mail client communications could be compromised, including e-mail forgery and packet sniffing. You learned there that you could use encryption and digital signatures to solve those issues. In this section, you get to see ways in which e-mail servers are exploited and measures that can be used to secure them. E-mail servers are typically compromised in the following ways:

- **Packet sniffing.**   E-mail generally moves through the Internet and other networks between e-mail servers, and also between e-mail clients and servers. E-mail servers relay e-mail to one another over the Simple Mail Transfer Protocol (SMTP) that uses TCP port 25. E-mail clients most commonly check e-mail using one of two protocols: the Post Office Protocol version 3 (POP3) or Internet Message Access Protocol (IMAP). POP3 clients contact the e-mail server on TCP port 110 and IMAP clients contact the e-mail server on TCP port 143. By default, these network communications are not encrypted and data can be intercepted with a protocol analyzer.

- **DoS attacks.**   DoS attacks against e-mail servers typically involve programming flaws that cause them to stop responding for some reason when certain data is sent to them. A DoS attack can also occur when users on a network receive and execute a virus that overburdens the e-mail server with traffic.

- **Open relays.**   E-mail servers and other types of servers sometimes act as SMTP relay servers. This is convenient for users and other servers that need to transmit e-mail. However, it is also a security issue because people who send spam seek out SMTP relays.

To protect your e-mail servers from those exploits, you can take the following actions:

- **Use virus scanners.**   You should configure virus-scanning programs on all client and server computers on which e-mail is accessed. E-mail is a popular transmission method for viruses and other malicious software.

- **Use an e-mail relay or e-mail gateway to protect your mail server.**   *E-mail relays* or *e-mail gateways* can be used to scan, clean, and filter e-mail before it reaches your e-mail server. These products typically run on separate secured servers and reduce the amount of e-mail that your server has to process. The e-mail relay or gateway can be used to filter potential virus attachments, spam, and other undesirable or suspicious e-mail.

- **Check for, and close, open e-mail relays.**   There are scanning programs that you can use on your own network to check for open SMTP relay services so you can find them before spammers do.

More Info   For more detailed information on securing e-mail servers, see NIST Special Publication 800-45, titled "Guidelines on Electronic Mail Security."

DNS Servers

DNS is an integral part of most communications occurring over TCP/IP networks today. The DNS server converts friendly computer names (host names) into IP addresses so that communications can be correctly routed through the network. Client computers user DNS to locate Web servers, FTP servers, e-mail servers, and a wide variety of other servers and network services. DNS can be an important target for an attacker. The potential ways in which DNS can be exploited include the following:

- **Snooping around the DNS server.**   Anyone can query DNS, so limit the information you maintain there.

- **Stealing zone transfers.**   DNS servers are often configured to provide other DNS servers with updates. The DNS server receiving the update is typically referred to as a *secondary server*. The purpose of the secondary DNS server is to maintain a backup copy of the DNS database and to provide name resolution services for client computers. An attacker could potentially receive a zone transfer and use it to help map out your network and search for potential targets.

- **Zone update spoofing.** An attacker can potentially spoof the address of the real primary DNS server and send a bogus update to a secondary DNS server. Client computers using that falsely updated DNS server would receive incorrect information and network communications could be redirected to a location controlled by the attacker.

- **DNS spoofing.** The dsniff utility, mentioned in Chapter 6, has a subordinate tool called *dnsspoof* that allows an attacker to set up a bogus DNS server to answer client systems. If the DNS server is spoofed, clients receive bogus information when they request name resolutions. This enables the attacker to redirect traffic.

- **Dynamic DNS (DDNS) record spoofing.** *DDNS record spoofing* allows client computers to update DNS with their name and IP address. Attackers could use DDNS to overwrite records that belong to other systems, or at least put bogus records in the DNS server.

- **DNS cache poisoning.** DNS servers maintain caches of IP name resolutions, allowing the DNS server to quickly answer a DNS name query that it has previously answered. Flaws have been found in some DNS servers that allow attackers to insert bogus information into a DNS cache. This exploit is referred to as *DNS cache poisoning*.

To secure your DNS server from the types of exploits just listed, consider taking the following actions:

- **Use a separate DNS server for the perimeter network.** Don't put any information in your publicly accessible DNS server that you don't want to the public to see.

- **Restrict information in DNS.** Limit the amount of additional information you provide in DNS. Although DNS allows you to store additional *host information* in HINFO records, consider how an attacker could use that information.

- **Limit zone transfers.** Configure your DNS servers to only allow zone transfers to specific secondary servers.

- **Secure zone transfers.** Berkeley Internet Name Domain version 9 (BIND 9), a DNS version maintained by the Internet Software Consortium (ISC), allows zone transfers to be signed. Zone transfer signing allows secondary servers to verify the credentials of the primary server. Microsoft's Windows 2000 DNS implementation is integrated with its directory services architecture, which allows servers to verify credentials before accepting data.

- **Secure dynamic updates.** Microsoft's Windows 2000 DNS implementation allows for a cross-check of client computer credentials before allowing an update to take place. BIND version 9 is capable of supporting signed DNS updates from clients. Implementing either method gives you a more secure dynamic update because client credentials are established before an update is allowed. You can also choose to disable dynamic updates and instead enter IP addresses manually.

- **Use Secure DNS.** Both BIND 9 and Microsoft's Windows 2000 version of DNS implement DNS security, which allows client systems to be sure that they are communicating with the correct DNS server, which prevents DNS spoofing.

- **Prevent cache poisoning.** The correction for DNS cache poisoning is to get an updated version or security patch for your DNS server that does not allow the DNS cache to be poisoned.

File and Print Servers

Every major operating system vendor provides a way for you to share files and printers on your network. Although sharing files and printers is considered a necessary and reasonable activity, it is also a common way in which hackers gain information and unauthorized access.

Two of the most popular file sharing protocols are the *Network File System* (NFS) and *Server Message Block* (SMB). NFS is typically associated with UNIX networks, but there are add-ons to allow other operating environments, such as those from Microsoft and Novell, to share files over NFS. SMB is typically associated with Microsoft File and Printer Sharing, especially over the Network Basic Input/ Output System (NetBIOS). However, there are products, such as Samba, that allow other operating environments to share files over SMB.

Attackers can use both NFS and SMB/NetBIOS file and printer shares to gain inappropriate information and access to your network in the following ways:

- **Enumerating resources.** Attackers attempt to make unauthenticated connections to shared resources on the network.

- **Exploiting incorrectly configured shares.** Shares that are made available to anyone are easy targets for attackers. If permissions are configured incorrectly or too much permission is available for an easily exploited user account, attackers can do plenty of harm.

- **Packet sniffing.** Attackers might try to read data (printer files or data files) as they traverse the network.

Consider the following methods for securing your file and printer shares:

- **Block access to shares and related information at the firewall.**   Administrators commonly block TCP/UDP ports 137, 138, and 139, which are commonly used for NetBIOS names and sessions. Administrators also block NFS TCP/UDP port 2049. This prevents many of the exploits discussed in this section by preventing external attackers from making connections to internally shared resources.

- **Use the highest security and authentication levels available.**   Some systems allow you to use varying levels of authentication strength. For more secure configurations, use stronger authentication, as discussed in Chapter 7.

- **Verify share security.**   Use the rule of least privilege to secure your shares. If possible, further secure data beyond the share by limiting access using file system permissions or encryption.

- **Use VPNs.**   If you need to secure the data transmitted between clients and servers, use a VPN to encrypt communications, as covered in Chapter 5.

DHCP Servers

DHCP provides IP addresses automatically to client computers. When clients request an address, they broadcast a DHCP Discover packet on the network. DHCP servers respond with a DHCP Offer packet that contains a range of valid addresses from which the client can choose. The client chooses an address using a DHCP Request packet and the server acknowledges the request with a DHCP Acknowledge packet. Attackers can attempt to use or interrupt the DHCP address lease process in the following ways:

- **Rogue DHCP server.**   An attacker can use a rogue DHCP server to subvert client communications. Some DHCP servers even provide the address of the DNS server. If an attacker is able to configure a client computer with a bogus IP address, the attacker can misdirect the client to resources controlled by the attacker.

- **Leasing legitimate addresses to attackers.**   Attackers get a foothold on your network when they obtain a legitimate IP address. They immediately learn part of your internal addressing scheme and could make use of the address to attack other systems on your network.

Consider the following solutions to these issues:

- **Scan for rogue DHCP servers.**   You can use a protocol analyzer or configure an intrusion-detection system to discover DHCP Offer packets from unauthorized DHCP servers.

- **Configure DNS server information at the client.**   Client computers that have a preconfigured DNS address ignore additional options, such as DNS server IP address. If you set the DNS IP address on the client computer, a rogue DHCP server is unable to trick a client computer into calling a bogus DNS server.

- **Restrict address leases.**   You can configure most DHCP servers not to lease addresses to unknown adapters. Typically, you configure all of the allowed media access control (MAC) addresses as address reservations for your DHCP clients to prevent the server from leasing addresses to unknown systems.

- **Block DHCP at the firewall.**   DHCP and Boot Protocol (BOOTP) operate over TCP/UDP ports 67 and 68. To prevent your DHCP server from accidentally answering queries from outside your network, be sure that these ports are blocked at the firewall.

NNTP Servers

NNTP allows news clients to connect to news servers to read and post messages. NNTP can be used to share information among colleagues privately or to post articles to a public NNTP server. In addition to the problems common to almost all server software, such as buffer overflows, attacker exploits of NNTP can also include the following:

- **Browsing private NNTP servers.**   Attackers might connect to a private NNTP server to gain information that they shouldn't be able to see.

- **Targeted information gathering.**   In Chapter 6 you learned that spammers frequent public sites to collect e-mail addresses. When you post a message to an NNTP server, the information you post could be seen by an attacker looking to compromise your network. People using NNTP sites sometimes post accurate diagrams of their network for the purpose of asking a technical question. However, attackers might use such information to look for ways to exploit a network. They might even offer bogus advice to create a hole in the network's defenses. They could also use information gathered to help them conduct a social engineering attack, which is explained in Chapter 11.

The following are some ways to protect your organization from NNTP server exploits:

- **Block NNTP on the firewall.**   If you have a private NNTP server that should not be accessible to external users, block the NNTP port TCP/UDP 119 at the firewall.

- **Require authentication and encryption.**   If you are posting private information on an NNTP server, you should protect that information. Some NNTP servers allow you to configure user authentication that prevents anonymous or unauthenticated users from connecting to and browsing your NNTP server. You can also configure encrypted communications using Secure Sockets Layer/ Transport Layer Security (SSL/TLS) or set up a VPN between NNTP clients and servers to prevent packet sniffing of sensitive data.

- **Watch what you post.**   Don't post items on a public NNTP server that could compromise your network. If you manage an NNTP server, don't allow others to post sensitive information to the public.

Data Repositories

Data repositories are locations that hold information about your network or organization, such as user accounts, computer accounts, directories, maps, and so on. Attackers can use the information stored in data repositories to formulate attacks against your organization. Therefore, you must ensure that this information is as limited and restricted as possible, while still meeting the informational needs of your organization. Most techniques to protect this information involve authentication and encryption. The following sections cover securing directory services and databases.

Directory Services

In computer networking, a directory service is any information storage and retrieval process that provides information about an organization's network. The information in a directory service can include computer accounts, user accounts, mail accounts, service locations, and shared resource information. The *Lightweight Directory Access Protocol* (LDAP) is a common directory service on many networks today that organizes data in a hierarchical fashion. The top of the hierarchy is called the *LDAP root*. The *LDAP root server* creates the hierarchy and the rest of the structure (and resources) branch out from that location. LDAP uses objects to represent computers, user accounts, shared resources, services, and so on. These objects are usually referred to by a name called the *common name*. Objects are organized into containers called organizational units (OUs). The directory service hierarchy and the information it stores provide a good map of your network infrastructure. Although this is convenient and useful for legitimate users on your network, it can also be quite useful to an attacker.

There are two basic ways in which attackers try to compromise LDAP servers:

- **Information gathering.**   A directory service is used to store information about network resources. Attackers can use this information to examine your network structure, resources, and potential targets.
- **Packet sniffing.**   Information traveling over typical LDAP communications is not encrypted. Attackers can listen to information transferred over LDAP, thereby gaining information about your network.

To protect your LDAP hierarchy, consider implementing the following controls:

- **Configure strong authentication.**   The two most popular versions of LDAP are version 2 (LDAP v2) and version 3 (LDAP v3). Both versions support anonymous and simple authentication, which are not very secure. Anonymous authentication doesn't require a password at all, and simple authentication uses a password, but it is transmitted unencrypted over the network, meaning an attacker could use a protocol analyzer to compromise it. Strong authentication over LDAP v2 is provided through Kerberos version 4 authentication. Strong authentication over LDAP v3 is provided through *Simple Authentication and Security Layer* (SASL) communications defined in RFC 2222. Configure the strongest authentication that your version of LDAP supports to better protect your LDAP hierarchy.

- **Utilize encryption.**   Secure LDAP (LDAPS, formerly known as sldap) allows you to encrypt communications using SSL/TLS.

- **Block access to LDAP ports from the Internet.**   LDAP communications travel over TCP/UDP port 389, and LDAPS communications travel over TCP/UDP port 636. Be sure that attackers cannot listen to or make connections using these ports.

Note   Other ports are also used in LDAP communications. For example, Microsoft's Global Catalog Server is an LDAP server that operates over TCP/UDP ports 3268. Check your software vendor's documentation for an exact list of ports used.

Databases

As you know, database servers store data, and both the data and the database server are potential targets for an attacker. An attacker might seek to compromise or disrupt your database server communications, steal your data, or take over your database server. In addition to the common software problems described at the beginning of this lesson (such as buffer overflows), database servers can be exploited in the following ways:

- **Unexpected data queries or commands.**   Many database servers use Structured Query Language (SQL), which allows for the querying and posting of data. A SQL-savvy attacker might use SQL commands to make your database server do things that you didn't expect or want it to do. This is known as *SQL injection*.

- **Unauthenticated access.**   If you allow unauthenticated access to your database server, attackers can more easily connect to and attempt to exploit your database server.

- **Packet sniffing.**   Attackers might sniff data that is transferred to and from the database server.

Here are some items you should consider that could help to secure your database server:

- **Run test queries.**   Test the database to see if you can submit extraneous queries and attempt to access unauthorized information.

- **Use stored procedures.**   Instead of having Hypertext Markup Language (HTML) or Active Server Pages (ASP) build SQL query strings from user input, use stored procedures to prevent SQL injection.

- **Configure authenticated access.**   Don't allow unauthenticated connections to your database server, whenever possible. Use the strongest authentication that your database server allows.

- **Encrypt data transfers.**   If you are transferring private data to or from your database server, consider using an SSL/TLS connection or VPN to protect the data.

- **Block database ports at the firewall.**   If your database server should not be queried by external entities, block access to it on the firewall. Different database servers utilize different TCP/UDP ports to transfer information. Check your specific database to determine which ports you should block.

Exercise: Port Matching

Match the services in the left column with the correct TCP/UDP ports on which the service is provided in the right column:

1. DNS   a. 143
2. DHCP   b. 53
3. SMTP   c. 110
4. POP3   d. 25
5. IMAP   e. 67/68

Lesson Review

The following questions are intended to reinforce key information presented in this lesson. If you are unable to answer a question, review the lesson and then try the question again. Answers to the questions can be found in Appendix A, "Questions and Answers."

1. What are some ways to secure your network from exploits targeted at servers capable of dynamic DNS (DDNS)?

2. What steps can you take to secure DHCP servers and clients on your network?

3. How might an attacker use your FTP server to compromise another computer?

4. What are the differences in authentication support between LDAP v2 and LDAP v3?

5. What are the components in an LDAP hierarchy?

Lesson Summary

- The following security tips are common to all servers: research issues that are specific to your server and its applications, keep informed of security alerts and updates, enable logging mechanisms, enable user encryption, maintain backup copies of information, and use vulnerability scanning tools.

- General tips for securing Web servers include the following: reduce features, secure available features, isolate your public Web servers from your internal network by placing them in a perimeter network, protect your internal Web servers by blocking port 80 on the internal firewall, and carefully choose Web server directories and secure them appropriately.

- Security tips for FTP servers include the following: isolate your public FTP servers from the internal network by placing them in a perimeter network, protect your internal FTP servers by blocking TCP/UDP ports 21 and 20 on the internal firewall, don't allow unauthenticated write access, configure encrypted authentication and data transfer where possible, and monitor your FTP directories for unauthorized content.

- The following are some security tips for e-mail servers: use virus scanners to protect your systems from viruses, use an e-mail relay or gateway server to protect your e-mail server, reduce processing load, scan for unwanted content, and scan for and close open SMTP relays.

- Security tips for DNS servers include the following: use a separate DNS server for internal and perimeter network name resolution, restrict the information you place in DNS, limit zone transfers, secure zone transfers, secure dynamic updates, and use secure DNS when possible.

- The following are some security tips for DHCP: scan for rogue DHCP servers, configure DNS server information at the DHCP client, restrict address leases to known MAC addresses, and block DHCP ports at the firewall.

- Security tips for file and printer servers include the following: block access to shares and related information at the firewall, use the highest security and authentication levels available, and verify share security.

- Security tips for NNTP servers include the following: block NNTP at the internal firewall, require authentication and encryption on private servers, and consider the information you allow and post on NNTP servers.

- The following are some security tips for LDAP servers: configure strong authentication, implement SLADP when encryption is required, and block access to LDAP ports from external networks.

- Security tips for database servers include the following: run test queries against the server to check security, use stored procedures, configure authenticated access and restrict or disallow unauthenticated access, encrypt data transfers for confidential data, and block database ports at the firewall.

C H A P T E R   9

Operational Security

About This Chapter

Applications, protocols, and operating systems have a variety of security mechanisms built into them, but the overall security picture for a business network transcends these software elements and encompasses a wide range of other areas, including physical security, hardware selection and protection, privilege management, and overall business continuity planning. This chapter examines these elements and presents a high-level overview of how to organize and implement these forms of protection.

Before You Begin

You should review Chapter 1, "General Networking and Security Concepts," and Chapter 7, "User Security," before reading this chapter.

Lesson 1: Physical Security

When studying the more esoteric aspects of network security, it is sometimes easy to neglect the more obvious forms of protection. Installing bulletproof applications and protecting your data with sophisticated encryption algorithms is no help if an intruder can open the door to your computer center and walk off with your server. The physical security of your network is a given that is too often ignored by security specialists who are more interested in the technical aspects of protection.

After this lesson, you will be able to

- Understand the need for physical protection of network equipment
- List the most commonly used biometric technologies
- Understand how intruders use social engineering to penetrate network security measures
- Describe how wireless networks present greater security risks than cabled networks
- Understand how offsite backup storage and a secure recovery area can reduce down time in the event of a disaster

Estimated lesson time: 40 minutes

Access Control

In most cases, the term *access control* is used when referring to the mechanisms that regulate network access to computers, software, or other resources. However, security professionals must understand that the term applies equally to the physical access to computers and other equipment that users are granted. Protection against theft is certainly an important consideration; important servers and other equipment should always be kept under lock and key. However, there are other potential dangers that physical access control can protect against as well, including fire, natural disasters, and even simple accidents.

In one small office, the primary server was kept in the lobby so that the receptionist could conveniently change the backup tape every day. Not only did this arrangement expose the server to possible theft, but it also made the server into a piece of furniture that was promptly covered with potted plants. The receptionist diligently changed the backup tape each day, right after watering the plants. One day a planter overflowed and the entire business ground to a halt for several days until a new server could be purchased and installed.

Servers containing important data, routers, and other crucial networking components should always be kept in locked server closets or a secured computer center
to protect against theft and even overwatering of plants. However, all too often, the
so-called computer center in an office consists simply of the rooms occupied by the
IT department, perhaps with an extra air conditioning unit and a combination lock
on the door. Servers might be scattered amidst workers' desks and the "secured"
door left open during business hours, for the sake of convenience. Server closets
can be an equally inappropriate term, when computers have to share unheated storage space with cleaning supplies and other odds and ends.

Closing the combination-locked door of the computer center at night and leaving the
air conditioning on can provide a relatively secure environment that defeats the
casual thief, but IT workers are no less liable to spill their cups of coffee than anyone
else, and having the servers out in the open during working hours is an inherently
dangerous practice. In the same way, a closet that is regularly accessed by maintenance workers and other personnel affords little or no protection for your servers.

A properly designed computer center or server closet is one in which physical barriers prevent access by anyone but authorized personnel when they have specific
reason to access that equipment. Even authorized IT workers should not have to be
in the same room as sensitive networking equipment because their desks are nearby
or because they need to get a ream of printer paper or other supplies. In fact, servers and other components should require very little physical access at all, because
most maintenance and configuration tasks can be performed remotely.

An installation with proper physical security should use concentric rings of
increasingly strong physical barriers, with the most sensitive resources stored in the
central ring. The combination lock on the computer center door is still a good idea,
protecting the entire IT department from casual intruders. The door should be kept
closed and locked at all times, however, perhaps with a buzzer to enable screened
outsiders to come in.

Inside the computer center, the actual location of the servers and other critical components should be protected by still another locked door with monitored access. At
its simplest, this monitoring could take the form of a paper log in which users sign
in and out of the locked room. If more security is required, magnetic key cards,
video cameras, or even security guards could be substituted. The point is that no
one should be entering the secured area without a specific purpose, and without
their presence being logged for later reference.

Physical Barriers

The actual nature of the physical barriers used to secure networking equipment is also an important consideration. Typical office construction standards—hollow doors, flimsy drywall, and drop ceilings—might defeat the casual intruder, but they are easily penetrated by the determined interloper. A state-of-the-art electronic combination lock is of little value when someone can easily put a fist through the wall or crawl over the doorway through a drop ceiling into the secured area.

The inner rings of your security area should provide protection on all six sides of the room, meaning that doors should be solid and walls should be reinforced and run vertically from slab to slab, through drop ceilings and raised floors. In some cases, even these precautions might be insufficient against intruders with heavy tools; an alarm system or security cameras can provide additional protection.

Biometrics

For installations requiring extreme security, the standard mechanisms used to control access to the secured area, such as metal keys, magnetic key cards, combinations, and passwords, might be insufficient. Keys and key cards can be lost or stolen, and passwords and combinations can be written down, shared, or otherwise compromised. As you saw in Chapter 7, one alternative that has made its way from James Bond fiction to the real world is biometrics.

Biometric technologies can be used for two different purposes: verification and identification. Biometric verification essentially asks the system to indicate whether individuals actually are who they claim to be. Biometric identification is the process of establishing an individual's identity based on biometric information, essentially asking the system to indicate who the person is. Although both functions have their own complexities, most biometric security systems are designed to verify individuals because the process is inherently simpler.

The complexities involved in biometric identification depend largely on the size of the system's user base. When there are a relatively small number of individuals to be identified, the biometric scan can immediately isolate specific minutiae in the individual's physiology and compare them with a database of known records. When the system must authenticate any one of thousands of individuals, the scanned biometric data is typically categorized first, so that the sampling of the database to which it must compared is reduced. Biometric verification, on the other hand, does not have to compare a sampling to all of the records in an entire database, only to the one specific record belonging to whomever the individual being scanned claims to be.

Biometric authentication devices can use a number of different characteristics to identify individuals. Some of the biometric technologies in use today include the following:

- **Fingerprint matching.**   The fingerprint scan is the oldest biometric technology and still one of the most popular. Because every individual's fingerprints are unique, fingerprint scans can be used for identification or verification. The image enhancement technologies developed over the years have helped to eliminate many of the problems that resulted from inadequate scanning or variances in finger pressure and position during the scan.

- **Hand geometry.**   Hand geometry is a verification technique based on a scan of an individual's hand shape, taking into account various characteristics, such as length, thickness, and curvature of fingers. An individual's hand geometry is not unique, however, as fingerprints are, so this technique cannot be used for identification, only for verification. However, hand geometry scans are much faster, cleaner, and less invasive than fingerprint scans, making them a much more convenient mechanism.

- **Iris scans.**   A scan of the eyeball's iris pattern is usable for both verification and identification. The iris is the colored part of the eye surrounding the pupil. Iris scans are based on a high-resolution photograph of the eye taken from a distance of less than three feet. The pattern of the iris does not change over a person's lifetime and is unaffected by eyeglasses or contact lenses, making it a very reliable form of verification and identification that is almost impossible to mask or imitate.

- **Retinal scans.**   The retina is found on the rear of the eyeball, and it contains a pattern of veins that is unique to each individual. Even identical twins have different retinal patterns. More accurate than virtually any other biometric technology, including iris scanning, retinal scans are more invasive, requiring the individual to look directly into an infrared light, which shines through the eyeball, illuminating the anterior surface.

- **Speech recognition.**   Voice pattern matching is one of the more complex biometric functions, and it is also easier to spoof (with recordings) than the other technologies listed here. The process of matching voice patterns involves the creation of a voice model for the individual to be authenticated. The voice model is a baseline pattern that accounts for the variations in utterances spoken by the same person at different times.

- **Face recognition and facial thermograms.**   Facial recognition systems and thermograms are not yet as accurate as fingerprints and other unique human attributes, but they have the potential to become a fast and uninvasive biometric verification system.

Some of the biometric systems on the market use a combination of physiological factors for various reasons. For example, a system that can perform both hand geometry and fingerprint scans can use the former for rapid identity verifications and the latter for the identification of individuals. Other systems combine two or more biometric technologies to create a combined accuracy rate and performance time that exceeds those of the technologies working individually.

Social Engineering

All of the security mechanisms that you use on your network are essentially a compromise between the need to protect valuable resources and the need to provide people access to those resources with a minimum of inconvenience. It would not be difficult to assign complex 20-character passwords to all your user accounts, run all your network cables through heavy steel conduits, and seal your servers inside a bank vault. The result would almost certainly be greater security than you have now. However, the expense of the installation and the revolt of the users faced with the inconvenience of remembering the passwords and unlocking the vault makes extreme measures like these impractical.

Even though security policies are typically implemented and enforced by the management of an organization, security actually rests in the hands of the people that use the protected systems every day. The object of all your security procedures is to make people understand the importance of protecting sensitive resources and to urge them to work with you in providing that protection. No matter how stringent your password policies, for example, there's nothing you can do to stop users from writing down their passwords in inappropriate places or sharing them with the wrong people, except educate them about the dangers of these practices.

Social engineering is a term used to describe the process of circumventing security barriers by persuading authorized users to provide passwords or other sensitive information. In most cases users are duped into giving an intruder access to a protected system through a phone call in which the intruder claims to be an employee in another department, a customer, or a hardware vendor. A user might give out a seemingly innocent piece of information, which the intruder then uses to elicit more information from someone else.

For example, in the first phone call, an innocent user might supply the information that Terry Adams, manager of the IT department, is out on vacation for the week, and that Mark Lee is the acting manager. In the next call, to Mark Lee, the intruder might identify himself or herself as the IT manager of one of the company's other offices, saying that Terry Adams had promised to fax the details of the office's firewall configuration and asking for the information to be faxed to 212-555-1234. The intruder might identify himself or herself as a salesperson for a router manufacturer. By getting a network administrator to chat about current router needs, the intruder might get the information needed to penetrate the company's defenses.

Attitude is everything when it comes to social engineering. It is surprising how often these seemingly obvious and transparent techniques are effective at eliciting confidential information when the intruder is adept at sounding confused, hurried, confident, or imperious. Kevin Mitnick, probably the best known of the so-called computer hackers since his conviction for breaking into telephone company computers, stealing data, and abusing electronic communication systems, obtained confidential information using his social engineering skills as much as his technical expertise.

You can't protect your network against social engineers with locked doors, passwords, or firewalls. The only true protection is educating your users about the techniques used by social engineers and the need to verify people's identities before disclosing any information to them. However, a telephone system that is capable of recording calls for later examination (along with the standard "your call may be recorded for quality control purposes" disclaimer) can act as a deterrent.

Environment

The environment in which your network must operate is an important consideration in the design and construction of the network and the technologies that you select. The typical office environment is usually augmented with additional air conditioning, air filtration, humidity control, or power conditioning in places where high concentrations of sensitive equipment are located, such as data centers and server closets. This type of environmental planning is as important to the continued operation of your network as securing your resources against theft, destruction, and data loss.

Fire Suppression

Protecting sensitive equipment from theft and maintaining proper operating conditions is important, but fire is a major threat to the continued operation of network equipment. The damage caused by fire, and by standard firefighting techniques, can cause not only data and equipment loss, but also damage to the facilities themselves that can take a long time to repair before replacement equipment can even be installed.

For large installations, a fire suppression system should be mandatory in the data center or server room. In the event of a fire, these systems flood the room with an inert gas, displacing the oxygen that the fire needs to burn. This puts the fire out quickly and prevents firefighters from destroying electronic equipment with water or foam. Unfortunately, these systems also displace the oxygen that people need to breathe, so evacuation alarms and emergency air supplies are also a necessary part of the system.

Halon compounds were the fire suppression gases of choice for many years, until they were found to damage the ozone layer. Now, they are in the process of being phased out in most countries around the world. Today, Dupont markets a line of replacement products, such as FE-13 and FE-36, that are safer for the environment and less toxic to humans. These types of chemical fire suppressants are well suited for electrical fires.

Wireless Networking

Typical operating environments, such as factory floors and laboratories, might require special networking equipment, such as fiber optic cables for resistance to electromagnetic interference or wireless technologies to support roaming users or bypass obstacles that inhibit the installation of standard network cables. Recent developments in wireless networking technology, and particularly the 802.11b standard published by the Institute of Electrical and Electronic Engineers (IEEE), have led to explosive growth in the use of wireless networks, and the security hazards that accompany this growth should not be underestimated.

Location

Because the signals that most wireless networking technologies use today can penetrate walls and other barriers, it is entirely possible for clandestine users outside the building to access the network using their own equipment. When selecting and installing wireless networking components, and particularly access points that provide access to a cabled network, you should test carefully to ascertain the operational range of the devices and select locations for the antennae that are near the center of the building, as far away from the outside walls as possible. In cases where sensitive data might be transmitted over the wireless network, it is best to keep the transmission power of all the wireless devices to the minimum needed for effective operation, so that any intruders outside the building have a harder time connecting to the network.

Shielding

Another way of protecting a wireless network from unauthorized connections is to shield the operational area. This can also protect the wireless network from denial of service (DoS) attacks. Implementing a DoS attack on a wireless network is alarmingly easily. Because microwave ovens operate at the same frequency as IEEE 802.11b transceivers, simply bypassing the door switch on an oven so that it can operate with the door open enables you to generate up to 1000 watts of interference.

Depending on the transmission power of the wireless networking equipment and the materials used to construct the building, the walls themselves might function as an effective shield. In the future, buildings could be constructed with integrated shielding, enabling wireless networks to operate inside without fear of a security breach. The problem with using shielding to protect a wireless network is that the signals of other devices, such as cell phones and pagers, could be blocked as well.

Wireless Cells

Wireless technologies such as IEEE 802.11b are well suited to local area networking applications because their operational ranges are sufficient for a typical network installation and a potential intruder has to be relatively close to a transceiver to connect to the network. However, cellular technology has virtually unlimited range, and there are now many products available that enable portable computers to connect to a network located almost anywhere in the world. In addition, the Bluetooth short-range wireless products that are now coming to market will make it even simpler (and cheaper) for users to connect a laptop to a remote network using the cell phones in their pockets.

Although cellular networking is slower than IEEE 802.11b and its ilk, the potential security danger of this technology is far greater, because the intruder need not be anywhere close to the network installation to gain access to its resources. Before implementing any cellular-based wireless network, you should consider carefully how you are going to protect the network against outside intrusion.

Disaster Recovery

In a security context, a disaster is any occurrence that can prevent your network from operating normally or prevent your company from doing business. Disasters can be as simple as a hard disk failure or as catastrophic as a hurricane, and a properly designed network has a plan in place that covers both these extremes and everything in between.

Backups

Backing up your data should be the first thing that comes to mind when you think of disaster recovery. Making regular backups and testing them by performing regular restores is basic, but it is only the beginning of a good disaster recovery plan.

In most cases, network administrators use backups to recover files that were accidentally deleted. This is a simple task, in that you simply use the same software that created the backup in the first place. Beyond that, however, everyone understands that backups are also protection against disk failures, computer thefts, or disasters in which a computer is damaged or destroyed. Restoring from a backup in these events is more complicated, because you must first install the operating system and the backup software before you can even access the data stored on your backup tapes or other media.

Many network backup products have a disaster recovery feature (often available as an add-on product at an additional cost) that simplifies the process of performing a complete restore. These products enable you to boot a computer from a CD-ROM that contains only the operating system and backup software components needed to perform a simple restore job. Completing the job restores the entire operating system and the full backup software product, so the system performs normally after that. For a business in which server down time means lost money, these products are a good investment against further damage resulting from the original disaster.

Offsite Storage

A recent backup can be a lifesaver in the event of a drive failure or computer theft, but you must also plan for disasters that might result in the complete destruction of your computer center, your building, or even your city. Fires, floods, tornadoes, and other catastrophes can destroy your backup media as easily as they can destroy your computers, so keeping copies of your backups offsite is an essential part of any disaster recovery plan.

Tip   In addition to the backups of your data, your offsite cache should also include copies of your company's disaster recovery plans and all emergency policies and procedures. The time and money you spend to devise a comprehensive disaster recovery plan would only be wasted if your building burns down, destroying all copies of the plan.

Depending on how much protection you think you need, an offsite storage solution could be as simple as making an extra copy of your backup tapes and taking it home every night. If a fire should destroy the building, you would still have a copy of your data to restore from. You might also consider storing the offsite copies in a bank's safe deposit vault or in a fireproof safe or storage facility.

Secure Recovery

Making backups on a regular basis and storing copies offsite, even with a disaster recovery disk, protects your data, but that doesn't necessarily mean that you can be up and running in a matter of hours if a disaster should strike. Depending on the nature of the disaster, you might have to replace a drive, a server, or even the entire office where the server was located. This could mean days or even weeks of down time before you can even begin restoring your data.

However, there are solutions that can reduce your down time to a matter of hours, even in the event of a catastrophic disaster. *Secure recovery* refers to an alternate site that contains a replica of all or part of your network. Depending on your budget and the nature of your business, solutions can range from a mirror server running at a site in another city to a complete secure recovery area containing everything you need to keep your business going until you can replace your original equipment.

Alternate Sites

A number of companies specialize in business recovery services. Some are simply hosting services that run mirror servers for you in a protected environment in another city. Under normal conditions, the servers can take on some of your normal traffic load, but when disaster strikes and your primary server goes down, the mirror server takes over immediately. Other services can provide you with everything from computers to office space to temporary workers, and anything else you might need to keep your business operating during a crisis.

One of the additional benefits of these services is that they provide you with a test platform for your emergency procedures and a convenient means of staging emergency drills to test the efficacy of your plans and the readiness of your people.

It isn't always necessary to use a professional service to have an alternate site for your network, however. If your company has branch offices in other cities, you can arrange for each office to have a mirror server at another location. You can even enter into a mutual agreement with another company to host servers for each other in the event of an emergency.

All of these solutions are known as *hot sites*, or alternative sites where you have servers running all the time, for immediate use in the event of an emergency. For businesses with limited budgets where continuous operation is not as critical, a *cold site* might be sufficient. A cold site means you keep duplicate equipment in offsite storage, ready for use if disaster strikes. For example, if there is a fire in your office and you have offsite copies of your backups and an extra server in storage, you can rent some temporary office space, or even a hotel room, and be up and running in a matter of hours.

Disaster Recovery Plan

The most important tool to have when disaster strikes your network or your business is a well-organized and well-maintained recovery plan. It is critical for everyone in your company to know what has to be done to keep your business going in the event of an emergency, and who is going to be responsible for which tasks. Disasters are, by definition, unpredictable, and you have no way of knowing what hardware, software, and even human resources will be lost. If recent events have taught us anything, it is that disaster can strike without warning at any time, so planning for the worst is the prudent thing to do in any business.

Lesson Review

The following questions are intended to reinforce key information presented in this lesson. If you are unable to answer a question, review the lesson and then try the question again. Answers to the questions can be found in Appendix A, "Questions and Answers."

1. Why is a biometric device based on hand geometry suitable only for verifying users and not identifying them?

2. Which of the following attributes of cellular networking products make them a greater security risk than IEEE 802.11b wireless products?

   a. Lower cost

   b. Greater transmission range

   c. Less susceptibility to interference from walls and barriers

   d. Use of higher frequencies

3. What is the difference between a mirrored server stored at a hot site and one stored at a cold site?

Lesson Summary

- Network resources must be protected physically as well as technically.

- Proper physical security uses concentric rings of increasingly strong barriers as you approach the central ring.

- Biometric technologies provide an additional method for identifying and verifying users.

- Social engineering is the process of circumventing security barriers by persuading authorized users to provide passwords or other sensitive information.

- Fire suppression systems using inert gas minimize the damage caused by fire and firefighting techniques.

- Wireless networking presents additional security problems that can be minimized by judicious selection of power settings and careful antenna placement.

- Regular backups with offsite storage are an essential element of any disaster recovery plan.

- Maintaining mirror servers at distant sites provides an immediate failover capability.

Lesson 2: Privilege Management

Networks exist to provide hardware, software, and information resources to users. To protect those resources from damage and theft, you must limit user access to them. You grant some users full access to particular resources, whereas other users receive partial access. Some users get no access at all, and you might even want to prevent those users from knowing that the resources exist. The process of planning how to assign those resources to your users is called *privilege management*.

After this lesson, you will be able to

- Understand how to use groups and roles to manage user privileges
- Understand how centralized management can simplify the privilege management process
- Describe the differences between mandatory access control, discretionary access control, and role-based access control

Estimated lesson time: 20 minutes

Understanding User, Group, and Role Management

To grant users access to network resources, most operating systems use a set of rights or permissions. Each right or permission provides the user with a specific privilege. For example, a file system typically has two separate permissions that enable a user to read a file and write to it. When you grant users the read permission only, they can look at the file, but they cannot change it. If certain users have to be able to modify the file, you must grant them the write permission as well.

The object of privilege management is to grant each user the rights and permissions to the specific network resources he or she needs to perform his or her assigned tasks, and no more. As mentioned in Chapter 8, this is called the rule of least privilege (also known as the principle of least privilege). Restricting users' access only to what they need prevents unsophisticated or careless users from accidentally damaging or destroying valuable resources, and prevents unauthorized individuals from doing things they should not.

In theory, granting privileges to users is a simple task. For example, to give a user access to a particular file, you add an entry to that file's access control list (ACL) containing the user's name and the specific permissions you want that user to have. However, when you consider that a large organization can have thousands of files stored on its servers and thousands of users who need access to various files, the task of privilege management becomes very daunting indeed.

Using Groups

To simplify the process of managing privileges, network operating systems all make it possible to create groups of users. When users are members of a group, they inherit all privileges granted to that group. Therefore, if you have 50 users who all need access to one file, you can create a group with those 50 users as members, and then create one entry in the file's ACL granting privileges to that group. In this way, you are creating one ACL entry instead of 50, which simplifies the process considerably. In addition, the network resources themselves are typically arranged in a hierarchical structure, with permissions running downstream. File systems and directory services let you assign users permission to access a specific object, and the users then inherit access to all of the subordinates of that object.

These techniques can make the network administrator's life much easier, but it is important for administrators to learn how to manage users and groups properly and consistently. When deciding how to manage users and groups, network administrators should ask themselves questions such as these:

- How many groups should we create?
- What should the groups be called?
- What criteria should we use when creating groups of users?
- How many users should there be in each group?
- What privileges should be assigned to each group?

There are no right and wrong answers to these questions. What is important is that the organization create policies for user and group management and compel everyone involved to adhere to them. If one administrator starts creating groups based on the geographical location of the users' work areas, and another administrator starts creating groups based on the first letter of the users' surnames, chaos is sure to ensue.

Creating Groups

When creating groups, the obvious intent is to group users together that have the same needs. If the workers in the Order Entry department all need to look up names in the customer database, it's common sense to create a group with a name such as Order Entry and grant that group the privileges needed to read the database. This is known as *role-based privilege management*. You should create groups based on specific tasks that multiple workers have to perform and assign the appropriate privileges to those groups. From that point on, when users take on or are relieved of a task, you simply have to add users or remove them from the right group. Most medium- and large-sized organizations never assign privileges to individual users; all privileges are assigned using groups.

Group management is rarely as simple as this example, however. You might have a large number of order entry workers who must be able to read the customer database, and a handful of supervisors who also need to be able to modify entries in that database. This certainly does not mean that you should grant the entire Order Entry group permission to read and modify the database. Instead, you might create two groups, Order Entry Operators and Order Entry Supervisors, with only the supervisors having permission to change database entries. You then make everyone in the department a member of the Order Entry Operators group, but only those few supervisors should be members of the Order Entry Supervisors group. One user can function in many roles, and therefore can be a member of many groups. The privileges assigned to each group of which a user is a member are then combined to create the user's *effective permissions*.

The relationships between the privileges assigned to different groups can become complicated. For example, one group might explicitly grant a privilege whereas another group explicitly denies that same privilege. If one user is a member of both groups, what are the user's resulting effective privileges? The answer depends on the operating system in use. Most operating systems have a system of priorities that enable you to have one group's privileges override those of another.

Centralized and Decentralized Management

In the early days of network operating systems, every computer maintained its own user accounts, groups, and permissions. When users needed access to the resources of a particular server, an administrator had to create accounts for them on that server and add them to the appropriate groups. This is known as *decentralized management*, because each server controlled access to its own resources, and administrators had to travel to each server or access it remotely to manage accounts. For each server a user accessed, the computers performed a separate authentication procedure. In some cases, when a user had the same account name and password on multiple servers, the authentication process occurred in the background and was automatic and invisible, but this still meant a great deal of extra work for network administrators, who had to create all of the accounts. Decentralized management is still available on some operating systems that are intended for small networks, but they are not typically used in large organizations.

Single Sign-On

The standard today is for users to perform a single sign-on when starting a computer session, which grants them access to resources all over the network. In most cases, on private networks, the single sign-on is provided by a directory service, such as Microsoft's Active Directory directory service or Novell's Novell Directory Services. Directory services typically use a digital certificate to authenticate a user's identity and grant them access to the resources they need. Directory services provide centralized management, so administrators only have to create one account for each user, all of which are stored in the same place, and the users only have to type their account names and passwords once.

For Web applications, centralized management is provided by applications such as Microsoft Passport. Users perform a single sign-on that authenticates them with the Passport service, and this grants them access to applications at other Web sites where they are registered.

Auditing

In addition to controlling access to network resources, privilege management typically provides administrators with a means of tracking resource usage, called *auditing*. Depending on the operating system, auditing might enable the administrator to maintain records of what privileges a particular user processes, what resources the users accessed, and when. When access control is based on digital certificates, this provides a nonrepudiation service. A user cannot deny having accessed a particular resource named in the audit, because only that user had control of the certificate that granted access to the resource.

In most cases, auditing is an optional feature that you have to enable manually before the system retains any information. The operating system typically saves the audit information to a log file, which administrators should review on a regular basis. To control the amount of disk space consumed by the logs, it is often possible to specify how long information is retained in the log and how detailed the audit information saved to the log should be. It is common for administrators to assume that logging audit information with the greatest amount of detail is best, but this can make it difficult to review the logs later.

For example, logging every instance in which a user successfully accesses a network resource can result in a huge log file that takes a long time to review and yields little or no useful information. You can use this type of information if you are trying to determine how many users access the resource, but in most cases you would be better served by just logging the unsuccessful access attempts. This is likely to result in a much smaller log file, which you can quickly review to see if unauthorized users are attempting to access secured resources.

Reviewing the audit logs on a regular basis is often delegated to a junior administrator. If this is the case, your organization should have policies in place that specify exactly when specific log results should be escalated to someone higher in the management hierarchy. Retaining your audit logs for an extended period of time is also a good idea, because you might want to use them in the future to compile statistics regarding your network's resource access patterns.

Lesson Review

The following questions are intended to reinforce key information presented in this lesson. If you are unable to answer a question, review the lesson and then try the question again. Answers to the questions can be found in Appendix A, "Questions and Answers."

1. Which of the following statements about users and groups is true?

   a. A user can only be a member of one group.

   b. A user's effective permissions can be inherited from multiple groups.

   c. Creating groups enables the network administrator to create fewer user accounts.

   d. Groups cannot have conflicting privileges.

2. How does centralized administration reduce the workload of the network administrator?

   a. By reducing the number of resources to which users have to be granted privileges.

   b. By reducing the number of groups that need to be created.

   c. By reducing the number of users accounts that need to be created.

   d. By reducing the number of privileges that have to be granted to each user.

3. When you grant a user account the minimal required permission, what rule are you applying?

Lesson Summary

- Rather than assign privileges to individual users, operating systems typically enable administrators to create groups, of which users are members. Privileges granted to a group are inherited by all of its members.

- Creating groups is a matter of determining which users need to have the same privileges.

- Centralized management, in the form of directory services and other single sign-on applications, has simplified the privilege management process by enabling administrators to create one account for each user, instead of many.

- Auditing enables administrators to track the privileges granted to a user, the resources that the user has accessed, and the overall usage of a resource.

Lesson 3: Removable Media

Removable storage media, such as magnetic tape, CD-ROMs, various types of floppy disks, and even hard disks, are involved in security considerations for two different reasons:

- Removable media can be used to copy confidential information from your company servers and remove it from the facility without the opportunity for the information to be filtered or audited by a network gateway.
- Removable media are often used to store data for backup or archival purposes.

After this lesson, you will be able to

- Understand the security ramifications of using removable media
- List the various types of removable media and explain how they are typically used
- Describe how the various types of removable media can be protected

Estimated lesson time: 30 minutes

You must understand what steps you can take to prevent people from using removable media to carry data out of the office. As a storage solution for confidential data, you should know how to protect the information on the media, how best to store the media to keep the information intact, and how to effectively erase the media when necessary.

The following sections examine characteristics of the most commonly used removable media.

Magnetic Tape

Because of its low cost, its ability to hold a great deal of data, and its reasonably high speed, magnetic tape has been the storage medium of choice for system backup operations for decades. Many organizations also use magnetic tape for archiving data, and, prior to the widespread acceptance of CD-ROMs, tape was sometimes used for software distribution as well.

As a backup medium, magnetic tapes are an inexpensive, reliable, and compact storage medium. Today's tapes can survive rough handling and extreme conditions better than hard disks because they contain no electronics, and they are more durable than CD-ROMs, because the surface that holds the actual data is protected inside a plastic case. Easily storable, magnetic tape also makes an excellent archival medium.

Magnetic tapes and tape drives are available in a variety of sizes and formats, as shown in Table 9-1.

Table 9-1.   Magnetic Tape Technologies

Type	Tape Width	Cartridge Size	Capacity (Uncompressed)	Speed
Quarter-inch cartridge (QIC)	.25 inch	4 × 6 × 0.625 inches (data cartridge); 3.25 × 2.5 × 0.6 inches (minicartridge)	Up to 20 GB	2 to 120 MB/min
Digital audio tape (DAT)	4 mm	2.875 × 2.0625 × 0.375 inches	Up to 20 GB	3 to 144 MB/min
8 mm	8 mm	3.7 × 2.44 × 0.59 inches	Up to 60 GB	Up to 180 MB/min
Digital linear tape (DLT)	.50 inch	4.16 × 4.15 × 1 inches	Up to 40 GB	Up to 360 MB/min
Linear tape open (LTO), Ultrium media	.50 inch	4.0 × 4.16 × 0.87 inches	Up to 100 GB	Up to 1920 MB/min

Generally speaking, QIC drives are used for backing up stand-alone computers and DAT for basic network backups. DLT, 8mm, and LTO are higher end technologies in both performance and price, and they are used for networks that require larger tape capacities and higher data transfer speeds.

Protecting Magnetic Tape Data

Unlike most other computer storage media, magnetic tape drives are not random access devices and do not function in the same way as hard disks, CD-ROMs, and other technologies. You can't simply copy files to the tape using standard file management tools. You must use a special program that is designed to write to the tape drive. Although there are simple command-line tools that can accomplish this, in most cases, network administrators use a specialized network backup product to write data to tapes.

Virtually all backup software products provide the ability to password protect backup jobs, so that only someone with the password can perform a restore from a particular tape using the backup software. This provides minimal protection against someone with access to the backup software restoring the data from a tape for their own purposes. However, this password protection is a function of the backup software only. It is still possible to read the raw data from the tape using hardware and software designed for this purpose, and to then extract the data from it. For complete security, you should encrypt the data written to the tape, so that even in its raw form, an intruder cannot access the information.

Of course, removable media are also easier to secure physically than computers or hard disks. If you keep your backup and archive tapes in a locked vault, you might not feel the need to password protect or encrypt them.

Erasing Magnetic Tapes

Because magnetic tapes are not random access devices, erasing the data stored on them is relatively difficult. In most cases, the erase function built into a backup software application does nothing but delete the tape header, leaving the actual data intact. This causes the backup software to see the tape as blank, and the next backup job written to the tape overwrites the previous information. However, it is still possible to retrieve the raw data from the tape and access the information stored there.

Even running a powerful magnet or bulk eraser over a tape is not a sure method of deleting all of the data stored there. With the appropriate equipment, a knowledgeable technician can retrieve at least part of the information from a tape that has supposedly been erased in this way.

The only sure method of erasing the data from a magnetic tape is using one of the permanent data deletion programs on the market. These programs perform multiple overwrites on the tape to ensure that all vestiges of the data stored there are eradicated. Some backup software packages have a secure erase feature built in; in other cases you might need a third-party product.

Preventing Tape Abuse

Magnetic tape drives are not a common accessory on the average computer, so limiting access to them is not that difficult. In a business environment, usually only specific servers are equipped with tape drives, and these computers should always be secured to prevent unauthorized individuals from using the tape drives for their own purposes.

Writable CD-ROMs

Compact Disc-Recordable (CD-R) and Compact Disc-Rewritable (CD-RW) drives have become almost ubiquitous in the home computer market, and they are commonly found on business computers as well. Although they lack the great capacity of the higher end magnetic tape formats, CDs are suitable for small-scale backups and archive projects.

Standard CD-ROMs are made by pressing a pattern of *pits and lands* in the substrate of the disc material. CD-Rs and CD-RWs are somewhat different. They use the same patterns to encode the data, but instead of creating a physical impression on the disk, a CD-R or CD-RW drive works by using a laser to create the data pattern in a layer of photosensitive dye incorporated into the disk. On a CD-R, the changes that the laser makes to the dye are permanent, whereas in a CD-RW, the changes can be reversed, making it possible to erase the disk and write new data on it.

When a drive reads a CD-R or CD-RW, a laser located below the disc shines upward through the dye layer and bounces off a layer of reflective material, which is a coating of a metallic alloy (or sometimes even gold or platinum) on the top (or label side) of the disk. It is true that the bottom side of a CD is the "business end" of the disk, because that's where the laser is, but a scratch in the reflective top surface is far more likely to cause read problems than a scratch on the bottom, because the focal point of the laser is the top surface, where the reflective material is located.

Archiving Data

As an archival medium, the value of a CD-R or CD-RW depends on the type of dye used to create the photosensitive layer in the disk and the state of the reflective coating on the top surface. There are a number of different compounds that manufacturers use for the dye, including cyanine, phthalocyanine, metallized azo, and formazen. These dyes have different effective life ratings provided by the manufacturers, which are obviously not the result of empirical studies, as they often speak of CD-Rs and CD-RWs being able to hold data for 75 or 100 years or more. It is reasonably safe to assume that when shopping for blank CD-R and CD-RW discs, you get what you pay for. If you are planning to archive data on these discs and you want to maintain the data indefinitely, you should definitely pay a little more for high-quality discs rather than using a bargain brand.

The photosensitivity of the dye and the relative fragility of the reflective surface on CD-R and CD-RW discs also means that you must be careful how you store the media. You should not expose the disks to sunlight for extended periods, and you should always store them in paper sleeves to protect the surface. If you can purchase discs with an additional protective coating on the top surface, you should do so.

For sensitive data, you should take the same precautions with CD-Rs and CD-RWs that you would with magnetic tapes. You can password protect the data on a CD by putting the files into a protected compressed archive, or by encrypting the data if greater security is needed.

Preventing CD-R/CD-RW Abuse

The best way to prevent people from burning their own CD-Rs and CD-RWs that include the company's confidential information is to restrict access to the drives. Many computer manufacturers today provide CD-R or CD-RW drives in their systems for a minimal cost over the same system with a read-only CD-ROM drive. You should avoid purchasing computers like these, except for users that have a legitimate need to burn their own CDs. Whenever possible, the computers containing CD burners should be secured to prevent other users from accessing them. Placing the computers behind locked doors, password protecting the basic input/output system (BIOS), and instructing users on the need to lock down the computers whenever they are left unattended are all methods you can use to minimize the risk of your data being illicitly burned on CDs.

Erasing CD-Rs and CD-RWs

Obviously, only CD-RWs can be erased and used again, but like magnetic tapes and other media, CD burning software usually has a dual-function erase feature, providing quick erase and full erase options. The quick erase function, as with a tape, deletes only the index on the disk, leaving the actual data to be overwritten later when you use the disk again. A full erase overwrites every bit of data on the disk, but that doesn't necessarily mean that it is totally unrecoverable. Differences in laser track alignment, like differences in head alignment on a magnetic medium, can leave vestiges of the data behind after an erasure. A determined individual with the correct equipment might be able to recover this data, at least in part.

The surest way of erasing the data on a CD-RW, and the only way on a CD-R, is to physically destroy the disk, but even this can be problematic. Removing the reflective surface from the top of the disk certainly prevents it from being read. Scratching the surface heavily with a sharp object, such as a nail, and breaking the disk into pieces is usually sufficient for most purposes. Some people have devised more elaborate methods, for example, using belt or drum sanders to completely remove the surface. Remember, however, that although removing the reflective surface might prevent the disk from being read, the dye pattern inside the disk is still left intact. Theoretically, at least, someone could reapply a new reflective surface and recover the data from the disk.

Breaking a disk into many pieces is also an effective means of destroying the data in most cases. Some heavy-duty shredders are strong enough to handle CDs and effectively break them into a great many pieces. Someone with sufficient time and patience could try to reassemble the jigsaw puzzle of broken pieces, however, so this method is by no means foolproof.

Heating CDs in an oven or incinerating them can certainly destroy them beyond all hope of recovery, but this method is not recommended because the fumes emitted by the burning polycarbonate can be toxic to humans and are certainly not good for the environment. Placing a CD-R or CD-RW into a microwave oven for a five-second burst on the highest setting is reputed to render it unreadable, and it also provides an entertaining show of sparks that etch a pattern into the reflective surface. This method is not recommended either, however, because of fumes and possible damage to the microwave from arcing.

Hard Disks

Although hard disks have historically been considered permanent computer components, in recent years they have become a viable removable medium as well. Ever-increasing capacities and consistently lower prices have made the hard disk the most economical storage medium available, and the hard disk arrays now found in many computers make them much more portable than they used to be. As a result, you can now consider using a hard disk as a backup medium, but you should also be aware of the possibility that hard disks can conceivably be removed from the office.

A hard disk array is essentially a framework containing a backplane that connects the drives in the array to the computer's interface. Once you install the array in a computer (or buy a computer equipped with one) you can then purchase standard hard disks and plug them into the array. In some cases, you might have to purchase a caddy that contains each hard disk as well. Some hard disk arrays are even *hot pluggable*, meaning that you can insert them into the array and remove them without shutting down the computer.

Unlike the other removable media discussed earlier, a hard disk that is removed from a computer includes the drive mechanism as well as the storage medium itself. This makes the removable hard disk unit much more fragile than a tape cartridge or a CD, because you have exposed electronics and read/write heads that are in close proximity to the platters containing the data. Dropping a CD or tape on the floor probably will not do any damage, but a hard disk will almost certainly break if dropped.

This is not to say, however, that the data will be irretrievably lost. Even if the drive mechanism is broken, there are companies that specialize in reclaiming data from damaged hard disks. The service can be expensive, but if it means the difference between saving and losing your data, the expense might be worthwhile.

Protecting the data on a removable hard disk with passwords and encryption and erasing that data securely is no different than it is on a permanently mounted hard disk. As with magnetic tapes, hard disks typically erase data by removing the appropriate entries from the drive index, leaving the actual data itself in place on the drive platters. Recovering this so-called deleted data is easier on a hard disk than on most other media because there are several commercially available utilities that enable you to read the raw data stored on the drive. Even data that is actually erased from the drive can sometimes be recovered, due to variations in the positioning of the drive heads on the platters. Fortunately, there are also a large number of applications that enable you to permanently delete files from the drive by repeatedly overwriting them with other data until all vestiges of the information are removed.

To completely erase all of the data on a hard disk, you can also perform a low-level format, which is the closest thing to starting with a completely new, empty disk. However, before performing a low-level format on a modern Integrated Drive Electronics (IDE) or Small Computer System Interface (SCSI) drive, you should consult the manufacturer and use the software they supply and recommend.

To prevent users from carrying removable disks and the data they contain out of the facility, you should limit the use of hard disk arrays to servers and other computers that can be physically secured.

Floppy Disks

Floppy disk drives are still standard equipment on most computers, even though their functions are all but superfluous. With their small capacity and slow speed, floppy disks are not a suitable medium for backups or archives, and the introduction of the bootable CD-ROM has even made them unnecessary for booting the computer in the event of hard disk failure. However, floppy disks do provide a convenient medium that individuals can use to copy data from a computer's hard disk and carry it out of the facility.

The most foolproof method for preventing users from copying data to floppy disks is to simply disable them or remove them from the computers completely. There are various security products on the market that can lock down a floppy disk drive, either physically, with a lock and key, or with software.

Rendering a floppy disk unusable is rather easy. The plastic cases protecting the actual storage medium are easily broken, and doing so makes it impossible for the drive to accept them. However, the medium itself, a flexible disk of plastic material impregnated with magnetic particles, is made of stronger stuff. As with all magnetic media, exposing the disk to a powerful magnet erases most of the data, but could still leave recoverable artifacts. In addition, although the medium inside a floppy disk is notoriously prone to damage, due to its flexibility, completely destroying the data stored so that it cannot be retrieved by any means can be a problem. It is not practical to burn the disk, because of its fumes. Magnetizing and then shredding the disk is the most practical alternative. Cutting the medium up into small enough pieces makes it unlikely that someone would devote the time needed to reassemble them.

Flashcards

A flashcard is a small data storage device conforming to any one of several manufacturers' standards, including Compact Flash, Smart Media, and Memory Stick. The nature of the devices vary, ranging from postage-stamp–sized memory cards to tiny hard disks that plug into a portable computer's PC Card slot. Most of these storage media are used for digital devices other than computers, such as MP3 audio players and digital cameras, but it is often possible to access the storage medium with a computer by using an adapter of some kind.

Depending on the technology and the application for which they are used, flashcards can have capacities from a few kilobytes up to a gigabyte or more. Media like these, with high capacity and small size, are prime candidates for abuse by users trying to smuggle confidential data out of a secured facility. These media are not yet a major security problem, because they are an emerging technology and computers are not yet equipped to use them without additional support hardware.

As a backup or archival medium, flashcard media are not yet in general use, and they are not likely to be unless their prices are reduced dramatically. In cost per megabyte, flashcards are currently among the most expensive storage media on the market. As of yet, there is no standard for the protection of data stored on a flashcard. The devices for which they are designed do not protect the data in any way, but when the use of these devices becomes more common on computers, a means for password protecting or encrypting the data will likely be devised.

Smart Cards

A smart card is a credit-card–sized device that contains a small amount of memory for storage and for software, and sometimes an integrated circuit, enabling it to perform some basic processing functions. Unlike the other media discussed in this lesson, smart cards are not designed as a storage device on which users keep their data. Smart cards are always associated with a specific application and they are designed to perform specific functions.

Smart cards are used for a variety of different applications. The card can hold a person's medical history, or a digital certificate used to authenticate a person's identity, or be used for "electronic cash" in retail businesses. In virtually all cases, the information on the card is secured using encryption, and the overall purpose of the card is usually security related.

Because a card can be lost or stolen, security applications never rely on smart cards alone; they always use a password or a personal identification number (PIN) along with the card to identify a particular user. The user is expected to keep the password or PIN secure, and not store it with the card itself.

Exercise: Identifying Removable Storage Media Types

Match the removable storage media in the left column with the appropriate description in the right column.

1. Flashcards
2. Magnetic tape
3. Smart cards
4. CD-R
5. Floppy disks

   a. Typically contains encrypted data used to authenticate a user's identity

   b. Can only be erased by physical destruction

   c. No longer used for backups and data archiving, due to low capacity

   d. New storage technologies using very small form factors

   e. Traditional medium used for backups

Lesson Review

The following questions are intended to reinforce key information presented in this lesson. If you are unable to answer a question, review the lesson and then try the question again. Answers to the questions can be found in Appendix A, "Questions and Answers."

1. Which of the following magnetic tape formats has the greatest storage capacity?

   a. DAT

   b. LTO

   c. DLT

   d. QIC

2. What is the term used to describe a hard disk that you can remove from the computer without shutting the system down?

3. Which of the following removable media is typically used to carry users' digital certificates?

   a. Flashcards

   b. Smart cards

   c. CD-Rs

   d. Floppy disks

Lesson Summary

- Magnetic tape is the traditional storage medium of choice for backups and data archiving. Data stored on tapes can be secured using passwords or encryption, and the data can be completely and permanently erased if needed.

- CD-Rs and CD-RWs have become the most popular general-use removable storage media in recent years, due to their low cost and relatively high capacity. Data on CD-Rs and CD-RWs can be secured, and CD-RWs can be securely erased. CD-Rs must be physically destroyed to erase their data, and there is no practical destruction method at this time that is completely foolproof.

- The low cost and high capacity of hard disks have made them a viable solution for backups and archiving, now that drive arrays that allow quick removal of the device are common. Hard disks are relatively fragile compared to other storage media, however.

- Floppy disks are no longer a popular storage medium because of their slow speed and low capacity. In most cases, floppy disk drives can be removed from computers if an administrator wants to prevent users from copying confidential data.

- Flashcards are new technologies that store data in extremely compact form factors, making them a potential source of concern for security administrators.

- Smart cards are specialized data storage devices that are primarily used for authentication. They are encrypted to keep the information on them secure.

Lesson 4: Protecting Business Continuity

The continued survival of a business depends on its continued operation. When a business stops operating for any reason, it loses credibility as well as income. When an extended period of down time is caused by a disaster, whether technological, environmental, or social, in many cases businesses never reopen. *Business continuity management* is a term that has been coined to describe the review, planning, and implementation processes that a business must perform to keep operating in the face of any interruption.

After this lesson, you will be able to

- Understand the process of creating a business continuity plan
- List some of the fault-tolerance measures you can take to keep your business going in an emergency

Estimated lesson time: 15 minutes

To be effective, business continuity management (BCM) must transcend the technological concerns of the IT department and involve the entire company from the top down. Although a relatively minor disaster, such as a hard disk failure in a server, can cause the company to cease operations for a time, the object of BCM is to plan contingencies for truly catastrophic occurrences in which company resources of many different types can be affected.

As an example, what would you do if the building housing your company's offices was destroyed by a tornado in the middle of a workday? If your IT department has a properly implemented disaster recovery plan, you have backup copies of your vital company data stored offsite, and perhaps even servers located in different cities or stored in unaffected locations. However, before the business can be fully operational again, you might need to find new office space, and then replace dozens of desktop workstations, the telephone system, and hundreds of mundane items such as office furniture, stationery, and supplies. In a worst case scenario, you might even have to find replacement personnel.

In the aftermath of a major disaster, people are likely to be overwhelmed by the enormity of the tasks that confront them. Even if they are able to overcome the emotional shock of such an event, they might have a difficult time focusing on what has to be done. The idea behind BCM is to have a comprehensive plan worked out in advance that specifies what has to be done to keep the business operational, who will do what when disaster occurs, and how replacement materials will be obtained.

Creating a Business Continuity Plan

The process of creating a business continuity plan must be sponsored by individuals at the highest levels of the company and encompass the entire operation, not just the IT department. The primary steps of the initial planning phase should include the following:

- Identify the mission-critical processes that the business must perform to continue operating. Every business consists of multiple processes that together enable the company to produce a product or service and be compensated for it. By listing these separate processes, you can more easily prioritize the company's activities and identify the resources you need to proceed.

- Identify all of the resources required for the mission-critical processes to operate. The list of resources for each process should include raw materials, tools and other equipment, facilities, fixtures, utilities, and personnel; in short, it comprises everything necessary for the process to continue.

- Rate the relative importance of the mission-critical processes to the continuing operation of the business. Depending on the nature of the business, your first priority might be manufacturing your product, or it might be taking orders from customers. In any case, there will be certain processes that must continue uninterrupted if the business is to survive, and others that can withstand a temporary interruption.

- Decide on a course of action to be undertaken for each mission-critical process to plan for an interruption. For crucial processes, the course of action might include moving the process to a branch office or activating a fallback facility with backup equipment prepared for such an eventuality. For less crucial processes, the company might choose to purchase insurance to cover the financial losses resulting from the interruption, rather than take steps to maintain productivity. This can protect the company against immediate financial losses, but the company's reputation can still be damaged. For some processes, the chosen course of action might be no action at all.

The planning phase of the business continuity plan is by far the most complex part of the process. Once you have decided what you are going to do and how, implementing the plan is relatively easy.

Note   For more comprehensive information on business continuity planning, you might want to consult the ISO 17799 document, published by the International Organization for Standardization. This document is available for purchase at *http://www.iso-17799.com*.

Implementing Business Continuity Preparations

For some of the processes that are essential to the survival of your business, your plan probably calls for the preparation of fallbacks that you can use if your site is damaged. Depending on the nature of your business, on the importance of the process, and your budget, these fallbacks can range from simple backups of your data to preparations for an alternative site where you can conduct business.

Backups

As discussed in Lesson 1 of this chapter, backing up your data is the most fundamental type of business continuity measure. Virtually every resource used by your business can be replaced, with sufficient time and money, except for your data. To prepare for possible disaster, you should back up your data on a regular basis (preferably daily) and make arrangements to store a copy of the data offsite.

High Availability and Fault Tolerance

High availability and fault-tolerance mechanisms are measures that you can take to keep your business operating in the event of a systems failure. Data availability technologies such as a redundant array of independent disks (RAID) enable a server to continue operating without data loss when a hard disk fails. It is also possible to build more comprehensive fault-tolerant systems, such as clustered servers that share a client load, but if one server fails for any reason, the other ones continue operating and take up the slack.

Obviously, these systems can do little good if all of the components are located at the same site, and the entire building is destroyed by a fire or other disaster. For this reason, it is also possible to place mirrored servers at distant locations, connected by a wide are network (WAN) link. For some businesses, having a branch office in another city is a convenient way to create a fault-tolerant organization. You can have not only duplicate computers and technological components at the other site, but a complete office configuration that can keep vital business processes going.

If constructing and staffing a branch office is not a practical alternative for your business, you should plan in advance for how you are going to replace vital resources that could be destroyed in a disaster. To do this, your list of essential resources should include absolutely everything the business needs to operate, including incidentals such as furniture and office supplies. Although it might not be necessary to actually purchase all of these items in advance, you should establish where and how you will get them if you have to implement the plan. For example, if a hurricane destroys a large part of your city, there is likely to be a rush on purchases of new office equipment afterward, along with profiteering by unscrupulous merchants. Cultivating good relationships with vendors in advance (preferably large vendors that won't have their entire stock destroyed in the same disaster as the one that claims your office) might mean that you will be a preferred customer later.

Note   Although it might be difficult to contemplate, you should also consider that people are a vital company resource as well. A good relationship with an employment agency could make it easier for you to engage temporary replacement personnel, if needed.

Utilities

The are a number of services such as electricity, running water, and mail, that are essential to keeping a business running. However, these services can be interrupted. If your business absolutely must keep running, no matter what the circumstances, your business continuity plan should include fallback measures that enable you to compensate for interruptions in these services.

The uninterrupted power supply (UPS) units that people commonly use to protect servers and other equipment from power spikes and brief power outages are capable of supplying power for only a few minutes. To keep a business running in the event of an extended power failure, you must have either a large array of batteries, or more practically, a generator that is tied into the building's electrical supply lines. Backup generators are frequently equipped with failover switches that enable them to start automatically if the building's power supply fails.

Reliance on mail and other delivery services can be somewhat more problematic. If it is not practical to make deliveries yourself in the event of a disaster that interrupts the local mail and other courier services, it might be better to plan on having an office at a distant location where the utilities are intact, which you can activate in case of emergency.

Lesson Review

The following questions are intended to reinforce key information presented in this lesson. If you are unable to answer a question, review the lesson and then try the question again. Answers to the questions can be found in Appendix A, "Questions and Answers."

1. Name a hardware technology that enables a computer to continue operating despite the failure of a hard disk.

2. Utilities such as electric power are typically not included as part of a business continuity plan because their reliability rate is so high. (True or False?)

3. Which of the following statements is true about a business continuity management (BCM) effort?

   a. BCM is a company process that must involve all departments and all levels.

   b. BCM is an IT consideration that is devoted to keeping the company's computer network operational in the event of a disaster.

   c. Each department manager in a company should create an individual business continuity plan for that department.

   d. BCM is a government project that dictates preparatory requirements to individual businesses.

Lesson Summary

- Business continuity management (BCM) consists of the review, planning, and implementation processes that a business must perform to keep operating in the face of any sort of interruption. BCM transcends the IT department and must involve the entire company infrastructure.

- To create a business continuity plan, you must identify the mission-critical processes that your business needs to function.

- After outlining your business processes, you must then decide on a course of action for each process, whether to take steps to keep that process operating under any conditions, insure the business against the losses an interruption of that process can cause, or take no action at all.

- Backups with offsite media storage are the most fundamental business continuity tool.

- High availability and fault-tolerance technologies, such as RAID and server clustering, can keep a business operating despite a systems or hardware failure.

- Utilities, such as electric power, are frequently taken for granted, and compensation for outages should be a part of the business continuity plan.

C H A P T E R   1 0

Organizational Security

About This Chapter

This chapter discusses some of the critical tasks you must perform and items you need to have in place to improve organizational security. Your organization's total effort to create, implement, support, and improve security is called a security program. The success of your security program depends on good documentation, proper risk assessment, and buy-in from the employees in your organization. In this chapter, you learn what you must do to establish, maintain, and improve organizational security.

Before You Begin

You should understand all of the concepts presented in Chapter 4, "Network Infrastructure Security," Chapter 7, "User Security," and Chapter 8, "Security Baselines."

Lesson 1: Documentation

To establish your security program, you must begin with a foundation. This foundation typically comes in the form of documentation, which might be government regulations, industry standards, or other guidelines. The focus of this lesson is the information and documents required to establish your security program.

After this lesson, you will be able to

- Select appropriate standards and guidelines from which to create your organization's policies
- Select and create policies that make up your organization's security policy
- Create documentation that defines the appropriate use, maintenance, and disposal of your organization's information assets

Estimated lesson time: 60 minutes

In this lesson you are introduced to some resources available on the Internet to help you formulate security policy. This lesson is not a replacement for those truly excellent resources, but the goal here is to provide enough information for you to effectively answer questions regarding organizational policy. Further, after reading this section you should have a good base of knowledge from which to research, define, improve, and maintain security policy for your organization.

Standards, Guidelines, and the Common Criteria

Standards and guidelines outline rules for governing an organization and conducting business. Standards must be complied with, whereas guidelines are generally recommendations and best practices. Standards can be driven by regulatory policy; for example, standards for public buildings codes mandate lighted exit signs, fire extinguishers, and other fire safety equipment. Compliance with guidelines is not mandatory; for example, a guideline for maintaining a Web site might be to place contact information on every page of the Web site. Organizations commonly use both standards and guidelines when developing policies.

Note   Policies are discussed later in this lesson. Standards are sometimes called codes or regulations, as in fire safety codes or environmental regulations. Standards can also be presented as benchmarks or baselines, which were presented in Chapter 8.

A standard that is gaining popularity and importance in the world is the Common Criteria (CC), a standard for evaluating the security of computer and network devices. This standard was developed as a joint effort between organizations in

France, the Netherlands, Canada, Germany, the United States, and the United Kingdom. The International Organization for Standardization (ISO) also recognizes the CC as ISO 15408.

The CC is provided in three parts, which are available at *http://www.commoncriteria.org* and on the companion CD-ROM. A brief description of each part follows:

3 PARTS of (CC) Common Criteria

- **Part 1: Introduction and general model.**   This document (approximately 60 pages) is an introduction to the CC. The document defines the concepts and principles of security evaluation.

- **Part 2: Security functional requirements.**   This document (approximately 360 pages) defines functional components and a method for expressing functional requirements. The term Target of Evaluation (TOE) is used to describe the products that are evaluated.

- **Part 3: Security assurance requirements.**   This document (approximately 215 pages) defines assurance components and a standard method for expressing assurance requirements. Part 3 also specifies the evaluation rating scale called Evaluation Assurance Level (EAL), ranging from EAL1 (functionally tested) through EAL7 (formally verified design and tested).

More Info   You can learn more about the CC by reading the 43-page users' guide titled "Common Criteria for Information Technology Evaluation User Guide" from *http://csrc.nist.gov/cc/info/infolist.htm*. CC documentation is also provided on the companion CD-ROM. Prior to the implementation of the CC, the United States government used the Trusted Computer System Evaluation Criteria (TSEC), which is also known as the rainbow project. Information on the project is maintained at *http://www.radium.ncsc.mil/tpep*. However, the United States has discontinued use of TSEC in favor of CC.

Policies and Procedures

The focus of this lesson is types of information that should be documented for your organization. For the purpose of this lesson, a policy is a document that states the goals of an organization with regard to certain areas of operation. A policy often includes procedures, which outline methods for achieving or maintaining the stated goals of the policy. A policy is a statement of what to do and a procedure is a statement of how to do it. Policies and procedures are created and used to define how organizational assets should be acquired, utilized, maintained, and discarded.

Note   Policies regarding people as human assets typically use terms such as *hired*, *motivated*, and *retired* or *terminated* (instead of using the terms *acquired*, *maintained*, and *discarded*).

Security Policy

As previously mentioned, policies are often formulated in part from standards and guidelines. Policies are also derived from the business and life experience of people working with or for the organization. A *security policy* is a set of rules regarding access and use of an organization's technology and information assets. Security policy is often created using a series of subordinate policies.

The main purposes of security policy are the following:

- To inform network users, technical support, and management of the requirements for protecting technology and information assets
- To provide guidelines for acquiring, configuring, monitoring, and assessing technology assets (that is, computer systems and networking devices)

An excellent resource for learning about and implementing security policy is RFC 2196, "Site Security Handbook" You should take time to read RFC 2196 while preparing for the Security+ exam. This RFC should also be considered required reading for anyone who is responsible for establishing or maintaining the security of a network. The following sections describe the type of policies that you might expect to find in a security policy. (RFC articles can be found at *http://www.icann.rfceditor.org*.)

More Info   NIST Special Publication 800-12, "An Introduction to Computer Security: The NIST Handbook" covers security policy in Chapter 5, "Communications Security." (NIST articles can be found at *http://www.csrc.nist.gov/publications*.)

Computer Technology Purchasing Guidelines

Computer technology purchasing guidelines are used to protect the organization from equipment that could lead to a security breach. These guidelines specify security features that are required or preferred by the organization. For example, an organization might decide to require that all new systems have built-in smart card readers. These guidelines should supplement the existing purchasing policies and guidelines.

Access Policy

An *access policy* provides guidelines for all personnel regarding the rights, privileges, and restrictions for using the organization's technology and information assets. As an example, the access policy might define a warning message that should be displayed when a user logs on to a system belonging to the organization. The warning message might state that all information accessed, sent, or received through devices belonging to the organization can be monitored.

Accountability Policy

An *accountability policy* indicates the responsibilities of people in the organization. The policy explains that audits of information assets can and will be conducted. The responsibilities and capabilities of personnel designated to conduct the audits should also be described. The accountability policy might also include guidelines for handling incidents, such as who to contact, what to do, and what not to do when a possible intrusion or inappropriate use of equipment is discovered. If incident response is not addressed in this policy, it should refer to the official incident response policy (discussed later in this lesson).

Authentication Policy

An *authentication policy* describes the acceptable methods, equipment, and parameters for allowing access to resources. For example, the policy might specify which types of users are allowed to remotely access the organization's internal network. The policy might also establish the equipment necessary to connect to the organization, such as a modem and a smart card. Refer to Chapter 7 for more information on authentication types.

Password Policy

The *password policy* might be included in the authentication policy or it could be a separate document. The password policy describes how passwords should be managed. This policy establishes the following:

- **Password length.**   The minimum (and possibly maximum) acceptable password length.

- **Password complexity.**   The types of characters that can be used for passwords; for example, uppercase and lowercase letters and numbers, including the use of special characters such as @, #, $, %, ^, &, and *.

- **Password expiration.**   The length of time a password can be used before it must be changed to something else.

- **Password uniqueness.**   The number of unique passwords that a person must set before being able to use a previously used password.

- **Account lockout threshold.**   The number of incorrect logon attempts permitted before an account is locked out.

- **Account lockout duration.**   How long a locked out account remains locked out. This is typically an automated setting available in some operating systems. An account might be locked out for a certain number of minutes or indefinitely, requiring an administrator to reset the account.

Availability Statement

The *availability statement* sets expectations for the availability of organizational resources. The document should define hours of operation, times when the resources are scheduled for maintenance (down time), and the availability of redundant resources. The document should also describe shutdown, startup, and recovery procedures for organizational equipment.

Information Technology System and Network Maintenance Policy

An *information technology (IT) system and network maintenance policy* describes how maintenance personnel are allowed to handle and access the organization's equipment. Both internal and external personnel should be considered. The extent to which external maintenance is to be utilized should also be defined. The policy should determine whether remote maintenance is allowed and how it is to be controlled. Outsourcing and the management of outsourcing agreements, access, and partners should also be addressed in the policy.

Violations Reporting Policy

The *violations reporting policy* defines violations and how they should be reported. Violations should be defined and might include privacy issues, proper use of equipment, and information security. Include contact information for reporting each type of violation. You might consider setting up an anonymous reporting system to encourage violation reporting.

Firewall Policy

Firewall policy describes the type of network traffic and data that is and is not allowed to traverse the firewall. Firewall policy is typically created before or immediately following the acquisition of a firewall product because it is typically customized to address the specific capabilities of that product. If the policy is not created after the firewall product is purchased, it is often necessary to modify the policy to address specific settings and capabilities of the new firewall product. Further, if additional firewall products are added or capabilities are enhanced, the firewall policy should be updated to reflect the changes and new capabilities.

Some organizations create separate policies for each portion of the network instead of using a single firewall policy. For example, an organization might specify policy for the internal network, the perimeter network, and test labs with different firewall configurations for each area. Whether documented as separate policies or created as a single firewall policy, the types of network traffic allowed in each area of the network should be specified.

More Info   NIST Special Publication 800-41, "Guidelines on Firewall and Firewall Policy," provides more detailed information on establishing a firewall policy.

Antivirus Policy

The *antivirus policy* describes the organization's efforts to reduce the exposure to, damage from, and spreading of malicious software. The policy should state requirements of personnel to implement, update, and appropriately utilize antivirus software. Common countermeasures such as not opening suspicious attachments in e-mail messages, not downloading programs from unauthorized sources, and scanning all removable media before using it should also be part of the policy.

Privacy Policy

An organization's *privacy policy* explains reasonable expectations of privacy for clients, customers, and partners. This policy should detail such issues as monitoring of e-mail, maintaining logs of Web sites visited, and restrictions and exceptions for accessing users' files. If you don't define a privacy policy, people in the organization might assume they have privacy, which could result in managerial or legal conflicts in the future.

Protecting Confidential Data

The privacy policy should also address the confidentiality of client and employee records and all other data that could be considered personal or private. The policy should give specific examples of private information, such as client medical records or employee personnel files. The privacy policy should include general guidelines for how to identify private information. The proper handling and storage of private information should also be specified in the privacy policy.

Platform for Privacy Preferences (P3P)

The World Wide Web Consortium (W3C) developed the Platform for Privacy Preferences (P3P) as a way to standardize the presentation and evaluation of privacy policy over the Web. P3P allows client Web browsers to access, display, and automatically evaluate the privacy policy of a Web site and its pages. P3P-enabled client Web browsers can be used to display the privacy policy of a Web site or its pages. These client Web browsers can also be configured to block cookies based on the user-defined settings. P3P requires both P3P-enabled Web browsers and Web sites. Web site publishers can configure their Web pages to support P3P using a P3P editor that converts a written privacy policy into P3P-formatted code.

More Info   For more information on P3P, including links to tools, instructions, and software for downloading, visit *http://www.w3.org/P3P*.

Acceptable Use Policy

An *acceptable use policy* might be part of a security policy or a separate document. This policy defines the ways in which personnel might use the organization's equipment. The acceptable use policy should also clearly define ways in which equipment should not be used. Prohibited uses should be clearly stated in this policy, such as specific activities like playing computer games or browsing pornographic Web sites on company systems. Some organizations even list prohibited and authorized Web sites and newsgroups.

More Info   Alternate names for the acceptable use policy include *appropriate use policy* or *authorized use policy*. You can find sample policies through the "The SANS Security Policy Project" at *http://www.sans.org/newlook/resources/policies/policies.htm*. There are more than 20 different sample policies that you can download and customize for your organization.

Incident Response Policy

A *computer security incident* is an actual, suspected, or attempted compromise of any IT system. Any activity that threatens a computer system or violates a security policy can lead to an incident, including the following:

- System changes (hardware, firmware, or software) without the owner's consent. This includes viruses, automated attacks, and manual attacks.

- A denial of service (DoS) attack that disables a computer system, router, or some other infrastructure device or when the network bandwidth is overwhelmed due to a malicious activity.

- An attempted or successful unauthorized access of a system or its data.

- Unauthorized processing, storage, alteration, or destruction of data.

These incidents can cause confusion and some people might be inclined to panic in reaction to such events. An incident response policy is a document that helps people respond appropriately to an incident. The policy defines an incident and gives examples of incident types (as just shown). The policy also designates people who are primarily responsible for handling security incidents and how they can be contacted. Further, the policy should provide step-by-step instructions for dealing with, documenting, and disseminating incident-related information.

More Info   Chapter 11, "Incident Detection and Response," provides additional information on incident handling. For more information on developing an incident response policy, read NIST Special Publication 800-3 titled "Establishing a Computer Security Incident Response Capability (CSIRC)." RFC 2196 and RFC 2350 also provide guidelines for developing an incident response policy. For links to sample incident response policies, visit *http://www.all.net/books/ir*.

Service Level Agreement

A *service level agreement* (SLA) is a contract that defines business or technical support parameters that an IT outsourcing firm agrees to provide to its clients. SLAs usually indicate agreed-on levels of performance and consequences for failing to maintain them. Some examples of SLAs include the following:

- **Internet service provider SLA.**   Specifies bandwidth and connection availability guarantees.

- **Local area network (LAN) SLA.**   Defines the availability of LAN connectivity equipment and a response time for resolving issues.

- **Application service provider SLA.**   Covers the hosting of a specific application or service, such as a Web application, database application, or e-commerce service. These agreements typically have provisions for server up time, availability, and recovery or replacement times. Sometimes these agreements are referred to as colocation or hosting services.

- **Data center SLA.**   An agreement that covers the availability of the organization's data. This agreement typically specifies backup frequency, time to restore, and guarantees concerning the availability of the systems holding the data.
- **Hardware SLA.**   Covers repairing, replacing, or restoring computers and other covered equipment within a specified period of time.

Note   Each service provider can negotiate, name, and create SLAs for their organization. Specific agreements might not always be presented as shown here. Instead, the individual SLAs might be combined (or even further subdivided), depending on the service provider.

Human Resources Policy

The human resources (HR) department of most organizations manages the hiring, training, and termination of personnel. For the employees who require access to computers and the network, the IT department must be involved. The HR policy describes how the HR and IT departments work together to coordinate the activation, deactivation, group memberships, and privileges of user accounts based on employment status and job function. Many situations might require coordinated efforts between the HR and IT departments, especially the following:

- **New employee hired.**   A user account with appropriate access and group memberships must be created. Employees might also be asked to review the organization's policies, including the security policy.
- **Employee terminated.**   A user account should be deactivated or removed before the employee is terminated to prevent a disgruntled employee from damaging or deleting information. Many software vendors produce provisioning software that creates and activates user accounts for new employees and deactivates user passwords and accounts and quarantines files when employees leave the organization. An example of such software is Business Layers' eProvision Day One software.
- **Employee vacation or leave of absence.**   A user account should be disabled when an employee is expected to be absent for an extended period.
- **Employee status change.**   When an employee is transferred or has some other type of job function or reclassification, user account permissions or group membership changes might be required.
- **Employee education and training.**   HR is often responsible for employee education and training. The IT department must typically work with HR to educate all employees on basic IT security.

HR might also have employees read and sign a code of ethics that describes how employees should behave on the job and perform their duties. In part the code of ethics informs and reminds employees that they must help maintain the security of the organization. The following statements related to the security of the organization might be part of the code of ethics:

- I agree to protect the security of proprietary and private information that I handle.
- I agree to promote and follow organizational and informational security policies.
- I will report all suspected breaches of security.

More Info   You can see an example of a code of ethics at the Information Systems Security Association (ISSA) Web site at *http://www.issa.org/codeofethics.html*.

Due Care

Due care describes a minimum or customary practice of reasonably protecting assets. For example, a network security professional should know that a computer with active file shares and no firewall protection is likely to get a computer virus. The security professional would violate due care if he or she plugged that computer directly into the organization's production network without first performing a virus scan.

Due care can vary by industry and business. For example, an advertising agency would not typically have the same due care responsibilities as an organization that handles medical billing. Protecting competitive information and advertising plans of client companies is due care to an advertising agency; maintaining privacy of medical records is due care to a medical billing company.

Note   *Due diligence* and *due professional care* are other terms associated with due care. Due diligence is considered implementation and exercise of due care. In this chapter no distinction is drawn between due care and due professional care. However, other texts might choose to equate due care with commonsense behavior expressed by a certain group of people, whereas due professional care is related to the common practices and knowledge of professionals in a specific occupation.

The concept of due care should be included in your organization's documented policies. You can document it separately or even make it part of other policies. For example, the following information could be added to the privacy policy to explain due care when handling confidential client information:

- Encrypt confidential data on fixed and removable media.
- Never transmit confidential data over unencrypted connections.
- Never leave confidential information easily accessible to unauthorized personnel. For example, do not leave a client's medical records displayed on your workstation while away from your desk.

Potential consequences of not exercising due care should be outlined in your security policy as well. Typical consequences for due care violations include termination of employment and possible legal action against all responsible parties.

Separation of Duties

Separation of duties is a security concept advocating that it is more difficult for multiple people (as opposed to an individual) to successfully commit and conceal an unethical, fraudulent, or illegal act. This concept is commonly applied in the separation of the accounting function into two parts: accounts payable and accounts receivable. The idea is that there is reduced chance of fraud if the duty of generating an invoice and receiving payment on that invoice is separated. If one person generates and collects payments on invoices, that person could potentially modify figures on both sides to generate and steal excess revenues. Such deception would be more difficult to coordinate, achieve, and conceal if two or more people are involved in this process.

Separation of duty should be part of your organizational policies and structure. You could introduce the concept as part of your security policy, but you must build it into systems and processes throughout the company. For example, your organization might specify that no one can be allowed to access areas that contain sensitive or critical information alone.

Need to Know

Need to know is a basic security concept that holds that information should be limited to only those individuals who require it. The measure is to determine whether a person needs to know certain information to perform his or her job function appropriately. For example, if a storage room contains new PCs, only those people responsible for deploying the new PCs have a need to know those items are in the storage room. Of course, the storage room should also be locked and monitored.

Need to know also applies to requests for information, which should be documented and justified. This is especially true when the request for information is outside of normal business practices, such as the HR department requesting copies of invoices from the accounting department.

Systems Architecture Documentation

System architecture refers to the hardware and software that a computer uses. When systems are configured on a network, the systems architecture also refers to the network architecture. As stated in Chapter 4, you should document your network layout, connections, and system configuration so that you can identify suspicious changes to that structure. This also applies to individual hosts on your network. Your organization's documentation should include descriptions of how every system is configured. This allows people (especially auditors) to identify nonstandard configurations and potential security violations.

Items that should be documented for each system include the following:

- **Operating system.** This includes operating system version or revision, service packs or security updates applied, and any modifications to the default configuration.

- **Hardware.** This includes specifications of processor, motherboard, RAM, hard disk, and all attached peripheral devices.

- **Applications.** This includes all authorized applications. If your organization prohibits the use of certain applications, those applications should be specifically documented as well. Some organizations require that any application not specifically allowed be prohibited.

Change and Configuration Management Policy

A change and configuration management (CCM) policy is often part of a security policy, but it might be a separate document. The CCM policy should specify who is allowed to make changes to systems architecture. The policy should also specify how those changes should be documented and justified, and who must be notified. Everyone in the organization should be made aware of this policy so that there is no confusion of how such things should handled.

Logs

Your organizational security policy should require the use of logs to track equipment and maintenance and to ensure warranty and service agreement compliance. Logs help to ensure that required tasks are accomplished on a regular basis. They can also be used to track the movement of organizational assets. For example, a log could be used to track the possession of classified information (sign-in/sign-out log).

Inventories

Inventories verify the physical existence and availability of the organization's assets. During an inventory (or inventory documentation process) people walk around the organization and actually verify that assets are physically present. Some inventories are also used to evaluate condition and assign asset values. Inventories can also be a deterrent to theft and misuse. Consequently, inventories of valuable and classified information should be conducted frequently.

Classification Policy

A *classification policy* describes the appropriate handling and protection of your organization's information assets. Many organizations classify technology and documents into secret, confidential, private, and public categories. Such classifications are usually accompanied by appropriate policies, procedures, and handling instructions. The following items provide some example policy statements concerning classification:

- **Secret.**   A compromise of secret information is likely to seriously hinder business operations, reduce competitive advantages, and result in significant financial cost to the organization. All secret information and systems used to access secret information should be clearly marked. Secret information must be encrypted when stored or transmitted electronically. Only personnel with an established need to know and appropriate security clearance should access secret information or utilize systems with access to secret information. Personnel responsible for the compromise of secret information will be terminated and criminally prosecuted.

- **Confidential.**   A compromise of confidential information might hinder business operations, reduce competitive advantages, and result in financial loss to the organization. All confidential information and systems used to access confidential information should be clearly marked. Confidential information must be encrypted when stored or transmitted electronically. Only personnel with an established need to know should access confidential information or utilize systems with access to confidential information. Personnel responsible for the compromise of confidential information will be terminated and can be criminally prosecuted.

- **Private information.**   A compromise of private information could damage the reputation of the organization, its clients, and its employees. This might also result in legal action against the organization and those individuals responsible for the compromise of private information. All private information should be clearly marked and private information should not be accessible on public terminals. Only personnel with an established need to know should access private information or utilize systems with access to private information. Personnel responsible for the compromise of private information can be terminated and criminally prosecuted.

- **Public information.**   Access and distribution of public information is not restricted.

- **Notification.**   Any compromise of classified information (secret, confidential, private) should be reported immediately to the appropriate security personnel. The contact information of the appropriate security personnel should be provided as part of your classification program.

These are not the only classifications that an organization can use to control access to information. For example, classifications such as "For Internal Use Only" and "Eyes Only" might be used to restrict documents to internal personnel or specific personnel, respectively. The classification program of the organization should clearly specify the classification types, classification authorities, who to contact with questions and to report violations, and consequences of compromising classified information.

Note Top Secret is a classification typically used by governments when the nature of information can cause grave danger to the nation and those who protect it. If you work for an organization that accesses, maintains, or stores Top Secret information, you undoubtedly received education on the proper handling of that information.

Retention and Storage

Retention and storage policies and procedures might be established as part of the organization's classification policy or as a separate document. Government regulations often influence organizational policy in this area. Most organizations dictate that classified information is to be stored based on its classification. For example, an organization's policy might specify that secret information must be stored in a combination safe, whereas confidential and private information must be stored in a locking file cabinet or safe. The form of storage is often regulated. Data retention laws vary greatly by country and industry. For example, a health management organization might have a policy such as this one concerning patient records:

- Original documents concerning patient cases must be maintained for two years.
- After two years, patient records can be digitally scanned and stored on optical media.
- Burning or pulverization can be used to destroy patient records older than seven years.

Disposal and Destruction

Disposal and destruction policies and procedures might be established as part of the classification policy or as a separate document. As with retention and storage, disposal and destruction can be influenced by government regulations. Most organizations dictate different disposal procedures based on document classifications. For example, disposal of secret information requires burning or pulverization and confidential and private information requires at least crosscut shredding. Magnetic media, such as tapes and floppy disks, can usually be degaussed (magnetically erased) before disposal. Some organizations require degaussing for confidential media and physical destruction for media used for certain data classifications.

Exercise: Policy Purposes

Match the policy descriptions in the left column with the appropriate policy in the right column.

1. More people involved in a process reduce the likelihood that one of them will do something inappropriate.

2. International security standard.

3. Guidelines regarding organization's member privileges to information assets.

4. Defines responsibilities and capabilities of information auditors.

5. Describes hours of operation.

6. Describes the type of network traffic that is allowed into or out of the organization.

7. Policy explaining that employees can be held accountable for negligent actions such as transmitting patient medical records in cleartext instead of an encrypted format.

a. Firewall policy

b. Accountability policy

c. Common Criteria

d. Separation of duties

e. Access policy

f. Availability statement

g. Due care

Lesson Review

The following questions are intended to reinforce key information presented in this lesson. If you are unable to answer a question, review the lesson and then try the question again. Answers to the questions can be found in Appendix A, "Questions and Answers."

1. List requirements you might find in a password policy.

2. What items might be included in a privacy policy?

3. What type of policy would typically prohibit playing of computer games on organizational computers?

4. What is a computer security incident?

5. If you sign an agreement with another company to host an e-commerce solution for your organization, the company you signed with is a what?

Lesson Summary

- Documentation creates the foundation of your security plan. You can use standards, guidelines, and government regulations to help formulate your organizational policies and procedures.

- Common Criteria is an international standard for evaluating the security of computer and network devices. This standard is supported by many different countries and has ISO equivalent standard 15408.

- Security policy is created from multiple subordinate policies such as access policy, accountability policy, authentication policy, password policy, firewall policy, and many other policies concerning privacy, system availability, maintenance, violations reporting, and acceptable use of equipment.

Lesson 2: Risk Assessment

To properly prioritize the efforts of your security program, you must assess risk. *Risk* is the likelihood that a particular threat will exercise a specific vulnerability and cause damage to an asset. *Risk assessment* involves the evaluation of threats, vulnerabilities, and potential impact on assets. Properly assessing risk allows you to implement *security controls* based on the degree of risk to specific assets. Security controls include security policy and procedures, antivirus software, firewalls, and everything else your organization does or implements to protect its assets.

After this lesson, you will be able to

- Calculate risk
- Identify assets
- Assess threats
- Assess vulnerabilities

Estimated lesson time: 25 minutes

Calculating Risk

Calculating risk allows you to prioritize implementation and maintenance of security controls. The security controls that address the highest risk areas should be the highest priorities for implementation and maintenance. Calculating risk requires a series of subordinate assessments. These assessments are then multiplied to determine risk. The formula for calculating risk can be expressed as follows:

Threat × *Vulnerability* × *Impact* = *Risk*

More Info   Some formulas for calculating risk show impact as event cost or asset value. One reference for more information is "The Risk Equation" by Peter Tippet, available from the TruSecure Corporation's Web site at *http://www.trusecure.com.*

If any of the multiplied factors is zero, then the risk is zero. To calculate risk, you must assess threats, vulnerabilities, and impacts, as explained in the following sections. However, before you can make any of these assessments, you must first understand your organization's assets.

Asset Identification and Valuation

Asset identification and valuation is the process of identifying all of an organization's assets and assigning a value to them. Because asset valuation involves calculations of depreciation, accountants are usually responsible for assigning value. Asset valuations help security administrators assess risk and apply appropriate protections to assets. The following list identifies assets that are found in most organizations:

- **Personnel.**   People are often called the most important asset of an organization; this category includes users, maintenance personnel, and administrators.
- **Information system equipment.**   All information systems hardware including computers, servers, network cabling, routers, switches, hubs, and all related devices are assets to the organization.
- **Software.**   All types of computer software are assets, including operating systems, diagnostic utilities, office applications, and so on.
- **Information.**   All data is an asset to the organization. Be sure to include data in applications, databases, user accounts, home directories, backups, archives, and logs.
- **Documentation.**   All of the policies, procedures, and supporting information are valuable to the organization. At a minimum the documentation is worth the time that it would take to re-create it.
- **Furniture.**   Desks, chairs, couches, conference tables, rolling carts, and all other manner of furniture that the organization owns are assets.
- **Production machinery.**   Any machinery that is used to produce products must be considered an asset. For example, a restaurant typically has a kitchen with oven, stove, cooking utensils, and other equipment.
- **Vehicles.**   Company cars, vans, buses, and other vehicles are all assets.
- **Physical structures.**   All physical structures that the organization owns, such as buildings, office spaces, and production facilities are assets.
- **Other items.**   Supplies such as paper, ribbons, removable media, pens, pencils, and staplers are also part of the organization's assets.

Note   This list is certainly not complete for all organizations. Each organization must consider assets that might be unique to the organization.

Threat Assessment

A threat is anything that could potentially cause harm to an asset. To assess threats, you must identify them and then estimate the likelihood that they might compromise your assets.

Threat Identification

The actual threats that could affect an organization vary depending on the organization's locations, industry, physical security, and visibility. Threats can be grouped into three major subcategories: natural, environmental, and human. Here are some examples:

- **Natural.**   Natural threats include fires, floods, volcanic eruptions, earthquakes, tornadoes, mudslides, avalanches, thunderstorms, and other natural disasters.

- **Environmental.**   Environmental threats can include pollutants, chemical spills, long-term power outages, and other situations.

- **Human.**   Human threats include any intentional or unintentional human action that might cause harm to organizational assets. Human threats can be subdivided into many separate categories. Some examples are technological attacks, which can include viruses, worms, Trojans, malicious software uploads, and network-based attacks; social engineering attacks, which involve tricking or deceiving clients, customers, or members of the organization to attack organizational assets; and physical attacks, such as theft, vandalism, arson, and sabotage.

Threat Likelihood

Estimating the likelihood that a threat will compromise your organization is truly guesswork, but you can collect information concerning the potential for each threat. For example, if you are assessing the likelihood of a natural disaster, you can check local historical records concerning floods, fires, tornadoes, and the like. When assessing the likelihood of future technological attacks, you can check the statistics of previous technological attacks and extrapolate based on that information. The following Web sites can help you collect statistics on technology attacks:

- NIST ICAT statistics at *http://icat.nist.gov*
- CERT statistics at *http://www.cert.org/stats*
- Security Stats statistics at *http://www.securitystats.com*

If you want to use the risk formula presented earlier, you should assign a numeric value to the likelihood that a threat will affect your organization. For example, you could use a five-point rating scale such as this one:

Rating   Description

1   A low rating, denoting that there is no history of the threat ever attempting to compromise this organization or similar organizations. The threat is unlikely to affect the organization in the future.

2   A medium-low rating, indicating there is little history of the threat attempting to compromise similar organizations. There is a minimal chance that the threat will affect this organization in the future.

3   A medium rating, signifying there is some history of the threat compromising this organization or similar organizations. The threat might affect the organization in the future.

4   A medium-high rating, denoting there is notable history of the threat compromising this organization or similar organizations. The threat will likely affect this organization in the future.

5   A high rating, indicating there is significant history of the threat compromising this organization or similar organizations. The threat is very likely to affect this organization in the future.

Note   This scale is only a recommendation for assigning a numeric value to the likelihood of a threat. Many organizations decide to use a low, medium, and high scale without numerical assignment.

Impact Assessment

Assessing impact involves performing a monetary calculation of the costs incurred should a particular threat compromise your organization's assets. This includes damage, loss of time, exposure to legal liability, and any other costs of restoring the organization to the operational capabilities that existed before the compromise. Assessing impact is a matter of guesswork based on historical data, current security controls, and current costs. For example, you might determine that a fire in the computer lab is likely to result in a loss of 25 computers. The time required to reinstall those systems and clean up the computer lab and the cost of replacing the equipment are part of the impact. If this represents .01 percent of your organization's total assets, the impact might be .01. Some organizations might choose to assign impact as a specific monetary value, which is perfectly acceptable. Organizations might also choose to use a multipoint scale, such as this:

Rating	Description
1	A low rating concerning an annoyance or minor, superficial damage.
2	A medium-low rating, indicating a minor disruption or small (but measurable) loss of productivity.
3	A medium rating, indicating a loss of information or successful denial of service.
4	A medium-high rating, indicating a full loss of connectivity, serious disruption of business operations, or some other effect that seriously impedes business operations.
5	A high rating, representing a significant business loss (potential loss of the organization to function at all, loss of life, or serious physical injury).

Vulnerability Assessment

A vulnerability assessment is a calculation of how prepared the organization is to handle a specific threat. For example, if the threat is a hurricane and the organization's structure, windows, equipment, and personnel are all very well prepared to handle such an event, the vulnerability of the organization to a hurricane is probably low. Again, if you choose to use the risk assessment formula, you should assign a value to the organization's vulnerability. Here is a sample scale for doing so:

Rating	Description
1	A low rating, denoting that the organization is well prepared to handle the specified threat.
2	A medium-low rating, indicating the organization is mostly prepared to handle the threat; there are a few additional safety measures that could be taken.
3	A medium rating, signifying that the organization has some safety measures in place for this threat, but it is still somewhat vulnerable to the specified threat.
4	A medium-high rating, denoting that the organization has very few safety measures in place for this vulnerability. The organization is vulnerable to the specified threat.
5	A high rating, indicating that the organization has no safety measures in place for this threat. The organization is very vulnerable to the specified threat.

More Info   This lesson was a brief overview on how to calculate risk. For more information on assessing and managing risk, review NIST Special Publication 800-30, "Risk Management Guide for Information Technology Systems."

Exercise 1: Checking Security Statistics

In this exercise you use CERT and ICAT to track down vulnerability reports. You must have Internet connectivity and a Web browser to complete this exercise.

1. Open your Web browser and connect to *http://www.cert.org/stats*.
2. Compare the number of incidents reported in the 1990s to the year 2000. Notice there were far more incidents in that one year than in the preceding decade.
3. Add up all the incidents CERT reported from 1988 to the year 2000 and compare that number with what was reported in the year 2001 alone. You should find that CERT recorded over 4900 more incidents in 2001 than in the preceding 12 years combined.
4. Review the rest of the statistics on this Web page. Notice the number of vulnerabilities reported in 2001 was more than double those reported in 2000.
5. Point your Web browser to *http://icat.nist.gov*.
6. Locate and click the Statistics link once the page loads.
7. Notice there is a more detailed breakdown of vulnerabilities on this Web site than those that CERT provides. However, as you can see from the statistics, vulnerabilities increased considerably between the beginning of 2000 and the end of 2001.

Exercise 2: Calculating Risk Discussion

In this exercise assume that you have been assigned to calculate the risk of 100 client computers to a malicious code attack, such as a virus, worm, or Trojan horse. What types of information would be relevant to your assessment? How would you quantify this information?

Answers here can vary widely, but some things to consider include the following:

1. Understand the value of the assets: How much did the equipment cost? Does it store sensitive data? What is the value of the complete system?
2. You need to see the system architecture documentation: hardware, software, and network connectivity.
3. Research the types of vulnerabilities that apply to the specific systems and applications.

4. Consider existing protective implementations: Is there a virus scanner on each system and at the gateway? Do the systems allow removable media? How often are backups and drive images taken?

5. Risk can be quantified by determining the total value of each asset and estimating how much damage can be done if the assets are compromised in a malicious code attack (determine impact). Then multiply impact by an estimate of how likely the threat is to occur (threat). Then multiply that figure by how vulnerable the system is to compromise (vulnerability). Risk = Threat × Vulnerability × Impact.

Lesson Review

The following questions are intended to reinforce key information presented in this lesson. If you are unable to answer a question, review the lesson and then try the question again. Answers to the questions can be found in Appendix A, "Questions and Answers."

1. What is the formula for calculating risk?

2. Who is normally responsible for assigning value to assets?

3. List some resources for collecting technology threat statistics.

4. What is the purpose of an impact assessment?

5. What is a vulnerability assessment?

Lesson Summary

- Threat multiplied by vulnerability multiplied by impact equals risk. To calculate risk, you must first assess the value of your assets, determine the likelihood of potential threats attacking or affecting your organization, and estimate the damage that would be caused by a successful attack on your organization.

- Assets are typically identified and valued by accountants because depreciation in value is involved in some of these calculations. The security administrator must be able to identify assets and have some concept of their value to the organization.

- Identifying and categorizing threats is important because there are many possible threats to any given organization. The security administrator must assess the likelihood that each threat will affect the organization and then prioritize security controls accordingly.

- To properly assess risk, a security administrator must assess the vulnerabilities of the organization's assets. This means the security administrator must determine how exposed each resource is to the possible threats that exist in the world.

- The security administrator must also decide how susceptible each asset is to compromise. The question here is how much of a given asset could or probably would be compromised in an attack.

Lesson 3: Security Education

To establish, maintain, and improve organizational security, you must have a security education program for informing and involving people in the security program. Education also seeks to achieve user buy-in or support for the program. Without user support, your security program cannot be truly effective. A security education program typically involves three stages: security awareness, security training, and ongoing education. In this lesson you learn about the critical elements that are part of a successful security education program.

Note   Your risk assessment can help you determine which topics merit the most attention in your security education program.

After this lesson, you will be able to

- Establish an effective security communication program
- Create a security awareness program
- Define parameters for an effective security training program
- Facilitate ongoing security education

Estimated lesson time: 15 minutes

Communication

Communication is the first and most essential part of providing a security education program to the people in your organization. Support for the organizational security program must be clearly communicated and demonstrated by upper management. Further, supervisors and managers throughout the organization must communicate and demonstrate support for the organizational security program.

The person primarily responsible for the organizational security program (often called the *security officer*) must be visible and available to people in the organization. The security officer should ensure there are open lines of communication concerning organizational security. People in the organization should be able to freely ask questions about the security program. One way to facilitate this process is to have an internal Frequently Asked Questions (FAQ) board, which might even allow people to ask questions anonymously with the answers posted to the board.

Suspected or known security violation reporting should also be as open as possible. Some organizations develop anonymous submission programs that allow people to report security violations, express security concerns, or suggest improvements.

User Awareness

Once you are sure the communication lines are open between those in charge of the security program and the rest of the organization, you can begin a security awareness program. Security awareness is not security training. Security training, covered in the following section, is a formal process in which participants take a more active role. Security awareness is essentially a marketing campaign designed to focus attention on the security program. A good security awareness program can bring a change in attitudes about security and set the stage for future security training.

Awareness programs usually deal with simple messages or quick concepts. For example, a part of your security awareness program might be as simple as delivering a message that reads, "Security is everyone's responsibility." You can think of the security awareness program as an advertisement for the organizational security program.

The methods you use to deliver your advertisements should be ongoing, creative, and motivational. Repeating the same message exactly the same way tends to cause people to selectively ignore it. To increase the success of your awareness program, use multiple methods to deliver your messages. Here are some ideas:

- **Logon access banners.** These banners are displayed when the user logs on.
- **Audio/video.** These awareness materials are delivered on video, audio, computer-based, or Web-based formats.
- **Posters or flyers.** These can contain simple tips for complying with security policy and best practices, such as how to create strong passwords.
- **Promotional or specialty trinkets.** Part of your security awareness program could include giveaways or prizes that have security slogans on them.
- **Newsletters, magazines, and briefings.** Notes, tips, and articles are other methods for distributing a security awareness message.

Security awareness is presented at an informational level. The focus is on describing what security has to do with the individual and the organization. The learning objective at this stage is recognition and retention. As shown in the list, the delivery methods involve media such as videos, newsletters, and posters. Evaluations at the awareness stage might involve games such as crossword puzzles, word searches, and anagrams. You might even assess the success of your awareness program by using simple true–false or multiple-choice evaluations. Retention of information presented in awareness is often short term.

Training

As previously mentioned, security training is a more involved process in which participants engage in learning. The most effective security training is directly related to the participant's job and allows for hands-on experience. Of course, time and cost are also factors in determining how much training to do and how to most effectively present it. For example, assume everyone in your organization is expected to be able to send encrypted e-mail. However, only the records and accounting departments ever really need to do so. You might decide to provide hands-on classroom training to the records and accounting departments. For the other departments you might just perform a demonstration during a departmental meeting and issue general instructions on using secure e-mail in the organizational newsletter.

Security training is also presented at a knowledge level. The focus is on explaining how to implement security. Delivery methods typically involve lectures, demonstrations, case studies, and hands-on practice. Evaluations at this stage might employ multiple-choice questions and practical scenarios requiring recognition and hands-on problem resolution. Retention of this information is intermediate and could be long term, depending on how much of it is transferable to the person's job functions.

Education

As mentioned at the beginning of this lesson, education is the overall program of informing and involving people in the security program. Education is also considered a learning stage beyond training and awareness. People immersed in security education seek understanding and are often self-motivated. They want to learn the "why" of security concepts. For example, they might want to know why the organization decided to dictate six-character, mixed-case, alphanumeric passwords as a minimum.

People at the education stage of learning are likely to attend seminars, engage in discussions, and perform practical research. Retention of topics is usually long term due to the high involvement level of the participants. Evaluations of security education might involve essays, job performance reviews, and professional certification.

Online Resources

Throughout this book links to additional information are provided as online resources. In this section the focus is specifically on resources that can be used to supplement your security education program. The following list provides Web links to obtain additional information or support with your security education program:

- The NIST Computer Security Resource Center (CSRC) maintains a list of awareness, training, and education resources at *http://csrc.nist.gov/ATE.*

- NIST Special Publication 800-16, titled "Information Technology Security Training Requirements: A Role- and Performace-Based Model," is available at *http://csrc.nist.gov/publications/nistpubs.*

- The NIST Computer User's Guide to the Protection of Information Resources is available at *http://csrc.nist.gov/publications/nistpubs/500-171/sp500-171.txt.*

- The NIST Executive Guide to the Protection of Information Resources is available at *http://csrc.nist.gov/publications/nistpubs/500-169/sp500-169.txt.*

- The NIST Management Guide to the Protection of Information Resources is available at *http://csrc.nist.gov/publications/nistpubs/500-170/sp500-170.txt*.
- The National Oceanic and Atmospheric Administration (NOAA) Computer Users' Guide for Protecting Information Resources is available at *http://www.csp.noaa.gov/Users-Guide-2002*.
- The Security Awareness Corporation sells a variety of materials such as posters, screen savers, tutorials, and pamphlets, to help promote security awareness. They also have some free customizable materials available at *http://www.securityawareness.com*.
- Native Intelligence, Inc. offers a variety of security awareness program materials at *http://nativeintelligence.com/awareness*.

Exercise: Stages and Delivery Types

Match the numbered security education program stages in the left column to the appropriate lettered delivery types in the right column.

1. Awareness
2. Training
3. Education

  a. Research projects
  b. Demonstrations
  c. Logon banners
  d. Discussions
  e. Hands-on activities

Lesson Review

The following questions are intended to reinforce key information presented in this lesson. If you are unable to answer a question, review the lesson and then try the question again. Answers to the questions can be found in Appendix A, "Questions and Answers."

1. Which stage of the security education program is mostly marketing?

2. At which stage of the security education program are individuals most likely to be self-motivated?

3. Security training is most effective when it is _____?

Lesson Summary

- Communication lines must be open for a security program to be successful. Support from top executives and the security administrator should be quite evident throughout the organization. Organizational members should be encouraged to ask questions, express concerns, and report violations.

- Security awareness is largely a marketing effort to promote the organization's security program. This effort can be undertaken with logon banners, trinkets with messages, motivational slogans, and a variety of other attention-catching methods.

- Security training seeks to increase involvement and teach people how to accomplish tasks. Security training is most effective when it is hands-on and directly related to the participant's job.

- Security education is an ongoing effort. As organizational members move into discussing, researching, and fully participating, they are embracing the education stage.

C H A P T E R   1 1

Incident Detection and Response

About This Chapter

As discussed in Chapter 10, "Organizational Security," a computer security incident is an actual, suspected, or attempted compromise of any information technology system. Any activity that threatens a computer system or violates a security policy can lead to an incident. An *intrusion*, which is any compromise of your organization's confidentiality, integrity, and availability (C-I-A) triad, is one type of incident. In this chapter you learn how to identify and respond to computer security incidents.

Before You Begin

You should read and understand the topics covered in the following chapters before reading this chapter: Chapter 1, "General Networking and Security Concepts," Chapter 2, "TCP/IP Basics," Chapter 4, "Network Infrastructure Security," Chapter 6, "Application Security," Chapter 8, "Security Baselines," and Chapter 10.

Lesson 1: Attacks and Malicious Code

Throughout this book you've learned about various types of attacks that can be conducted against your organization. This lesson adds to and organizes previous discussions of attacks. The main objective of this lesson is to bring all of these topics together to improve your understanding of the many different ways in which your network might be attacked.

After this lesson, you will be able to

- Identify different network scanning methods to discover security weaknesses
- Recognize and help to protect your organization from denial of service (DoS) and distributed denial of service (DDoS) attacks
- Reduce the chance of successful password guessing attacks
- Compare and contrast different types of malicious code

Estimated lesson time: 60 minutes

Scanning

Scanning might not always be considered an attack. Web search engines scan the Internet looking for pages to index. Some Internet users scan the Internet looking for publicly accessible resources, such as game servers. However, attackers also use scanning to identify potential targets for attack and to locate vulnerable resources. Scanning can provide attackers with the following information:

- Network topology
- Types of traffic allowed through the firewall
- Active hosts on a network
- Operating systems running on a target computer
- Types of connectivity devices present on a network
- Type of applications that are running on a network
- Software version numbers and patch levels
- Account information

Attackers also use vulnerability scanners that probe for specific exploits that could exist on any computer or connectivity device on the network. By collecting all of this information, an attacker can begin to craft a specific attack. When scanners are used for this purpose, the act of scanning is considered part of the attack. In the following section you learn about scanning utilities and different types of scans that can be used to find security holes on your network.

More Info   Laura Chappell provides a good overview of scanning techniques and consequences in her article "You're Being Watched: Cyber-Crime Scans," available at *http://www.nwconnection.com/2001_03/cybercrime*.

Scanners

As mentioned in Chapter 8, you should use vulnerability scanners on your own network to identify vulnerabilities and fix them before attackers can exploit them. There are many different network scanners that can be downloaded from the Web. These are some examples:

- Advanced Administrative Tools from G-Lock Software.
- Xprobe2 from Sys-Security Tools.
- GFI LANguard Network Security Scanner.
- Network Mapper (NMAP), a network scanning utility that runs on a wide variety of operating systems.
- Computer Cops, which provides several different scanners, including a Web-based version of NMAP.
- Foundstone offers several scanning tools, such as BOping, SuperScan, ScanLine, SNScan, and DDosping. Each tool includes a description of its scanning capabilities.
- Nessus offers a free vulnerability scanner.
- The Arirang CGI scanner is designed specifically to identify Common Gateway Interface (CGI) vulnerabilities.
- Internet Security Scanner (ISS) and Security Administrator Tool for Analyzing Networks (SATAN).
- Microsoft Baseline Security Analyzer (MBSA) and the Microsoft Network Security Hot Fix Checker (HFNetChk).
- EtherPeek and AiroPeek are available from WildPackets Inc.
- Sniffer software products are available at *http://www.sniffer.com*.

Once you've acquired the appropriate scanning tools, you can begin to check your network for vulnerabilities. The following sections discuss types of scanning that might be performed against resources on your network.

ARP Scanning

As discussed in earlier chapters, Address Resolution Protocol (ARP) addresses are used in all Internet Protocol (IP)-based communication between computers. ARP converts IP addresses into media access control (MAC) addresses so that network adapters can communicate with one another on a network. Attackers can use ARP to map out the number of active hosts on a network by sending ARP broadcast packets to all the possible address of a particular segment. By design, all active hosts must respond to the ARP broadcast with their MAC addresses. Although you would not want to prevent hosts from responding to ARP broadcasts, you could set your intrusion detection system (IDS) to trigger an alert if a particular host sends an excessive number of ARP broadcasts.

Figure 11-1 shows evidence of an ARP scan as captured by Microsoft's Network Monitor. In the figure, the local host is sending ARP scan, which you can see in the Source MAC Address column (Src MAC Addr). The scan proceeds sequentially from the local host through all possible addresses. If this were an actual attack, the attacker would be monitoring ARP replies to determine which hosts were active. An attacker might also use the discovered MAC addresses to spoof the MAC address on his or her computer to defeat MAC address filtering, which can be enabled on many types of switches and wireless access points.

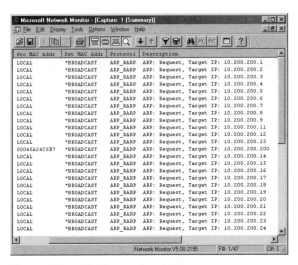

Figure 11-1. Evidence of an ARP scan

ICMP Scanning

Internet Control Message Protocol (ICMP) provides error and information messages for IP-based networks. ICMP scans, like ARP scans, can also be used to identify active hosts on the network. The following ICMP scans can be used to detect devices on your network:

- **ICMP echo.** This type of scan is also known as a ping sweep or ping scan because the ping utility utilizes ICMP echo requests to locate hosts. Attackers looking for targets often attempt use a ping sweep to find hosts that respond to ICMP echo requests, which identifies them as active devices on the network. Request for Comments (RFC) 792 describes the ICMP echo request and reply. (RFC articles can be found at *http://www.icann.rfceditor.org*.) Figure 11-2 illustrates a ping sweep using the NMAP port scanner.

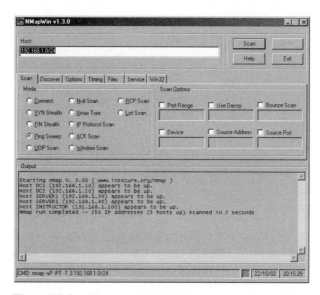

Figure 11-2.   Ping sweep example

- **ICMP router solicitation.** Often, routers are configured not to respond to ping sweeps, but another type of ICMP request can be used to locate routers on the network. Client systems use this to locate routers on the network, but so can attackers. ICMP router solicitation is described in RFC 1256.

- **ICMP address mask scan.** Hosts that cannot determine the appropriate IP subnet mask for their subnet use the ICMP address mask request. This type of request is not typically used today because hosts are configured with their IP addresses and subnet masks locally or from Dynamic Host Configuration Protocol (DHCP) servers. However, because the functionality still exists within the IP version 4 (IPv4) protocol stack, attackers can try to utilize these messages to receive replies from active hosts on the segment. RFC 950 describes ICMP address mask request and reply messages.

UDP Scanning

Attackers use User Datagram Protocol (UDP) port scans to identify potentially exploitable services that a target is running. Exploitable services such as chargen, daytime, and echo (discussed in Chapter 8) run over UDP and could be discovered in such a scan. Figure 11-3 illustrates a UDP scan against a single target host using the NMAP port scanner.

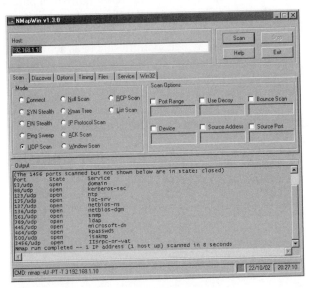

Figure 11-3. Example of a UDP scan

As you can see in the figure, the target of the scan, which is a Microsoft Windows 2000 Server computer, has 12 different UDP ports open. By examining these ports, a skilled attacker can determine many things about the target, including these:

- UDP port 53 (domain) indicates that the target is a Domain Name System (DNS) server.

- UDP port 161 is used for Simple Network Management Protocol (SNMP), a management service that the attacker could potentially exploit to find out even more information about the host and potentially the network.

- UDP port 3456 is used for IISRPC, indicating that the server is running Internet Information Services (IIS) Remote Procedure Call (RPC). Based on this, the attacker could make a good guess that the system is likely a Microsoft operating system and might be running Web and File Transfer Protocol (FTP) services. The attacker could follow up by attempting exploits against all of these services and focused attacks for Microsoft systems.

- UDP ports 88 for Kerberos, 123 for Network Time Protocol (NTP), 389 for Lightweight Directory Access Protocol (LDAP), and 464 for Kerberos passwords (kpass) are indications that the target is probably an Active Directory domain controller.

- UDP ports 137 and 138 are used for Network Basic Input/Output Service (NetBIOS). UDP 445 is used for Server Message Block (SMB) over TCP/IP. The presence of these ports and services is indicative of a server that is enabled for Microsoft networking.

Note   Attackers might be able to use UDP ports 137 and 138 to conduct *NetBIOS enumeration*, which allows them to list users, groups, shares, and other resources available on such servers. The NetBIOS enumeration (NBTEnum) utility written by NTSleuth helps to exploit NetBIOS services. Microsoft has implemented additional security features in its latest products to better protect systems from such exploits. To prevent NetBIOS enumeration from external networks, close these ports on your firewall. To reduce the exploitation of NetBIOS enumeration of Microsoft systems on internal networks, disable file and printer sharing and increase the RestrictAnonymous value in the Windows registry. See Microsoft Knowledge Base Article Q246261, "How to Use the RestrictAnonymous Registry Value in Windows 2000."

The results of this UDP scan tell the attacker a lot and present several avenues for attack. If you are a security administrator and you see such results, you should first seek to remove or disable all unnecessary services. Once all unnecessary services are removed or disabled, ensure that the latest security updates have been applied.

TCP Scanning

Attackers use Transmission Control Protocol (TCP) scans to identify active hosts and connectivity devices on the network. Like UDP scans, TCP scans also identify potentially exploitable services on the network. As described in Chapter 2, TCP uses a three-way handshake process to create a connection between client and server. Once the connection is created, TCP maintains the connection until it is terminated by either host. TCP scans can exploit the connection-oriented behavior of TCP. The following sections describe different TCP scans that can be used to identify active hosts and services on a target system or network.

Connect

TCP connect scans (also called *vanilla TCP connect scans*) are used to identify potential targets and services. This type of scan utilizes the full TCP three-way handshake. The attacker sends a TCP connection request with synchronize (SYN) segment and awaits a synchronize-acknowledgment (SYN-ACK) or reset (RST) response from the target host. If the target's TCP port is closed, the response is RST. If the target's TCP port is open, then a SYN-ACK is returned. If the attacker receives a SYN-ACK, the attacker knows the service is available. The attacker then sends the final ACK segment to complete the TCP handshake. Although most IDS implementations can detect TCP connect scans, successful connections are less likely to be identified as suspicious. However, if many connections are made sequentially, in a short period of time, or from a single host, these connections could trigger an IDS alarm. Many attackers know this and consequently spread their scans over a day, a week, or an even longer period of time. Sometimes the only way to identify a scan is to look historically at all the ports a particular host has attempted to contact. Of course, a savvy attacker would try to bounce scans off different hosts or use spoofed addresses to make identifying and tracking the scan much more difficult.

Note   FTP bouncing was discussed in Chapter 8. FTP bounce is a method that attackers use to protect their identity when scanning your network, by bouncing the scan off a vulnerable FTP server.

Half-Open

Half-open scans (also called *SYN* or *SYN stealth scans*) achieve the same goal as TCP connect scans: identifying potential targets and listening TCP services. However, the half-open scan is not as "polite" as the connect scan because the scanning device or attacker never sends the final ACK packet. This leaves the target of the scan with several TCP ports in a half-open state, hence the name of this type of scan. Half-open scans reduce the amount of time the attacker has to wait to get scan results, because the scanning tool doesn't need to send the final ACK packet. The net effect is that the target service in this case waits for an ACK response, but eventually gives up and expires (times out) the connection request.

Half-open TCP ports are also symptoms of a *SYN flood* or *SYN-ACK attack*. SYN floods are classified as DoS attacks because their objective is to stop the server from responding to legitimate client requests. During a SYN flood, the attacker attempts to send TCP connection request packets to a specific TCP port or ports faster than the target server can expire them. A SYN flood consumes all of the server's available TCP connection resources so that it is unable to service new client requests. One way to reduce the effects of such an attack is to reduce the time that a TCP port waits for an ACK response.

More Info   For more information on SYN attacks, review CERT Advisory CA-1996-21, "TCP SYN Flooding and IP Spoofing Attacks," available at *http://www.cert.org/advisories/CA-1996-21.html*.

FIN

When a basic firewall or router blocks other TCP scans, the TCP *FIN scan* might succeed. The FIN scan, like other TCP scans, is used to identify listening TCP ports based on a response, or lack of a response, to a finish (FIN) packet. Attackers send the TCP FIN packet to the target host, even though they haven't previously made any connections to the target. If the target responds with an RST packet, the TCP port solicited is closed. If the target has an open TCP port, it discards the packet and doesn't respond. No response is an indication of an open port (or at least a potentially open port), so an attacker can then follow up with other scans, connection attempts, or attempts to exploit services on the target system.

XMAS

Another derivative TCP scan designed to bypass basic firewalls or routers with filtering capabilities is the *XMAS scan* (also called a *Xmas tree scans*). This scan uses a series of varied TCP packets to identify listening TCP ports on target devices. Some characteristics of XMAS scan packets include TCP sequence numbers of zero, and FIN, urgent (URG), or push (PSH) flags set. Target devices send a TCP RST packet if their ports are closed. Target devices discard XMAS packets and provide no response when the TCP port is open.

Note   A derivative of the XMAS scan, known as a Full-XMAS scan, sends packets with all TCP flags set (FIN, URG, PSH, ACK, RST, and SYN).

NULL

Yet another TCP scan designed to penetrate firewalls and filtering routers is the TCP *NULL scan*. A NULL scan is similar to the XMAS scan in that TCP sequence numbers are zero, but the NULL scan passes no flags at all. As with the XMAS and FIN scans, if a port is closed, the target sends an RST packet. If the port is open, the target discards the packet without a response.

ACK

TCP *ACK scans* are often used instead of ping sweeps to identify active hosts on the network. If an RST packet is returned, the client port is unfiltered by a firewall and might even have a service available on that port. If no response is returned, or the response returned is an ICMP destination unreachable message, then the port is probably filtered by a firewall.

Note   A derivative of the ACK scan called the *Window scan* identifies active hosts on the network and tries to further identify the host operating system or device manufacturer by its default TCP window size.

Fragmentation

Fragmentation, described in Chapter 2, is the process of dividing one large packet into two or more smaller packets. This is legitimately done to send packets from a network that supports large packet sizes to a network that supports smaller packet sizes. For example, fragmentation is commonly used between Token Ring networks and Ethernet networks because Ethernet networks typically support a maximum packet size of just over 1500 bytes, whereas Token Ring networks support packet sizes of 4500 bytes or more.

Attackers might try to use fragmentation to allow SYN, FIN, XMAS, or NULL scans to bypass a filtering firewall, router, or IDS. In this case, the purpose of fragmentation is to hide the true intention of the packets traveling into the network. If the router or firewall doesn't reject fragments or doesn't reassemble the fragmented packets, it cannot protect hosts on the other side of the device from being scanned.

DoS/DDoS

DoS and DDoS attacks were first introduced in Chapter 1, and they are mentioned throughout the book. As you know, DoS and DDoS attacks seek to disrupt normal operations. Essentially, a DoS attack is any attack that consumes or disables resources in an attempt to hinder or disrupt some operation or function. Some DoS attacks target specific software flaws and others attempt to consume resources so that legitimate users cannot utilize a service.

DDoS attacks are DoS attacks conducted simultaneously from multiple computers. DDoS attacks are often conducted using other compromised computers running *zombie software*, which is any software under the remote command of an attacker. A computer running zombie software is known as a zombie or zombie host. Zombies are often computers that don't belong to the attacker, but instead are computers that the attacker was able to compromise. The actual owner of the computer often does not know that his or her system is running zombie software and attacking other computers.

More Info   Trinoo and Tribe Flood Network (TFN) are two DDoS tools that attackers can use to take over client computers and make them zombie hosts. You can learn more about these tools from the CERT article "Distributed Denial of Service Tools," available at *http://www.cert.org/incident_notes/IN-99-07.html*.

Spoofing

Spoofing attacks are discussed throughout this book. As you know, spoofing is pretending to be someone else by impersonating, masquerading, or mimicking that person. Here are some of the forms of spoofing discussed in this book:

- IP address spoofing is forging the IP source address in one or more IP packets to show that the packet came from a source other than the true source of the packet.

- ARP cache poisoning or spoofing is a method for placing incorrect information in computers' ARP caches to misroute packets.

- RIP spoofing uses the Routing Information Protocol (RIP) to update routing tables with bogus information.

There are other forms of spoofing as well. For example, Web spoofing occurs when an attacker sets up a Web page or Web site that looks like a legitimate Web site. The attacker then attempts to redirect other systems to this location in an attempt to steal passwords, credit cards, or other potentially valuable information. In the following sections, you'll see how spoofing is used in several different types of DoS attacks.

DoS Examples

There are two basic types of DoS attacks: those that attack a specific software flaw, called flaw exploitation attacks, and those that seek to consume resources, called flooding attacks. You've already seen an example of each type of attack in this book. An example flaw exploitation attack is the echo and chargen attack described in Chapter 8, which places those services in continuous loops. The SYN flood attack, mentioned earlier in this chapter, is an example of a flooding attack. There are several well-known types of DoS attacks that can help to further your understanding. The following list describes several examples of both types of DoS attacks:

- The *ping of death* (POD) is a flaw exploitation attack in which the attacker sends an ICMP echo request that is larger than 65,536 bytes to a target. Of course, the attacker cannot send a single oversized packet to a remote location because it wouldn't be routable or legal on the network. The attacker fragments the oversized packet into smaller packets. Several vendor implementations of the IP protocol stack were not originally designed to handle oversized packets. Some targets of POD attacks would become unresponsive, crash, or restart. All major software and network equipment vendors have since updated their IP protocol stacks so that they are not vulnerable to POD attacks. Alternate names and derivatives of the POD attack include *long ICMP*, *jolt*, *sPING*, *ICMP bug*, and *IceNewk*. For more information on POD, see CERT Advisory CA-1996-26, "Denial-of-Service Attack via Ping," available at *http://www.cert.org/advisories/CA-1996-26.html*.

- *Teardrop* (also called a *fragmentation attack*) is a flaw exploitation attack that involves two or more IP fragments that cannot be properly assembled due to improperly configured fragment offset numbers. Some targets of the teardrop attack would become unresponsive, crash, or restart. All major software and network equipment vendors have since updated their IP protocol stacks so that they are not vulnerable to teardrop attacks. Alternate names or derivatives of the teardrop attack include *targa*, *SYNdrop*, *Boink*, *Nestea Bonk*, *TearDrop2*, and *NewTear*. For more information on teardrop, see CERT Advisory CA-1997-28, "IP Denial-of-Service Attacks," available at *http://www.cert.org/advisories/CA-1997-28.html*.

- *Land* is a flaw exploitation attack in which an attacker sends a forged packet with the same destination and source address and port. Some targets of the land attack would become unresponsive, crash, or restart. All major software and network equipment vendors have since updated their IP protocol stacks so that they are not vulnerable to land attacks. For more information on land attacks, see CERT Advisory CA-1997-28, "IP Denial-of-Service Attacks," available at *http://www.cert.org/advisories/CA-1997-28.html*.

- *ICMP flood* is a DoS attack that attempts to overwhelm the target with ICMP packets so that it cannot service them, making it unresponsive. This can be done as a DDoS attack using multiple zombie hosts or by spoofing the source address of an ICMP echo request packet, as discussed later.

- *UDP flood* is very much like an ICMP flood, except that the protocol attacked is UDP. The attacker sends a large number of UDP packets to random ports on the target. The target responds with RST packets or ACK packets, depending on whether a service is configured for the particular port. If an attacker is able to send enough of these packets, the target system could become unresponsive, crash, or reboot. This can be done as a DDoS attack using multiple zombie hosts or by spoofing the source address of a UDP service request packet, as discussed later. For more information on UDP floods, see CERT Advisory CA-1996-01, "UDP Port Denial-of-Service Attack," available at *http://www.cert.org/advisories/CA-1996-01.html*.

- *Smurf* is a specific type of ICMP flood attack that involves sending spoofed ICMP echo packets. In this attack, the attacker spoofs the IP address of the target in an ICMP echo request packet to the broadcast address of a segment where the target is a zombie network on the Internet. For example, if the target is 192.168.1.1 on segment 192.168.1.0, the attacker would send an ICMP echo request with the forged source address 192.168.1.1 to a destination address 192.168.1.255, which is the broadcast address for the segment on which the host is located. Every system on that segment then replies to the target with an ICMP echo reply message. If the attacker sends enough of these packets, the target could be overwhelmed by ICMP echo replies and become unresponsive. For more information on smurf attacks, see CERT Advisory CA-1998-01, "Smurf IP Denial-of-Service Attacks," available at *http://www.cert.org/advisories/CA-1998-01.html* and the Smurf FAQ at *http://www.iops.org/Documents/smurf-faq.html*.

- A *fraggle* is a variation of the smurf attack that uses UDP service request packets instead of ICMP packets. The details and method of the attack are identical, except that the UDP protocol and UDP echo packets are used.

Protection

Protecting systems from DoS flaw exploitation attacks usually involves applying a security update to the system or removing the attacked service. Protecting systems from DoS and DDoS floods is not as simple because the functionality exploited is not a flaw. However, firewalls and filtering routers can sometimes be used to help prevent certain DoS attacks. Here are three basic firewall and router measures that can be used to mitigate the effects of a DoS attack:

- **Egress filtering.**   Place a filter on outgoing traffic to prevent internal subnet addresses from being spoofed. If a packet coming from a specific internal subnet doesn't have a source address from that subnet, have the firewall or router drop the packet. This prevents resources from your organization from being used to attack resources on other internal subnets or even resources that belong to other organizations outside of your network.

- **Ingress filtering.** Packets from external sources with IP source addresses from internal subnets are usually DoS attacks. Configure your routers to drop all incoming packets with source addresses of internal systems or private IP address sources (as defined in RFC 1918).

- **Disable IP-directed broadcasts.** As you read earlier, smurf attacks use a ping to the broadcast address of an IP subnet. Routers should be configured to drop such packets and not respond to these requests.

More Info You can learn more about these measures in the Computer Incident Advisory Capability (CIAC) bulletin "DDoS Mediation Action List," available at *http://www.ciac.org/ciac/bulletins/k-032.shtml*, and RFC 2644, available at *http://rfc-editor.org*.

IDS software, covered in the next lesson, also helps to alert you to and might even automatically respond to a DoS attack. Some software vendors have created anti-DoS tools that might also help to protect your network from DoS attacks. Here are some examples:

- Asta Networks' Vantage Systems
- Arbor Networks' Peakflow
- Captus Networks' CaptIO
- Top Layer's AppSafe

In addition to configuring filters and adding software to help protect against DoS attacks, you should develop an understanding with your Internet service provider (ISP). If all of your efforts to prevent a DoS attack fail, you can then get help from your ISP to reduce the effects of a DoS attack. The ISP's help is useful when external attacks are inbound or when you discover that your internal clients are compromised and attacking resources of other organizations. Of course, your ISP can't help you if your internal hosts and subnets are under attack from one another (using only the internal network).

More Info When it comes to DoS attacks that rely on half-open ports, such as SYN floods, reducing the amount of time that a port waits for an ACK helps to reduce or prevent that type of attack. For more information on what you can do to reduce or prevent DoS attacks, see "Managing the Threat of Denial-of-Service Attacks," available from CERT at *http://www.cert.org/archive/pdf/Managing_DoS.pdf*.

Source Routing

Source routing, defined in RFC 791, is a technique that allows the sender or source of a packet to identify the route that the packet should take through the network. Typically, a router determines where the next hop should be for a packet to reach its destination. However, when source routing is used, the sender determines some or all of the hops that the packet should take across the network. In strict source routing, the sender must specify the entire route that the packet must take, but this is almost never done. Instead, a *loose source and record route* (LSRR) is typically used, in which the sender gives one or more hops that the packet must traverse.

Unfortunately, source routing allows an attacker to attempt to evade security controls on a network by routing packets around filtering routers (and possibly firewalls). This security concern is described in RFC 1812, along with a potential solution. RFC 1812 specifies that all routers must support source route options in packets, but they can also include a feature that allows the router to discard such packets. Although this feature must not be enabled by default, network administrators could specifically configure their routers to discard packets that specify routing information.

Man-in-the-Middle

In Chapter 1 and Chapter 2, you learned that man-in-the-middle attacks occur when an attacker successfully inserts an intermediary system between two communicating hosts. This allows the attacker to listen to and possibly modify communications passing between the two systems. There are several different tools that an attacker can utilize to conduct a man-in-the-middle attack, including the following:

- **SMBRelay.**   Mentioned in Chapter 8, the SMBRelay tool is used between two SMB hosts (typically Microsoft or Microsoft-compatible networking systems). Windows 2000 and later Microsoft operating systems allow for SMB signing, which helps to thwart man-in-the-middle attempts.

- **SSHmitm.**   SSHmitm is part of the dsniff toolkit (mentioned in Chapters 4, 6, and 8). SSHmitm exploits Secure Shell (SSH) version 1 traffic by acting as a proxy between SSH sessions. This tool can capture information and encrypted logins. To prevent this exploit, use SSH version 2. See CERT Vulnerability Note VU#684820 at *http://www.kb.cert.org/vuls/id/684820* for more information.

- **webmitm.**   webmitm is also part of the dsniff toolkit. This tool proxies Hypertext Transfer Protocol (HTTP) version 1.0 and Secure HTTP (HTTPS) communications and captures information and encrypted logins. To prevent this exploit, use HTTP version 1.1–compatible Web clients and servers.

Back Door

A back door is a program or account that allows security measures to be circumvented. At one time, back doors were common in many products because vendors installed them to make supporting clients easier. Of course, once attackers discovered them, attacking that equipment or software was also easier. In addition to finding pre-established back doors, many attackers can create or obtain back door software that helps them exploit systems.

For instance, Trojan horse programs might be used as back doors. An example of this is a program called Apher Trojan, which was advertised as a virus scanner update to several victims. Instead, the Apher Trojan installed Backdoor.Death.25, a back door program that allows an attacker to remotely control the victim's computer.

A root kit is a type of back door that is used to give root access to UNIX and Linux computers. The "root" user is the unrestricted account for managing all aspects of the system. There are root kit programs for other operating systems as well, even though these operating systems call their unrestricted user account something else, such as administrator or superuser. Root kits often replace multiple programs on their target operating systems so that attackers can access and remotely control the target easily through several different services. Some files are also used to repair each other. In this way, if the victim discovers one of the replaced files and deletes it, the other root kit files on the system can re-create or repair the deleted file. Most antivirus scanners are able to detect back doors and root kits.

More Info   You can learn more about back doors and root kits from any major software vendor that has virus-scanning products. Symantec, McAfee, and Panda Security all maintain virus lists that you can search. For example, a search on Symantec's virus encyclopedia for "back door" yields 576 results. Other well-known back door programs include NetBus, SubSeven, and BackOrifice.

Password Guessing

Password guessing attacks are discussed throughout this book. Chapter 1 introduced the concept of dictionary attacks, in which a password-guessing or password-cracking program uses a preexisting list of words to try to guess a password. Originally, dictionary attacks were limited to words found in a dictionary, but they have since evolved to include names, numbers, and special characters. Further, modern dictionary attacks are not limited to any type of character set or combination. For example, a user named Sharon might decide that $haRon54 is a good password because it includes a dollar sign, an uppercase letter, and two numbers. However, a dictionary attack might discover such a password quite easily because the substitution of $ for S is so common that dictionary scanners often include this feature. Further, the numbers in this password are likely Sharon's birth year without the leading two digits (presumably 19). Here again a dictionary attack would likely add two- and four-digit years to the end of common names.

Where the dictionary attack fails, the brute force attack usually succeeds. A brute force attack goes beyond using a substitution list by running different combinations of characters until they compromise the password using mathematical algorithms.

Cracking a complex password (described in Chapter 4) can take a long time, possibly as long as many years. However, the amount of time that it takes depends on how many systems are attempting to crack the password. If an attacker is able to compromise 20,000 host computers to try different password combinations, the time it might normally take could be reduced to minutes.

Note Crack, John The Ripper, passwd, and other password-checking tools for UNIX systems are available from *ftp://coast.cs.purdue.edu/pub/tools/unix/pwdutils*. The L0phtcrack password-checking tool for Windows is available from @stake at *http://www.atstake.com*.

Password guessing is made much more difficult when system administrators use secure password policies (as described in Chapter 4 and again in Chapter 10). If the attacker is only allowed to take three guesses per hour, and the password is complex, there is a greatly reduced chance the password can be cracked. This is especially true if there is a system administrator or IDS watching for password threshold violations. The password policy might even specify that the account be locked out after a certain number of incorrect guesses within a specific time span. This makes online guessing of complex passwords virtually impossible. In such a case the attacker might attempt to capture a packet exchange that includes a password hash being passed across the network. The attacker could then attempt to decode the password offline.

Note If an attacker attempts to guess the password for a user account that is used for a service (such as an account that is used to automatically back up servers), a password guessing attack could become a DoS attack. If the service account is locked out, then the service cannot perform its job. The same principal could be applied to all user accounts. If an attacker obtained a list of user accounts and then attempted to log on incorrectly to each account multiple times, each user could be prevented from logging on for a certain period of time. Administrators must monitor account lockout activity to mitigate the effect of such attacks.

Another way to thwart password guessing is to simply not use passwords. For example, many organizations implement smart cards to increase security. These credit-card-sized access cards contain a computer chip that stores a digital certificate. This digital certificate is used to grant access to a system or network. Smart cards typically require an additional form of security such as a personal identification number (PIN) or biometric identifier. This reduces the chance that an unauthorized individual could use the card if it is lost or stolen. For example, when the user inserts the smart card into the reader, he or she must enter a PIN, provide a thumbprint, or have a retinal scan performed before accessing the network. If a smart card is lost or stolen, the security administrator can revoke the certificate as soon as he or she is aware of the loss.

Replay Attack

Replay attacks involve listening to and repeating data passed on the network. An attacker tries to capture packets containing passwords or digital signatures as they pass between two hosts on the network using a protocol analyzer. The attacker then filters the data and extracts the portion of the packet that contains the password, encryption key, or digital signature. Later, the attacker resends (replays) that information in an attempt to gain access to a secured resource.

An actual replay attack is more difficult than just capturing and repeating information. The attacker must accurately predict or guess TCP sequence numbers to make this work. However, it is possible for an attacker to guess correctly or use a script or utility that automatically makes guesses until the correct sequence is determined.

The following is a list of reported replay vulnerabilities that might help to further your understanding of these attacks:

- **Compromise SSH passwords.**   The CERT vulnerability note (VU#565052) titled "Passwords Sent Via SSH Encrypted with RC4 Can Be Easily Cracked" describes how SSH sessions can be replayed (*http://www.kb.cert.org/vuls/id/565052*). The actual solution to this problem is not to use the weak RC4 encryption algorithm, which is discussed in the next section.

- **Compromise Web sessions.**   Attackers who are able to capture packets between Web clients and servers using nonencrypted session identifiers or unsecured cookies are vulnerable to replay attacks. This is further described on the Open Web Application Security Project (OWASP) Web site at *http://www.owasp.org/asac/auth-session/replay.shtml*.

- **Compromise SMB authentication.**   CVE-1999-0391, available at *http://icat.nist.gov*, describes how SMB authentication packets from Microsoft Windows 95 and Microsoft Windows 98 can be reused, which could allow an attacker to gain access to a system.

- **Compromise virtual private network (VPN) connections.**   The Internet Security Systems report titled "vpn-replay-attack (7870)" describes a VPN exploit for UNIX and Linux systems, available at *http://www.iss.net/security_center/static/7870.php*.

To protect yourself and your organization's network from replay attacks, ensure that the latest security updates are applied to your existing software. Use the latest and most secure encryption techniques for all connections that involve authentication. For example, IPSec (covered in Chapter 5, "Communications Security") can provide antireplay services through the Authentication Header (AH) or Encapsulating Security Payload (ESP).

Encryption Breaking

Researchers and attackers have broken many encryption algorithms. For example, the RC4 encryption standard and the Wired Equivalent Privacy standard (based on RC4) implement weak encryption keys that can be broken in a very short time. In 1997, Ian Goldberg, at that time a graduate student at the University of California, Berkeley, used 250 computers to break 40-bit RC4 in less than four hours.

Mathematical Attacks

Time and processing speed are the only factors determining the security of an encryption algorithm. *Mathematical* or *brute force attacks* can be used to break any encryption algorithm. As you read in the previous section, 40-bit encryption was quickly broken in 1997. Two years later, the 56-bit Data Encryption Standard (DES) was broken in less than 23 hours by a team from the Electronic Frontier Foundation and Distributed.Net. Although every algorithm is vulnerable to brute force attacks, longer key lengths provide better security. Visit *http://www.eff.org/ DESCracker* for more information on this topic.

Birthday Paradox

The *birthday paradox* or *birthday attack* is more of a theory than an actual attack. The birthday paradox, simply stated, is that in every group of 23 people there is more than a 50 percent chance that two people share the same birthday. If you translate this concept into password or encryption breaking, there is better than a 50 percent chance that two passwords in any group of 23 are the same. Of course, that alone doesn't allow you to discover a password or encryption key, nor does it tell you which two of the possible 253 pairs match. Remember also that there is better than a 40 percent chance that none of the pairs match in that particular group.

Theoretical examples of the birthday paradox are not typically applied to breaking passwords or encryption keys. Instead, they are usually proposed as methods for deception on digitally signed documents. A common scenario used to explain how a birthday attack might be carried out is as follows:

1. An unscrupulous person (attacker) creates two contracts: one that is acceptable to the target of the attack and one that is unacceptable.

2. The attacker then creates multiple subtly different versions of each document until a document pair with matching hash codes is produced (think back to your experience with MD5 encryption in Chapter 8).

3. The sender then submits the acceptable contract to the recipient for approval.

4. If the recipient doesn't make any changes to the contract, but does acknowledge that he or she agrees to the terms, the attacker can substitute the unacceptable document for the acceptable document at some future time (because they both have matching hash codes).

One way to avoid a birthday attack is for a document recipient to always make a change to that document and compute a hash value. This way, the recipient also has a digital record of the transaction. Further, the stronger the encryption algorithm, the more costly and difficult it is for the attacker to create a false version.

Hijacking

Session hijacking was described in Chapter 2 as a situation in which communications between two computers (client and server) are taken over by a third (attacker's) computer. The session is essentially stolen from the client. The attacker's computer bumps the client system off its session and begins communicating with the server without going through the full authentication process, gaining access to a secured resource without authentication.

Researchers and attackers discovered methods for hijacking TCP connections, terminal connections, and wireless connections. The following documents describe hijacking exploits in greater detail:

- CERT Advisory CA-1995-01, "IP Spoofing Attacks and Hijacked Terminal Connections," at *http://www.cert.org/advisories/CA-1995-01.html*
- CERT Advisory CA-2001-09, "Statistical Weaknesses in TCP/IP Initial Sequence Numbers," at *http://www.cert.org/advisories/CA-2001-09.html*

Software Exploitation

Software exploitations were covered in detail in Chapter 6 and Chapter 8. As you probably recall from those chapters, buffer overflows are the most common exploit discovered. In addition to buffer overruns, there are many other types of software vulnerabilities, including cross-site scripting, in which Web sites inadvertently include malicious Hypertext Markup Language (HTML) code in their Web pages. Attackers often place the code there in successful attempts at compromising the Web page. This issue is described in CERT Advisory CA-2000-02, "Malicious HTML Tags Embedded in Client Web Requests," available at *http://www.cert.org/advisories/CA-2000-02.html*. The SANS organization and the United States Federal Bureau of Investigation (FBI) maintain a list of the top 20 reported vulnerabilities at *http://www.sans.org/top20*. This Web location also includes links to resources to help you discover these vulnerabilities and increase the security of your network.

Social Engineering

Social engineering was introduced in Chapter 1, and subsequently discussed throughout the book, as any method of attack that relies on the deception or exploitation of people. The example scenario presented in Chapter 1 illustrates a situation in which an attacker could compromise a user's password. A common way for an attacker to do this is to pretend to be part of the technical support staff for the organization. The attacker then contacts a user, explaining that he or she needs the user's password to perform some maintenance or troubleshooting activity on that user's system or the network.

Many other forms of social engineering exist, most conducted over the telephone. However, an attacker might be bold enough to take a part-time job cleaning offices, for example, to search for passwords that are written down. Employees should be advised that company security is in their hands (as explained in Chapter 10). They must realize that writing a password down or giving it to someone else puts the whole organization's information security systems at risk.

One devious example of how networks can be compromised is something that happened to a large ISP. An attacker called an ISP pretending to need technical support. During the conversation, the attacker mentioned that he was selling his car. The technical support person expressed interest in the car, so the attacker said that he would send a picture of the vehicle attached to an e-mail. The technical support person opened the attachment, believing it was a picture of an automobile. However, the attachment was instead a back door program that gave the attacker access to the entire internal network.

You can learn more about social engineering and see more examples of social engineering attacks from the following sources:

- CERT Incident Note IN-2002-03, titled "Social Engineering Attacks Via IRC and Instant Messaging," available at *http://www.cert.org/incident_notes/IN-2002-03.html*
- CERT Advisory CA-1991-04, titled "Social Engineering," available from *http://www.cert.org/advisories/CA-1991-04.html*
- VIGILANTe Corporation's Security Resources Social Engineering information page located at *http://www.vigilante.com/inetsecurity/socialengineering.htm*

The main method for protecting your organization from social engineering attacks is educating users about these attacks. Also, ensure that there is a clear organizational security policy that explains precautions users must take in handling their passwords, including simple rules, such as the following:

- Don't give your password to anyone for any reason.
- Don't write your password down.
- Don't allow others to watch you enter your password.
- Don't allow security cameras or video cameras to be aimed at your keyboard when you enter your password.
- Report any suspected password violations or attempts to violate passwords to your security administrator.

Malicious Code

Malicious code, or malware, is a common name applied to all forms of unwanted and destructive software, such as viruses, worms, and Trojans. The best way to protect yourself and your organization from malicious code is to install virus scanners and keep definition (signature) files current. You can deploy individual virus scanners on each computer and install virus-scanning gateways at your network perimeter (as mentioned in Chapter 6).

Various types of malicious code have been discussed throughout this book. The remainder of this section brings all of that information together in a simple bulleted list. There are also a few new terms in this list. You should commit all of the following terms and definitions to memory:

- **Dropper.**   A dropper is a virus carrier program or file. When the dropper is executed or opened, it creates a virus. Virus authors often use droppers to shield their programs from virus scanners. Droppers are also called injectors.

- **Hoax.**   A hoax is false virus warning that people believe is real. These hoaxes are typically spread through e-mail messages. Hoaxes were discussed in Chapter 6.

- **Joke.**   A joke is a nondestructive program that is propagated like malicious code. People usually consider this type of program annoying or funny.

- **Logic bomb.**   A logic bomb is a destructive program that goes off when a predetermined event takes place, such as the user typing a certain series of keystrokes, changing a file, or occurrence of a certain time and date. A logic bomb that is triggered at a certain date and time is also called a *time bomb*.

- **Multipartite virus.**   A multipartite virus infects multiple locations on a system. These viruses typically infect memory first and then copy themselves to multiple other locations, such as the boot sector of each hard disk, files, and executables on the system.

- **Polymorphic virus.**   A polymorphic virus, or mutating virus, changes or mutates as it copies itself to other files or programs. The goal is to make it difficult to detect and remove the virus.

- **Sparse virus.**   A sparse virus doesn't immediately infect files. Instead, it waits a certain period of time (or for some other condition to be met) before it infects a program. For example, the sparse virus might wait until a file is accessed 50 times or until it reaches 500 MB in size. This makes the virus more difficult to detect. A sparse virus is also called a sparse infector.

- **Stealth virus.**   A stealth virus attempts to hide itself from detection attempts by deceiving people or virus scanning software. When a person or virus scanner attempts to view the virus-infected file, the stealth virus intercepts the disk access request and feeds the person or virus scanner an uninfected version of the file. The virus might also report the uninfected file size of certain files, which prevents people and virus scanners from noticing that a file is too large.

Of course, the virus must be resident in memory to perform this action, so a good virus scanner can detect a stealth virus. Stealth viruses are also called interrupt interceptors.

- **Trojan horse.** A Trojan horse is a seemingly useful (or harmless) program that performs malicious or illicit action when activated, such as destroying files.

- **Virus.** A virus is malicious code that infects or attaches itself to other objects or programs. All viruses have some form of replication mechanism, which is how they propagate.

- **Wild.** Wild is a descriptor for malicious code that exists outside of virus and antivirus labs. Malicious code is "in the wild" when it is infecting unsuspecting computer users. The opposite of malicious code in the wild is malicious code in the zoo, discussed later. You can learn more about viruses reported to be in the wild from the WildList Organization International at *http://www.wildlist.org*.

- **Worm.** A worm is malicious code that replicates by making copies of itself on the same computer or by sending copies of itself to another computer. Worms, unlike viruses, do not infect other program files on a computer. All worms have some form of replication mechanism, which is how they propagate.

- **Zoo.** Zoo is a descriptor for malicious code that only exists inside a virus or antivirus lab. The opposite of malicious code in the zoo is malicious code in the wild.

More Info   The terms and definitions you need to know are covered in this section. For more comprehensive and up-to-date lists of malicious code terminology, visit virus-scanning software vendor Web sites, such as Symantec, McAfee, F-Secure, and Panda Security. You can also find several glossaries online by performing a search for "virus glossary" at your favorite Internet search engine. If you would like to test your virus-scanning software, you can download the European Institute of Computer Anti-Virus Research (EICAR) Standard Anti-Virus Test File, which is available from *http://www.eicar.org*.

Exercise: Attacks and Scans

Match the types of attacks or scans in the left column with the appropriate descriptions in the right column.

1. Ping sweep
2. SYN flood
3. Fraggle
4. POD
5. XMAS
6. Smurf
7. Teardrop
8. Connect
9. Half-open

a. ICMP attack that involves spoofing and flooding
b. UDP attack that involves spoofing and flooding
c. ICMP echo reply scan
d. Scan that completes the TCP handshake
e. Scan that leaves off the final ACK
f. DoS or DDoS attack that leaves open TCP ports
g. Scan that passes multiple TCP flags
h. Attack with oversized ICMP echo reply packets
i. Attack with IP fragments that cannot be reassembled

Lesson Review

The following questions are intended to reinforce key information presented in this lesson. If you are unable to answer a question, review the lesson and then try the question again. Answers to the questions can be found in Appendix A, "Questions and Answers."

1. What are some ways you can combat DoS attacks?

2. How can LSRR be used to avoid security devices?

3. What can attackers use replay attacks to compromise?

4. What type of attacks can be waged against encryption keys and secure hashes?

5. What type of sessions can be hijacked?

Lesson Summary

- Attackers typically use scanners to locate potential targets and security weaknesses. You can better protect your network by running scanners on it to find and correct weaknesses before attackers. Remove all unnecessary services and patch all discovered vulnerabilities.

- There are numerous types of DoS and DDoS attacks that attackers can use in attempts to hinder business operations of a target organization. You can reduce the effectiveness of many of these attacks by configuring appropriate filtering rules on your firewalls and routers. Also, maintain a good relationship with your ISP to ensure that you can mitigate a successful DoS attack.

- Source routing can be used by an attacker to route packets around security devices on your network. To prevent this, configure your routers to drop packets that contain LSRR information.

- Password guessing and encryption breaking can both be accomplished by brute force. To prevent such attacks from being successful, employ the latest and strongest encryption mechanisms and longest key lengths practical. If you must use passwords, ensure that you educate your users on creating secure passwords that cannot be easily broken by a dictionary attack. Ensure that users know not to write passwords down or share them with other people. Implement strong password policies, so that users must change their passwords frequently.

Lesson 2: Intrusion Detection Systems

Intrusion detection is the process of monitoring and evaluating computer events and network traffic for signs of intrusions. In Chapter 4, you learned that an IDS is a hardware device with software that is used to detect unauthorized activity on your network. IDS implementations can log and alert you to unauthorized activity on your network. IDS software can be implemented on individual hosts, servers, at the network perimeter, or throughout the entire network. This lesson takes a more detailed look at IDS's.

After this lesson you will be able to

- Classify IDS roles as host-based or network-based
- Select appropriate IDS response types
- Identify steps in a staged IDS deployment

Estimated lesson time: 60 minutes

An IDS can be implemented as a network intrusion detection system (NIDS), system integrity verifier (SIV), or log file monitor (LFM). A brief explanation of each is reiterated here:

- A NIDS monitors network traffic and traffic patterns to discover someone attempting a DoS attack, port scans, or attempts to guess the password to a secured resource.
- An SIV monitors a single system's file structure to determine if (and when) an attacker modifies, deletes, or changes a system file. An alternate name for SIV IDS is *target-based IDS*.
- An LFM parses system log entries (from one or more systems) to identify possible system attacks or compromises.

These functions are not the only way in which IDS implementations are classified. The most common and simplified categorization of IDS implementations is to separate them into host-based and network-based IDS. There are also subordinate classifications that separate the ways in which IDS implementations detect and respond to intrusions. The remainder of this lesson explores network-based and host-based IDS, detection methods, and response types.

More Info   The Internet Engineering Task Force (IETF) put together the Intrusion Detection Working Group (IDWG) to draft documents defining IDS requirements, language, and framework. You can learn more about this work group and the documents produced at the Intrusion Detection Exchange Format Web site at *http:// www.ietf.org/html.charters/idwg-charter.html.*

Network-Based IDS

As the basic description of NIDS just given conveys, network-based IDS's detect attacks by capturing and analyzing network traffic. A single NIDS can protect multiple hosts by listening to traffic on one network segment. NIDS implementations often utilize sensors (hosts running IDS software) at various points on a network. These sensors monitor and analyze network traffic at their locations and report potential attacks to a central management console. The sensors are commonly bastion hosts limited to running only the IDS sensor software. These hosts are often designed to operate in a mode, sometimes called stealth mode, that is difficult for attackers to detect. IDS can do the following:

- **Increase overall security.**   The more layers of protection you have on your network, the safer the network is from attack.

- **Protect multiple systems.**   A few well-placed NIDS's can protect a large network because they monitor all traffic on their subnet.

- **Allow monitoring traffic inside your firewall.**   Some attacks come from the inside. A firewall at the threshold of your network or even at the perimeter network is not going to protect internal client systems from each other. NIDS can help you to discover internal attacks.

- **Alert you to incoming attacks.**   By monitoring network traffic, NIDS can alert you when an attack is taking place, such as an attempt to overflow a buffer.

- **Detect slow attacks.**   NIDS can keep track of suspicious activities over a long period of time. For example, if an attacker conducts a scan over a period of a week or month, NIDS can keep track of this and report when a certain threshold is met or exceeded.

- **Delayed analysis.**   Some NIDS's allow you to capture packets now for later forensic investigation, sometimes referred to as *honeynet mode*.

- **Take corrective action.**   Some NIDS's can actually do something beyond logging and alerting you to attacks. For example, some NIDS's could be used to change the configuration of a client or firewall to eliminate a possible attack.

In addition, NIDS's have a low impact on network traffic because they don't act as gateways. They collect and analyze traffic as it passes by, but they don't restrict the flow of network traffic.

Although NIDS's are flexible, powerful, and increasingly advanced detection and response mechanisms, they are not a panacea for network security issues. They have limitations, which include the following:

- **Processing speed.**   Just like every device on the network, NIDS's have limited processing power and collection capabilities. NIDS's can drop packets and misdiagnose network issues if they are overwhelmed with packets to analyze. Ensure that the NIDS you select can keep up with the network on which you are planning to place it.

- **Issues with segmentation.**   NIDS's listen to the traffic on a given network segment. NIDS capability is reduced when a switch, virtual local area network (VLAN), or router is used to reduce network traffic. The solution to this problem typically involves adding sensors to each segment. In the case of a switch, plug the NIDS into the monitoring port, which allows it to receive all traffic passing through the switch.

- **Issues with encryption.**   The payload of an encrypted packet is difficult to analyze. Most NIDS's don't decrypt packets, so attacks that are encrypted tend to bypass NIDS detection mechanisms. Later in the lesson, we cover potential solutions to this issue.

- **Attack success.**   Most NIDS's cannot determine whether an attack was successful; they report only that an attack was initiated. This means that network administrators must follow up to check if an attacked system was compromised.

- **False positives and missed detections.**   A NIDS can only discover what it is programmed to discover. If an event appears to be an attack, a NIDS reports it. If a real attack doesn't appear to be an attack, a NIDS won't detect it. Detection methods and related issues are discussed later in this lesson.

- **NIDS attacks.**   Some creative software engineers have developed tools to fool NIDS's or even attack them. Such tools are discussed later in this lesson.

NIDS Examples

Many different organizations produce NIDS's. Some are free and others cost thousands of dollars. Amazingly, the saying "you get what you pay for" doesn't seem to apply to NIDS's. The free NIDS's are sometimes rated higher than the commercial ones (see the *MCP Magazine* article "Barbarians at the Gate" by Saoutine, Perfiliev, and Corti, available at *http://www.mcpmag.com*). Here are some examples:

- Snort is a free open-source NIDS.
- Enterasys Networks' Dragon is a commercial NIDS.
- Realsecure is a commercial NIDS available from Internet Security Systems.
- NetProwler is a commercial NIDS available from Symantec.
- NFR NID is a commercial NIDS from NFR Security.
- Argus is a free network-monitoring tool for UNIX-based systems, and includes intrusion detection capabilities.
- SWATCH (Simple WATCHer) is a free LFM for UNIX-based systems.

More Info   For more information on NIDS, visit the SANS IDS FAQ at *http://www.sans.org/newlook/resources/IDFAQ/ID_FAQ.htm.*

NIDS Attack and Evasion

As you learned in Chapter 4, attackers might attempt to attack, bypass, disable, or fool those systems. There are several publicly available tools for attacking or confusing NIDS's. Here are some examples and descriptions of NIDS attack tools:

■ Stick launches a direct attack against the NIDS using a Snort signature file that is used to identify attacks. The attack causes a large number of false alarms, which reduces the system resources of the NIDS. So many false alarms could cause a real alarm to go unnoticed by security administrators or the real alarm might not even be logged by the NIDS due to lack of system resources.

■ Fragroute is a NIDS evasion tool that hides attacks from the NIDS by obfuscating attack packets. The tool intercepts, modifies, rewrites, and reorders packets so that the NIDS cannot identify them.

■ Tribe Flood Network 2000 is a DDoS attack tool that uses encryption, decoy packets, and IP address spoofing to avoid NDIS identification. (DDoS attacks are described in more detail in the next lesson.)

Host-Based IDS

A host-based IDS (HIDS) is installed on individual computers to protect those individual systems. HIDS's are much more reliable than NIDS's in detecting attacks on individual systems. HIDS typically utilize operating system audit trails and system logs. Operating system audit trails, generated by the core of the operating system (kernel), are quite reliable for tracking system events. System logs also track system events and are smaller and easier to interpret. However, system logs are sometimes modified by attackers, so focusing on both audit trails and system logs provides a double-checking feature.

Many HIDS's are part of personal firewall software. *Personal firewalls*, or *host wrappers*, can examine all network packets, connection attempts, and logon attempts to their host machines. In addition, HIDS's can check the integrity of system files (and other files) to ensure that they are not tampered with. Some HIDS's are also designed to report intrusion attempts to a central IDS console located somewhere else on the network. This configuration allows a security administrator to monitor multiple host systems from one location. There are several benefits to using a HIDS on a network to protect your systems, including these:

■ They are better than NIDS's at monitoring and keeping track of local system events.

- They aren't typically hindered by encrypted attacks. HIDS's can read transmitted packets before they are encrypted and received packets after they are decrypted.

- They can help to detect software integrity breaches, such as Trojan horse software, file modifications, and so on.

- Because HIDS's only protect a single system, switches, VPNs, and routers do not affect their functionality.

Although HIDS's have several benefits, they also have limitations, such as these:

- **Difficult to manage.**   HIDS's are more difficult to manage than NIDS's in large networks because they must be configured and controlled on individual systems.

- **Susceptible to DoS attacks.**   Attacks against the HIDS-protected host might affect the HIDS itself. DoS attacks against the host might disrupt or disable the HIDS. A successful attack against a host protected by a HIDS could potentially disable and destroy evidence collected by the HIDS.

- **Require host resources.**   HIDS's require resources from the protected host. HIDS's need extra hard disk space to store logs and tracking information. HIDS's must also utilize processor time and memory to analyze packets, user-issued commands, audit trails, and system logs to protect the client.

Application-Based IDS

In an effort to increase security, software and hardware vendors are increasingly likely to integrate IDS into their products. (See "IDS at the Crossroads," *Information Security Magazine*, June 2002, available at *http://www.infosecuritymag.com*.) One example of this is a breed of HIDS known as *application-based IDS*. An application-based IDS analyzes the events occurring within a specific software application using the application's transaction log files. An application-based IDS is able to detect suspicious behavior that might go unnoticed by other forms of IDS because application-based IDS can analyze interactions between the user, the data, and the application.

There are several benefits to using an application-based IDS, which include the following:

- **Monitor user/application interaction.**   Application-based IDS's can monitor the interaction between the user and the application, which could allow for the tracing of unauthorized activities.

- **Unaffected by encryption.**   Application-based IDS's read and analyze application transactions and commands, so they are completely unaffected by network encryption and decryption.

As with any IDS, there are also limitations to application-based IDS's, such as these:

- **Vulnerable to attack.**   Similar to a HIDS, an application-based IDS is close to the potential target of attack, the protected application. If the application is under attack, the logs that the application-based IDS analyzes (or the application-based IDS software itself) might be targeted in that attack.
- **Difficulty detecting malicious software.**   Unlike HIDS's, application-based IDS's typically won't identify Trojan horses or other malicious software because they focus on a specific application's security, not the overall security of the host or network, as do HIDS and NIDS, respectively.

HIDS Examples

Several software vendors produce HIDS's and personal firewalls that include a HIDS. The following list is a sample of some of those HIDS's and personal firewalls:

- BlackICE Defender, a personal firewall and IDS product from Internet Security Systems.
- Zone Alarm, a personal firewall and IDS product from Zone Labs.
- Symantec Host Intrusion Detection System from Symantec.
- Host Intrusion Detection system from NFR Security.
- TCPWrappers for Unix systems.
- Host-based intrusion detection tools from Foundstone, such as fport, filewatch, attacker, and carbonite.
- Tripwire, a file and directory integrity-checking tool from Tripwire Security.

Note   There are many other tools for many different operating systems that can help you discover intrusions. Sometimes these tools are grouped as forensic analysis tools and sometimes they are deemed intrusion detection tools. Any tool that can analyze file or directory integrity could be considered an intrusion detection tool, such as Message Digest 5 (MD5), Pretty Good Privacy (PGP), backup software, imaging software, and file comparison utilities (WINDIFF and DIFF). Further, tools that display processes or open connections could also be used for intrusion detection. This includes lsof, ps, tlist, sclist, and TCPView.

Detection Methods

There are two basic methods for detecting and analyzing attacks that IDS's utilize. The first and most commonly implemented method is called *misuse detection*. This type of detection requires the IDS to identify a predefined attack pattern. The second method is *anomaly detection*, which involves recognizing something suspicious or atypical. Each method has benefits and limitations, which are discussed in the following two sections. More recent IDS implementations increasingly use both methods.

Misuse Detection

A misuse detection in IDS (also called *signature-based detection*) works a lot like a virus scanner. A virus scanner locates viruses by identifying the virus programming code within a file, in memory, attached to e-mail, or somewhere else on a system's removable or fixed media. Misuse detection involves identifying an *attack signature*, which is some indicator that a specific attack is occurring. Misuse detectors analyze system activity, looking for events that match a predefined pattern of attack. Misuse detectors must have their attack signatures updated as new attack types are discovered. Again, this is similar to virus scanners, which must have their virus signature files updated.

The benefits of misuse detectors include the following:

- They can quickly identify defined attacks.
- They help system administrators track attacks.
- They don't generate many false alarms because they are programmed to recognize situations that are typically attacks. Of course, as you saw earlier, some attackers create fake attacks, which generate false alarms. Of course, these false alarms are still evidence of an attack (at least against the IDS).

Misuse detectors also have limitations, such as the following:

- They require updated attack signature files because they can only detect predefined attacks based on those signatures. Some misuse detectors employ *state-based detection*, which allows them to recognize variations of specific attacks.
- They can be targeted for attack with virus signature files (as with Stick, described previously).

Anomaly Detection

Anomaly detectors identify unusual activities or situations, called anomalies. Anomaly detectors classify abnormalities as potential attacks. To determine what is normal and what is not, an anomaly detector must gather information about the systems and networks on which it operates. Once enough information is available, the anomaly detector can identify abnormalities based on historical data.

The benefits of anomaly detectors are as follows:

- They don't need to rely on predefined attack signature files to identify attacks.
- They can help to identify attack patterns that can be turned into attack signatures for misuse detectors.

The limitations of anomaly detectors include the following:

- They require more experienced security administrators because the detector can only point out abnormalities, which might or might not be attacks. The security administrator must make the final determination of whether the anomaly is an attack or not.
- They are more likely to produce false alarms than misuse detectors because not all irregularities are actual attacks.
- They require more administrative involvement than misuse detectors.

Response Types

Once an IDS implementation has obtained and analyzed event information that could indicate a possible attack, it generates a response. That response might be sending an alert to an administrator, writing information to a log file, or reconfiguring the firewall or other devices. The response depends on the capabilities and configuration of the IDS. IDS responses can be active, passive, or a combination of the two.

Active Response

An IDS *active response* (also called *active detection*) is an automatic action that a system takes when it recognizes an attack. The response might be innocuous, such as increasing information collection; moderate, such as reconfiguring the network; or severe, such as launching a counterattack against the intruder.

Of all the active response types, increasing information collection is the safest because it is unlikely to cause the organization any additional problems. In such a response, the IDS might increase logging activities or the number of packets captured for analysis. The additional information can be used to help determine the identity of the attacker, origination point of the attack, number of targeted systems, and so on. Further, the organization can use the information to pursue legal action against the attacker and assist with forensic analysis (described in Lesson 3).

Reconfiguring the network is a more complex response than increasing logging. The objective is to stop the attack as soon as it is identified. For example, when the IDS detects an attack, it might reconfigure firewall filters, isolate a host on a particular VLAN, or reroute network packets. The benefit is that the IDS might be able to stop an attack in progress. The drawback is that the network might be reconfigured because of a false alarm or an attack on the IDS. If an attacker can determine what your IDS does when it is attacked, the attacker could use that reconfiguration against you in some way. For example, if the IDS simply closes ports when they are attacked, an attacker could attack all ports to shut down a particular device, causing a DoS condition.

Automatic counterattacks are the most dangerous active response because they can bring an organization more trouble than the original suspected attack. The counterattack might be an attempt to probe or disable the intruder's computer or site. However, there are several problems that can arise from such attempts. For example, a counterattack might enable the intruder to avoid legal prosecution for the initial intrusion that led to the counterattack, or the intruder could take legal action against your organization for the counterattack. Further, attackers often spoof the credentials of other people, so the counterattack might further injure an innocent party, which could also result in legal action against your organization.

Passive Response

An IDS *passive response* (or *passive detection*) is much less complex than active response. Passive responses leave the response to the intrusion in the hands of the system or security administrator. A passive response involves alerting the administrator that an attack might be taking place. This means the IDS might activate an alarm or send a network alert, e-mail, or page indicating that a threshold was exceeded or an attack signature was identified. The administrator can then determine whether the attack is legitimate and how best to respond.

IDS Deployment

Before you can effectively deploy an IDS, you must understand your network infrastructure and organizational security policies. Also, initial IDS deployments are best done in a staged approach because they are typically high-maintenance at first. Until you learn how to adapt IDS alert thresholds and configuration parameters to your organization, implementing an IDS throughout the organization (large-scale deployment) is inadvisable. The staged approach also gives personnel time to adapt to the new technology, which is especially important for the people who are expected to investigate alerts and monitor IDS logs. For example, consider the following four-stage approach:

1. **Deploy a limited NIDS.**   A NIDS can protect multiple hosts from a single location. You can improve the security of your entire network and begin to customize an IDS for your network by deploying a NIDS. If your NIDS implementation comes with a management console, deploy the console before you begin adding sensors. Get comfortable with the reporting, alarms, and thresholds of your NIDS implementation.

2. **Deploy NIDS sensors.**   Incrementally deploy sensors throughout your network. Each time you deploy a new sensor, take time to understand the differences in traffic, reporting, logging, and alerts that you receive from that sensor. Figure 11-4 illustrates ideas for sensor placement on an example network (discussed in greater detail later).

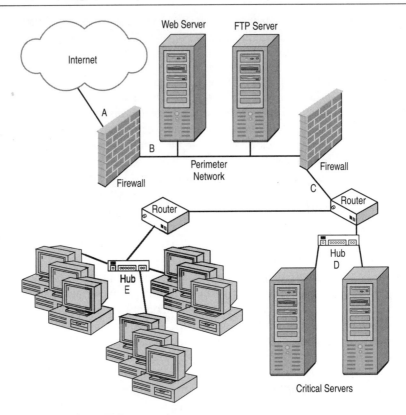

Figure 11-4.   NIDS sensor placement

3. **Deploy a limited HIDS.**   A HIDS can generate many alerts and could be quite difficult to manage if the initial deployment is done on a large scale. Deploy a HIDS only to critical hosts or servers at first. Again, take time to understand the reporting, logging, and alerts that you receive from your hosts. If your HIDS implementation allows for a management console, deploy and configure it before you add additional hosts.

4. **Fully deploy a HIDS.**   Once you are comfortable with the HIDS on your critical servers, you can optionally roll out the HIDS to all client systems. Such a rollout makes every host independently capable of recognizing potential attacks. However, many organizations opt not to deploy the HIDS on all systems because doing so could be quite expensive. Wide-scale HIDS deployment usually involves additional software licenses, higher deployment costs, and increased technical support time.

Figure 11-4 illustrates locations (A, B, C, D, and E) where NIDS sensors could be deployed on a sample network. The advantages of deploying these NIDS sensors in each location are discussed here:

- **Location A.**   This location is outside the organizational network and perimeter firewall, which means it can document any inbound attack against the organization's network. This is a good place to gather information on possible incoming attacks and provide ongoing justification for new security measures. A sensor in this area could also be used to track outgoing attacks originating inside the organization. However, this area is also highly likely to generate false alarms and could require very high maintenance. Organizations that decide to place NIDS sensors here often configure the IDS to be least sensitive or to simply log potential attacks instead of activating alerts. Many organizations choose not to configure a NIDS at this location because their firewall logs are sufficient for gathering information from this location.

- **Location B.**   This location is ideal for a NIDS to protect the perimeter network. Attacks that successfully traverse or bypass the external firewall can be picked up here. A NIDS sensor can help to protect the Web, FTP, and other servers that typically reside in the perimeter network. A sensor here can also detect outbound attacks. These sensors are typically configured for low to moderate sensitivity, because otherwise they typically generate too many false alarms.

- **Location C.**   NIDS sensors at this location protect the organization's internal network. They can catch attacks that successfully traverse or bypass the internal firewall. In addition, sensors at this location can detect internal and outbound attacks, and they are typically configured for moderate to high sensitivity.

- **Location D.**   A sensor at this location can protect critical servers from compromise. The advantage of placing a sensor here is that it can catch internal and external attacks. Sensors are typically configured for maximum sensitivity at this location.

- **Location E.**   A sensor at this location gathers a large amount of internal traffic, which helps to detect potential internal attacks. Sensors at this location are typically configured for moderate to high sensitivity.

More Info   NIST Special Publication 800-31 titled "Intrusion Detection Systems (IDS)" provides more detail on many of the topics discussed in this lesson. (NIST articles are available at at *http://csrc.nist.gov/publications*).

Exercise: IDS Staged Deployment Steps

Place the following staged IDS deployment steps in the appropriate order:

1. Deploy a HIDS to critical hosts
2. Fully deploy a HIDS
3. Fully deploy a NIDS
4. Partially deploy a NIDS

Lesson Review

The following questions are intended to reinforce key information presented in this lesson. If you are unable to answer a question, review the lesson and then try the question again. Answers to the questions can be found in Appendix A, "Questions and Answers."

1. What are the main differences between NIDS, SIVs, and LFMs?

2. What are the benefits of NIDS's?

3. What are some problems with NIDS's?

4. What are some ways that attackers try to avoid detection?

5. What benefits do HIDS's and application-based IDS's have over NIDS's?

Lesson Summary

- Intrusion detection systems (IDS's) can collect and analyze information in different ways. Some analyze information from the network, others from system files, and still others from log files. Many IDS's analyze information from multiple sources.

- IDS's can be network-based, host-based, or application-based. NIDS's are able to protect a larger number of systems and are easier to implement than HIDS's. However, NIDS's are limited by their processing power and ability to decode packets quickly. NIDS's also have trouble with encryption, VLANs, and encrypted tunnels. HIDS's are able to work around encryption and provide better individual host protection. However, HIDS's might be compromised during an attack on the target and might lose valuable information. Application-based IDS's are best for detecting specific attacks on applications and are not limited by data encryption. However, like HIDS's, they can be compromised or disabled in an attack.

- Typical IDS responses are passive, allowing the administrator to take action when an incident occurs. Active IDS responses have different levels of severity. The most benign level is to increase logging. An intermediate level is to reconfigure the network in some way as a response to an attack. This has the drawback of potentially creating a security hole or disrupting normal operations. The most severe active response is to launch a counterattack. This could cause the organization additional difficulties, especially if the counterattack is launched against an innocent party.

- IDS deployment is best done in stages. This allows network staff to customize and become familiar with IDS implementations. The NIDS should be deployed first. Once the NIDS is fully configured and deployed, the HIDS can be deployed to critical hosts. After critical hosts are successfully configured and running with a HIDS, a full HIDS deployment can be contemplated.

Lesson 3: Incident Response

In Chapter 10 you learned that an incident response policy should be part of your organization's security policy. This incident response policy should cover how personnel are expected to deal with computer security incidents, events that result from any type of attack, which includes intruders and malicious code. In previous lessons you learned about different types of attacks and ways they might be detected. In this lesson you learn how computer security incidents resulting from an attack or intrusion should be handled.

After this lesson, you will be able to

- Organize and coordinate a response team
- Select appropriate forensic activities in response to an intrusion
- Maintain a chain of custody and preserve evidence

Estimated lesson time: 30 minutes

CSIRT

When a computer security incident occurs, some person or group should take the lead in receiving, reviewing, and responding to incident reports and activity. In an organization, this is typically the person designated as the security officer. Some organizations appoint teams to handle security incidents. Such a team is often called a *computer security incident response team* (CSIRT). A CSIRT could be an ad hoc team, assembled only when an incident is reported, or a formal team supported by a corporation, governmental body, educational institution, or some other type of organization.

If an organization doesn't have its own CSIRT, there are usually external teams that can help. There are CSIRTs throughout the world ready to assist network administrators with computer security incidents. The Forum of Incident Response and Security Teams (FIRST), at *http://www.first.org*, maintains a list of contact information of incident response teams. If you cannot find a team that covers your organization, you can contact CERT (*http://www.cert.org*) to report new viruses and major security incidents. If you establish a CSIRT, you should contact FIRST to identify your team to other teams and establish a reporting chain.

More Info   For more information, see RFC 2350, "Expectations for Computer Security Incident Response"; CERTs CSIRT FAQ at *http://www.cert.org/csirts/ csirt_faq.html*; NIST Special Publication 800-3, "Establishing a Computer Security Incident Response Capability (CSIRC)"; and "Electronic Crime Scene Investigation: A Guide for First Responders," available at *www.ncjrs.org/pdffiles1/nij/ 187736.pdf*.

Incident Response Basics

Every organization should have an incident response policy. All users should know who to contact if they think an incident is occurring. In many cases, the information you see in this lesson should be part of your incident response policy. If you are responsible for creating or maintaining this policy, you should review this lesson and all of the referenced documents when creating, modifying, or improving that policy. Thorough documentation helps ensure that you and the members of your organization are able to respond appropriately during a security incident.

One of the first things that you should do is prioritize your response. This means protecting the most important resources first. Here is an example of a priority list for responding to an incident:

1. Protect people's lives and safety.
2. Protect classified and sensitive data first.
3. Protect other data.
4. Protect hardware and software.
5. Minimize disruption of business services and operations.

The actual steps that you must take to accomplish those tasks depends on the situation. One common first step is to remove a compromised system from the network. Although doing so technically changes the system's configuration, it also mitigates the harm that an attacker or malicious code can cause. If you don't remove a compromised system from the network, and that system is used to infect or attack other systems, you could be held responsible for damages.

Forensics

Computer forensics describes the investigation and analysis of computer security incidents with the interests of gathering and preserving potential legal evidence. This section describes the components and important aspects of computer forensic investigation. In this section you learn the basics about collecting evidence, maintaining a chain of custody, and preserving evidence.

Collection of Evidence

When an incident occurs, you should immediately begin to collect evidence. This evidence can help you learn from the intrusion and improve your systems, their operation, and your staff's capabilities. Evidence might be required for the following reasons:

- To locate, educate, reprimand, or terminate negligent or responsible employees.
- To prosecute attackers for computer crimes or misuses.
- To describe your situation and obtain help from other CSIRTs.

Note If you live in the United States, you can contact your state's attorneys general's office or local law enforcement office to learn about requirements for handling computer evidence.

Point of Contact

Appoint someone as the point of contact to be responsible for maintaining contact with law enforcement and other CSIRTs. This person should coordinate all activities and disseminate information appropriately to internal and external personnel. The point of contact should also be responsible for coordinating the collection of evidence to ensure that it is done in accordance with all laws and legal regulations.

Work Carefully

Before you begin work on a compromised system, consider what your actions might mean to the present state of the system. When gathering evidence, concentrate on not altering anything and meticulously document all of your actions for later reference. This is often difficult because you might need to disconnect the system from the network to stop the malicious activity. If you do not, you might be held liable for damage done to other systems or organizations.

When possible, analyze a replica of the system instead of the original. For example, make an image of the system's hard disk, or make and restore a backup to another system. Do your best to ensure that your image copying or backup doesn't change the current state of the compromised system. Some courts might require the original compromised system as evidence.

Note You shouldn't conduct your investigation from a compromised computer. Once a system is compromised, none of the components can be trusted. Some forensic software manufacturers produce software that allows you to analyze a system from another computer. This allows you to inspect files, logs, and data without actually modifying the compromised system. Forensic tools are discussed next.

Forensic Tools

Many of the tools you need to conduct a forensic investigation are often part of the operating system you are using. However, the built-in operating system tools might not be as effective or easy to use as tools specifically made for forensic investigation. There are many different software providers producing and maintaining forensic tools, some of which are listed below. You can find out more about these products by doing an Internet search on the company or software name.

- Foundstone, which provides a list of free forensic software for Windows operating systems.
- Computer Cop, which provides forensic tools for Windows operating systems.
- ASR Data, which provides forensic tools for Macintosh, Linux, and BeOS.

- EnCase, from Guidance Software.

- The Cybersnitch Web site, which maintains a set of links to forensic software organized by operating system called The Ultimate Collection of Forensic Software (TUCOFS).

Collect All Available Information

All information concerning the incident must be recorded and securely stored. You should establish, examine, and preserve an audit trail. An audit trail is a record of who accessed a computer and what operations he or she performed. Some software products create audit trails automatically. Sometimes you might have to pull an audit trail together from a variety of sources such as system logs, network logs, file access times, IDS logs, and system administrator logs and notes.

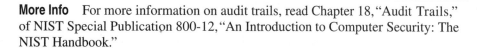

More Info   For more information on audit trails, read Chapter 18, "Audit Trails," of NIST Special Publication 800-12, "An Introduction to Computer Security: The NIST Handbook."

In addition to acquiring and protecting the audit trail, you should collect other potential evidence. This includes any information that addresses the who, what, where, when, why, and how of a situation, such as the following:

- Obtain and protect the latest partial and full system backups.

- Take a pictures or screen shots of all evidence, such as messages displayed on the computer, signs of visible damage, and anything else that is out of place or suspicious.

- Obtain and protect any security videos, audios, or reports from periods of time surrounding and including the incident.

- Recover as many deleted, encrypted, or damaged files related to the intrusion as possible.

You should create and maintain a written log for each and every incident response activity. Examples of what you should document include the following:

- Name of the system or systems compromised

- Time, date, and location of each activity

- Specific actions taken

- Identities of the people performing each action

- What each person said

- Who was notified and what information was disseminated

- What actions each notified person, group, or organization took

- Who had access to the system, physical location, and evidence

- What data was collected and who analyzed it

Realize that all evidence is subject to subpoena at any legal proceeding. Ensure that you document each incident separately and that your documentation is thorough and professional.

Chain of Custody

A chain of custody must be maintained for all evidence. A documented chain of custody shows who collected and had access to each piece of evidence. Failure to maintain this chain of custody might invalidate your evidence. The documentation must be meticulous and verifiable, including dates, times, locations, and the verified identities of every person handling evidence. This includes any time evidence is accessed or moved while in storage. Further, anyone accessing stored evidence should provide a legitimate, verifiable, and documented purpose for doing so.

Preservation of Evidence

Protecting the evidence you gather is critical. As mentioned previously, work carefully and change as little as possible. Try to conduct your investigation on a separate system that is a restored backup or imaged version of the compromised system. Everything you do must be thoroughly documented. Follow these rules to preserve evidence:

- Archive and retain all information concerning an intrusion until the investigation and any legal proceedings are complete.

- Preserve all critical information onsite and offsite. Make copies of all logs, system hard disks, policies, procedures, system and network configurations, photographs, cryptographic checksums, databases, and system backups. Offsite storage preserves evidence in the event of a natural disaster or subsequent intrusion.

- Define, document, and follow a strict procedure for securing and accessing evidence both onsite and offsite.

Legal Action

Coordinate all of your activities with your organization's upper management and legal counsel (if available). Legal counsel can advise you of your options—both civil and criminal—in pursuing legal action. If you plan to pursue legal action, you must contact the appropriate law enforcement agencies immediately. Their reports and verifications are often required to prove that an incident actually occurred. Further, they might be able to support you in collecting information and preserving evidence. You should also collaborate with other CSIRTs, which might be able to provide additional experience and guidance.

Exercise: Incident Response Priority

Organize the following incident response actions into an appropriate priority:

a. Minimize the effect of the attack on the organization's business activities
b. Protect all other data
c. Protect classified and sensitive data
d. Protect hardware and software
e. Protect human life and prevent people from being injured

Lesson Review

The following questions are intended to reinforce key information presented in this lesson. If you are unable to answer a question, review the lesson and then try the question again. Answers to the questions can be found in Appendix A, "Questions and Answers."

1. What should you do when organizing a CSIRT?

2. What are the main points you should keep in mind when performing computer forensics?

3. Why is unplugging a compromised system from the network usually a prudent action?

Lesson Summary

- CSIRTs can be either formalized or ad hoc teams. CSIRTs help an organization deal with computer security incidents and possibly protect other organizations from compromise. There are CSIRTs all over the world that are willing to work with network administrators and other CSIRTs to help reduce the damage caused by attackers and malicious code.

- Computer forensics is the investigation and analysis of computer security incidents with the objective of collecting evidence. Evidence must be gathered carefully so that other evidence is not disturbed. When possible, systems should be analyzed by making images or backups to avoid disturbing a system that might be used as evidence in a legal proceeding.

- A chain of custody is required to prove that evidence is preserved and unaltered. Without a chain of custody, evidence might be considered invalid. Evidence must be carefully preserved with plenty of documentation, including logs, reports, pictures, backups, and system images. Two copies of all evidence that can be duplicated should be maintained. One copy should be maintained onsite and one copy should be held offsite to protect evidence in case of a natural disaster or subsequent attack.

A P P E N D I X   A

Questions and Answers

Chapter 1: General Networking and Security Concepts

Lesson 1: The Big Picture

▶ **Lesson Review**

1. Although there is a need for information security, and there is a small chance of getting hacked, there is not normally any damage done and the cost to the company that is hacked is relatively minor. (True or False?)

   False. Most computers that are connected to the Internet have been scanned, and many have been attacked. Recent studies show that computer hackers cost U.S. businesses almost 6 cents of every dollar of revenue.

2. You work for a company that sells tea and tea supplies. The total annual sales for the company are $5 million. The sales of tea total $2 million and the sales of tea supplies total $3 million. The tea has a very interesting taste that cannot be duplicated. Which of the following should be considered when placing a value on the tea formula, and why?

   a. How the tea is produced

   b. What the total annual sales of the tea is

   c. Where the tea formula is stored

   d. How many people in the company have access to the tea formula

   b. In this case, the value of the asset can be based on the total sales of the tea. The sales of tea supplies would not be included in the worth of the tea formula.

3. You work for a company that sells tea and tea supplies. The total annual sales for the company are $5 million. The sales of tea total $2 million and the sales of tea supplies total $3 million. The tea has a very interesting taste that cannot be duplicated. The marketing group for your company has a marketing plan that is expected to double the sales of the tea from $2 million to $4 million. What is the real value of the tea formula? What is the perceived value of the marketing plan?

The real value of the tea formula is $2 million because that is the current sales of the tea. The perceived value of the marketing plan is $2 million because that is the projected increase the market plan is expected to provide.

4. When talking about information security, what are the three cornerstones of the C-I-A triad?

The three cornerstones of the C-I-A triad are confidentiality, integrity, and availability.

5. List the sequence in which you perform the following steps when creating a risk management plan.

   a. Identify the vulnerabilities to your C-I-A triad

   b. Identify the value of your C-I-A triad

   c. Identify the threats to your C-I-A triad

   d. Identify how you can mitigate the risks

   b, c, a, d

Lesson 2: Identifying Threats

Page 18   ▶   **Lesson Review**

1. You are responsible for creating a mitigation plan for threats to your company's information security. Which of the following should your mitigation plan identify as threats from fabricated and natural disasters? (Select all that apply.)

   a. Incomplete backups

   b. Power outages

   c. Your building flooding

   d. A virus infecting the servers at your company

   e. A fire in your building

   b, c, e. Although all of these are threats that should be considered in your mitigation plan, the ones that can be identified as fabricated or natural are power outages, flooding, and fire. Each of these could be man-made or could occur naturally.

2. When determining the risk posed by a threat, external threats are more dangerous than internal threats. (True or False?)

False. Threats from internal sources can be just as damaging to your C-I-A triad as threats from external sources, so the risk is the same.

3. Select all the attacks that are based on using malicious code:

a. Trojan horse

b. Social engineering

c. Virus

d. Novice

e. Worm

a, c, e. A Trojan horse, virus, and worm are all examples of malicious code. Social engineering is an attack type, but is based on a person gaining access to your information using trickery of some sort. A novice is a hacker wantto-be that does not have the talent of a hacker.

Lesson 3: Intrusion Points

Page 22   ▶ **Lesson Review**

1. Your company has a high-speed Internet connection that can be used to access the Internet and allows people on the Internet to access your company's Web site. Each user also has a modem that he or she can use for Internet access in case the high-speed connection fails. Users can select the Web browser they want to use and are allowed to manage their own computers. Which of the following are intrusion points for the hacker?

a. The high-speed connection

b. The Web browser on each of the client's computers

c. The modem that each user has

d. The Web server for your company's Web site

a, b, c, d. All of these are intrusion points that can be used to gain access to your company's information.

2. When accessing Web sites, an intruder might exploit a Web server using the HTTP protocol. (True or False?)

True. HTTP is a protocol used to access a Web server. An intruder might be able to exploit the Web server using the HTTP protocol.

3. It is always better to have several access points to the Internet so that if a hacker takes one down your company still has access. (True or False?)

False. The fewer the connections to the Internet, the fewer intrusion points a hacker can use to gain access to your company's information.

Lesson 4: Defending Against Threats

Page 28   ▶   **Lesson Review**

1. Your company has a high-speed Internet connection that can be used to access the Internet and allows people on the Internet to access your company's Web site. Each user also has a modem that he or she can use for Internet access in case the high-speed connection fails. Users can select the Web browser they want to use and are allowed to manage their own computers. Which of the following are things you could do to defend against intrusion?

   a. Increase the number of Web browsers that can be used to make it more difficult for a hacker to identify and exploit the Web browser application.

   b. Limit the number of Web browsers that can be used to one or two so that you can better manage application updates.

   c. Have each user access the Internet using his or her modem so that hackers will be confused by the number of physical connections your company has to the Internet.

   d. Minimize the number of physical connection points to the Internet by removing the modem connections.

   b, d. One way is to limit the types of applications that are used. This makes keeping up with current security patches and service packs easier. Another way to defend against intrusion is to minimize the number of intrusion points available to a hacker.

2. Your company wants to make sure that anyone with an administrator account for the network requires a more stringent form of user authentication than regular users. Name three methods that can be used.

   Biometric authentication, smart card authentication, or certificate-based authentication.

3. Auditing is used to secure the network and systems on your network. (True or False?)

   False. Auditing does not secure the network and systems, but does record information that can be used to secure a network or system. By auditing, you record certain activity. This record can then be used to identify attack types and secure against them.

Lesson 5: Organizational and Operational Security

Page 32   ▶   **Lesson Review**

1. You discover that an intruder has compromised your company's C-I-A triad. Of the choices listed below, which is the most appropriate action you should take in response to this threat, and why?

   a. Attempt to identify the person that compromised the system.

   b. Preserve the log files for a forensics expert.

   c. Empty the log files so that you can try to capture specific data if another attack occurs.

   d. Leave any log files with the company's receptionist so that the forensics expert can find them.

   b. If your C-I-A triad is compromised, then your job is to secure potential evidence and not destroy any of the evidence. A forensics expert should be called in to attempt to identify the person who breached security and ensure that the chain of custody for the evidence is not broken.

2. If an employee is fired, what should you do as an information security specialist?

   You should ensure that the user cannot access the network and systems. You can do this by disabling the user's account or by changing the password on the account.

Chapter 2: TCP/IP Basics

Lesson 1: Basic TCP/IP Principles

Page 54   ▶   **Exercise 2: Identifying Information Captured Using Network Monitor**

In this exercise, you will view and identify information captured using Microsoft Network Monitor on a system running the Microsoft Windows XP operating system. Figure 2-11 shows the results of a network capture when viewing the home page at *http://www.ietf.org*.

Refer to Figure 2-11 and provide the missing information in the list below.

- Ethernet frame length: **365 (0x016D)**
- IP version: **4 (0x4)**
- Application-level protocol in use: **HTTP**
- First octet of the source IP address: **12**
- First octet of the destination IP address: **132**

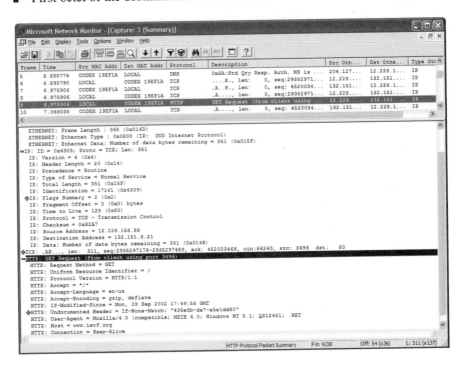

Page 55   ▶   **Lesson Review**

1. After each layer of the DARPA communications model shown below, list the TCP/IP protocols that that particular layer uses.

Application Layer

Telnet, FTP, SMTP, NetBios

Transport Layer

TCP, UDP

Internet Layer

IP, ICMP, IGMP, ARP, RARP

Network Interface Layer

Ethernet, Token Ring, FDDI

2. Place the following TCP/IP communications steps in the correct order:

a. The IP protocol adds a header to the packet and passes the packet to the next lower layer.

b. The Transport layer protocol adds a header to the Application layer request and passes the packet to the next lower layer.

c. The network interface adds header and trailer information to the packet and places it on the network.

d. An application is started that requests communications with a computer on the network. The application forms a packet and passes the request to the next lower layer.

e. The Transport layer strips the header and passes the packet to the next higher layer.

f. The Network Interface layer receives the packet from the network, strips the header and trailer information, and passes the packet to the next higher layer.

g. The Internet layer strips the header and passes the packet to the next higher layer.

h. The Application layer strips the header and passes the information to the application.

Correct order is d, b, a, c, f, g, e, h

3. What protocol and field store the address of the destination computer?

a. The source address of the Ethernet II frame

b. The destination address of the Ethernet II frame

c. The source address of the IP datagram

d. The destination address of the IP datagram

d

4. Which header contains a field that specifies the total size of a frame?

   a. Transport layer header

   b. Internet layer header

   c. Network Interface layer header

   d. All of the above

   c

Lesson 2: TCP/IP Layers and Vulnerabilities

Page 61   ▶   **Lesson Review**

1. At what layer of the DARPA communication model can a DoS attack occur?

   a. Network Interface layer

   b. Internet layer

   c. Transport layer

   d. Application layer

   e. All of the above

   f. None of the above

   e. DoS attacks can occur at any layer. The DoS attack overloads the system that is being attacked.

2. An attack occurs that attempts to disrupt a computer by sending TCP handshake packets in the wrong order. At what communications layer would this attack occur?

   a. Network Interface layer

   b. Internet layer

   c. Transport layer

   d. Application layer

   c

Chapter 3: Certificate Basics

Lesson 1: Understanding Cryptography

Page 71   ▶   **Lesson Review**

1. Select the answer that best describes cryptography.

    a. Cryptography is encrypting messages with a secure hash function to provide information security.

    b. Cryptography is decrypting messages with a secure hash function to provide information security.

    c. Cryptography is encrypting and decrypting data to provide information security.

    d. Cryptography is providing information confidentiality using a shared secret, also known as an asymmetric key pair.

    c

2. Which of the following best describes a key?

    a. A procedure for solving a mathematical problem in a fixed number of steps

    b. A set of instructions that govern ciphering or deciphering messages

    c. A one-way mathematical function that creates a fixed-sized representation of data

    d. An algebraic equation for solving a mathematical problem in a fixed number of steps

    b

3. What is a procedure for solving a mathematical problem in a fixed number of steps?

    a. A secure hash function

    b. A symmetric key

    c. An asymmetric key

    d. An algorithm

    d

4. Match the term to the definition:

1. Symmetric key
2. Asymmetric key pair
3. Secure hash function
4. Algorithm

a. A procedure for solving a mathematical problem in a fixed number of steps

b. A one-way mathematical function that creates a fixed-sized representation of data

c. Two keys that form a key pair; one key is used to encrypt data, and the other key is used to decrypt data

d. A single key is used for encrypting and decrypting data, and everyone that is allowed to encrypt and decrypt the data has a copy of the key

1-d; 2-c; 3-b; 4-a

Lesson 2: Using Cryptography

Page 76   ▶   **Lesson Review**

1. Which is the best mechanism for providing confidentiality?

a. Secure hash function

b. Symmetric key

c. Asymmetric key

d. Algorithm

b

2. You need to send an e-mail message to someone and ensure that the integrity is verifiable when it arrives. Which would best provide that capability?

a. Using a secure hash function to create a message digest

b. Using an asymmetric public key to create a digital signature

c. Using a symmetric key to create a digital signature

d. Using an algorithm to create a message digest

a

3. You need to provide a method to allow the receiver of an e-mail to be able to authenticate that a message came from a specific person. Which would best provide that capability?

a. Using a secure hash function to create a message digest

b. Using an asymmetric key pair to create and validate a message digest

c. Using a symmetric key to create and validate a message digest

d. Using an algorithm to create a message digest

b

4. You need to provide a mechanism that can establish nonrepudiation when sending e-mail to a business partner. Which would best provide that capability?

   a. Using a secure hash function to create and validate a digital signature

   b. Using an asymmetric key pair to create and validate a digital signature

   c. Using a symmetric key to create and validate a digital signature

   d. Using an algorithm to create and validate a digital signature

   b

Lesson 3: Identifying the Components of a Public Key Infrastructure

Page 84   ▶   **Lesson Review**

1. Which best describes a PKI?

   a. A digital representation of information that identifies you as a relevant entity by a TTP

   b. An entity that is recognized as an authority trusted by one or more users or processes to issue and manage a certificate

   c. Uses asymmetric key pairs and combines software, encryption technologies, and services to provide a means of protecting the security of communications and business transactions

   d. A list of certificates issued by a CA that are no longer valid

   c

2. Which best describes a certificate?

   a. A digital representation of information that identifies you as a relevant entity by a TTP

   b. An entity that is recognized as an authority trusted by one or more users or processes to issue and manage a certificate

   c. Uses asymmetric key pairs and combines software, encryption technologies, and services to provide a means of protecting the security of communications and business transactions

   d. A list of certificates issued by a CA that are no longer valid

   a

3. Which best describes a CA?

   a. A digital representation of information that identifies you as a relevant entity by a TTP

   b. An entity that is recognized as an authority trusted by one or more users or processes to issue and manage a certificate

   c. Uses asymmetric key pairs and combines software, encryption technologies, and services to provide a means of protecting the security of communications and business transactions

   d. A list of certificates issued by a CA that are no longer valid

   b

4. What are some reasons a certificate might be placed on a CRL? Select all correct answers.

   a. The certificate owner lost the private key.

   b. The certificate owner is going on a business trip and wants the certificate expiration refreshed so it does not expire.

   c. The certificate owner left the company.

   d. The certificate owner changed names.

   e. The certificate owner lost the public key.

   a, c, d

Lesson 4: Understanding CA Trust Models

Page 92 ▶ **Lesson Review**

1. You are the security specialist for your company and you have just installed a third CA. Each CA supports three different geographical locations. You are attempting to access a server that was issued a certificate by the new CA, but your certificate is not being accepted. Which is the best way to solve the problem?

   a. Have the new CA issue you a certificate

   b. Have the new CA and each of the old CAs issue a certificate to each other

   c. Reinstall the software on the new CA

   d. Make the new CA a bridge CA

   b

2. Which statements are true of a mesh architecture? Select all that apply.

   a. Connects mesh and hierarchical architectures together.

   b. There is a top-level CA known as a root CA.

   c. Multiple peer CAs issue certificates to each other.

   d. Does not issue certificates to end users.

   c

3. Which statements are true of a hierarchical architecture? Select all that apply.

   a. Connects mesh and hierarchical architectures together.

   b. There is a top-level CA known as a root CA.

   c. Multiple peer CAs issue certificates to each other.

   d. Does not issue certificates to end users.

   b

4. Which statements are true of a bridge CA? Select all that apply.

   a. Connects mesh and hierarchical architectures together.

   b. There is a top-level CA known as a root CA.

   c. Multiple peer CAs issue certificates to each other.

   d. Does not issue certificates to end users.

   a, d

Lesson 5: Understanding Certificate Life Cycle and Key Management

Page 98   ▶   **Lesson Review**

1. Match each portion of the certificate life cycle with the answer that best describes it.

1. Enrollment	a. CA distributes the CA to the user
2. Distribution	b. Involves tracking the creation, expiration, and revocation of certificates
3. Validation	
4. Revocation	c. A request is initiated by users requesting certificates from a CA
5. Renewal	d. Occurs when a certificate reaches the expiration date
6. Destruction	
7. Auditing	e. CA adds the certificate to its certificate revocation list
	f. Verifying that the signature is valid, that a trusted CA has issued the certificate, that the certificate can be used for its intended purpose, and determining if the certificate has been revoked
	g. The process of deleting the certificate after it has been published on the CRL

   1-c; 2-a; 3-f; 4-e; 5-d; 6-g; 7-b

Chapter 4: Network Infrastructure Security

Lesson 1: Understanding Network Infrastructure Security

Page 103   ▶   **Review Questions**

1. List three or more items that are considered part of a network infrastructure.

   Cables, connectivity devices such as hubs, routers, switches, firewalls, and hosts, and servers on the network.

2. What are some of the actions you might take to secure your physical network infrastructure?

    You could hire security guards; install sensors, alarms, and closed-circuit TV cameras and monitors; use physical access badges and security cards; install backup electrical power; protect network cables; lock wiring closets and server rooms; encase equipment in protective housings; use tamper-proof seals on equipment casing; install fences and parking lot gates; maintain fire-extinguishing and detection systems appropriate for your equipment and facility; and ensure that buildings meet appropriate construction standards.

3. In addition to physical attacks, what other types of attacks might be directed against your network infrastructure?

    Attacks against the electronic configuration of equipment are also possible. For example, an attack against a router might involve rewriting the routing table.

4. Name other security threats that are not related to people attacking your network.

    Other security threats not related to people attacking your network are fires, floods, tornadoes, earthquakes, mudslides, volcanic eruptions, and other natural disasters.

Lesson 2: Securing Network Cabling

Page 107   ▶   **Exercise: Identifying Cable Vulnerabilities**

Match the cable type in the left column with the compromise it's susceptible to in the right column. More than one compromise might apply to any given cable type.

1. Fiber optic   a. EMI and RFI
2. Twisted-pair   b. Breaking or cutting
3. Coaxial   c. Eavesdropping

1-b

2-a, b, c

3-a, b, c

Page 107   ▶   **Lesson Review**

1. What techniques can be used to sabotage coaxial and twisted-pair networks?

    Removing terminators, cutting the cable, or using heat or an energy-generating motor or device to disrupt communications with EMI and RFI.

2. Which coaxial and twisted-pair sabotage methods do not work on fiber optic cable?

    EMI and RFI don't affect fiber optic cable. Fiber optic cable doesn't use terminators either, so you cannot simply remove a terminator to disrupt communications (as you could on a coaxial network cable).

3. List eavesdropping methods for each type of cable: twisted-pair, coaxial, and fiber optic.

Twisted-pair cable can be eavesdropped on by adding a hub (or adding a cable to an existing hub). Coaxial cable can be eavesdropped on by adding a station to the bus. Also, more sophisticated technology would allow you to collect data transmissions by tapping into either the twisted-pair cable or coaxial cable. Fiber optic cable cannot be easily eavesdropped on. Someone would have to insert a station or signal-repeating device (repeater) to compromise a fiber optic connection between two points. This would result in some type of outage, making it easily detectable.

4. What methods can you use to help protect your network from eavesdropping?

Documentation and routine checks are the best method for protecting your network from eavesdropping. In addition, network-monitoring equipment can alert you to the presence of rogue connections. Be sure to investigate all outages because an outage might be used to insert a rogue device on the network.

Lesson 3: Securing Connectivity Devices

Page 125   ▶   **Exercise: Identifying Network Infrastructure Exploits**

Match the equipment exploits in the left column with the appropriate devices in the right column. Some exploits can be used on multiple device types.

1. Physical sabotage

2. Overwriting MAC-to-IP address mappings

3. Rerouting cables

4. Packet sniffing

5. EMI and RFI

a. Routers

b. Switches and bridges

c. Hubs

d. Hosts on the network

e. Wireless AP

f. ARP cache

1-a, b, c, d, e

2-a, d, e

Overwriting MAC-to-IP address mappings applies to the ARP cache. Routers, wireless APs, and hosts on the network maintain ARP caches, so they are also vulnerable to ARP cache poisoning.

3-a, b, c, d, e

4-a, b, c, d, e

5-a, b, c, d, e

Page 125   ▶   **Lesson review**

1. List security issues that are common to managed hubs, switches, and routers.

   Hubs, switches, and routers are all physical devices. They can be disrupted by power outages and physical sabotage. This includes damaging the devices and rerouting cables to the devices.

2. Describe security issues that are common to switches and routers.

   Switches and routers maintain tables, which could be potentially exploited and incorrectly configured. Also, switches and routers are physical devices (as previously mentioned), so they are vulnerable to all of the issues stated in the answer to question 1.

3. How might an attacker compromise a firewall implementation?

   Attackers could find an exploit in the firewall software, determine a way to circumvent the firewall, or discover an incorrectly configured firewall.

4. List ways in which a PBX can be compromised.

   PBXs are often compromised because they are left with default passwords. Other vulnerabilities might include problems with PBX software that has not been updated, maintenance or remote administration back doors that have not been plugged, and passwords that are easy to guess.

5. What are the security implementations available for wireless networks?

   802.11b authentication, Extensible Authentication Protocol over LANs (EAPOL), and Wired Equivalent Privacy (WEP) encryption.

Lesson 4: Exploring Secure Topologies

Page 137   ▶   **Exercise: Selecting Infrastructure Security Measures**

Each of the statements in the left column describes a technology discussed in this chapter. Match the terms in the right column with the descriptions in the left column.

1. Used to secure and encrypt network data transmitted between partner networks	a. Perimeter network
2. The area between the internal and external network typically used to provide semisecure services to the external network	b. NAT
	c. VPN
3. A device that can be used to create screened subnets and separate the internal network from the external network	d. Firewall
4. Can mask your internal IP address range and allow multiple hosts to share a single IP address	

1-c; 2-a; 3-d; 4-b

Page 137   ▶   **Lesson Review**

1. What is the purpose of dividing a network into security zones?

    Security zones enable administrators to better protect internal resources from external attacks. Different security measures can be used to protect resources based on the function they are expected to provide.

2. What are the major benefits of a perimeter network?

    The main benefit of a perimeter network is that it separates the services that your organization provides to external customers from those provided to internal customers and employees. By making this separation, you can use tighter security controls to secure the internal network and place appropriate focus on securing and monitoring resources in the perimeter network.

3. How can NAT be used to protect your network?

    NAT can protect your internal addressing schedule (and even individual hosts) from attackers on the external network. This doesn't mean that NAT protects individual hosts from attack, but it can make the job of mapping your internal network more difficult for attackers.

4. How are VPNs used?

    VPNs are used to encrypt communication (data) over networks. They are typically used between partner networks or for secure remote connections.

5. What are the benefits of VLANs?

    VLANs reduce broadcast traffic and make it easier for you to reconfigure your network. From a security standpoint, VLANs can make it more difficult for an attacker to map your network.

Lesson 5: Securing and Monitoring Network Resources

Page 144   ▶   **Exercise: Identifying Security Devices**

Match the term in the right column with the most appropriate statement in the left column:

1. Can help to secure your data if your laptop is stolen   a. Honeypot
2. Helps you to learn attacker techniques and potential future exploits   b. IDS
3. Alerts you when a recognized attack is underway   c. Motion-sensing alarm
4. Helps you to keep your laptop from being stolen   d. Data encryption

1-d; 2-a; 3-b; 4-c

Page 144   ▶   **Lesson Review**

1. What security methods are common to workstations and servers?

    Install virus-scanning software and keep virus definition files up to date, monitor system logs for errors, configure logging or auditing for critical system resources and data, limit access to workstations to a specific user or set of users, control access to local and shared resources, remove unnecessary applications and services, configure automated or centralized backup systems, and ensure the latest operating system and application security fixes are applied and kept current.

2. What security steps are typically implemented on mobile devices that aren't usually necessary on workstations and servers?

    Antitheft devices, additional identifying marks or colors, and data encryption.

3. What tools can you use to monitor your network infrastructure devices?

    SNMP management devices, intrusion detection systems, and honeypots.

4. What security benefits does an intrusion detection system provide?

    Warnings about possible attacks, protection from known or recognized attacks, protection of critical system files, and logging of attack information.

5. How can you use a honeypot to help protect your network?

    You can use a honeypot to learn about new exploits that an attacker might soon attempt. You can also prove that attackers are after your network, which might motivate you and those who control your budget to implement tighter (and possibly more expensive) security measures.

Chapter 5: Communications Security

Lesson 1: Understanding Remote Access Connectivity

Page 154   ▶   **Lesson Review**

1. What are two types of remote access connectivity solutions?

    Remote access connectivity can be provided through telephone lines and the Internet.

2. What security concerns must you consider when providing remote access connectivity solutions?

    The security concerns you must consider are how to manage devices not physically connected to your network, and how to secure the communications link between the remote computer and your network.

3. A technique used to identify modems connected to telephone lines is known as
    a. Callback Control Protocol
    b. War dialing
    c. War driving
    d. War walking

    b

Lesson 2: Providing Secure Remote Access

Page 171 ▶ **Lesson Review**

1. During port-based access control interaction, an authenticator
    a. Enforces authentication before it allows user access to the services
    b. Requests access to the services
    c. Checks the supplicant's credentials
    d. Allows data exchange between two ports

    a

2. Which protocols support VPN tunneling?
    a. PPP
    b. PPTP
    c. TCP
    d. SLIP

    b

3. A RADIUS server can only provide authentication for one remote access server. (True or False?)

    False. A RADIUS server provides centralized authentication for any number of remote access servers.

4. Select all of the following that are advantages of TACACS+:
    a. Provides a standard method for managing dissimilar networks
    b. Provides distributed user validation for users attempting to gain access to a router or access server
    c. Provides centralized validation for users attempting to gain access to a router or access server
    d. Runs over UDP for more efficient communications

    a, c

5. The L2TP protocol uses which port?

    a. 443

    b. 80

    c. 1701

    d. 29

    c

6. Which do SSH protect against?

    a. NFS mounting

    b. Packet spoofing

    c. Password sniffing

    d. Internet attacks

    b, c

Lesson 3: Understanding Wireless Standards and Protocols

Page 184   ▶   **Exercise 1: Identifying Maximum Wireless Speeds**

In this exercise, you match the wireless standard with the maximum speed it supports.

1. 802.11a
2. 802.11b
3. 802.11c

a. 22 Mbps transmitting at 2.4 GHz

b. 22 GHz transmitting at 2.4 GHz

c. 54 Mbps transmitting at 2.4 GHz

d. 54 GHz transmitting at 2.4 Mbps

e. 11 Mbps transmitting at 2.4 GHz

f. 11 GHz transmitting at 2.4 Mbps

1-c; 2-e; 3-a

▶ **Exercise 2: Identifying Key Wireless Access Terms**

Match the term in the left column with the most appropriate statement in the right column.

1. ESS	a. The mechanism created in the 802.11 standard that utilizes a cryptographic security countermeasure to provide confidentiality, and has the added benefit of becoming an authentication mechanism.
2. WTLS	
3. 802.1x	
4. BSS	
5. WEP	b. Security layer is based on standard Transport Layer Security (TLS).
6. WAP	

a. The mechanism created in the 802.11 standard that utilizes a cryptographic security countermeasure to provide confidentiality, and has the added benefit of becoming an authentication mechanism.

b. Security layer is based on standard Transport Layer Security (TLS).

c. A suite of protocols used for securing communications in layers 3 through 7. The communications model can be compared to the seven-layer OSI model.

d. The APs talk amongst themselves forwarding traffic from one BSS to another, as well as switch the roaming devices from one BSS to another.

e. Wireless devices (notebooks and handhelds) no longer communicate in ad hoc mode. Instead, all traffic from one device destined for another device is relayed through the AP.

f. A standard for port-based network access control that provides authenticated network access to 802.11 wireless networks and wired Ethernet networks.

1-d; 2-b; 3-f; 4-e; 5-a; 6-c

Page 185   ▶ **Lesson Review**

1. What is the maximum transport speed supported by the 802.11b standard?

   a. 2.4 GHz

   b. 2 Mbps

   c. 11 Mbps

   d. 10 Mbps

   c

2. What is the encryption method employed by WEP? What is the maximum bit encryption supported?

   a. RC4

   b. RC5

   c. 64-bit encryption

   d. 128-bit encryption

   a, d

Chapter 6: Application Security

Lesson 1: E-Mail Security

Page 199 ► **Lesson review**

1. Name two ways in which you can increase the privacy of e-mail.

   Implement encryption and digital signatures. This can be done using PGP or S/MIME-enabled software.

2. What are some steps you should take to protect your organization from the exploitation of e-mail vulnerabilities?

   Review security alerts and bulletins for information on new exploits and software patches. Install and test new e-mail software security patches as they are made available.

3. What can you do to help your organization combat spam?

   Configure spam filters on mail gateways and clients. Participate in programs to collect and reduce spam (such as those sponsored by the FTC or antispam organizations like spam.org and junkbusters.org). You might also follow the advice of spam.org: Never respond to spam. Don't post your address on a Web site. Use a second e-mail address in newsgroups. Don't provide your e-mail address without knowing how it will be used. Use a spam filter. Don't buy anything solicited through spam.

4. What steps can you take to reduce your organization's exposure to e-mail scams?

   Review common scam postings on Web sites like scambusters.org, ccmostwanted.com, and ftc.gov. Educate your organization's users on ways to identify scams, such as showing them the FTC article titled "FTC Names Its Dirty Dozen: 12 Scams Most Likely to Arrive Via Bulk Email." Create policies that prohibit users from following instructions in common scams, such as giving out account numbers.

5. How can you reduce the propagation of e-mail hoaxes?

   Don't forward any unconfirmed information, especially if it was forwarded to you. Use Web sites like hoaxbusters.org to determine whether such e-mail is a known hoax. Learn to recognize and teach others the five tell-tale signs of an e-mail hoax: an indication of urgent information or request, a request to tell all your friends, some form of bogus corroboration to imply that the hoax isn't a hoax, prognostication of dire consequences if the e-mail is not forwarded or the steps are not followed, and the e-mail has been forwarded to others and has a history or several angle brackets (>>>>) in the message body.

Lesson 2: Web Security

Page 214   ▶   **Exercise: Application Security Solutions**

Match the security issues in the left column with the products or specifications that address those issues in the right column:

1. E-mail forgery
2. Clear text e-mail
3. Sniffing Web connection packets
4. Clear text IM
5. Buffer overflows
6. Cleartext cookie transmission

a. PKI-enabled IM applications
b. Secure coding practices
c. PGP
d. SSL/TLS
e. S/MIME
f. Security patches

E-mail forgery is addressed by PGP and S/MIME, both of which can be used to create digital signatures. Cleartext e-mail is also addressed by PGP and S/MIME, both of which can be used to encrypt e-mail. Sniffing Web connection packets is addressed by SSL/TLS, which can be used to encrypt those communications. Clear text IM is addressed by PKI IM applications. Buffer overflows are rectified by secure coding practices and security patches. Cleartext cookie transmission can be encrypted by SSL/TLS.

Page 214   ▶   **Lesson review**

1. How might you secure communications between a Web browser and client?

   Web communications are typically secured with SSL/TLS encryption. Another standard (not as popular as SSL/TLS) to secure Web communications is S-HTTP.

2. What is a software developer's defense against buffer overflows? How should a security administrator handle buffer overflows?

   Applying secure coding practices is the software developer's best defense against buffer overflows. Security administrators should test and apply security patches that correct buffer overflows as soon as they are available. If a security administrator knows of a buffer overflow issue that has not been corrected, he or she should consider disabling that application until a security patch is available.

3. What type of CGI exploits do attackers look for?

   Well-known or sample scripts on Web servers; finding CGI scripts that are in directories to which the attacker can gain access and run; using SSI to compromise CGI scripts; working around a client-side preprocessor (such as a Java applet) and sending data directly to CGI applications in hopes of exploiting them.

4. What types of security issues can arise from cookies?

Cookies can provide an attacker with a look at how your Web server processes and tracks data. Cookies that are used for authentication, storing private data, or feeding information into other programs might be compromised or stolen.

5. What problems does signing active content seek to solve? What security issues might still exist in signed content?

Signing active content allows the user to verify the entity that created it. However, simply being able to verify who developed the application is not a guarantee that the creator is honest and used secure coding practices. The security of the application is not guaranteed, just the identity of its creator. Signed content could still be a malicious program or a legitimate program with a security hole.

Lesson 3: File Transfer

Page 220   ▶   **Lesson review**

1. What are the main security concerns of client/server FTP communications?

Standard FTP communications use unencrypted authentication and data transfer that can be easily packet sniffed. This could result in a compromise of user names, passwords, and possibly private programs and data.

2. How can you mitigate the security concerns regarding FTP?

Secure FTP and Kerberized FTP can be used to encrypt FTP authentication and communication.

3. What are some of the dangers of using file-trading utilities?

File-trading utilities are often used to transfer copyrighted material. Further, they could be used to transfer Trojan horse software.

Chapter 7: User Security

Lesson 1: Understanding Authentication

Page 237

▶ **Exercise 1: Following a Cross-Realm Authentication**

In this exercise, place the steps in order as they would occur in the following scenario.

Scenario: You are a user who has authenticated in one realm and you wish to access a service registered in another realm.

1. The client contacts the RTGS and requests a session ticket to access the remote service.
2. The client contacts a TGS and requests a TGT for the remote realm.
3. The client accesses the service.
4. The AS authenticates the client and provides the client with a TGT.
5. The client (user) sends a registration request to an AS.

   5, 4, 2, 1, 3

▶ **Exercise 2: Reviewing Kerberos Terminology**

In this exercise, match the terms in the left column with the correct definitions in the right column.

a. Realm

b. Authentication server (AS)

c. Ticket-granting ticket (TGT)

d. Ticket-granting service (TGS)

e. Kerberos Distribution Center (KDC)

1. What a AS and TGS form together

2. The ticket a client receives that allows them to request session tickets

3. The service that a client requests a session ticket from

4. The service that registers a client and provides them with a TGT

5. The logical boundary that is formed by an AS and TGS

   a-5; b-4; c-2; d-3; e-1

Page 238

▶ **Lesson Review**

1. What type of authentication does Kerberos provide?
   a. One-way authentication
   b. Mutual authentication
   c. Direct authentication
   d. Indirect authentication

   b

2. With CHAP authentication, what information does a client return in response to a challenge? (Select all that apply)

a. Session ID

b. Random string of data

c. User name

d. Encrypted challenge

e. Password

a, c, d, e

3. Select the answer that best describes token authentication:

a. Something you have

b. Something you know

c. Something you are

a

4. Select the answer that best describes user name and password authentication:

a. Something you have

b. Something you know

c. Something you are

b

5. Select the answer that best describes biometric authentication:

a. Something you have

b. Something you know

c. Something you are

c

Lesson 2: Understanding Access Control Models

Page 243   ▶   **Exercise: Identifying Authentication Methods**

In this exercise, match the authentication methods in the left columns with the correct definitions in the right column.

a. RBAC

b. DAC

c. MAC

1. Permits the owner of an object (such as a process, file, or folder) to manage access control at his or her own discretion.

2. Access to an object is restricted based on the sensitivity of the object (defined by the label that is assigned), and granted through authorization (clearance) to access that level of data.

3. Access is based on the role a user plays in the organization.

a-3; b-1; c-2

Page 243   ▶   **Lesson Review**

1. With discretionary access control (DAC), there is no mechanism for creating and enforcing rules regarding access control. Access is configured at the discretion of the owner of the object. (True or False?)

   True

2. Which description best fits role-based access control (RBAC)?

   a. Access control is configured at the discretion of the object's owner.

   b. Access to an object is restricted based on the sensitivity of the object and is granted through authorization.

   c. Access is granted based on the user's role.

   c

3. Which description best fits discretionary access control (DAC)?

   a. Access control is configured at the discretion of the object's owner.

   b. Access to an object is restricted based on the sensitivity of the object and is granted through authorization.

   c. Access is granted based on the user's role.

   a

4. Which description best fits mandatory access control (MAC)?

   a. Access control is configured at the discretion of the object's owner.

   b. Access to an object is restricted based on the sensitivity of the object and is granted through authorization.

   c. Access is granted based on the user's role.

   b

Chapter 8: Security Baselines

Lesson 1: Network Device and Operating System Hardening

Page 260   ▶   **Lesson Review**

1. How can you stop certain protocols from traversing your routers?

   Access control lists (ACLs) can be used to prevent specific protocols from traversing your routers.

2. What can you do to make it more difficult for an attacker to sniff your network?

   Permanently disabling the promiscuous mode of the network card makes a network scanner useless on the compromised system. If you cannot permanently disable promiscuous mode, you might be able to disable it temporarily. The attacker would have to be sophisticated enough (and obtain the required access) to re-enable promiscuous mode. Other things that you can do include enabling encryption between connections, using network switching, and physically securing connection points to your network.

3. What can you do to secure your computer's file system?

   Be sure to use a file system that supports file and folder permissions. Configure the permissions according to the rule of least privilege.

4. What is the purpose of disabling unnecessary systems, programs, processes, protocols, and services?

   You should disable all unnecessary systems, programs, processes, protocols, and services to reduce the avenues by which an attacker could potentially exploit your network.

5. Why is it imperative that you monitor security alerts?

   New vulnerabilities are discovered frequently and vendor patches are released to correct them. If you do not monitor vulnerability alerts, you might miss an update and allow your organization to fall vulnerable to an attack that could have been prevented.

Lesson 2: Server Application Hardening

Page 275   ▶   **Exercise: Port Matching**

Match the services in the left column with the correct TCP/UDP ports on which the service is provided in the right column:

1. DNS   a. 143
2. DHCP   b. 53
3. SMTP   c. 110
4. POP3   d. 25
5. IMAP   e. 67/68

1-b; 2-e; 3-d; 4-c; 5-a

▶ **Lesson Review**

1. What are some ways to secure your network from exploits targeted at servers capable of dynamic DNS (DDNS)?

   There are essentially two methods for protecting your network from DDNS exploits: Disabling DDNSand implementing DNS security, so that client identities can be verified before they can update the DNS server.

2. What steps can you take to secure DHCP servers and clients on your network?

   Configure reservations for DHCP clients on the DHCP server. Configure client options on the client, instead of relying on the DHCP server, which could potentially be replaced by a rogue DHCP server. You should block DHCP requests from traversing the firewall by blocking UDP/TCP ports 67 and 68.

3. How might an attacker use your FTP server to compromise another computer?

   Some FTP servers are susceptible to port bouncing, which allows an attacker to bounce a scan off of your FTP server and direct it to another computer. This enables the attacker to scan another computer without giving away his or her source IP address to that client.

4. What are the differences in authentication support between LDAP v2 and LDAP v3?

   LDAP v2 supports simple, anonymous, and Kerberos version 4 authentication. LDAP v3 supports simple, anonymous, and SASL authentication.

5. What are the components in an LDAP hierarchy?

   LDAP root, organizational units, and objects.

Chapter 9: Operational Security

Lesson 1: Physical Security

▶ **Lesson Review**

1. Why is a biometric device based on hand geometry suitable only for verifying users and not identifying them?

   Hand geometry can only be used to verify users because the characteristics of the hand that are measured by the device are not unique to each individual.

2. Which of the following attributes of cellular networking products make them a greater security risk than IEEE 802.11b wireless products?

   a. Lower cost

   b. Greater transmission range

   c. Less susceptibility to interference from walls and barriers

   d. Use of higher frequencies

   b

3. What is the difference between a mirrored server stored at a hot site and one stored at a cold site?

The server at the hot site is running continuously, whereas the server at the cold site is only stored there, and is not running.

Lesson 2: Privilege Management

Page 296   ▶   **Lesson Review**

1. Which of the following statements about users and groups is true?

   a. A user can only be a member of one group.

   b. A user's effective permissions can be inherited from multiple groups.

   c. Creating groups enables the network administrator to create fewer user accounts.

   d. Groups cannot have conflicting privileges.

   b

2. How does centralized administration reduce the workload of the network administrator?

   a. By reducing the number of resources to which users have to be granted privileges.

   b. By reducing the number of groups that need to be created.

   c. By reducing the number of users accounts that need to be created.

   d. By reducing the number of privileges that have to be granted to each user.

   c

3. When you grant a user account the minimal required permission, what rule are you applying?

   Rule of least privilege.

Lesson 3: Removable Media

Page 305 ▶ **Exercise: Identifying Removable Storage Media Types**

Match the removable storage media in the left column with the appropriate description in the right column.

1. Flashcards
2. Magnetic tape
3. Smart cards
4. CD-R
5. Floppy disks

a. Typically contains encrypted data used to authenticate a user's identity

b. Can only be erased by physical destruction

c. No longer used for backups and data archiving, due to low capacity

d. New storage technologies using very small form factors

e. Traditional medium used for backups

1-d; 2-e; 3-a; 4-b; 5-c

Page 306 ▶ **Lesson review**

1. Which of the following magnetic tape formats has the greatest storage capacity?

   a. DAT

   b. LTO

   c. DLT

   d. QIC

   b

2. What is the term used to describe a hard disk that you can remove from the computer without shutting the system down?

   Hot pluggable.

3. Which of the following removable media is typically used to carry users' digital certificates?

   a. Flashcards

   b. Smart cards

   c. CD-Rs

   d. Floppy disks

   b

Lesson 4: Protecting Business Continuity

Page 311   ▶   **Lesson Review**

1. Name a hardware technology that enables a computer to continue operating despite the failure of a hard disk.

   Redundant array of independent disks (RAID).

2. Utilities such as electric power are typically not included as part of a business continuity plan because their reliability rate is so high. (True or False?)

   False. Utilities should be included in a business continuity plan if a business absolutely requires them to operate.

3. Which of the following statements is true about a business continuity management (BCM) effort?

   a. BCM is a company process that must involve all departments and all levels.

   b. BCM is an IT consideration that is devoted to keeping the company's computer network operational in the event of a disaster.

   c. Each department manager in a company should create an individual business continuity plan for that department.

   d. BCM is a government project that dictates preparatory requirements to individual businesses.

   a

Chapter 10: Organizational Security

Lesson 1: Documentation

Page 327

▶ **Exercise: Policy Purposes**

Match the policy descriptions in the left column with the appropriate policy in the right column.

1. More people involved in a process reduce the likelihood that one of them will do something inappropriate.

2. International security standard.

3. Guidelines regarding organization's member privileges to information assets.

4. Defines responsibilities and capabilities of information auditors.

5. Describes hours of operation.

6. Describes the type of network traffic that is allowed into or out of the organization.

7. Policy explaining that employees can be held accountable for negligent actions such as transmitting patient medical records in cleartext instead of an encrypted format.

a. Firewall policy

b. Accountability policy

c. Common Criteria

d. Separation of duties

e. Access policy

f. Availability statement

g. Due care

1-d; 2-c; 3-e; 4-b; 5-f; 6-a; 7-e

Page 327

▶ **Lesson Review**

1. List requirements you might find in a password policy.

   Requirements for password length, complexity, expiration, uniqueness, lockout threshold, and lockout duration.

2. What items might be included in a privacy policy?

   The policy might include information concerning protections for customer, client, and employee data. Descriptions concerning the type of information that can be audited and monitored, such as e-mail and visited Web sites, can also be part of this policy. The policy can be used to inform employees that they are being watched, so they don't expect they have complete privacy at work.

3. What type of policy would typically prohibit playing of computer games on organizational computers?

Acceptable use policy.

4. What is a computer security incident?

An actual, suspected, or attempted compromise of any IT system.

5. If you sign an agreement with another company to host an e-commerce solution for your organization, the company you signed with is a what?

Application service provider.

Lesson 2: Risk Assessment

Page 335   ▶   **Lesson Review**

1. What is the formula for calculating risk?

Threat × Vulnerability × Impact = Risk

2. Who is normally responsible for assigning value to assets?

Accountants.

3. List some resources for collecting technology threat statistics.

CERT (http://www.cert.org), ICAT (http://icat.nist.gov), Security Statistics (http://www.securitystats.com).

4. What is the purpose of an impact assessment?

Establish how costly an exploited vulnerability might be for the organization.

5. What is a vulnerability assessment?

A determination of how susceptible the organization or asset is to a threat.

Lesson 3: Security Education

Page 340   ▶   **Exercise: Stages and Delivery Types**

Match the numbered security education program stages in the left column to the appropriate lettered delivery types in the right column.

1. Awareness	a. Research projects
2. Training	b. Demonstrations
3. Education	c. Logon banners
	d. Discussions
	e. Hands-on activities

1-c; 2-b, e; 3-a, d

Page 341   ▶ **Lesson review**

1. Which stage of the security education program is mostly marketing?
   Awareness.

2. At which stage of the security education program are individuals most likely to be self-motivated?
   Education.

3. Security training is most effective when it is _____?
   Hands-on and related to the person's job.

Chapter 11: Incident Detection and Response

Lesson 1: Attacks and Malicious Code

Page 364   ▶ **Exercise: Attacks and Scans**

Match the types of attacks or scans in the left column with the appropriate descriptions in the right column.

1. Ping sweep	a. ICMP attack that involves spoofing and flooding
2. SYN flood	b. UDP attack that involves spoofing and flooding
3. Fraggle	c. ICMP echo reply scan
4. POD	d. Scan that completes the TCP handshake
5. XMAS	e. Scan that leaves off the final ACK
6. Smurf	f. DoS or DDoS attack that leaves open TCP ports
7. Teardrop	g. Scan that passes multiple TCP flags
8. Connect	h. Attack with oversized ICMP echo reply packets
9. Half-open	i. Attack with IP fragments that cannot be reassembled

1-c; 2-f; 3-b; 4-h; 5-g; 6-a; 7-i; 8-d; 9-e

Page 365   ▶ **Lesson Review**

1. What are some ways you can combat DoS attacks?

   Configure routers for appropriate ingress and egress filtering and to deny IP-directed broadcasts. Apply all software patches to hosts to protect your IP stack. Coordinate with your ISP to stop or reduce DoS attacks that involve systems outside your organization.

2. How can LSRR be used to avoid security devices?

   Attackers can configure LSRR on client packets to route packets around security devices. To protect your systems from this, configure routers to discard packets that specify LSRRs, if possible.

3. What can attackers use replay attacks to compromise?

   Attackers can use replay attacks to compromise passwords, encryption keys, authentication, VPNs, and sessions.

4. What type of attacks can be waged against encryption keys and secure hashes?

   Replay attacks and mathematical or brute force attacks (birthday attacks).

5. What type of sessions can be hijacked?

   Potentially any session, but the ones discussed in this lesson are TCP, terminal connections, and wireless connections.

Lesson 2: Intrusion Detection Systems

Page 378   ▶   **Exercise: IDS Staged Deployment Steps**

Place the following staged IDS deployment steps in the appropriate order:

a. Deploy a HIDS to critical hosts

b. Fully deploy a HIDS

c. Fully deploy a NIDS

d. Partially deploy a NIDS

d, c, a, b

Page 378   ▶   **Lesson Review**

1. What are the main differences between NIDS's, SIVs, and LFMs?

   Network intrusion detection systems (NIDS's) monitor and analyze network traffic for intrusions. System integrity verifiers (SIVs) monitor single systems for changes to files and file structures. Log file monitors (LFMs) monitor log files for intrusions.

2. What are the benefits of NIDS's?

   NIDS's increase overall security. They can protect multiple systems, allow monitoring inside the firewall, and alert you to incoming attacks. These systems also detect slow attacks. NIDS's can take corrective action and they have a low impact on network traffic.

3. What are some problems with NIDS's?

   They have system limitations that might prevent them from collecting and analyzing every event. They only collect the traffic that passes by, so you need to consider how switches and VLANs affect their ability to perform. NIDS's cannot usually decrypt packets for analysis and they cannot typically determine attack success. In addition, they can generate false positives.

4. What are some ways that attackers try to avoid detection?

There are specific attacks used against IDS systems, such as sending an overabundance of attack signatures. Setting off multiple IDS alarms might give an attacker enough time to bypass the IDS with an undetected attack. Some attackers use fragmentation to disguise the true intention of their packets traversing the network. Others use encryption to obfuscate communications. Further, some attackers might attempt to route packets around the NIDS with LSRR (as described in the previous lesson).

5. What benefits do HIDS's and application-based IDS's have over NIDS's?

They are not limited by encryption, so they see packets or information before encryption and after decryption. They are closer to the target, which means they can collect more accurate information. They help to detect software integrity breaches, file modifications, Trojan horse software, and other effects of attacks. VPNs don't affect the function of HIDS's either.

Lesson 3: Incident Response

Page 385   ▶   **Exercise: Incident Response Priority**

Organize the following incident response actions into an appropriate priority:

a. Minimize the effect of the attack on the organization's business activities

b. Protect all other data

c. Protect classified and sensitive data

d. Protect hardware and software

e. Protect human life and prevent people from being injured

e, c, b, d, a

Page 385   ▶   **Lesson Review**

1. What should you do when organizing a CSIRT?

Decide whether you should formalize a team or create an ad hoc team as necessary. If you establish a formal team, contact FIRST to identify your team and establish a reporting chain. Ensure your team reviews RFC 2350, CERTs CSIRT FAQ, NISTs SP 800-3, and "Electronic Crime Scene Investigation: A Guide for First Responders."

2. What are the main points you should keep in mind when performing computer forensics?

Change as little as possible, examine the system from a backup or image if possible instead of using the actual system, document and preserve all evidence, and maintain documented chain of custody.

3. Why is unplugging a compromised system from the network usually a prudent action?

An attacker or malicious code could cause more damage if a compromised system is left plugged into the network. This could leave the organization and responsible people liable for damages.

A P P E N D I X   B

Ports and Protocol IDs

This appendix presents a list of Transmission Control Protocol (TCP) and User Datagram Protocol (UDP) ports and Internet Protocol (IP) IDs that you should know. This appendix is not a comprehensive list of all available port and protocol IDs, but it does include the important ones that you should know.

Ports

There are a couple of reasons to know TCP and UDP port numbers. First, you often need to allow or deny certain ports when configuring a firewall or routers. Second, there are several ports that are commonly attacked and exploited that should be disabled whenever possible. You can keep up with commonly exploited ports by visiting the SANS Common Vulnerable Ports list, which is Appendix A of the SANS/ FBI Top 20 List (*http://www.sans.org/top20*). Table B-1 lists the ports and related services that you should know.

Table B-1.   TCP and UDP Port Numbers

Ports and Protocols	Services
20 TCP	File Transfer Protocol (FTP) data port
21 TCP	FTP control port
22 TCP	Secure Shell (SSH)
23 TCP	Telnet
25 TCP	Simple Mail Transfer Protocol (SMTP)
53 UDP	Domain Name Service (DNS) lookup
53 TCP	DNS zone transfer
67 UDP	Bootstrap protocol server; Dynamic Host Configuration Protocol (DHCP) server
68 UDP	Bootstrap protocol client; DHCP client
69 UDP	Trivial File Transfer Protocol (TFTP)
80 TCP	Hypertext Transfer Protocol (HTTP)
88 TCP	Kerberos

Table B-1. TCP and UDP Port Numbers *(continued)*

Ports and Protocols	Services
109 TCP	Post Office Protocol (POP) version 2
110 TCP	POP version 3
111 TCP	Sun Remote Procedure Call (RPC) and Network File System (NFS)
119 TCP	Network News Transfer Protocol (NNTP)
123 TCP/UDP	Network Time Protocol (NTP)
135 TCP	End point mapper (epmap) and NT RPC services
137 TCP/UDP	NetBIOS over TCP/IP name service (NetBIOS-ns)
138 UDP	NetBIOS over TCP/IP datagram service (NetBIOS-ds)
139 TCP	NetBIOS over TCP/IP session service NetBIOS-ssn)
143 TCP	Internet Message Access Protocol (IMAP)
161 UDP	Simple Network Management Protocol (SNMP)
162 UDP	SNMP Trap
389 TCP	Lightweight Directory Access Protocol (LDAP)
443 TCP	Transport Layer Security (TLS)/Secure Sockets Layer (SSL)
445 TCP/UDP	Microsoft DS (NetBIOS service)
500 TCP/UDP	Internet Key Exchange (IKE) protocol; Internet Security Association and Key Management Protocol (ISAKMP)
514 UDP	UNIX Syslog (system logging)
1701 UDP	Layer 2 Tunneling Protocol (L2TP)
1723 TCP	Point to Point Tunneling Protocol (PPTP)
2049 TCP	Sun NFS
3389 TCP	Microsoft Terminal Services MS WBT Server
5631 TCP	PCAnywhere Data
5632 UDP	PCAnywhere Status

The Internet Assigned Numbers Authority (IANA) has reserved both TCP and UDP ports for all of these protocols except syslog. This table illustrates the most commonly used port numbers and protocols. For a complete list of ports check the IANA Web site at *http://www.iana.org/assignments/port-numbers*.

Protocol Numbers

You sometimes need to know protocol IDs when configuring routers or firewalls. For example, you might need to know a specific protocol ID to allow a certain protocol through your firewall. If you would like to read a detailed example, read Microsoft Knowledge Base article Q233256 "How to Enable IPSec Traffic Through a Firewall." Table B-2 lists the IP protocol identifiers you should remember.

Table B-2.   Protocol Numbers

IP Protocol Identification Number	Used for
1	Internet Control Message Protocol (ICMP)
6	TCP
17	UDP
47	Generic Routing Encapsulation (GRE), which is used in PPTP connections
50	Authentication Header (AH) used with Internet Protocol Security (IPSec)
51	Encapsulating Security Payload (ESP) used with IPSec

For a complete list of protocol IDs check the IANA Web site at *http://www.iana.org/assignments/protocol-numbers*.

Glossary

Numbers

8.3 compatible file name A file name that has a maximum of 8 characters followed by a period and 3-character extension, such as myfile22.txt.

802.11a A wireless communication standard that supports a maximum speed of 54 Mbps.

802.11b A wireless communication standard that supports a maximum speed of 11 Mbps; fallback speeds 5, 2, and 1 Mbps.

802.11g A draft standard which provides 54Mbps wireless networking capabilities, similar to that of 802.11a but in the same band as 802.11b, to offer higher Wi-Fi compatible data-rates for wireless local area networks (WLANs).

A

acceptable use policy Defines the ways in which personnel can use the organization's equipment.

access control Refers to the mechanisms that regulate network access to computers, software, or other resources. However, the security professional must understand that the term applies equally to the physical access that users are granted to computers and other equipment.

access control list (ACL) A rule list that tells the router or firewall how to deal with network packets the router receives.

access point (AP) A device that provides a central connection point for one or more wireless network devices.

access policy Provides guidelines for all personnel regarding the rights, privileges and restrictions for using the organization's technology and information assets.

accountability policy Indicates the responsibilities of people in the organization. The policy explains that audits of information assets can and will be conducted.

ACK scans TCP scans used to identify active hosts on the network.

ACK segment The final packet of a TCP three-way handshake. The information sent includes the source and destination ports, sequence number, acknowledgment number, ACK flags, and window size.

active content Small executables or script code, which is rendered within the client's Web browser. For example, some banks offer mortgage calculators on their Web sites. Active content is also known as dynamic content.

active detection *See* active response.

active response An automatic action that a system takes when it recognizes an attack. The response might be innocuous, such as increasing information collection; moderate, such as reconfiguring the network; or severe, such as launching a counter-attack against the intruder.

ActiveX A set of technologies from Microsoft that enables interactive content for the World Wide Web.

ad hoc mode A wireless device mode that is used for peer-to-peer communications.

administrator Any person responsible for the day-to-day operation of system and network resources.

algorithm Procedure for solving a mathematical problem. This can require that the same procedure be repeated several times to solve the problem, such as when determining the greatest common denominator of two numbers.

anomaly detection A method that involves recognizing something suspicious or atypical.

anonymous FTP Servers do not require authentication and instead have users log in as "anonymous" and then enter their e-mail address as the password.

anti-virus policy Describes the organization's efforts to reduce the exposure to, damage from, and spreading of malicious software. The policy should state requirements of personnel to implement, update, and appropriately utilize anti-virus software.

application hardening Making an application more secure, which includes applying the latest security patches and enforcing user-level security if available. Applications on a system can be client applications, such as a Web browser, or server applications, such as a Web server application.

application service povider SLA Covers the hosting of a specific application or service, such as Web application, database application, or e-commerce service. These agreements typically have provisions for server up time, availability, and recovery or replacement times. Sometimes these agreements are referred to as co-location or hosting services.

application-based IDS Form of intrustion detection system (IDS) that analyzes the events occurring within a specific software application. This type of IDS typically analyzes the application's transaction log files.

appropriate use policy *See* acceptable use policy.

ARP cache A portion of system memory dedicated to media access control (MAC) to Internet Protocol (IP) address resolution.

ARP cache poisoning Adding bogus entries to the ARP cache on a host computer.

Arpspoof A utility in the dsniff suite of utilities that helps to spoof ARP caches.

asymmetric algorithm Encryption algorithm that utilizes two keys. The key that encrypted the plaintext cannot be used to decrypt the ciphertext. Examples include Diffie-Hellman and RSA.

asymmetric key pair Two keys that form a key pair; one key is used to encrypt data, and the other key is used to decrypt data.

attack An attempt to bypass security controls on a computer. The attack could alter, release, or deny data.

attack signature An indicator that a specific attack is occurring; used by misuse detectors.

auditing To capture security-related events in a log file.

Authentication Header (AH) Another name for IP protocol 51, which provides integrity and authenticity for packets, but not confidentiality.

authentication policy Describes the acceptable methods, equipment, and parameters for allowing access to resources.

authentication server (AS) In a Kerberos realm, the AS is the server that registers all valid users (clients) and services in the realm. The AS provides each client a ticket granting ticket (TGT) that is used to request a ticket from a ticket granting server (TGS).

authenticator A role in which a LAN port enforces authentication before it allows user access to the services that can be accessed through that port.

Authenticator Port Access Entity (PAE) The authenticator PAE enforces authentication before it allows access to resources located off of that port.

authenticators A series of bits, symbol, or group of symbols that are inserted into a transmission or message in a predetermined manner and are then used for validation. Authenticators are typically valid for 5 minutes. An authenticator can only be used once, which prevents someone from intercepting an authenticator and then reusing it.

Authenticode Used in Internet Explorer to check for digital signatures before downloading ActiveX components.

authorized use policy *See* acceptable use policy.

availability Ensures that information and systems can be accessed when needed by authorized personnel.

availability statement Sets expectations for the availability of organizational resources. The document should define hours of operation, times when the resources are scheduled for maintenance (down-time), and the availability of redundant resources.

B

basic service set (BSS) A portion of a wireless network that acts as a single Ethernet collision domain. When using a BSS, wireless devices can communicate with each other directly or through a single access point.

bastion host A host computer that is exposed to the Internet by a three-pronged firewall or because it is placed between the firewall and the external network. This host should have a secure configuration.

biometric authentication Automated method of identifying a person based on a physical characteristic, such as a thumbprint or the retina of their eye.

birthday attack A translation of the birthday paradox into an attack that involves creating multiple versions of two opposing documents in hopes of getting two copies that have the same digital signature or hash. The two documents can then be switched as a form of attack against people agreeing to the first, but not the second.

birthday paradox The theory that in every group of 23 people there is more than a 50 percent chance that two people share the same birthday.

blind FTP Servers or directories that allow write access, but not file listings (read access).

bridge CA A certification authority that connects mesh and hierarchical architectures together. This allows different companies to have their own trust architecture, and then have a single connection using a bridge CA.

broadcast domain A segment, subnet, or virtual local area network (VLAN) that doesn't filter broadcast traffic. Each host on a broadcast domain can broadcast packets to all other hosts on the broadcast domain.

brute force attack Attacks that use mathematical algorithms to break encryption keys, passwords, or other logical security measures with brute force; trying every combination available.

bytestream Segmentation and reassembly of Application layer data into datagrams that the source and destination computers support.

C

Callback Control Protocol (CBCP) Allows your remote access servers or clients to negotiate a callback with the other end.

certificate A digital representation of information that identifies you and is issued by CAs, which are often a trusted third party (TTP).

certificate publication point A location where certificates are stored and published.

certificate revocation list (CRL) A signed, time-stamped list of server serial numbers of CA public key certificates that have been revoked. The CRL is necessary to allow CAs to accept and reject certificates that were issued by a different CA.

certification authority (CA) A computer that issues digital certificates, maintains a list of invalid certificates, and maintains a list of invalid CAs.

chain of custody Procedures (especially documentation) to ensure the integrity of the information collected by tracking its handling and storage from the point of collection to final disposition of the evidence.

Challenge Handshake Authentication Protocol (CHAP) A protocol that can be used when a remote client needs to authenticate itself to a network server or when two routers need to authenticate themselves to each other to begin a Point-to-Point Protocol (PPP) session. Challenge includes the session ID and a random string of data to the remote client. The remote client uses a Message Digest function (MD5) hash to return: the username, an encrypted challenge, session ID, and password.

checksum A computation applied to a file that results in a string that can be used to check the integrity of a downloaded file.

ciphertext Information that is encrypted.

classification policy The appropriate handling and protection of your organization's information assets.

commercial CA Operated by a certificate-issuing company; provides certificates to the general public, or for use when communicating with other entities.

Common Gateway Interface (CGI) Programs that are commonly used on Web servers to produce dynamic content. CGI is a specification for transferring information between an application and a Web server. For example, CGIs are frequently used to perform data input, search, and retrieval functions on databases.

Common Internet File System (CIFS) The revised version of Server Message Block; see SMB.

complex passwords Have mixed case, alphanumeric, and multiple characters. Such passwords are difficult to guess or crack with a password-cracking program.

computer forensics The investigation and analysis of computer security incidents in the interest of gathering and preserving potential legal evidence.

computer security incident An actual, suspected, or attempted compromise of any information technology system. Any activity that threatens a computer system or violates a security policy can lead to an incident.

computer security incident response team (CSIRT) A team of people assembled to respond to computer security incidents.

computer technology purchasing guidelines Guidelines used to protect the organization from equipment that could lead to a security breach. These guidelines specify security features that are required or preferred by the organization.

confidentiality Private or secret. Confidentiality ensures that only authorized personnel access information. One way to provide confidentiality is to encrypt data.

connection protocol (SSH-CONN) A protocol that runs over the user authentication protocol and multiplexes the encrypted tunnel into several logical channels.

connection-oriented Means that the source and destination computer establish a connection and then transfer data. This ensures reliable delivery of the data to the destination computer.

cookie A small amount of data that a Web server stores about a user on the user's own computer; also known as a magic cookie.

cracker Someone who breaks security on an automated information system or a network. Crackers are typically doing something mischievous or malicious, and although they might be trying to break into a system for what they consider a good and higher cause, they are still breaking into a system.

cross-realm authentication The capability of users in one realm to be authenticated and access services in another realm.

cryptanalyst A person who has skill working at breaking codes or encryptions; code breaker.

cryptographic key Consists of a set of instructions that govern ciphering or deciphering messages, and can include a random or pseudo-random number.

cryptography Secret writing, or the enciphering and deciphering of messages in secret code or cipher. With respect to information security, cryptography is a branch of mathematics concerned with transforming or concealing data to provide information security using mathematical algorithms. Cryptography is currently one of the ways that you protect your confidentiality-integrity-availability (C-I-A) triad.

cyclic redundancy check (CRC) Provides a bit-level integrity check for the packet. This ensures that the packet arrived without transmission-related damage. Also known as the frame check sequence (FCS).

D

data center SLA An agreement that covers the availability of organization's data. This agreement typically specifies backup frequency, time to restore, and guarantees concerning the availability of the systems holding the data.

decryption Process of decoding the encrypted message.

default allow rule Allows all inbound traffic, except that specifically denied.

default deny rule Denies all inbound traffic except that specifically allowed.

defense-in-breadth A variety of security devices at multiple levels of the network infrastructure.

defense-in-depth Multiple security devices at multiple levels of the network infrastructure.

denial of service (DoS) A type of attack that renders a service inoperative. For instance, a DoS attack can make a popular Web site unavailable for some length of time.

digital certificates An electronic credential used to authenticate users.

directory enumeration When attackers browse a Web server's directory structure and available files looking for potential intrusion points.

discretionary access control (DAC) Permits the owner of an object (such as a process, file, or folder) to manage access control at their own discretion.

distribution system (DS) Forms the spine of the wireless LAN, making the decisions whether to forward traffic from one Basic Service Set (BSS) to the wired network or back out to another access point or BSS.

DMZ *See* perimeter network.

DNS cache poisoning When attackers exploit a flaws in a DNS server by placing bogus entries in the DNS cache.

dropper A virus carrier program or file. When the dropper is executed or opened it creates a virus. Virus authors often use droppers to shield their programs from virus scanners. Droppers are also called Injectors.

due care A minimum or customary practice of reasonably protecting assets.

Dynamic DNS (DDNS) record spoofing When attackers use DDNS to overwrite records that belong to other systems, or put bogus records in the DNS server.

E

eavesdropping The act of capturing and decoding network transmissions.

electromagnetic interference (EMI) Noise spread over the whole electromagnetic spectrum. This can affect the reception of electronic transmissions of audio, video, radio, television, and network data. EMI can lead to the malfunctioning of other sensitive electrical and electronic equipment.

e-mail gateway Servers running software that can scan, clean, and filter e-mail before it reaches your e-mail server. Also known as an e-mail relay.

EMI/RFI *See* electromagnetic interference (EMI) and radio frequency interference (RFI).

Encapsulating Security Payload (ESP) Another name for IPSec protocol ID 50, which provides confidentiality, authenticity, and integrity.

enrolling A setup procedure for biometric authentication in which an administrator stores the user's biological feature that will be used later to verify the user's identity. This is typically acquired by using a sensor (hardware device) that can record the particular feature, such as a thumbprint scanner.

extended service set (ESS) A wireless networking implementation that has more than one basic service set (BSS) available. This allows users to move between multiple infrastructure BSSs. In an ESS, the access points talk amongst themselves, forwarding traffic from one BSS to another, as well as switch the roaming devices from one BSS to another.

Extensible Authentication Protocol Over LAN (EAPOL) The 802.1x defines a standard for encapsulating EAP messages so that they can be handled directly by a LAN MAC service. 802.1x tries

to make authentication more encompassing, rather than enforcing specific mechanisms on the devices. Because of this, 802.1x uses Extensible Authentication Protocol to receive authentication information.

Extensible Authentication Protocol Over Wireless (EAPOW) When EAPOL messages are encapsulated over 802.11 wireless frames.

external access points Network components that connect your company to the Internet and applications that are used to communicate across the Internet communications protocols.

F

false acceptance rate (FAR) The percentage of unauthorized users who are incorrectly identified as valid users during biologic authentication. Also known as type 2 errors.

false rejection rate (FRR) The percentage of authorized users who are incorrectly rejected during biologic authentication. Also known as type 1 errors.

file allocation table (FAT) A file system type available for Microsoft and other operating systems that doesn't support file or directory-level security.

FIN scan A TCP scan used to identify listening TCP ports based on a response, or lack of a response, to a finish (FIN) packet.

firewall policy Describes the type of network traffic and data that is and is not allowed to traverse the firewall.

forensics The investigation and analysis of a computer for the purpose of gathering and preserving evidence.

Forum of Incident Response and Security Teams (FIRST) An organization that coordinates CSIRTs world wide.

frag attack *See* fragmentation attack.

fraggle A specific type of UDP flood DoS attack that involves sending spoofed UDP echo packets to a subnet. The spoofed address is the target of the attack and all hosts on the subnet reply to the target.

fragmentation Breaking a single IP datagram into several smaller datagrams for transport across "small-packet" networks. This allows packets to travel from a source computer to a destination computer across various types of networks.

fragmentation attack Any attack that involves sending fragmented packets as a form of attack or IDS deception. *See* teardrop.

frame check sequence (FCS) *See* cyclic redundancy check.

FTP bounce An exploit in which attackers run scans against other computers through an FTP server.

H

hacker Someone who can write code to provide a solution to a problem. The code is not always written eloquently, but does provide a solution to a difficult problem and is created quickly

half-open scans TCP scan that identifies potential targets and listening TCP services. Doesn't send the final ACK packet in the TCP three-way handshake, which leaves the target of the scan with TCP ports in an open and waiting state for a short period of time.

hash One-way mathematical function (OWF) that creates a fixed-sized value (known as a hash or message digest) based on a variable-sized unit of data. A hashing algorithm will always produce the same hash value based on the same input data and never have two different data units produce the same hash value.

hidden fields Used to pass data between CGI applications through the client browser. The browser itself never displays the data (hence the name hidden field).

HINFO record A DNS record that stores additional information about a host computer, such as where it is located or who manages it.

hoax A false virus warning that people believe is real. These hoaxes are typically spread through e-mail messages.

honeynet mode A type and mode of intrusion detection that allows you to capture packets for later forensic investigation.

honeynets Networks of honeypot systems or a single honeypot system that simulates a network of vulnerable devices.

honeypots Systems that have no production value and are designed to be targets for attackers. They help administrators learn about attacks and attack methods.

host membership query An IGMP protocol datagram that a router sends at intervals to verify that computers on a segment are still listening for multicast traffic.

host membership report An IGMP protocol message that a computer sends to the router it is configured to use requesting multicast messages be forwarded.

host spoofing A situation in which an attacker uses the IP address of another system in order to attack that system or to hide his or her identity.

host wrappers *See* personal firewalls.

host-based IDS (HIDS) Software installed on individual computers to protect those individual systems.

I

ICAT A database of computer vulnerabilities and exploits maintained at http://icat.nist.gov. ICAT originally stood for Internet Categorization of Attacks Toolkit. However, it is not an acronym today because the focus of the toolset has changed.

ICMP flood A DoS attack that attempts to over-whelm the target with ICMP packets so that it can-not service them and becomes unresponsive.

IEEE 802.11 A set of standards that cover wireless networking.

IEEE 802.1x A standard for port-based network access control that provides authenticated network access to 802.11 wireless networks and wired Ethernet networks.

information technology system and network maintenance policy Describes how maintenance personnel are allowed to handle and access the organization's equipment. Both internal and exter-nal personnel should be considered.

infrastructure mode A wireless mode used when wireless devices communicate with a wireless access point.

instant messaging (IM) A popular method by which people communicate today. IM allows peo-ple to send pop-up messages, files, audio, and video between computers.

integrity Ensures that information is accessed and modified only by authorized people.

internal access points Systems that are not in a secured room and systems that do not have any local security configured.

Internet Group Management Protocol (IGMP) A protocol designed to allow for communication with multiple hosts at one time.

Internet Protocol Security (IPSec) A standard secu-rity protocol that provides privacy, integrity and authenticity for network traffic in the following situations: end-to-end security for IP unicast traf-fic, from client-to-server, server-to-server and cli-ent-to-client using IPSec transport mode; remote access VPN client and gateway functions using L2TP secured by IPSec transport mode; site-to-site VPN connections, across outsourced private WAN or Internet- based connections using L2TP/IPSec or IPSec tunnel mode.

Internet Security Scanner (ISS) A software utility for vulnerability scanning.

Internet service provider SLA Specifies bandwidth and connection availability guarantees.

intrusion Any compromise of your organization's C-I-A triad.

intrusion detection A process of monitoring and evaluating computer events and network traffic for signs of intrusions.

intrusion detection system (IDS) A hardware device with software that is used to detect unau-thorized activity on your network.

intrusion points Areas that provide an access point to your company's information.

IP spoofing A situation in which an attacker uses the IP address of another system to attack that sys-tem or to hide his or her identity.

IPSec transport mode IPSec mode that secures an existing IP packet from source to destination.

IPSec tunnel mode IPSec mode that puts an exist-ing IP packet inside a new IP packet that is sent to a tunnel end point in the IPSec format.

J

Java A programming language created by Sun Microsystems.

Java applets Small self-contained Java programs.

Java Virtual Machine (VM) A software component that takes the plain-text Java code and translates it to native instructions on the client system.

JavaScript Netscape's object-based scripting lan-guage, which is commonly used to communicate with other components or to accept user input. JavaScript is typically embedded inside an HTML page and read by a client browser. A "SCRIPT" tag inside HTML coding is used to note the use of JavaScript. An "APPLET" tag is used to call Java applets inside HTML.

joke A non-destructive program that is propagated like malicious code. People usually consider this type of program annoying or funny.

K

Kerberized FTP Provides secure authentication between the FTP client and server. Kerberized FTP also encrypts file transfers. To use Kerberized FTP the FTP client and FTP server must be Kerberized.

Kerberos protocol A secure asymmetric encryption method that is used to encrypt client/server authentication.

Kerberos v4 authentication The strongest authentication allowed in LDAP v2.

key Set of instructions that govern ciphering or deciphering messages.

key and certification management tools Tools for auditing and administering digital certificates.

Key Distribution Center (KDC) Contains the information that allows Kerberos clients to authenticate.

key life cycle There are five stages in the key life cycle: certificate enrollment, certificate distribution, certificate revocation, certificate renewal, and certificate auditing.

L

land A flaw exploitation attack where an attacker sends a forged packet with the same destination and source address and port.

Layer 2 Tunneling Protocol (L2TP) A widely implemented tunneling protocol. L2TP encapsulates PPP frames to be sent over IP, X.25, frame relay, or Asynchronous Transfer Mode (ATM) networks. When configured to use IP as its transport, L2TP can be used as a VPN tunneling protocol over the Internet. L2TP over IP uses UDP port 1701 and includes a series of L2TP control messages for tunnel maintenance.

Layer 3 switches Routers that are VLAN aware (meaning they can pass VLAN frames without actually routing traffic).

layered defense A layered approach to building a defense that includes securing the network infrastructure, communications protocols, servers, applications that run on the servers, and the file system. It should also include some form of user authentication.

LDAP root The logical top of an LDAP hierarchy.

LDAP root server Creates the hierarchy and the rest of the structure (and resources) branch out from that location.

LDAP version 2 (LDAP v2) The second version of the LDAP protocol that supports anonymous and simple authentication, as well as Kerberos v4 authentication.

LDAP version 3 (LDAP v3) The third version of the LDAP protocol that supports anonymous and simple authentication, as well as Simple Authentication and Security Layer (SASL).

Lightweight Directory Access Protocol (LDAP) A common directory service on many networks today. LDAP organizes data in a hierarchical fashion. LDAP uses objects to represent computers, user accounts, shared resources, services, and so on.

local area network (LAN) SLA Defines the availability of LAN connectivity equipment and a response time for resolving issues.

log file monitor (LFM) Software that parses system log entries (from one or more systems) to identify possible system attacks or compromises.

logic bomb A destructive program that goes off when a predetermined event takes place, such as the user typing a certain series of keystrokes, changing a file, or at a certain time and date.

long file name (LFN) A file name that can be up to 255 characters.

loose source and record route (LSRR) Defined in RFC 791, is a technique that allows the sender or source of a packet to set a preferred route for a packet to take through the network.

M

Macof A script that can be used to flood a network segment and its connectivity equipment (such as switches and bridges) with random MAC addresses. This makes it difficult for the device to build and maintain tables that allow it to appropriately route packets.

Mailsnarf A utility that helps to compromise e-mail transfers and messages.

malicious code Software or firmware that is intentionally placed in a system for an unauthorized purpose.

man-in-the-middle (MITM) An attack where an attacker's computer captures the communications between two computers and impersonates them both.

mandatory access control (MAC) Access to an object is restricted based on the sensitivity of the object (defined by the label that is assigned), and granted through authorization (clearance) to access that level of data.

mathematical attack *See* brute force.

mesh architecture A certificate structure in which multiple peer certification authorities issue certificates to each other. To certify, they create certificates for each other.

Microsoft Baseline Security Analyzer (MBSA) A software utility for vulnerability scanning.

Microsoft Challenge Handshake Authentication Protocol (MS-CHAP) Microsoft Corporation's implementation of the CHAP protocol, provides greater security than CHAP, and Microsoft networking domain logon support capabilities. MS-CHAP uses the Message Digest 4 (MD4) hash made up of the challenge string, session ID, and the MD-4 hashed password.

Microsoft Challenge Handshake Authentication Protocol version 2 (MS-CHAPv.2) Version 2 of Microsoft's MS CHAP protocol that has a larger initial encryption key size than MS-CHAP and also supports a bi-directional challenge. This allows the client to send a challenge to the remote access server. MS-CHAP v.2 also uses MD4 for hashing of the password.

Microsoft Network Security Hot Fix Checker (HFNetChk). A software utility for vulnerability scanning.

misuse detection Intrusion detection system (IDS) detection method for identifying attacks based on attack signatures.

mitigation Making something less harmful or less painful in order to lessen your risks.

Msgsnarf A utility that helps to compromise instant messenger programs.

multicast Sending data packets to multiple host computers at once.

multi-factor authentication Authentication that involves multiple factors to grant access to an authorized user. There are three basic factor types: Type 1 is something you know, such as a password; Type 2 is something you have, such as a smart card; Type 3 is something you are, such as a fingerprint.

multipartite virus A virus that infects multiple locations on a system. A multipartite virus typically infects memory first and then copies itself to multiple other locations, such as the boot sector of each hard disk, files, and executables on the system.

mutual authentication A situation in which both the server and client must authenticate with one another.

N

NetBIOS enumeration A method for discovering resources available on a Windows network, such as users, groups, shares, and other resources.

NetBIOS Enumeration (NBTEnum) Utility A utility written by NTSleuth that helps to exploit Net-BIOS services. Microsoft has implemented additional security features in their latest products to better protect systems from such exploits.

network administrator Any person responsible for the day-to-day operation of system and network resources.

Network File System (NFS) A file sharing protocol typically associated with UNIX networks, but there are add-ons to allow other operating environments, such as those from Microsoft and Novell, to share files over NFS.

Network Information Service (NIS) A server service that provides a master accounts database for users on a UNIX-based network.

network infrastructure All of the wiring, networking devices, and networking services that provide connectivity between the computers in a network.

network service A program that is used to provide some function for another computer or network device on the network.

network-based intrusion detection system (NIDS) Software and hardware that monitors network traffic and traffic patterns to discover someone attempting a denial-of-service attack, port scans, or attempts to guess the password to a secured resource.

nonrepudiation Prevents an individual or process from denying that he, she, or it performed a task or sent data.

novice Someone who aspires to be a hacker or cracker, but does not have the technical skills. Typically, a novice will go to a Web site created by a hacker or cracker and run a program that attacks a network or computer system.

NTFS A file system type available for Microsoft and other operating systems that supports file- and directory-level security.

null scan A TCP scan that passes no TCP flags designed to penetrate firewalls and filtering routers.

P

P3P A standard that defines a method for client Web browsers to access, display, and automatically evaluate the privacy policy of a Web site and its pages.

packet spoofing A situation in which an attacker modifies a data packet to make it appear that it originated from a different host.

Password Authentication Protocol (PAP) An authentication protocol that requires a password, but the password is sent in cleartext, and is therefore is not a very secure authentication mechanism.

password guessing An attack that involves guessing a user name and password in an attempt to gain access to a network or system. There are password programs available that attempt to break a password using a brute force technique, and others that try passwords against a dictionary.

password policy A policy that describes how passwords should be managed.

password sniffing The act of capturing and decoding network packets that contain passwords as they are transmitted across the network.

perceived value Potential value of a product or asset.

perimeter network A separate network segment and set of resources between an internal and external network. The purpose of the perimeter network is to provide services to the public without compromising the security of the private network. Also known as DMZ or screened subnet.

personal firewalls Protect individual host computers from network attacks. Some personal firewalls also have host intrusion detection software built-in.

ping of death (POD) A flaw exploitation attack in which the attacker sends an ICMP echo request that is larger than 65,536 bytes as multiple fragmented packets to the target host.

plaintext Information that is not encrypted.

Point-to-Point Tunneling Protocol (PPTP) A tunneling protocol created by the PPTP Industry Forum (US Robotics [now 3Com], 3Com/Primary Access, Ascend, Microsoft, and ECI Telematics).

polymorphic virus A virus that changes or mutates as it copies itself to other files or programs. The goal is to make it difficult to detect and remove the virus.

port A single point of connection to the network.

Port Access Entity (PAE) The PAE controls the algorithms and protocols that are associated with the authentication mechanisms for a port.

port mirroring A function that allows a switch port (or multiple switch ports) to propagate traffic to the mirrored port (chosen by the administrator). In this way, all traffic traversing that switch port (or all of the switch ports) is duplicated on the mirrored port.

Pretty Good Privacy (PGP) Software that can be used to encrypt or digitally sign data.

principal Any unique entity to which Kerberos can assign tickets.

principal CA A certification authority that connects with a bridge CA.

privacy policy Explains reasonable expectations of privacy for clients, customers, and partners. This policy should detail such issues as monitoring of email, maintaining logs of Web sites visited, and restrictions and exceptions for accessing users' files.

private CA A certificate authority that issues certificates for an organization's private use, such as when an employee attempts to gain access to an internal server or gain access remotely.

private key Secret key that only the private key holder has. It is used to decrypt information encrypted with the public key, and also to create a digital signature.

promiscuous mode A condition that a network adapter can be placed in to gather all passing information.

protocol analyzer A device (or computer software program) that allows its user to capture and decode network traffic. Also called a data sniffer, network sniffer, packet sniffer, or another derivative of these names.

public FTP servers File Transfer Protocol (FTP) servers that are typically open to everyone on the Internet.

public key Provided to many people and used to validate that a message came from the private key holder or to encrypt data to send the private key holder.

public key infrastructure (PKI) Security infrastructure that uses asymmetric key pairs and combines software, encryption technologies, and services to provide a means of protecting the security of communications and business transactions. RFC 2459 defines the X.509 PKI, which is the PKI defined for use on the Internet.

public key-enabled applications and services Applications and services that support using certificates.

R

radio frequency interference (RFI) is noise occurring over the part of the energy spectrum used specifically for broadcasting. This affects reception of radio broadcasts. RFI may lead to the malfunctioning of other sensitive electrical and electronic equipment.

RADIUS proxy server A remote access service provider that is able to authenticate remote dial-in connections by contacting another system's accounts database.

RADIUS server A remote access service provider that is able to authenticate remote dial-in connections.

real value Actual value of a product or asset.

realm An organizational boundary that is formed to provide authentication boundaries. Each realm has an authentication server (AS) and a ticket granting server (TGS). Also known as a Kerberos realm.

registration authority (RA) An entity that is designed to verify certificate contents for a CA.

Remote Authentication and Dial-In User Service (RADIUS) Used for providing authentication, authorization, and accounting services for remote access services and separates the remote access server functions from the user authentication server functions. UDP-based; authentication and authorization together.

remote ticket granting server (RTGS) A Kerberos-enabled server that grants the session tickets used by remote clients to start a session with a service.

RIP spoofing Forging the Routing Information Protocol (RIP) packets to tell the router to send packets to an unauthorized network.

risk Exposure to loss or possible injury. With information security, the risk is that your company's information will fall prey to outside forces and cause your company losses in time, money, and reputation.

risk assessment the evaluation of threats, vulnerabilities, and potential impact on assets.

risk management The complete process used to identify, control, and mitigate the impact of uncertain events.

role-based access control (RBAC) Access is based on the role a user plays in the organization. For instance a human resources manager would need access to information that a department manager would not need access to, and both would need access to some common information.

root CA A certification authority (CA) at the top of a CA hierarchy that issues certificates to subordinate CAs. Those CAs can then issue certificates to other CAs, and so on. The CAs at each level can issue certificates to subordinate CAs or users.

rule of least privilege An administrative philosophy that dictates users and groups should be given only the necessary permissions to perform their jobs or a certain task and nothing more.

S

S/MIME (Secure Multipurpose Internet Mail Extensions) This specification is similar to PGP in that it seeks to enable the encryption and digital signing of e-mail messages. S/MIME is designed and marketed for integration into e-mail and messaging products.

screened host *See* bastion host.

screened subnet *See* perimeter network.

script injection When attackers place malicious scripts on target systems to subvert communications, such as redirecting cookies to the attacker's system.

secure coding practices Applying secure coding practices means designing programs with security in mind.

Secure FTP A type of File Transfer Protocol (FTP) program that supports SSL/TLS encryption for FTP communications. SSL/TLS encryption protects the transfer of the password and all data between the client and server. Also known as SFTP, S/FTP, or S-FTP.

secure hash function One-way mathematical function that creates a fixed-sized representation of data.

secure mail Configure the Secure Multipurpose Internet Mail Extensions (S/MIME) protocol to ensure the integrity, origin, and confidentiality of e-mail messages.

Secure Shell (SSH) A protocol and software package originally developed at the Helsinki University of Technology and is a secure, low-level Transport protocol. SSH allows users to log on to a remote computer over the network, execute commands on it, and move files from one computer to another while providing strong authentication and secure communications over unsecured channels.

Secure Sockets Layer *See* Transport Layer Security.

secure Web communications The use of certificates with Secure Sockets Layer (SSL) or Transport Layer Security (TLS) protocols for authenticating and encrypting communications between servers and clients.

security administrator Any person who is responsible for the security of information and information technology.

Security Administrator Tool for Analyzing Networks (SATAN) A software utility for vulnerability scanning.

security controls Everything an organization does or implements to protect its assets including security policy and procedures, anti-virus software, and firewalls.

security officer The person primarily responsible for the organizational security program.

security policy Set of rules regarding access and use of an organization's technology and information assets. Security policy is often created using a series of subordinate policies.

security zones Security zones help organizations classify, prioritize, and focus on security issues based on the services that are required in each zone.

Server Message Block (SMB) A file sharing and communication protocol used on Microsoft and compatible networks.

server-side includes (SSI) A capability available to many Web servers that allows one document to be inserted into another. In addition, data can be fed into or out of another program if SSI is enabled where programs are stored. Attackers might be able to use SSI to compromise your scripts.

service level agreement (SLA) A contract that defines business or technical support parameters that an IT outsourcing firm agrees to provide its clients.

session hijacking An attack that occurs after a source and destination computer have established a communications link. A third computer disables the ability of one the computers to communicate, and then imitates that computer.

shared secret *See* symmetric algorithm.

Shiva Password Authentication Protocol (SPAP) An authentication protocol that incorporates a reversible encryption mechanism. SPAP is more secure than PAP, but does not provide protection against remote server impersonation.

signature-based detection A process of identifying viruses or computer attacks based on attack signatures.

Simple Authentication and Security Layer (SASL) The strongest authentication allowed in LDAP v3.

Simple Network Management Protocol (SNMP) A protocol and service used for remote management of hosts on a TCP/IP network.

smurf A specific type of ICMP flood DoS attack that involves sending spoofed ICMP echo packets to a subnet. The spoofed address is the target of the attack and all hosts on the subnet reply to the target.

social engineering A term used to describe the process of circumventing security barriers by persuading authorized users to provide passwords or other sensitive information.

Software Development Kit (SDK) Programming guide that explain the structures, functions, and methods for developing programs for specific platforms.

source routing Defined in RFC 791, is a technique that allows the sender or source of a packet to identify the route that the packet should take through the network.

sparse virus A sparse virus doesn't immediately infect files. Instead, it waits a certain period of time (or for some other condition to be met) before it infects a program.

spoofing Pretending to be someone else by impersonating, masquerading, or mimicking that person.

state-based detection A form of detection employed by misuse detectors that allows recognition of attack variations or derivative attacks.

stealth scans *See* half-open scans.

stealth virus A type of virus that attempts to hide itself from detection attempts by deceiving people or virus-scanning software. When a person or virus scanner attempts to view the virus-infected file, the stealth virus intercepts the disk access request and feeds the person or virus scanner an uninfected version of the file.

supplicant A role in which a LAN port requests access to the services that can be accessed through the authenticator's port.

supplicant Port Access Entity (PAE) The supplicant PAE tries to access the services that are allowed by the authenticator.

symmetric algorithms Encryption algorithms that use the same key for encrypting and decrypting data, and everyone that is allowed to encrypt and

decrypt the data has a copy of the key. This is also known as a shared secret. Examples are Data Encryption Standard (DES), Triple DES (3DES), and Advanced Encryption Standard (AES).

symmetric key A single key used for encrypting and decrypting data, and everyone that is allowed to encrypt and decrypt the data has a copy of the key.

SYN flood *See* SYN-ACK attack.

SYN scan *See* half-open scans.

SYN segment The first segment of the three-way handshake. The information sent by computer1 includes source and destination port, starting sequence number, the receive buffer size, maximum TCP segment size, and the supported TCP options.

SYN-ACK attack DoS attack in which an attacker attempts to send TCP connection request packets to a specific TCP port or ports faster than the target server can expire them. A successful SYN flood consumes all of the target's available TCP connection resources so that it is unable to service new client requests.

SYN-ACK segment The reply to a SYN segment, which is the second step of the TCP three-way handshake process. The information sent includes source and destination port, starting sequence number, acknowledgment number, the receive buffer size, maximum TCP segment size, and an acknowledgment.

system hardening Making a system more secure. This includes removing unused services, ensuring that the latest security patches and service packs are installed, and limiting the number of people with administrative permissions.

system integrity verifier (SIV) Software that monitors a single system's file structure to determine if (and when) an attacker modifies, deletes, or changes a system file. An alternate name for SIV IDS is target-based IDS.

T

TACACS *See* Terminal Access Controller Access Control System Plus.

TACACS+ *See* Terminal Access Controller Access Control System Plus.

TCP connect scans Scans used to identify potential targets and services. This type of scan utilizes the full TCP three-way handshake.

teardrop A fragmentation attack that involves two or more IP fragments that cannot be properly assembled due to improperly configured fragment offset numbers.

Terminal Access Controller Access Control System Plus (TACACS+) An authentication protocol that allows a remote access server to communicate with an authentication server. The system is used to determine whether a dial-in user should be allowed to access the network. Previous versions of TACACS+ were TACACS and XTACACS. Although they share similar names and have the same goals, the older versions are not compatible with the newer TACACS+ protocol.

three-way handshake The process that two computers use when establishing TCP communication sessions. This process involves the passing of three packets (SYN, SYN-ACK, ACK), hence the name three-way handshake.

ticket A block of data that allows a user to prove their identity to a service. Each ticket is stored in a ticket cache on the user's local computer and is time stamped.

ticket cache A portion of memory that stores all of a user's Kerberos tickets. This cache is separate from the cache of the application that is using the ticket. By having the tickets in their own cache, users need only provide their credentials once per session, even if several applications are using that ticket to access a service.

ticket granting server (TGS) A Kerberos-enabled server that grants the session tickets used by clients to start a session with a service.

ticket granting ticket (TGT) A ticket that is granted as part of the Kerberos authentication process and is stored in the ticket cache. The TGT is used to get other tickets that are specific to a service.

token A device that can be issued to a user for use in the authentication process. For example, there are token devices that, when enabled, synchronize with a server. Tokens are often small handheld devices, with or without keypads. They can range in size from a credit card to a small pocket calculator.

Transport Layer Security (TLS) A secure replacement for Secure Sockets Layer (SSL) that allows for certificate-based authentication and encryption for Hypertext Transfer Protocol (HTTP) or Web-based protocols.

Transport-layer protocol (SSH-TRANS) A protocol that provides secure authentication, confidentiality, and network integrity. The possibility of SSH-TRANS providing encryption is also available. Transport is typically run over a TCP/IP connection, but can also be used on top of another reliable data stream.

Tribe Flood Network (TFN) DDoS tool that attackers can use for taking over client computers and making them zombie hosts.

Trinoo DDoS tool that attackers can use for taking over client computers and making them zombie hosts.

Trojan horse A seemingly useful or benign program that when activated performs malicious or illicit action, such as destroying files.

trust A relationship that allows a CA to trust a certificate issued by another CA.

trust path A logical path that links several certification authorities together so that the trust relationship can extend beyond two certification authorities that have formed a trust.

trusted third party (TTP) An entity trusted by other entities with respect to security-related services and activities.

tunneling Encapsulating one protocol or data set into another protocol or data set. The purpose might be to encrypt communications or simply provide compatibility between two different types of networks.

U

UDP flood A DoS attack that attempts to overwhelm the target with UDP packets so that it cannot service them and becomes unresponsive.

user authentication protocol (SSH-USERAUTH) Authenticates the client-side user to the server. It runs over the Transport-layer protocol.

V

verifying A comparison in biologic authentication in which the data collected by a sensor at a computer or other secured resource is compared with the information stored during enrolling to grant or deny access.

violations reporting policy Defines violations and how they should be reported. Violations should be defined and can include privacy issues, proper use of equipment, and information security.

virtual local area network (VLAN) Distinct segments or portions of a network designed to control broadcast traffic. Each VLAN is considered a broadcast domain because all hosts on a VLAN are able to send broadcast traffic to all hosts on a VLAN. Broadcast traffic is not allowed to pass beyond the logical confines of the VLAN.

virtual private network (VPN) A secure connection between a remote computer and a server on a private network that uses the Internet as its network medium.

virus Malicious code that can replicate, but not propagate itself. A virus requires an installation vector (such as an e-mail message or floppy disk), which is how it infects or attaches itself to other objects or programs. All viruses have some form of replication mechanism, which is how they propagate.

vulnerability A weakness in your information security that could be exploited by a threat; that is, a weakness in your systems and network security, processes, and procedures.

W

war dialing A technique used to dial all of the telephone numbers in a specified range, and then record those that have a modem connected. Once the phone numbers that have modems are identified, an attacker can redial the system and attempt to break into the computer system.

war driving A technique in which a person with a portable device drives around attempting to locate wireless access points.

Web spoofing When an attacker sets up a Web page or Web site that looks like a legitimate Web site. The attacker then attempts to redirect other systems to this location in an attempt to steal passwords, credit cards, or gather other potentially valuable information.

wild A descriptor for malicious code that exists outside of virus and anti-virus labs. Malicious code is "in the wild" when it is infecting unsuspecting computer users.

window scan A TCP scan that is a derivative of an ACK scan used to identify active hosts on the network and tries to further identify the host operating system or device manufacturer by its default TCP window size.

Wired Equivalent Privacy (WEP) A mechanism created in the 802.11 standard that utilizes a cryptographic security countermeasure to provide confidentiality, and has the added benefit of becoming an authentication mechanism.

wireless access point *See* access point.

Wireless Application Environment (WAE) The top layer of the Wireless Application Protocol (WAP) model.

Wireless Application Protocol (WAP) Provides a suite of protocols used for securing communications in layers 3 through 7. The communications model can be compared to the seven-layer OSI model.

Wireless Datagram Protocol (WDP) Provides a consistent interface between over-the-air protocols.

Wireless Markup Language (WML) A programming language based on the Extensible Markup Language (XML).

Wireless Session Protocol (WSP) This protocol uses a token-based version of HTTP to support operations over limited bandwidth.

Wireless Transaction Protocol (WTP) This supports multiple message types and limits the overhead of packaging sequencing.

Wireless Transport Layer Security (WTLS) The security layer of the WAP, providing privacy, data integrity, and authentication for WAP services.

worm Malicious code that replicates by making copies of itself on the same computer or by sending copies of itself to another computer. Worms, unlike viruses, do not infect other program files on a computer. All worms have some form of replication mechanism, which is how they propagate.

X

XMAS scan TCP scan designed to bypass basic firewalls or routers with filtering capabilities. This scan uses a series of varied TCP packets to identify listening TCP ports on target devices. Also known as the XMAS tree scan.

XTACACS *See* Terminal Access Controller Access Control System Plus.

Index

A

Antique Lockplate

The earliest lock in existence is an Egyptian lock made of wood, found with its key in the ruins of Nineveh, in ancient Assyria. In construction it is the prototype of the modern cylinder lock. Locks and keys are also mentioned in the Old Testament, and the Greeks and Romans used locks of simple design. Medieval artisans designed locks of exquisite detail, the perforations and carvings often having no relation to the working of the lock.* The beautiful **antique lockplate** on the cover of this book is another elegant example of security at work.

At Microsoft Press, we use tools to illustrate our books for software developers and IT professionals. Tools very simply and powerfully symbolize human inventiveness. They're a metaphor for people extending their capabilities, precision, and reach. From simple calipers and pliers to digital micrometers and lasers, these stylized illustrations give each book a visual identity, and a personality to the series. With tools and knowledge, there's no limit to creativity and innovation. Our tagline says it all: *the tools you need to put technology to work*.

The CompTIA Authorized Quality Curriculum Program

The logo of the CompTIA Authorized Curriculum Program and the status of this or other training material as "Authorized" under the CompTIA Authorized Curriculum Program signifies that, in CompTIA's opinion, such training material covers the content of the CompTIA's related certification exam. CompTIA has not reviewed or approved the accuracy of the contents of this training material and specifically disclaims any warranties of merchantability or fitness for a particular purpose. CompTIA makes no guarantee concerning the success of persons using any such "Authorized" or other training material in order to prepare for any CompTIA certification exam.

The contents of this training material were created for the CompTIA Security+ exam covering CompTIA certification exam objectives that were current as of December, 2002.

How to Become CompTIA Certified

This training material can help you prepare for and pass a related CompTIA certification exam or exams. In order to achieve CompTIA certification, you must register for and pass a CompTIA certification exam or exams.

In order to become CompTIA certified, you must:

(1) Select a certification exam provider. For more information please visit
      http://www.comptia.org/certification/general_information/test_locations.asp.

(2) Register for and schedule a time to take the CompTIA certification exam(s) at a convenient location.

(3) Read and sign the Candidate Agreement, which will be presented at the time of the exam(s). The text of the Candidate Agreement can be found at
      http://www.comptia.org/certification/general_information/candidate_agreement.asp.

(4) Take and pass the CompTIA certification exam(s).

For more information about CompTIA's certifications, such as their industry acceptance, benefits, or program news, please visit *http://www.comptia.org/certification/default.asp.*

CompTIA is a non-profit information technology (IT) trade association. CompTIA's certifications are designed by subject matter experts from across the IT industry. Each CompTIA certification is vendor-neutral, covers multiple technologies, and requires demonstration of skills and knowledge widely sought after by the IT industry.

To contact CompTIA with any questions or comments:
Please call + 1-630-268-1818
questions@comptia.org

ProCert Labs Tested Service Mark

Choose Wisely: Look for courseware that bears the ProCert Labs Tested service mark. It assures that the course is designed to effectively teach the principles needed to pass your professional certification exam.

Courseware that bears this symbol has been tested and approved by ProCert Labs and is verified to include 100 percent of the information needed to pass the associated certification exam. In addition, this course has passed a thorough testing for Instructional Design Integrity.

ProCert Labs is an independent third-party quality assurance laboratory.

MICROSOFT LICENSE AGREEMENT

Book Companion CD

SOFTWARE PRODUCT LICENSE

The SOFTWARE PRODUCT is protected by United States copyright laws and international copyright treaties, as well as other intellectual property laws and treaties. The SOFTWARE PRODUCT is licensed, not sold.

1. **GRANT OF LICENSE.** This EULA grants you the following rights:

   a. **Software Product.** You may install and use one copy of the SOFTWARE PRODUCT on a single computer. The primary user of the computer on which the SOFTWARE PRODUCT is installed may make a second copy for his or her exclusive use on a portable computer.

   b. **Storage/Network Use.** You may also store or install a copy of the SOFTWARE PRODUCT on a storage device, such as a network server, used only to install or run the SOFTWARE PRODUCT on your other computers over an internal network; however, you must acquire and dedicate a license for each separate computer on which the SOFTWARE PRODUCT is installed or run from the storage device. A license for the SOFTWARE PRODUCT may not be shared or used concurrently on different computers.

   c. **License Pak.** If you have acquired this EULA in a Microsoft License Pak, you may make the number of additional copies of the computer software portion of the SOFTWARE PRODUCT authorized on the printed copy of this EULA, and you may use each copy in the manner specified above. You are also entitled to make a corresponding number of secondary copies for portable computer use as specified above.

   d. **Sample Code.** Solely with respect to portions, if any, of the SOFTWARE PRODUCT that are identified within the SOFTWARE PRODUCT as sample code (the "SAMPLE CODE"):

      i. **Use and Modification.** Microsoft grants you the right to use and modify the source code version of the SAMPLE CODE, *provided* you comply with subsection (d)(iii) below. You may not distribute the SAMPLE CODE, or any modified version of the SAMPLE CODE, in source code form.

      ii. **Redistributable Files.** Provided you comply with subsection (d)(iii) below, Microsoft grants you a nonexclusive, royalty-free right to reproduce and distribute the object code version of the SAMPLE CODE and of any modified SAMPLE CODE, other than SAMPLE CODE, or any modified version thereof, designated as not redistributable in the Readme file that forms a part of the SOFTWARE PRODUCT (the "Non-Redistributable Sample Code"). All SAMPLE CODE other than the Non-Redistributable Sample Code is collectively referred to as the "REDISTRIBUTABLES."

      iii. **Redistribution Requirements.** If you redistribute the REDISTRIBUTABLES, you agree to: (i) distribute the REDISTRIBUTABLES in object code form only in conjunction with and as a part of your software application product; (ii) not use Microsoft's name, logo, or trademarks to market your software application product; (iii) include a valid copyright notice on your software application product; (iv) indemnify, hold harmless, and defend Microsoft from and against any claims or lawsuits, including attorney's fees, that arise or result from the use or distribution of your software application product; and (v) not permit further distribution of the REDISTRIBUTABLES by your end user. Contact Microsoft for the applicable royalties due and other licensing terms for all other uses and/or distribution of the REDISTRIBUTABLES.

2. **DESCRIPTION OF OTHER RIGHTS AND LIMITATIONS.**

   - **Limitations on Reverse Engineering, Decompilation, and Disassembly.** You may not reverse engineer, decompile, or disassemble the SOFTWARE PRODUCT, except and only to the extent that such activity is expressly permitted by applicable law notwithstanding this limitation.

   - **Separation of Components.** The SOFTWARE PRODUCT is licensed as a single product. Its component parts may not be separated for use on more than one computer.

   - **Rental.** You may not rent, lease, or lend the SOFTWARE PRODUCT.

- **Support Services.** Microsoft may, but is not obligated to, provide you with support services related to the SOFTWARE PRODUCT ("Support Services"). Use of Support Services is governed by the Microsoft policies and programs described in the user manual, in "online" documentation, and/or in other Microsoft-provided materials. Any supplemental software code provided to you as part of the Support Services shall be considered part of the SOFTWARE PRODUCT and subject to the terms and conditions of this EULA. With respect to technical information you provide to Microsoft as part of the Support Services, Microsoft may use such information for its business purposes, including for product support and development. Microsoft will not utilize such technical information in a form that personally identifies you.

- **Software Transfer.** You may permanently transfer all of your rights under this EULA, provided you retain no copies, you transfer all of the SOFTWARE PRODUCT (including all component parts, the media and printed materials, any upgrades, this EULA, and, if applicable, the Certificate of Authenticity), **and** the recipient agrees to the terms of this EULA.

- **Termination.** Without prejudice to any other rights, Microsoft may terminate this EULA if you fail to comply with the terms and conditions of this EULA. In such event, you must destroy all copies of the SOFTWARE PRODUCT and all of its component parts.

3. **COPYRIGHT.** All title and copyrights in and to the SOFTWARE PRODUCT (including but not limited to any images, photographs, animations, video, audio, music, text, SAMPLE CODE, REDISTRIBUTABLES, and "applets" incorporated into the SOFTWARE PRODUCT) and any copies of the SOFTWARE PRODUCT are owned by Microsoft or its suppliers. The SOFTWARE PRODUCT is protected by copyright laws and international treaty provisions. Therefore, you must treat the SOFTWARE PRODUCT like any other copyrighted material **except** that you may install the SOFTWARE PRODUCT on a single computer provided you keep the original solely for backup or archival purposes. You may not copy the printed materials accompanying the SOFTWARE PRODUCT.

4. **U.S. GOVERNMENT RESTRICTED RIGHTS.** The SOFTWARE PRODUCT and documentation are provided with RESTRICTED RIGHTS. Use, duplication, or disclosure by the Government is subject to restrictions as set forth in subparagraph (c)(1)(ii) of the Rights in Technical Data and Computer Software clause at DFARS 252.227-7013 or subparagraphs (c)(1) and (2) of the Commercial Computer Software—Restricted Rights at 48 CFR 52.227-19, as applicable. Manufacturer is Microsoft Corporation/One Microsoft Way/Redmond, WA 98052-6399.

5. **EXPORT RESTRICTIONS.** You agree that you will not export or re-export the SOFTWARE PRODUCT, any part thereof, or any process or service that is the direct product of the SOFTWARE PRODUCT (the foregoing collectively referred to as the "Restricted Components"), to any country, person, entity, or end user subject to U.S. export restrictions. You specifically agree not to export or re-export any of the Restricted Components (i) to any country to which the U.S. has embargoed or restricted the export of goods or services, which currently include, but are not necessarily limited to, Cuba, Iran, Iraq, Libya, North Korea, Sudan, and Syria, or to any national of any such country, wherever located, who intends to transmit or transport the Restricted Components back to such country; (ii) to any end user who you know or have reason to know will utilize the Restricted Components in the design, development, or production of nuclear, chemical, or biological weapons; or (iii) to any end user who has been prohibited from participating in U.S. export transactions by any federal agency of the U.S. government. You warrant and represent that neither the BXA nor any other U.S. federal agency has suspended, revoked, or denied your export privileges.

DISCLAIMER OF WARRANTY

NO WARRANTIES OR CONDITIONS. MICROSOFT EXPRESSLY DISCLAIMS ANY WARRANTY OR CONDITION FOR THE SOFTWARE PRODUCT. THE SOFTWARE PRODUCT AND ANY RELATED DOCUMENTATION ARE PROVIDED "AS IS" WITHOUT WARRANTY OR CONDITION OF ANY KIND, EITHER EXPRESS OR IMPLIED, INCLUDING, WITHOUT LIMITATION, THE IMPLIED WARRANTIES OF MERCHANTABILITY, FITNESS FOR A PARTICULAR PURPOSE, OR NONINFRINGEMENT. THE ENTIRE RISK ARISING OUT OF USE OR PERFORMANCE OF THE SOFTWARE PRODUCT REMAINS WITH YOU.

LIMITATION OF LIABILITY. TO THE MAXIMUM EXTENT PERMITTED BY APPLICABLE LAW, IN NO EVENT SHALL MICROSOFT OR ITS SUPPLIERS BE LIABLE FOR ANY SPECIAL, INCIDENTAL, INDIRECT, OR CONSEQUENTIAL DAMAGES WHATSOEVER (INCLUDING, WITHOUT LIMITATION, DAMAGES FOR LOSS OF BUSINESS PROFITS, BUSINESS INTERRUPTION, LOSS OF BUSINESS INFORMATION, OR ANY OTHER PECUNIARY LOSS) ARISING OUT OF THE USE OF OR INABILITY TO USE THE SOFTWARE PRODUCT OR THE PROVISION OF OR FAILURE TO PROVIDE SUPPORT SERVICES, EVEN IF MICROSOFT HAS BEEN ADVISED OF THE POSSIBILITY OF SUCH DAMAGES. IN ANY CASE, MICROSOFT'S ENTIRE LIABILITY UNDER ANY PROVISION OF THIS EULA SHALL BE LIMITED TO THE GREATER OF THE AMOUNT ACTUALLY PAID BY YOU FOR THE SOFTWARE PRODUCT OR US$5.00; PROVIDED, HOWEVER, IF YOU HAVE ENTERED INTO A MICROSOFT SUPPORT SERVICES AGREEMENT, MICROSOFT'S ENTIRE LIABILITY REGARDING SUPPORT SERVICES SHALL BE GOVERNED BY THE TERMS OF THAT AGREEMENT. BECAUSE SOME STATES AND JURISDICTIONS DO NOT ALLOW THE EXCLUSION OR LIMITATION OF LIABILITY, THE ABOVE LIMITATION MAY NOT APPLY TO YOU.

MISCELLANEOUS

This EULA is governed by the laws of the State of Washington USA, except and only to the extent that applicable law mandates governing law of a different jurisdiction.

Should you have any questions concerning this EULA, or if you desire to contact Microsoft for any reason, please contact the Microsoft subsidiary serving your country, or write: Microsoft Sales Information Center/One Microsoft Way/Redmond, WA 98052-6399.

PN 097-0002296

System Requirements

To get the most out of the *Security+ Certification Training Kit* and the Supplemental Course Materials CD-ROM, you will need a computer equipped with the following minimum configuration listed below.

- 133-MHz Intel-based Pentium level processor

- 64 MB RAM

- 650 MB (minimum) to 1.5 GB (optimum) free space on a 2-GB hard disk space.

- 8x CD-ROM drive or faster

- Mouse or pointing device

- Display system capable of 800 x 600 resolution or better

- Internet connection

For the best viewing experience of the *Security+ Certification Training Kit* eBook, and to perform some of the exercises in this book, the following system configuration is recommended:

- Microsoft Windows 95, 98, Me, Windows NT, or Windows 2000

- Pentium II (or similar) with 266 MHz or higher processor